THE
TAO
AT
WORK

ON
LEADING
AND
FOLLOWING

STANLEY M. HERMAN

THE
TAO
AT
WORK

ON
LEADING
AND
FOLLOWING

 JOSSEY-BASS PUBLISHERS
SAN FRANCISCO

Substantial discounts on bulk quantities of Jossey-Bass books are available to corporations, professional associations, and other organizations. For details and discount information, contact the special sales department at Jossey-Bass Inc., Publishers. (415) 433-1740; Fax (415) 433-0499.

For sales outside the United States, please contact your local Paramount Publishing International Office.

Manufactured in the United States of America. Printed on acid-free paper.

Illustrations: Polly Becker

Library of Congress Cataloging-in-Publication Data

Herman, Stanley M., date.
    The Tao at work : on leading and following /
Stanley M. Herman.
        p.   cm.
    "Most of this book is a version of a twenty-five-hundred-year-old tract, dictated by a person named Lao-tzu, called the Tao"—Introd.
    ISBN 1-55542-709-X
    1. Management—Philosophy. 2. Taoism. I. Lao-tzu.
Tao te ching. II. Title.
HD38.H4625   1994
658—dc20   94-5609
                                          CIP

FIRST EDITION
HB Printing   10 9 8 7 6 5 4 3 2 1   *Code 9469*

To Michael David Herman

September 16, 1955   February 17, 1994

INTRODUCTION

While in the midst of coping with difficulty, complexity, and pressure, it's useful to pause from time to time and remind yourself of the obvious. This book is about the obvious.

I suppose that, in some measure, I have always been captivated by the obvious. It has usually seemed such a sound base on which to build intelligent complexity—when that needs to be done—and such a comfortable place to return to when I need some relief from complexity or a "sanity check" of its relevance.

Most of this book is a version of a twenty-five-hundred-year-old tract, dictated by a person named Lao-tzu, called the Tao (translation: the way along which one passes in going from one place to another). In Taoist folklore, as Lao-tzu is about to depart his city, possibly for the last time, the gatekeeper at the city wall asks him if he is willing to leave a legacy of his wisdom for those who are to come. Lao-tzu is at first reluctant, but eventually he bows to the gatekeeper's urging and recites eighty-one verses, which the gatekeeper writes down. From that time to the present, those eighty-one verses have been translated and interpreted time and time again throughout the world. Probably no other work has inspired as many versions.

Because of the nature of Chinese character writing (a single character can represent a large number of things and ideas), it is literally impossible to translate Lao-tzu's verses without interpreting them. The Tao focuses on ultimacy—the diamond-hard core of what "the system" is about and how it runs. As the Tao focuses your attention on that subject, it also points out methods and processes for getting to that diamond-hard core. And it does so in surprisingly practical ways. Practicality is the key to this version of Lao-tzu's work. It will teach you nothing new, only remind you of things you already know.

ABOUT THE STORIES

Each interpretation of the Tao is, of course, flavored by its author's particular biases and style. This one is no exception. Some authors attempt to explain Lao-tzu's thought in relation to that of other philosophers, both Western and Eastern. My choice has been instead to use stories of life in contemporary organizations to illuminate the messages, especially as they apply to the marketplaces of our everyday lives. Many of these stories have roots in the folktales of other cultures, including Greek, Ukrainian, Chinese, and Japanese. But their trunks and branches are shaped by the lives and experiences of people I have known—and you will recognize.

This book can be especially useful to people in transition. For those of you who feel harassed and dissatisfied by your current life and work styles, it offers an opportunity to adjust your balance. It points to the serenity in both solitary sunsets at the beach and turbulence of a perplexing crisis at the office.

There are a number of ways of reading a book. If you use the "slotting process," you pick out familiar messages—those that seem to confirm the ideas you already hold in your head—and slot them into your model of the world. Slotting reinforces the model. Or you might use the "argument process," where you consider what you read and argue with it in your mind. The argument process can be a useful way of learning, providing you continue the argument rather than chop it off after you've had your say. Or you can use the "suspended judgment process," in which you pay particular attention to the things that don't fit your current model, or don't even seem to make sense. Then you just wait to see what happens.

One other note: You will find "discontinuities" in the verses—abrupt changes in subject matter in a single verse. In rendering Lao-tzu's verses from their traditional form, I faced a choice about whether to cut these apparent discontinuities which, at first glance, may seem to throw the reader off or dilute the main message. One early reviewer advised that—in this age of soundbites—I should keep it simple. I considered that advice but decided to stay with the Tao's style. If these ideas are not entirely linear or sequential, well, neither is Lao-tzu—or life in general, for that matter. To help you with the "breaks" I have used a small device ⌒ to show that a pause may be appropriate.

This is a dipping-into book. If you keep it within easy reach you can open it at random and see what it has to say to you at the moment. If you like to muse you can take on a few verses at a time, or even a single one.

ACKNOWLEDGMENTS

The two major inspirations for this version of the Tao were:

Tao: A New Way of Thinking by Chang Chung-yuan. New York: Harper & Row (1975).

The Way of Life According to Lao Tzu, translated by Witter Bynner. New York: Capricorn Books (1944).

Thanks to Kit Bristol for what he said, John Lockwood for what he did, and Ram Dass for what he wrote.

And, once again, to Sarah Polster, who edited, contributed, and had fun.

1

You can choose how you think and what you act upon. You can center your attention on what is real and valid according to your own observations and experiences, or you can become a contributor to the latest, most fashionable Tower of Babel.

If you choose to be a tower builder, you put on the uniform of a particular profession or trade or political movement or social or economic group. You go along and get along. You pledge allegiance to your group's slogans and interpret events according to its generalizations.

If you choose to be a reality hunter, you place yourself somewhat apart from the popular view and concentrate on discovering what is going on beneath the slogans.

Both courses have their advantages and disadvantages. If you choose to help build the tower, sooner or later you will be disappointed. What is supposed to happen (according to the slogans) doesn't happen, and you are thrown on your own devices. If you choose to be a reality hunter you will find the hunt is not an easy one, and at times it can get lonesome.

Some choose one course and some the other to travel their lives. A few recognize that both have validity. To respect popular generalizations but not depend on them is healthy. To increase your capacity for coping with their crucial exceptions is a skill. The important moves in your life are made when you depart from your usual pattern, whether by necessity or choice.

2

Many people are reflexive partisans. They instantly compare, contrast, and form opinions for or against everything that comes over their horizon. They join causes and take positions. They wave their arms about politics, social issues, economics, ethics, and other people. Once a reflexive partisan takes a position or chooses a side, it becomes the flag of his ego. His own personal sense of victory or defeat, worthiness or worthlessness, becomes dependent on his cause.

It is better not to set your stance too soon or champion it too adamantly. As time winds forward there will be more to see than can be seen at present—but only if your eyes remain open.

A contributor to the latest and most fashionable Tower of Babel

For a wiser course, take a moment to recognize the foundation for other opinions along the continuum before you choose a position. If you are able, consider the continuum itself. Comprehending all opinions will enable you to better govern the arena of debate.

3

It is better not to overpraise people for capable performance, but rather to think of capable performance as nothing special. Whether as a parent or a leader, encouraging others to compete for your favorable recognition is a limiting tactic. It is better just to provide an environment that allows people to do what they are best able to do in the best ways they can, and to help excellence become natural.

A sound leader concentrates on producing what is required, simplifying issues, providing well—but not overly well—for her people, and clearing their minds of prejudices and useless habits. The best leaders and parents perform these functions in an entertaining rather than a solemn way.

THE LEGEND

THIS WAS ONE of the earliest stories he told us. His name was William O. (for Orville) Boyd, though, come to think of it, a lot of people knew him by another name, especially in his early days at the company. Back then they called him "Wild Old Boyd." Now people just call him Bill. He has mellowed some over the years.

A bunch of us—about a dozen people who worked in the division—used to meet for lunch pretty regularly, and once a month or so we would go out to dinner together. Bill was a sturdy old guy who still said what he meant, and it didn't matter much who was there to hear him. The saying about him was, "Don't ask him a question if you don't want the answer." During his career he had held a lot of jobs. He had been involved in everything from marketing to product development to human resources, but his real love was being involved in making products. He once told us that even as a kid he was always interested more than anything else in what things were about and how they worked.

Bill had been a production general foreman for almost ten years when I met him. There were a lot of people who thought he could have gone a lot further up the chain of command if he had wanted to. But he chose to stay close to where the product was, and where most of the people were. If you asked him about his career he would say that he was a level higher than he ever expected to be, and two lower than he ought to be. Then he would grin, and you wouldn't know if he was serious or just making a remark.

One night we were at dinner at Dante's, an Italian restaurant near the plant. The conversation got around to the early days of the company, so of course we talked about Gary Newhouse. Gary was the person most responsible for turning the company from a run-of-the-mill, midsized producer of me-too computer peripherals into a Fortune 200 information-technology giant. He was a genuine legend. People still talked about what the company might be like now if he hadn't been forced out. Then Jennifer asked Bill if he had known Gary.

Bill said he remembered him well. He recalled that when Gary was in his early twenties he was made section head of a group of thirty or so technical and support people. A hot new product this group had designed was failing in the field. The product's failure had caused a damaging disruption in the business of one of the company's biggest customers. Gary and his group were faced with a crisis: A solution had to be found fast, and it would require an around-the-clock effort from everyone.

Bill continued his story: I was a teenaged technician when I first met Gary. I was in a different department, and one of my jobs as the junior member was to schedule meeting times for the conference rooms shared by the departments on our floor. Gary came to me to schedule a meeting. He wanted to call his people together to tell them about their challenge and what it would require of all of them. But all the conference rooms in the building were already occupied or reserved.

I explained the situation to him and told him I would call around to see if anyone would be willing to delay a meeting, but he would have to be patient for a while until I could get in touch with people. But Gary was not a patient type. He said he didn't have the time, and then right before my eyes he climbed to the top of his desk in the big, open bull pen that housed both his section and others. He shouted over the din for the attention of his team and made his speech right there. I couldn't help but listen, nor could most of the other people in the bay. Listening to him made me decide to volunteer my help, if they wanted it.

Well, the long and the short of it was that they solved the problem in fifty round the clock hours and won a strong customer endorsement. Gary had a barbecue dinner at his house for his whole team and the rest of us who had helped out. A few people called for him to make a speech, but he wouldn't do it. He just tipped his glass and said, "Here's to us." A couple of months later Gary was promoted.

Gary wasn't an easy boss. He was a strong disciplinarian with a stainless-steel will, and he demanded more of both himself and others than just about any other manager at his level. People worked harder for him than they had ever worked before, yet turnover in his section was low. He bucked the company system regularly and seemed to do outrageous things as a matter of course. And his people delighted in talking about him and his latest exploits.

One story in particular was told over and over again at the company as Gary kept climbing higher in the management hierarchy. On his way to a vacation trek in Peru one year, the plane in which he was flying, an old DC-3, developed engine trouble over a dense jungle. After circling for several minutes the pilot finally found a clearing and managed a reasonably soft belly-landing. Injuries to the passengers were relatively minor. Gary's wrist was sprained, and he splinted it himself using a rolled-up airline magazine and some tape he had in his briefcase.

What was most alarming about the situation, as the passengers soon learned, was that the copilot had been unable to establish definite radio contact with any airfield before they went down. As far as the passengers knew they were alone and abandoned in the middle of a Peruvian jungle. Some of them panicked. Others

14

seemed to freeze into a kind of paralysis of despair. Their only thought was that they sit and wait to be found when their flight failed to arrive at its destination.

Gary surveyed the area with the pilot and copilot, and all three agreed that the plane would be difficult to spot under the canopy of treetops. According to several passengers who were later interviewed, it took Gary only twenty minutes to gather everyone together, mount one of the plane's wings, and make a speech. He convinced them that they could and would walk out of the jungle and back to civilization. As one passenger said later, "He made it seem almost matter-of-fact." It took Gary and the group three days, but they did make the long, difficult march, and except for mosquito bites no one suffered any further injuries.

Gary became an executive vice president, and he continued to be smart, demanding, and lucky. His reputation made him seem tough to some and terrifying to others. Yet people from all parts of the company seemed to be standing in line to transfer into his organization. It was fun and exciting and successful. There were opportunities and generous budgets. For a lot of midlevel managers, a meeting with Gary was an event— like meeting an NFL quarterback. Even when he skinned you with that whiplike mind of his, you could go back to your peers and show the scars proudly.

When Gary was appointed president and chief operating officer of the company, his mind seemed to grow even sharper. He had a vision for the company's future, and he had the business sense and the instincts to determine what was crucial and what was irrelevant in getting to it. He had about zero tolerance for irrelevance and for people who brought irrelevancies to him, no matter who they were—and that included some pretty powerful people in the financial community. Gary engineered several acquisitions that were instrumental in moving the company into the front ranks of its industry, but in the process he bruised the egos of several major investment bankers.

When the company's CEO retired a few years later, most of us expected that Gary would succeed him, but it didn't happen. A more conservative person was picked. Gary still tried to mobilize support among the board of directors for his plans, but his style had generated too many opponents. Instead they appointed him vice chairman of the board, a job with more title than authority, and in which he no longer held operating responsibility. About a year later, I remember, a major business magazine commented on the "seeming decline of company energy," and for more than two years the company did indeed seem to get pretty lethargic.

Gary sensed a new chance and, like Napoleon, attempted to come back from exile. He tried again to win the board to his vision. For a while it looked as though he might succeed, but the forces against him were still too strong. Soon afterward, at sixty-two, Gary retired and made plans to sail around the world in a small boat. Just before his scheduled departure Gary was interviewed by a prominent business columnist. Sensing a hot story of high-level corporate conflict, he asked Gary if, in light of his long career with the company, he felt any bitterness about the way he had been treated.

Gary seemed surprised by the question; then he said, "No bitterness at all. It was a hell of a trip." He smiled and pointed at a model of his sailboat, resting at a corner of his desk. "And now," he said, "I'm getting ready to start another one."

Bill seemed to have ended the story just in time, as the waiter arrived with our wine, but nobody moved. Bill folded his big hand around his glass and said that about a year after Gary retired, the company was awarded two large contracts and started to hire again. ❖

No matter what the conditions, an outstanding leader realizes that his interconnections with those he leads, those who lead him, and the situation he faces are perfect.

A sound leader knows too that he ought not call those he leads from too far ahead, nor demand of them abruptly what they find too unfamiliar or uncomfortable to give. Ego and compulsion to control are enemies of sound leadership. Asserting your position by maligning the opposition is of limited use. A loud assertion of your position and importance may be exhilarating, but it can freeze your maneuverability.

Be cautious of the leader who shines too brilliantly. He may dazzle for a while, but when his glitter fades, those who have not illuminated their own paths will be left in the dark. A driving wind pushes what is before it only when it blows ceaselessly. It imparts none of its energy, but only exhausts both itself and the objects of its force. When it stops blowing, what is before it stops moving. So it is with a driving leader.

5

Whether the situations in your life are proceeding well or poorly for you at this moment is a matter of cyclicality. Both triumph and disappointment are parts of the whole of your experience, which keeps unfolding. It is the same with families and organizations.

Organizations and the behavior of people within them persist. Making, buying, selling, administering, and serving continue through generations. When you enter organization life you are entering a stream that has been flowing for a long while before you arrived and will continue after you have gone. That is significant and should be respected. Stirring up change should be done selectively and with prudence. There will always be unforeseen consequences.

Debates, feuds, and antagonisms are seldom about what they seem to be about. Since that is the case, trying to settle such issues logically will often prove fruitless. Treat the problem by moving it out of the way or going around it, if possible.

Remind yourself often that you will favor the behaviors of some people and not those of others—and that your approval or disapproval is irrelevant. What is required is that you take care of what is yours to deal with.

6

Young or old, beginner or master, there is still time to reach your best goal. You need only discover what it is and recognize the inexhaustible opportunities for its realization.

As green sticks give birth to buds that blossom into splendid flowers, so do the most unexceptional occupations contain the buds of excellence. They require only proficient nurturing to ripen.

The ordinary and the comfortable is the base from which the outstanding arises. After every exertion that meets the special demands of crisis or golden opportunity, the ordinary and the comfortable is the foundation to which each of us returns to spend most of our time. The sound leader does not neglect the apparently unexceptional. She understands that green sticks may bring forth the blossoms of prominent achievements.

A driving wind pushes
what is before it only
when it blows ceaselessly

7

Though he understands his significance to himself, an outstanding leader is not an end unto himself. He is available to the interests of others and requires no indemnifications.

Roles, policies, responsibilities, and duties are like the rafters, joists, and studs of a house. They provide a framework. Nevertheless, within a good framework some bad may be done. More important, within a bad framework some good may be done. The outstanding leader finds opportunity to serve within either framework; thus he never stops advancing.

8

Whatever his level in the hierarchy, the sound leader stands as high within it as he can in what he does, and as low within it as he is able in terms of personal pride in his position and achievements. Large egos tend to high ambition and showy claims. They sort other people and conditions only as items favorable or unfavorable to themselves and their interests. Great prides trumpet great accomplishments and obscure great failures, rise on great euphorias and sink in great despondencies. In all this tide of drama the pleasures of the ordinary are often lost.

The sound leader refines his ego to more moderate proportions. While he may lead through momentous events, he travels his road more evenly. He pauses to engage his friendliness, focuses his attention on maintaining his straightforwardness, and remembers to value the substance of both his own and others' work. Insisting on no sorting of those for or against him, he himself is not so sorted.

9

Ever climbing, ever reaching.
Ever striving, ever surpassing. Ever gaining, ever accumulating. Ever the same. For some these alone are the ways to attain. And so for fifty years or more they repeat the pattern until stopped by circumstances, by disillusion, or by death.

There are alternatives—a less locked and linear point of view. The reconsideration of ever onward and upward, and the revaluing of pauses and side paths. The recollection that attainment can also be the filling of holes, and that each of us has a different whole to fill.

10

If you are a skilled planner, can you trust yourself without a plan? Can you trust your spontaneous self to carry you through? If you are able to control important events, can you allow smaller ones to go their own way?

If you can lead courageously, can you follow humbly? If you can roar and charge forward like a tiger, can you wait patiently and nourish like a cow? Has your thirst for praise and recognition been sufficiently quenched that you can achieve significant deeds and allow the credit to flow to others? And all of this without exertion?

If you have these skills, generate them but do not cling to them, develop them but do not depend on them, lead them but do not compel them.

This is the way.

11

Notice and make use of spaces:

Silence

Unpredictability

Openness

What is not said

What is outside the boxes on the organization chart

These spaces often define intent and meaning.

JANEY-SUE GETS EVEN

O NE DAY IN EARLY OCTOBER Larry Berline just sat there at the table and twirled angel-hair pasta around his fork without eating a bite. Bill asked him if something was wrong with the food. Larry said no, the food was fine, but he was so upset he couldn't taste it anyway. Larry was a young programmer in software development. He said his supervisor had just dumped a load of abuse on him for a mistake that hadn't been his fault at all, and no matter how hard he had tried to explain, the boss wasn't in a mood to listen. He said he wished he knew a way to get through to the guy.

Bill nodded sympathetically, then he told us about Janey-Sue Waddleton. Janey-Sue, who was still under thirty, Bill said, already had a reputation in the company; it arrived at the plant even before she did. Everybody had somehow heard that she was born in Enid, Oklahoma, and had gone to MIT and then, for her MBA, to Harvard Business School—both on scholarships. After that she'd been hired directly into corporate headquarters. And now she was assigned here at our plant as manager of developmental projects.

Everybody had opinions about her: Some thought she was awesome and a lot of others spent time waiting for her to fall on her face.

One time, after Janey-Sue had been at the plant for about six months, she was assigned the responsibility of preparing the product development plan for a particularly important project. The plan was to be presented by her boss to the company's executive office, and a date was set on their agenda. To assure the accuracy and quality of the presentation, Janey-Sue and her unit worked many extra hours to ensure their data were correct and that the presentation would respond to the needs of the executive office.

But when the time came to translate the information into an appropriate presentation, a cascade of problems began. First, the graphics were incorrectly prepared by the graphic design department, which resulted in a two-day delay. Then, when the designs were corrected, the photo-processing equipment for making the slides broke down. The graphics department told Janey-Sue that no replacement parts would be available for ten days, which was seven days later than the scheduled presentation. Janey-Sue decided to send the work out to a local vendor. She insisted on a delivery date that would allow an extra day before the presentation, in case final corrections were needed.

On the morning of the scheduled delivery date, however, Janey-Sue's boss called her at home and asked her to fly to a nearby city right away to handle an emergency assignment. She never had an opportunity to inspect the slides. Later that afternoon, Janey-Sue's boss called her department and asked to see the slides. Since Janey-Sue wasn't there, one of the young engineers in her outer office took the call, found the envelope that had recently been delivered, and rushed it up to the boss's office. The slides were of very poor quality.

When Janey-Sue returned to her office two days later, weary from her long hours of work on the emergency, she was immediately called to her boss's office. In front of some of her peers, who happened to be in the room on another matter, her boss criticized Janey-Sue severely for the low quality of the slides. Janey-Sue said nothing.

In mid-March, at a staff meeting, it was discovered that the division's marketing manager had missed an important product feature in his advertising campaign for one of the division's new products. Without quite saying so the marketing manager hinted broadly that part of the fault lay with Janey-Sue's department for not having provided him with timely information on the feature. In fact this was not so. Janey-Sue, however, said nothing.

In April, on a warm spring day, Janey-Sue was again called to her boss's office. He greeted her warmly, shook her hand, and congratulated her, in front of a large group of upper-echelon managers, for continuing her department's concentration on a small program that most people had written off as impractical. The yield from the prototype product that had just been tested was almost six times better than had been predicted. She was assured that the accomplishment wouldn't be forgotten at bonus time. She graciously received the smiles and congratulations of everyone in the room. It was only after some thought that Janey-Sue recalled she had meant to cancel the project but under the pressures of the last few months she had forgotten to do so. She said nothing. ❖❖

Notice and make use of spaces

12

Data can overload, rumors can confuse, biases blind. The struggle to climb the pyramid can cost you your peace and self-regard. And success brings no relief.

Therefore, a sensible person does her best and allows the victory that is her due to unfold itself. Though action surrounds her, at heart she is quiet.

13

Success or failure

Failure or success

Fear of failure

Need for success

They drive human striving, reward and punish human pride, and obscure what is necessary for wholeness.

Regard the satisfaction of your ego as your central purpose and you feel the elation of triumph and the anguish of failure. Make your ego stiff and you carry the weight of heavy armor. Hold your ego closed and you must keep constant vigil for its safety. Allow your ego's walls permeability and experience the winning of the world.

14

For some, intellect is the means for bringing all things under control. To comprehend cause and effect, they collect data and sort them, measure them and interpret them, classify them and predict them.

When considering the future remember the remote past. One who is aware of the stream of causes, back to the primeval cause and forward to the ultimate cause, is less concerned about causes. She knows that causes can be traced, but ultimately the cause of the causes cannot be.

Yet there are no accidents. Each thing happens, according to the laws of nature, because it must, for reasons that make it inevitable. And this is the way the system has always been—causes that are traceable but ultimately unknowable. Know this and become master of all moments.

15

Alert to problems and opportunities, addressing them with prudence and calm. Solid in principle and fluid in execution. Open to ever-changing possibilities. Generous and considerate. These are the qualities.

Flowing with one's natural stream, accepting one's rapids and whirlpools, becalmings and stagnant pools. Stroking hard without compulsion, resting patiently, awaiting clarity that is sure to come. These are their applications.

BACK TO THE MAIL ROOM

THE ATMOSPHERE IN OUR division at the time was pretty tense. We were behind schedule on several projects and over budget on some others. The general manager had already demoted one of the project leaders, and he seemed on the warpath most of the time. A bunch of us met at Robbie's Bistro, which serves great seafood, and we were discussing whether a person would be better off keeping a low profile in these times rather than speaking his mind. Tom thought the best strategy was to go along and get along. He claimed that agreeing with the boss never did anybody much harm, while disagreeing with the boss seldom did anyone much good.

Bill grinned and said he had some experience on that subject. He told us about a time when he had just earned his engineering degree and had been promoted from technician to management trainee. At that time, Bill said, the trainees were assigned to a variety of jobs. Some of the assignments were appealing and interesting, like working with a project team, and some were nothing but routine "dog work," like sorting mail.

Bill continued: I was one of the lucky ones at first, and I got to work as a staff assistant to the division VP. In the course of the assignment I had a fair number of contacts with him, and we got along well—at least I thought so. Well, one day I happened to be in his office taking notes for him while he reviewed one of the division's programs. Suddenly he came up with this idea for cutting about three percent out of the program's costs. He was very excited, and I guess he couldn't wait to tell someone about it, so he told me.

I was just a junior engineer at the time, but when I was a technician I had been involved with that program and I knew the idea wouldn't work.

Bill paused and glanced at Tom, and Tom couldn't resist asking, "What did you do?"

I told him my opinion was that it wouldn't work, and then told him why. I just dumped a whole bucket of reasons right out on his desk.

What happened?

Two days later I got assigned to the mail room to mend my opinions.

"Sure," said Tom, triumph glowing from his eyes. "And that ought to be a lesson to us all."

But Bill hadn't finished. Tuesday of the following week, he said, I got a call from the boss's secretary, who said he wanted to see me in an hour. When I went in he told me that he was reassigning me to the staff assistant job. He also dropped a couple of hints that he had decided not to implement his idea about cost reduction. Instead he had some other ideas that he thought would address the cost issue. He didn't mention what they were, and I just sat there and didn't say much. Before I left he said he was glad to have me back on board, and he invited me to dinner at his house the next weekend.

"Yep," beamed Tom, "what a difference a little discretion can make."

Bill went on: I was single at the time, living mostly on fast food and TV dinners, so I really enjoyed the meal. After dinner the boss, his wife, and I sat around and talked. The boss was feeling pretty mellow, and after a while he invited me into his study. He poured us a couple of snifters of a brand of cognac I couldn't afford, and as we sat and sipped he talked about the division. Then he stood up and told me he was going to do something that he didn't often do. He was going to allow me to be one of the first people in the company to see his new strategic plan for the division.

"Hey," said Tom, "that's a real sign of respect!"

Well, said Bill, I thought about it for a minute, then I put down my glass, stood up, and went to get my coat. My boss asked where I was going. Heading home, I said. I'll have to be up early tomorrow to get to the mail room on time.

Tom just shook his head sadly from side to side, but try as he might he couldn't hide his grin. ❖

16

Every now and then, consider your life as a whole (including your death). For some, absolutely the most difficult thing of all is to learn that they are no better than anyone else; for others, it is that they are no worse than anyone else.

If you are able, reflect a little as well that you are no better or worse than all else that appears before you, composed of subatomic particles that are tracks of energy. All are contained together, within "the system."

If that view seems too abstract, too lacking in power, too passive or fatalistic, reflect further. Destiny does not lack power, nor is it often passive. Blindness and anxiety are the costs of denying destiny. Understanding destiny is enlightenment. It does not require your surrender but rather your embrace. In return it offers the knowledge of your immortality.

17

The best leader seldom interferes. Less desirable is the one who is well known and admired by everyone. Worse is the one who is feared, and worst the one held in contempt.

To become an excellent leader, you have to abandon addiction to praise from above and flattery from below. The excellent leader leads least. He studies the distinctive skills and natural inclinations of both those above and those below, and he directs their attention to accomplish what is required to benefit all. When this has been done, all declare they have been part of a worthwhile purpose.

18

In our times, questions of right and wrong or benign and wicked are seldom asked. Rather, in these times, issues of legality predominate. But legality only defines the margins, within which people display their arts of avoidance and their crafts of manipulation.

Rules and laws do not reform people or make them ethical. Nor do charitable guidelines make them generous. Nor does adherence to the codes of loyalty and duty make them honorable.

19

In the practices of management, simplicity is enjoying a revival. A sound leader will revive his own simplicity as well.

Reduce the layers of hierarchy and the details of policy, and encourage people to find their own best ways. Curtail the output of data and train people to concentrate on what is important. Cut the number of committees and encourage individuals to assume responsibility. Lower the level for approvals and those above can attend to their primary business.

Dispense with so many formalities and rituals and people will find their reward in concentrating on the substance.

20

The case is often made that contemporary issues are highly complex and one must not oversimplify them. But often, too, issues are made to seem more complex than they are. By sleight of hand and mind, many in our society acquire prestige and grow wealthy perpetuating complexity.

I, however, am the son of a truck driver, and were I not otherwise engaged I might now be

Abandon addiction to praise from above and flattery from below

driving, too. When I hear complex explanations I am not convinced, unless I
am convinced, and I am convinced only by the simple.

People say, "How naive, how illogical." But I continue, out of tune with this popular chorus, direct in words and deeds, not an insider or an "old boy," still only an apprentice learning the truck driver's trade.

These are the apprentice's lessons: To forsake my high dramas and the inner-head soliloquies that animate them. To reduce immense, broad issues to smaller, narrower ones. To make choices rather than decisions, and to watch the pattern of these choices point to my new directions.

I have allowed my cleared vision to reveal new possibilities that have changed my old questions or dissolved them. And I have found the part of me that knows full well that all will be well, whichever choice I make.

21

Perspectives abound: The worker, the supervisor; the engineer, the salesman; the bold, the cautious; the analyst, the activist. Each gathers information and molds it into a form that suits his singular disposition. Each form is constructed from the materials of that person's interests, experiences, and feelings. Thus opinions are derived and closely held.

But opinions are no more than runoff from that enormous hidden stream that moves all things along. Competent people make sense of their opinions, superior people make sense of many opinions, outstanding people realize the source of opinions.

22

Quick and easy success can dull your edge. Establishing your image can slow your moves. Maintaining your position can leave you behind. Refining your data can blunt your instincts. There is danger in complacency.

Deviating from the shortest path, one better learns the geography. Advancing more slowly, one has time to know the inhabitants. Bending to pressure, one remains unbroken and may later spring back vigorously.

Driving one's self less, one may be carried by the drive of well-selected others. Recognizing one's self as no more or less than an equal, others may credit one's specialness.

23

In every life things are bound to go up and down. In nature the weather changes from fair to stormy and then to fair again. In the stock market and in the fortunes of sports teams there are wins and there are losses.

One year a person who is capable works hard and is promoted. A second person who is capable works hard and is not. And a third person who is not capable and avoids work, but who plays political games cleverly, is also promoted. How unfair, one might say.

But the tide turns, the season changes, and the pendulum swings, all according to their own schedules. The world is fair only on its own terms. It is not obliged to conform to yours.

If you identify yourself with winning then winning will identify with you. If you identify yourself with losing then losing will identify with you.

A sound leader chooses her course and follows its varied turns without regrets. She performs her work as well as she can, dispensing kindness when she can and justice when it is required. When she finds herself badly used by others she changes what she can, protects what she can, and endures what she must. Until the tide turns, the season changes, and the pendulum swings.

YOU NEVER KNOW

THERE WERE TIMES WHEN Bill could be exasperating. Craig Lopez had just heard that he was going to be transferred, and he didn't have much choice about it. Several of us were sympathizing with him while he complained about what a rotten deal he was getting. Craig didn't like the city they were sending him to, and he was convinced that his being so far away from headquarters would soon put his career on the shelf. As he saw it, the move would be the first step on his way down. We tried to reassure him, but we weren't getting anywhere. Then someone turned to Bill in desperation and asked him if he had any suggestions.

Well, I don't know if I mentioned this before, Bill said, but my daughter Janice left her job a while ago. She didn't have any choice, she was laid off. Bill's face was a pitcherful of gloom.

Since we were all in a sympathetic mood anyway, it wasn't long before someone said that that was too bad.

It could have been worse, Bill said. She got another offer in a couple of weeks; it even paid better.

That's great! someone said.

Bill said that it would have been, except that she had to move to a different city, just like Craig. Bill's gloomy face got a little gloomier.

If she hated that half as much as I do, said Craig, that must have been a tough decision for her.

Bill's shoulder twitched in a small shrug. Actually, he explained, it turned out she had been wanting to spend some time away from her boyfriend. They'd been talking about moving in together, and she wanted to think about it for a while.

Really, Craig said suddenly. You could see he was getting involved in the story. That can be a good idea—time away in another place, maybe dating some other people, that can be helpful.

Bill looked up at Craig and seemed all at once brighter-eyed. That's just what happened, he said. After a few months Janice found out that she really did want to live with him. He's offered to finance them both until she gets a job in the city. They may even get married.

Right! said Craig, who was savoring his own good judgment. I'm glad it turned out well.

No sooner had he said it than Bill clouded up again and looked like the gloom pitcher was about to run over. The trouble is, he explained, they just couldn't come to an agreement on where they were going to live. He wanted to keep his apartment, but Janice didn't like it and wanted to find a new place so they could start together fresh. They became very polarized about the subject and had some real arguments.

That's too bad, Craig sort of mumbled warily. He was beginning to look a little glassy-eyed.

Actually, said Bill, who looked like he could go on forever and might just do it, they decided just a few days ago to find a new place, and this morning Janice called and said they found one they both like very much.

Uh-huh, murmured Craig. We could hardly hear him. Bill's saga kept marching on.

Unfortunately the rent is very high. They could afford it if she were working, but they want to save some for a house too. And then they're talking about starting a family. Bill tapered off and it was real quiet for what seemed like a very long time. Then Bill looked directly at Craig, and this time you couldn't tell whether he was gloomy or happy.

When Craig couldn't hold out any longer he had to ask: Well, Bill, how did it finally turn out?

Good question, Bill said, good question.

24

Self-confidence sends a strong signal when it is quiet. When broadcast at high volume, it turns to static. The leader who is her own publicist is no more likely to convince her audience than her client. In advancing toward the peak, a leader who throws her weight around is more likely to lose her footing. One who carries her weight in proper balance is more likely to hold the trail.

When her early advances have been made in long, easy strides, a young person may come to expect the same in the future. Thus, considering only her past, she values only one direction—forward; only one speed—fast; and only one mood—"look at me." But the trail is long, and wiser travelers learn to move from side to side occasionally, to slow the pace, or even to retreat at times. And they learn to feel as comfortable in the background as in the front.

25

Like a surfer on a wave or a skier on a slope, each of us rides the world. There is no other possibility. How we ride the world is our way.

All ways start in silence and emptiness, like bowls, or empty warehouses waiting to be filled. This is a place before the separation of thinking, feeling, and willing begins. It has no name. When the silence and emptiness stir to gather together into things, it is called chaos. Life is what it is called when thinking is created. Thus are formed the subject matters of the mind and spirit, as well as persons to perceive them and energy for their motion.

Each person's way is a marvel of intricacy and significance. So too are the way of the earth and the way of the spirit. In an endless network, each way sparks and is sparked by all others, and thus maintains life.

26

In the midst of the crisis —surrounded by its perils, stressed by its demands, confused by its issues, worried by its consequences— step aside and breathe. As all athletes know, tightening does not improve performance, distraction slows, anxiety makes you miss.

Step aside and breathe. Take a break. Still the closed-loop message that speeds inside your head, and listen for a moment to silence. Then, afterward, hear a fresher message.

At the peak of success, in the midst of acclaim, admiration by peers, congratulations by superiors, let it all wash over you like an invigorating shower. Then be done with it. Enjoy but do not cling. Step aside and breathe.

27

A sound leader is economical and elegant in his use of resources.
He knows how to best use imperfect people. He understands their traits and foibles without condemning them. He assesses people continually, but never concludes he knows the total of their worth. His ability to place the right people in the right jobs at the right times is hardly noticed.

Some leaders are the beneficiaries of extraordinary gifts. They lead by unfathomable combinations of personal charm, brilliance of mind, and forcefulness of character. Like powerful magnets, they draw others to them without effort. These leaders, too, can be mistaken.

If you want to correct another person's character or behavior, first find within yourself the same trait or conduct. Then you and the other person can learn together what needs

In every life things are
bound to go up and down

to be done. If you only lecture to others about what is best, you are as far off the road as those to whom you lecture. Appreciate the competent, value the unskilled.

28

A person who can both plunge ahead and wait patiently can foster the appropriate strategy. One who values expansion and appreciates contraction is better able to perceive the possibilities latent in others. He can manage diversity, distinguishing between those who are best at risking and creating, those who are best at caution and maintaining, and those who are best at toughness and compelling. As he respects all, he can modulate the entrepreneur, stimulate the bureaucrat, and temper the autocrat.

Only one who is high in stature and low in vanity can truly grasp the worlds of those he leads, and because of this he is an endless source of usefulness to them.

The capacity for such nondiscrimination grows within the leader. Such a leader can lead the many, not only the few.

29

Those who talk of making changes but do not first take time to see how matters stand now have nothing to build on, and their efforts usually fail. Pronouncing the old ways of doing things "irrational" or "dysfunctional" is more a commentary on the commentator than on the old ways. All apparent irrationalities serve one or many people's interests.

A sound leader pursues change carefully and he knows when to let be—whether old ways, other people, or himself. Be wary of aims too extreme and plans too vast. Inertia is a powerful force to reckon with.

In all nature and among all people and organizations there is uniqueness. As no two snowflakes or fingerprints are the same, neither are two persons, families, organizations, or cultures.

A sound leader is most often moderate.

30

An organization will not endure for the long term when its leaders depend on aggression as a constant strategy. Aggression has consequences—even when it is successful it breeds enemies. Weak enemies may combine and become strong. Circumstances may change the battleground; advantages once held may be lost.

Aggression mobilizes antagonisms, both in the opposition and among a leader's own people. Such a surge of hostile thoughts takes on a life of its own and gives rise to unforeseen hostile actions that cannot be controlled. Aggression will often bring disorder and devastation to the aggressor as well as to his victim, from which recovery is slow.

Wise generals are reluctant to war. When circumstances require conflict, wise leaders will devote themselves to it but not esteem it. Even in victory, a wise leader will not dwell on self-congratulation or encourage celebrations. He will recognize that his winning was inevitable, merely an outcome of circumstances, not a cause for personal pride.

Neither will the sensible leader flaunt his power. When power is prized too much, it stiffens into chains of command and symbols of authority. This breeds bureaucracy and rigidity, and so perish creativity and adaptation. Bureaucracy and rigidity have caused the downfall of organizations from ancient empires to modern megacorporations.

31

When conflict is required do not stir emotions against the opponent or glorify your superior technology. When these are done, followers—like stampeding cattle—will run amok, and bitterness and turmoil will be the yield.

Quiet concentration on limited objectives, free from the confusions of passion, will more likely bring success and durable reconciliation. Graciousness in victory is better than the domination of antagonists. The leader who turns as swiftly as he can from the needs of conflict to the opportunities of reconciliation is useful for the longer term.

The vital person can exercise superior energy without making enemies or damaging opponents. The leader with a drive to obliterate her enemies is dangerous and unloved, even by her allies—they will cast her out as soon as they are able.

VICTORY

THE WHOLE PLANT was talking about the feud between the marketing and design departments. They squabbled with each other about every issue, and when there weren't any issues at hand, they seemed to invent them. It started between the two department heads at a staff meeting. They crossed swords on some issue that no one remembers anymore, but the battle spread throughout their organizations and continues now as a full-scale war.

Bill recalled that once, back about ten years ago, there were two vice presidents in the company. Both were able and ambitious, and both were generally considered to be the strongest candidates for the next promotion. Their battles with each other were notorious, and, on a scale of one to ten, the cooperation between their divisions was a negative number. Since the production of the company's newest and most important product, on time and on budget, depended on their close cooperation, the feud was an important problem. Just about everything was tried to get them together, including bringing in an outside facilitator to arbitrate between them. But nothing had worked. The company president, who had been trying to keep out of it as much as he could, finally decided, reluctantly, that he had to make a choice between them. He asked one VP to resign and placed both divisions under the other VP's authority.

When the news was out that this VP was the clear winner (by a knockout), her supporters inside her old division came to her, congratulating and praising her and generally whooping it up. They told each other there would now be a new regime; they talked about how right they had been all along and how wrong the other division had been. They worked furiously to develop and present proposals that called for the dismemberment of the other division and the assignment of key functions to themselves. They seemed to think of the VP as their general who had just won the war, and now they wanted her to take apart the defeated enemy's empire. They proposed a hundred changes, but the VP politely declined almost all of them.

Instead she made personal calls on many people in the other division and asked them what courses of action they believed in and what resources they needed to pursue those courses. When she could, she gave them support; when she couldn't, she told them why not and offered alternatives. Gradually she changed their old policies and ways of operating, but she didn't replace their old regulations with a set of new ones. Instead, she gave the new group and her old division some time to work out a new integration between them. Overall, she left a lot of open spaces for exploration.

In time the environment cooled, and the people in both divisions were less prone to put each other down. Pretty quickly, under the pressures of tight deadlines and with no rewards for feuding, they began to improve their collaboration. The new product was brought in on time, though it was about fourteen percent over budget. There were some all-night parties when that happened, Bill told us, and there were people from both divisions at most of them. ❖❖

32

What is in the world has always been in the world. Nothing new is made; only names are changed and viewpoints from which they are seen. Worldly people discriminate endlessly. They judge what is better or worse, invent titles, rank, and status, and struggle (or complain) to obtain what they think they do not have. All of this activity is part of the way the world works.

Some people mistake these discriminations for the substance of their lives. To get what they think they do not have they push against stone walls, exhausting their energy and capacities. Thus they fail to notice the possibilities that lie beyond their current points of view.

When leaders remember the way of the world they bring wisdom to their leadership. Recognizing the familiar courses and turnings of people's discriminations, they compare the present to the past, anticipate points of discord, and help people discover unnoticed harmony.

33

Knowing others and what moves them provides the tools of power. Knowing yourself and what moves you brings the diamond core of mastery. Overcoming others demonstrates your power. Self-mastery has no need for demonstration.

Leaving greed behind, content to optimize, you have no need to maximize. Independent of the habits of ostentation, you less exhaust the earth. Reflecting on your source and destination, you sight eternity and lose all fear of death.

34

World that contains so much:

Activity and rest

Laughter and tears

Predator and prey

Abundance and scarcity

Love and loneliness

And all of us within it, without exception
or exemption.

While encompassing us, the world does not
control us. Whether praised or cursed or just
ignored, the world continues to do its duty.
How generous the world is.

Can a person equal the world?

35

**When you have traveled the
way for a time,** some of those you
meet will perceive it and be more content in
your presence. They will feel they have found
a safe and healthy place.

Others will not notice, or may grow restless,
anxious to return to tumult. Ego is compelling,
but by its nature eventually trips itself to
humiliation. Excitement is appealing, but by its
nature grinds itself down.

The Tao is matter-of-fact and requires no embellishment. It is hardly noticeable, but it lasts forever.

36

Power is most secure when not displayed

Large egos are vulnerable to slight

Aggression is vulnerable to counterattack

High status is vulnerable to failure.

Still, power is the flour of change

Egos provide its yeast

Aggression gives the heat for baking and

Status turns the oven on.

And so the Tao makes bread.

37

In the midst of action hides tranquility. Those who find it act without exertion, allowing their natures to select their choices and motions.

Leaders who know tranquility are neither obsessed by maximum yields nor compelled toward self-righteous destinations. Setting aside the weighty burden of an ultimate goal, they guide people more gracefully through both difficult and easy times, continuing without concluding.

Though it must be sought, tranquility cannot be found by hunting. It eludes the hunter until, of its own free will, it seeks out the one who awaits it.

38

The person who is sound and confident meets others without hidden intention.
The person dedicated to courtesy meets others with practiced warmth and solicitude. The person dedicated to obeying the rules meets others ethically. The one anxious to avoid punishment meets them legally. The person eager for acceptance meets others according to the fashion of the day.

To meet others courteously

To meet others ethically

To meet others legally

To meet others according to the fashion of the day

Each of these, in our time, is expertly promoted and elaborated by renowned authorities. And so declines the quality of our lives.

The person of stamina is neither duped nor confused. He has his sureness. He owns his yes and his no.

BEEJAY'S ELEPHANT

O N ANOTHER NIGHT OUR group
went out to dinner. It was a long evening, and
the longer it went on the more relaxed it got.
Toward the late hours, like kids telling ghost stories, we
began talking about weird things that had happened
around the plant. Jennifer said there was one new piece
of computerized equipment that, no matter how many
times they calibrated it, always slid back to the same
mistake. They called in the service people, who even
changed some parts, but the same thing kept happening.
Other people told other stories, about things like undis-
coverable software glitches or people they knew who
always seemed to be at the right place at the right time,
and they wondered how anybody could be that lucky.
Each story seemed to be getting a bit richer than the one
before, until they fairly dripped with exaggeration.

Then Bill told his story. It seems there was this one
time when a peculiar thing happened in the marketing
department. You know, Bill said, those marketing people sometimes have pretty rich imaginations. But anyway, there was a customer relations manager named

Beejay who had an elephant that sat on her desk and talked to her.

At first, nobody in the office gave it more than passing notice. *They* couldn't hear it talk. Bill told us how from time to time he would pass by her desk and notice the intense look on Beejay's face. She seemed to be leaning toward the elephant, and sometimes she seemed to move her lips a little. Well, we all put it down to an idiosyncrasy, Bill said, and since most of us had one or two of our own, and since Beejay seemed so normal in most other ways, no one paid much attention.

One day though, Bill continued, after I got to know Beejay pretty well, we were sitting at lunch, after everybody else had left, and I asked her about the elephant statue. She said that it was a real elephant, and told me that it talked to her sometimes.

It didn't *look* real, and she explained that that was because it was good at disguising itself. She said that it didn't like to draw much notice, and so it had made itself into a five-inch high ivory statue of an elephant. She said it could have made itself into something entirely different if it had wanted to.

Well, from time to time Beejay and I talked about the elephant and Beejay told me more about it. She said the nice thing about her elephant was that when she asked for advice, her elephant would usually give it to her, and it was almost always good advice. For instance, once she had been unsure about whether or not she was qualified for a new supervisor job that had been posted. She wondered if it would be a good idea or a bad idea to let her boss and the human resources department know that she wanted to apply. She asked the elephant, and it advised her to go full speed ahead. She took its advice, and she got the job.

The thing that was less nice about Beejay's elephant was that it would sometimes give her its opinions and advice when she didn't ask for them or even really want to hear them. For instance, when she had insisted one time on getting her own way in a meeting with her new staff, though some of them clearly wanted to go in another direction, she came away feeling like a powerful leader. But later, as she thought about it more, she worried that she had been too autocratic. It was a serious issue to her, and it made her feel important to have important things like that to worry about.

Then suddenly, out of the blue, Beejay heard her elephant laughing at her. Beejay told me that, to her ears, the laughter was so loud that she looked around to see if anyone else could hear it. Beejay asked her elephant why it was laughing. "This is a serious issue," she told it. "Can a supervisor really get the best from her staff if she acts autocratically and stifles their initiative? And what about the ethical issues of abusing power?"

The elephant seemed to raise its trunk a little, and it said, "Beejay, my dear. You aren't nearly as powerful as you think you are, and other people aren't nearly as helpless." And though Beejay asked it to explain further, that's all it would say.

As if that weren't bad enough: About a month later Beejay came out of a meeting with her boss feeling frustrated, resentful, and angry because her boss had turned down her proposal. Later, when the anger and resentment had worn off, she felt only frustrated and powerless—and very sorry for herself. She slumped down at her desk and brooded on how little authority she really had around here. Suddenly she was again jarred by the sound of her elephant's rolling chuckle. And she heard it say, "Beejay, you aren't nearly as helpless as you think you are, and other people aren't nearly as powerful."

"C'mon Bill," Max asked, "do you really expect us to believe that?"

"Which part?" asked Bill. ❖

The leader with a drive to obliterate enemies is dangerous and unloved, even by her allies—they will cast her out as soon as they are able

39

Once upon a time the simple could be seen: That all reality is virtual. That chaos encompasses order, and order chaos. That clarity and peace interweave elegantly with difficulty and battle, and that spirit is the sinew that binds all the world together.

From these conditions arise the billion others with which we live. Failing to recall that this is so, you miss the world's significance, the direction of its change, its uses and its destination. And so you may feel lost and frightened.

Through his deeds a great leader reminds people of their possibilities. His greatness rises not upon the tower of spectacular achievement but from the foundation of the ordinary. He stands not above but among those he leads, upon the same earthy foundation, and beneath him lies the solid rock.

All leaders announce themselves as servants of those they lead. For some these protestations only mask their pride. The great leader recognizes his leadership is a duty no more important than any other.

40

Each person lives, then dies—acts and then is still. Wherever action leads and whatever it achieves, stillness comes. Action and stillness are part of a whole, each requiring the other in order to know itself—as large requires small, as night requires day.

41

Some people perceive the way at once and join it. Others glimpse its direction and discuss it in admiring words. But, as if it were a dazzling panther, they keep their distance from it. And some people ridicule the way with great enthusiasm. If the way were not embraced by some, avoided by some, and laughed at by some, it would not be itself.

Those who laugh at the way can list its faults: pointless, of no practical use, not for these times or cultures. What is important to those who laugh is what can be counted. The core of life is of no concern. Acquisition is the focus of existence. Complexity is a fascination. And people's doings are all that can be discerned.

But eternity is claimed by the one who opens to know the whole. Strength and endurance are his who can feel the core of life. Skill is his who can go straight to the simple center. And laughter is his who can hear the greatest joke.

42

The way is perfect as it is

And so will it be perfect as it changes.

The way is always in balance

For every force a counterforce

For every inhale an exhale.

Creation arises from nothing,

Stands as one and

Then divides in two,

Male and female.

And from the male and female combination

Off spring the billion variations.

All of this together, in ferment and at rest,

Are the way, the system of our world.

Modesty is functional, boastfulness is risky.

Force bears consequences.

43

Dissolving elaborate falsehoods,
cutting through misinformation and guile—this
is critical thinking. Still, critical thinking cannot
penetrate to the reality of a situation.
Penetrating to reality cannot be perfected by
exercise, only by granting yourself permission.

Thinking is not seizing ideas, but permitting
them to dance before you. Saying does not
always require your words; silence speaks as
well. Nor does action always require your
exertion. As small flowers and great oaks are
drawn toward the sun without effort, so allow
truth to unfold itself. Allowance without force
is valuable.

DRAGONS AND VALUES

SOME SENIOR MANAGERS from another company in our industry were involved once in a bribery scandal with a minister of a Central American government. Things were very stirred up because of this all over the industry—the top management of most companies, including ours, decided to give values and ethics courses to everybody, with lots of examples of what was acceptable behavior and what wasn't. Ethics was the topic of the day, and some people became very sensitive about impropriety, especially the appearance of impropriety. George was one of them.

George was a fairly new member of the lunch crew. He was a young, bright guy with strong convictions about what was right and what was wrong. He was also pretty quick to let you know his opinions. His critical remarks hit people sometimes, but the group was pretty free and open with one another, and George didn't bother anyone too much. You could tell Bill was fond of him. Bill made it a point to include him in conversations, and he showed real interest in George's views.

I had the impression that George reminded him of himself at that age.

One time Bill, George, and I were assigned to fly out to the Midwest and work on a customer problem. We met with a couple of the customer's representatives all day at their branch office. The problem was the failure of one of the products we supplied them. During a coffee break, George and the customer's engineers began to talk about values and ethics. They all agreed the whole country seemed to be in pretty sad shape in that area, what with scandals of one kind and another, violence in the streets, and a lack of direction from our leadership. Just about everybody agreed that people needed to concentrate more on the subject of values or we could expect to see the whole social structure go down the tubes before very long. Just before it was time to go back to work, Bill remarked that there were two kinds of values, ideal and operational, and it was best not to confuse them. I didn't really understand him at the time, but I did before the night was over.

We went to dinner with them after a long, tough day. It was a good dinner, in pleasant company, and at the end of the meal Bill paid the check. It had once been the customary thing to do, but that was before the bribery scandal and all the values and ethics courses. I was sitting across the table from George, and I noticed right away that he could hardly believe his eyes. His shoulders hunched, his mouth popped open, and for a minute I thought he was going to detonate, but with

great effort he held his peace. In fact, he became totally quiet and stayed that way until we dropped the customers off at their hotel. As soon as they were out of
the cab, George seemed to take a big, deep breath, and
then he proceeded to climb all over Bill. How could
you do that? he demanded. After all we talked about,
how could you pay that check?

I could see Bill wince. I knew paying the check had just
been an old habit and he hadn't even thought about it,
but George didn't see that or didn't care. He kept after
Bill: What about ethics and values? What are the customer's reps going to think?

Bill just sat and listened to George dump on him. After
what seemed a long time, when George had finally run
down a bit, Bill asked, "George, Do you think I was
trying to bribe them?" George said, "That's not the
question." "It's my question," said Bill.

George said he knew Bill wasn't trying to bribe them,
but still it could be misunderstood. They could think
you were attempting to get them to go easy on us.
Paying that check could be misinterpreted by someone
else. Bill sighed, and then admitted it was possible.
"Exactly!" said George triumphantly.

Bill sighed again and then he said, I suppose that's
been a heavy load. George looked puzzled and asked
Bill what he meant. Well, said Bill, I put that check
down at the restaurant; you apparently are still carrying it. George started to respond, but his sense of

humor cracked through and he smiled a little. Then he admitted that that might to some degree be true. The cab got to the hotel about then. It was late, but we decided on a cup of coffee so we went to the coffee shop. After we settled in, George asked Bill if he thought appearances were unimportant.

No, I think they can be important, Bill said, but I guess my operational values got the better of my ideal ones at dinner. They sometimes do. But then again, he continued, it could be worse—if my ideal values got too big, they might get in the way of me seeing my operational ones. Like this Chinese fellow I heard about, he added. Bill had this little glint starting at the corner of his eyes. What Chinese fellow, George wanted to know; he had his own twinkle.

Bill sipped his coffee and began his story: About six years ago we worked on a joint venture with a Chinese firm. One of their people, a woman named Chan, told me a story that she said went back about five hundred years. As I recall it, there was an important man in town who admired dragons. You might say that he so revered them that, in his mind, the regime of a dragon was his highest value. The man always attended town council meetings and, year after year, as the townspeople considered their problems, he kept saying that if the town only had its own dragon, the dragon would set things right. It would make the town's unruly youth settle down. It would clean up the criminal element and eliminate opium smoking, and it would eradicate political corruption. The man made his case so forcefully that the town council was very impressed.

Not only the council was impressed, according to Ms. Chan—eventually the man's speeches attracted the attention of the ancient dragon goddess. She was so persuaded by his words that she decided to assign one of her dragons to the town. The next morning the dragon she sent showed up at the man's window to receive its instructions.

Bill picked up his coffee cup and studied the cold residue at its bottom. George waited awhile, then shrugged. "You win," he said. "What happened then?"

Bill frowned thoughtfully. Well, the dragon rumbled a few times and snorted out a fiery plume to announce its arrival. The man, hearing the commotion and attracted by the glow, pulled back his curtains and looked out to see his dragon right there before his eyes. At which point he died of fright. ❖

44

Whether seeking fame or wealth or victories, the one less driven by acquisitiveness is less captured by fixation, pays less cost to conscience and to self-esteem.

The one who values himself and others knows how to be content, what is enough, the price of things, how to say no, when to slow and ease the strain; he respects the long view and can accommodate it.

The one who hacks his way most quickly dulls himself. The one who carves his way lasts longer. The one who finds the spaces and flows through them, longest of all.

45

Great organizations invariably decline. Great monuments eventually decay. Great accomplishments are always surpassed. All that is achieved invites its own eclipse.

As long as life continues there is more to be or do. Thus, the perfect being unattainable, why rush to reach it? When tired, rest. When rested, act. These are the guidelines for a suitable life.

46

Where the Tao is understood
moderation and steadiness are valued. Where
excess is esteemed, aggressive strategies rule
the day. Men who accumulate cumbersome
empires are honored more than those who
carefully tend to smaller enterprises.

In such times discontent reigns, ambition runs
rampant, domination is the mode. So,
turbulence increases and in a while shakes the
overgrown down. Only those who know
contentment are immune. They walk through
peace and turbulence on dependable legs.

In the midst of
action hides
tranquility

47

It is not necessary to possess all the data to know your best course. Without exhaustive inspection of each and every factor, what feels right and good your spirit will announce.

There are times when data are no use, when information distances, and learnedness obscures the heart of certainty. The keen-minded, without hurrying to meetings knows the crucial issues, without analysis recognizes the choices, without programs does what needs doing. The best of all action stems from the fact of being.

48

Experts, to guard against misfortune, toil daily, carefully stacking up their stores of expertise. Like ammunition wagons, they display armaments suitable for all eventualities.

Those who scrutinize the Tao are not experts, nor do they seek to pile up knowledge or wisdom. Those who study the Tao discard the nonessentials and concentrate more intently on the core. Like riflemen, they sight their targets, knowing that there is no need to fire.

ARCHERS AND TARGETS

A VERY WELL KNOWN EXPERT on strategic planning was scheduled to visit the plant. He had impressive credentials. He was an officer or a board member in three out of four of the most prominent industry associations, taught at one of the most prestigious business schools in the country, had written books, and had even been interviewed on TV. People were expecting important input from him, and rumor had it that he had a long-term contract with top management. A few of us were sitting around after lunch, talking about the upcoming visit. Everyone around the table was hoping something useful would come out of it. We all agreed that the business needed some changes and corrections, and most of us had some ideas about what they ought to be.

Bill hadn't said much, and several people noticed. Finally, someone asked him what he thought. Bill said he wasn't against experts, he just thought they had a tendency to wear out after a while, and people ought not hold it against them, as often seemed to happen. By that time he had our attention and he was on his way.

He said that when he thought about experts it always reminded him of when his niece, Sandy, was a graduate student in economics. She decided to write her thesis on trends in investment forecasting, and one of the people she wanted to interview was John Zalhn, the investment advisor.

Tom said, I remember him. I heard him talk once. He was really a hot item a while back. People used to search him out, and he got big bucks for speeches.

Jennifer said, There were investment clubs all over the country that followed his advice. People staked fortunes on his predictions. I always wondered what happened to him.

Well, said Bill, one year Zalhn's forecasts went downhill. And so they did the next year, and the year after that. After a couple more years, Zalhn's renown was gone, and he just faded from the financial scene.

Despite his decline, Bill continued, Zalhn was very important to his niece's research theories, so she tracked him down and found he was living near a small town in Vermont. She called him, and he invited her to come up to talk. They sat in his beautiful garden, and after some introductory questions Sandy asked him to explain what he believed were the most influential factors in the decline of his forecasts. Having prepared herself well, Sandy arrayed a list of reasons that various authorities had proposed earlier. She asked whether it was a misreading of economic cycles, changes in monetary policy by the Federal

Reserve, the globalization of the world economy, or some other element entirely. Each time Sandy mentioned a factor Zalhn would agree, or he would say he supposed he had missed taking that factor into account sufficiently. After Zalhn had admitted he was probably at fault on just about every factor she mentioned, Sandy was getting pretty exasperated. Finally she asked, if he had to pick the single most important factor that accounted for his decline, what would it be? Zalhn responded quick as a flash—he said he guessed it was a change of luck.

Bill said that on her way back from Vermont, Sandy was enjoying the scenery as she drove toward home. Once, glancing out her window, she spotted a bull's-eye target painted on the side of a barn. When she got closer she saw an arrow right in the center of the target. Less than a mile down the road was another barn and on its side a similar target was painted, with another arrow lodged dead center.

Sandy was impressed as she travelled through this small New England county. On almost every barn she passed she saw a bull's-eye, and at the dead center of each there was an arrow. She wondered who this magnificent archer might be, so she stopped at a combination gas station and general store and asked around. The people talked about the archer with respect, even awe; but Sandy got the impression that no one was entirely sure who the archer was, because they had never seen him shooting. A few of the locals thought he shot only at night.

Just before Sandy was about to drive out of the station a tall, handsome woman in her mid fifties approached her car and said that she knew the archer. She said he was a well-known, high-level government advisor who lived in a very pricey house on top of a high hill, and archery was his hobby. The woman said she hadn't wanted to talk about him in the store but she told Sandy his name. Sandy recognized it immediately and decided that while she was in the neighborhood she would visit him.

She searched until she found the house. The archer was a short, slightly built person who wore glasses that seemed to Sandy to be quite strong. His appearance was not at all what she expected, so after some introductions and chatting, she asked him if he would be willing to explain his unerring accuracy with the bow and arrow.

The archer considered her request for a long time. He said that he seldom revealed his method to people, but that was because very few ever asked him. Most people, he said, were more interested in his record than in how he achieved it. Sandy waited expectantly.

Finally he nodded and told her that his method had two steps: First, shoot the arrow at the side of a barn. Second, after it landed, paint the bull's-eye around it. Sandy thanked him, then drove home. ❖

49

A sound person has fewer opinions and attends more closely the opinions of others.

She admires what she approves and can admire what she does not approve as well. She can discover the untruth within truth and the truth within untruth.

She understands the minds of others because she is not diverted into judging them. Because she accepts them, she is able to discover their intelligence even when it dwells beneath their foolishness.

50

People, in immense numbers, are busy being born and dying. Fearful, many strive for impregnability. Seeing only death at the end of life, they long for immortality; perceiving no other means than through their progeny, they propagate.

But those who know the way know they live in immortality now. In the midst of danger they are not threatened. Confident of their invincibility, they allow themselves to be vulnerable. They do not fear because there is no place in them for death to dwell.

51

All things are created in the Tao, given their shapes and natures and their movement. Each thing moves according to its shape and nature, and all things move according to their interactions with each other.

The Tao does not push all things, nor does it pull them. It is satisfied, as a parent

to give them birth

to watch over them

to furnish nourishment for their growth

to accord them opportunity

to provide the arena for their play.

For this the Tao expects no reward.

52

Words are the beginning of the world. Words form thoughts and thoughts make things. But, what is there before words?

The womb, the bowl, the emptiness, containing all.

When you are on fire with words, smothered by thoughts, entangled in things, reality becomes obscured by smoke. For a moment, set aside your words and thoughts and things. Cherish emptiness, for it quenches the fire of words and clears the view. Then you will know the whole, emptiness and fullness.

The one who knows the whole may use it all, the visible and concealed, present and future, action and nonaction. With such an advantage, you will never lose.

SIMPLE-MINDED

BILL SAID HE FIRST MET Abner when Abner was about twenty-two. He had a soft-spoken, open-faced style, and he had a reputation as a country boy, sort of naive. Not many people took him seriously. Then—the next thing anyone knew—people walking down the hall were pointing him out as the guy who had just won the division a major contract. Rumor had it that the customer had signed because the CEO had been personally impressed by Abner.

Abner still didn't get a lot of credit from the "in" people in the division. They figured it was an accident. One guy said that Abner was so dumb he didn't know it couldn't be done—so he did it. But then Abner had a couple of repeats, and most of his critics got very quiet.

When you got to know Abner he really wasn't dumb at all, of course. He just had a bias for the simple. Abner had a knack for shaking off complications like a dog shakes off water. In his simplicity, he sometimes noticed things that other people didn't bother to notice. For instance, when everyone in the industry was talking about how important service after sale was, Abner did his own simple tally among his customers. He found out that for a big segment of his market, time of delivery was more important.

After he had landed a number of impressive contracts, Abner won a reputation as a top gun and a rising star in the division. But Bill didn't remember any time when he used it to throw his weight around. He still had a lot of that open vulnerable quality. Bill said he used to enjoy teasing him every once in a while.

Once, Bill said, I asked Abner how he got to be so modest. Had his parents told him that pride was a sin? Abner said he didn't think he was modest, it was more that he didn't feel he could claim much personal credit for what he did. When I asked him what he meant, he said he just got quiet in his mind, then stepped into the middle of the people and information going on and let nature take its course. ❖

53

Knowing the way as broad and straight and clear, why would I deviate from it? Because men are fascinated by the indirect and devious. Through the indirect and devious men may acquire reputation, wealth, and power. Devoted to reputation, wealth, and power, they acquire greed.

Greed breeds inequality. So are spawned riches and poverty, elite and rabble, selfishness and want. Pursuing reputation, wealth, and power men are, in turn, pursued. Enmeshed in greed, they may quickly lose the straightest way.

54

Do not be concerned that others do not follow the way or value it. The way has endured since the beginning and will continue ever after, whether cheered or jeered.

There is no need to reform the world.

Reform yourself, you reform your family.

Reform yourself, you reform your workplace.

Reform yourself, you reform your nation.

Reform yourself, you reform the world.

Thus by yourself you accomplish all change, in family, workplace, nation, and the world. Not by the power of the sword you wield but of the lens through which you view.

55

The one who walks the way is not complex. He is able to withstand attack, whether blunt or subtle. Whether required to press forward or to yield, his power is evident. He is as unthreatening as a child, yet his potential can be sensed.

Though he suffers a hundred frustrations, his stamina raises him up again. Though he is forced a hundred times to shout his case, his voice remains inexhaustible and fresh.

Striving with all his might he does not revere his success nor brood its lack. He leads a charmed life, at ease with events. It is not his will that makes him strong, but his nature. Depending on his will, he would weaken.

**Thinking is not
seizing ideas, but
permitting them to
dance before you**

56

Those who hold wisdom do not scatter words. Those who scatter words do not hold wisdom.

Being,

quietly, without explanation,

releasing one's hold,

untangling one's ties,

clearing one's head,

accustoming one's vision,

grounding one's self,

These are the means of the Tao.

The one unswayed by passion, profit, or praise is champion.

Following the way, he has become the way.

57

Calm at rest, composed in action, steady in tumult. Do only what is required; change only what must be changed. Flowing downhill, water follows its easiest route. It disturbs only what it needs to, but whether brook or torrent, always reaches its destination.

Make battle rare, for every action provokes reaction. Prefer to guide through equilibrium, the balancing of forces. From the whisper touch of snowflake to the mighty roar of avalanche, gravity does its work. The earth supports all with minimum intervention.

Regulation brings obstruction, which impedes creativity and disables initiative.

Preparing for conflict encourages aggression.

Conspiracy and deceit among leaders breed wariness and cunning among followers.

Increasing the number of laws stimulates evasion and lawbreaking.

A wise leader remembers: When I hold no pretensions to righteousness, those with whom I do not interfere reach their own balance. When I enforce no regulations, people do not rebel. When I promulgate no fashionable new teachings, others pursue what is understandable, direct, and effective. When I preach no complicated theories of human nature, people may learn to understand themselves.

PERSONALITIES

BILL SAID IT WAS A SQUABBLE that had gone on so long and so loud that it had reached the top levels of the company. It was about the product specification sheets, which weren't up-to-date, hadn't been for months, and were rapidly becoming useless to the people they were supposed to help.

The division general manager set up a meeting between the product support department manager and the process documentation department manager. He asked Arlene Goldman, who was head of production—and Bill's boss at the time—to arbitrate at the meeting. He admitted to Arlene that he didn't envy her. He said he would no more want to get between those two groups than he would want to get into a swamp full of mosquitoes. Arlene had a reputation for fair-mindedness, Bill said, and just looking like she did—sort of big and powerful and friendly, like an aunt you wish you had—made her a likely choice for assignments like this. Arlene asked Bill to sit in on the session with her. She said it would be good for him.

Actually, Bill said, he thought that she wanted him for moral support and to be her "gofer."

Well, the way it started out, Bill continued, we knew right away that the managers of the two departments weren't going to be a lot of fun to work with. The one from product support said that his department couldn't do its job because they weren't getting up-to-date documentation, and they hadn't been getting it for six months. He knew it was six months because that was when Larry Humphries, who had been in charge of specifications, had left the process documentation department. He didn't say a word about Bruce Salaway, who had replaced Larry, but he had a long list of complaints about the service from then on. He said the only solution was to transfer the function, and the most natural place for it, he added coolly, was inside the product support department.

The other manager denied most of the complaints. And for those he didn't deny, he had his own long lists of explanations and justifications that always seemed to pin the fault on other departments. He claimed the data they provided were usually inaccurate to start with. In fact, he insisted, the records showed that forty-five percent of the data the process documentation department received contained serious errors. He also said he had already spoken with the managers of those other departments, and had their assurance that they would improve their accuracy. This, he guaranteed, would soon solve any remaining problems.

Arlene and I spent the better part of the afternoon listening to the two of them argue with and sometimes rant at each other. They both seemed to be locked into their positions. The product support manager insisted over and over that specifications documentation ought to be transferred to his department, and the process documentation manager defended himself by claiming the problems didn't exist or that they were someone else's fault. Finally, Arlene gently called a halt and suggested we set up another meeting for the following week.

In the meantime, at her suggestion, she and I did some research. We found out some interesting things. For instance, the error rate in the data was seventeen percent, not very good, but not the forty-five percent the process documentation manager had claimed. For another thing, none of the other department managers we spoke with remembered having a discussion with the process documentation manager about improving their accuracy rate, though some of them did admit wistfully that they probably ought to do better. We also learned that the product support manager had made his recommendation for transferring the specifications documentation process to product support three years earlier. The idea was totally unworkable. Government regulations required all product documentation to be produced in the same department that develops the products. That had been fully explained to product support not once, but several times in the past few years.

I have to admit, Bill said, that I was pretty discouraged about the whole situation, even a little disgusted. I told Arlene that it seemed to me she was dealing with one manager who was unwilling to understand a simple fact of life, and another who was a congenital prevaricator or at best an exaggerator. I finished up by saying that I thought helping these two get together on a reasonable agreement was about as hopeless as trying to purify our city's particularly polluted river.

Arlene heard me out, then clucked her tongue against her teeth a couple of times and asked, "What if we all could get past the personalities? Why do you think two seasoned managers are behaving this way?"

"Maybe," she said, "the product support manager just can't think of any other way to get through to the process documentation manager, so he's trying to threaten process documentation with having the function taken away, even though it can't happen. It's just a kind of bluff. And process documentation, feeling pressed to the wall, makes these exaggerated claims of his for the same kind of reason." She looked at me with those wide, brown eyes. "Do you think, if we let go of judging their virtues, we can find some way to work out this situation?"

It turned out to be a rhetorical question, because I couldn't think of a thing. But Arlene could. She remembered the product support manager had not seemed unhappy about the service he got when Larry Humphries was in charge of specifications. Arlene had

97

worked earlier with both Humphries and his replacement, Bruce Salaway. Humphries was a stickler for detail, she said, and Salaway was more of a broad-brush person. She thought it was just the wrong job for Salaway, and that there might be a way to arrange a transfer for him to a job that was a better fit. Then he could be replaced with someone who was more like Humphries.

By this time I was getting with Arlene's program, and I liked it. I suggested that, on the other side of the equation, it was pretty clear that the product development manager was loading a lot of wishful thinking into his tall tales. I thought we might be able to help some of it to come true by using our influence with the other departments to get them to concentrate on improving their accuracy. Arlene nodded and said there might be a deal in there somewhere, and we began to plan the next meeting.

The way it turned out, it took two more meetings before the product support and process documentation managers worked out an agreement that was pretty much, but not exactly, along the lines we had speculated about. Two months later they were both congratulated by the division general manager in a staff meeting. He called them an example of the kind of cooperation that ought to be the norm in this division. Arlene didn't get any public credit at all, but she didn't seem to mind. ❖

58

When a leader steadily concentrates her people's attention toward a desired destination and then allows them to find their own way to it, they become purposeful and invested.

When a leader insists that her own view prevail, her followers waver. When compliance is enforced, followers soon learn evasion and avoidance.

No person can forecast ultimate consequences. From apparent misfortune springs unforeseen opportunity. In the midst of success lie the unseen seeds of decline, awaiting only the irrigation of complacency. Who can tell where a road will turn, or when?

In organizations where images are made of smoke, and people sing slogans to drown out facts, illusion reigns until it crashes. The sound person knows her mind, but does not demean the minds of others. She is strong but not dominating. She is enlightened but not dazzling.

59

A wise leader, like a wise parent, guides others according to their natures, and according to her own. Though versed in current knowledge, she is not filled up with mind-made models of efficiency or probity.

An empty mind has space to receive; a full mind does not. Regularly practice an empty mind. Forget your learning and it will remember you. Set aside your skillfulness and skillfulness will better serve you. The master of an empty mind is the master of the future. For her no challenge is too severe, no high office too daunting.

An empty mind empowers endurance, longevity, and limitless scope.

60

Within an empty mind dirty tricks lose their sting, deceit is turned to good use, destructive purposes are neutralized, and no damage is done. Though opponents seek to do each other harm, they do each other good. Opponents require each other.

Within an empty mind the struggle's use can be perceived, and the opponents' alliance is recognized.

61

Large organizations flourish when they provide opportunity and benefit to smaller ones. Great endeavors remain accessible and accepting; thus people flow to them as rivers flow to seas. Causes flourish when they allow more than they demand; thus they remain supple rather than grow rigid.

When a great endeavor adopts the precepts of a lesser one, it gains both ideas and the devotion of the lesser one's adherents. When a lesser endeavor recognizes its lesser-ness, it gains both perspective and potency. Thus, by providing open space for the flow of change, each endeavor may prevail.

A sound leader brings people together and helps them to do what each does best. Some will be best at initiating and directing, others at analyzing and suggesting, others at implementing and participating. A sound leader assures that all get what they need.

62

Nothing is excluded, no one is cast out of Tao. One person values the honorable, another disdains it. Tao holds both firm and safe, nevertheless. People may incline toward lying, cheating, exploiting, lusting—at least a thousand vices, yet none are rejected.

Though in our time great systems of technology have been conceived, great networks of information connected, and great economic and political empires founded, still they do not provide what Tao provides.

Tao provides certainty that persists through ages of systems, networks, and empires. It is a free resource to all, but chooses its moment to present itself to each, sinner and saint alike.

63

Particular factors, special conditions, and exceptional situations affect outcomes. The ability to distinguish is required to glean triumph from failure.

When your head is not bent by anxiety, opportunities can be perceived more clearly. Complicated problems are best penetrated by plain thinking. Arduous projects are best begun with easy steps. Intense controversies are most readily resolved in lesser details. Great issues turn on small pivots.

Therefore, the wise person does not concentrate long on intractable dilemmas, but rather on small and simple choices. Solving small problems prevents their growth into intractable dilemmas.

Promises made too easily are hard to fulfill. Deny problems, and problems multiply. Underestimate difficulty, and difficulty escalates. Facing troubles early and sensibly, the wise person manages well. His problems and difficulties do not compound.

64

Resist the lure of scattered motion, better hold to single-goal devotion.

Issues young and plain are easy to disperse,

with time to age and gather weight, predicaments are worse.

Early prevention is a general rule,

radical correction a harsher tool.

Confronting crises before they are born,

resources are less used up and worn.

Still, though you hold this guideline so,

no one can assure where life will go.

Despite the use of care and plan,

who can predict the fortunes of a man?

On prosperity's broadest plain, with clearest skies,

nine layers of difficulty may suddenly arise.

Or a thousand miles of change begin

with a single thought that sparks within.

All lives require thoughtful care,

in this world in which predictability is rare.

Frightened of disorder some must
grasp control,

others more willingly sail their ocean's roll.

Best recall that care and ease are one,

though neither must be overdone.

They endure the trying times, standing firm
as stone,

who with unerring sense,

know when to act and when to leave alone.

65

**Scholarship costs the scholar
dearly** when concepts are made to
substitute for observation. When people band
together in favor of some special notion, they
frequently come to pride themselves in the
eloquence of their explanations and blind
themselves to contrary evidence. When this
happens, more harm is done than good.

Attempting to steer an organization according
to a currently stylish chart, leaders are often
caught in an unanticipated whirlpool that
seizes the rudder from their hands. Spinning

uncontrollably, their vision is confused. Sailing the perimeter of any paradigm, a leader is better able to sight his true horizon and control his course. Those who can employ the current of the whirlpool while lightly skimming its periphery are most skilled.

In the midst of daily and ordinary things,

to possess old wisdom,

to know with certainty

at the mind of minds,

the heart of hearts,

the soul of souls,

the place where all is well,

That is the ever-surging source of sound management.

66

The mightiest lakes and seas are always at the lower places of the earth. By being low, they accept all that flows to them from higher places and are thus enriched. A leader with true humility, who has no fear of seeming low, has no requirement to station himself high. He too accepts all that flows to him and perceives its value.

A modest leader can follow the direction of his followers and discern its worth. Then, when he directs his followers, his direction is in harmony with theirs. Appreciating each follower's needs, he seldom impedes.

IN PURSUIT OF THE BOSS'S JOB

ONE OF THE DEPARTMENT managers had just been promoted to head a division, and people were buzzing about it like a swarm of wasps. There were many who thought she was the most political person in the company and that it was an outrage that she got the job. Bill didn't seem quite so upset, because he thought she was also one of the better department managers. He said the situation reminded him of the story of Dan and his boss.

Bill described how Dan had coveted his boss's job and had been trying to get it for almost two years. His effort included a considerable amount of political maneuvering, as well as hard work. For instance, Dan was always alert for opportunities to ask other people small questions about his boss's ideas—questions that just managed to dull the ideas' luster. One time when Dan met with the division finance manager, he casually asked whether it seemed likely that the new project his boss had proposed could be kept within budget. Dan could see that the question started some wheels turning in the finance manager's head. At other times Dan made it a point to stop by his boss's boss's office and casually drop suggestions that could add a new and better wrinkle to one of the ongoing projects in his department. Dan was particularly active when his boss was out of town on business trips. During those trips Dan made it a point to be in the office and to make contact with the senior managers and VPs as much as he could.

It seemed to Dan his tactics had gradually been winning points, but it was a slow process. He was convinced that if he only had the chance, he could run the department better than it had ever been run before. He thought often and intensely about that. Then, suddenly, the opportunity of a lifetime presented itself. Dan's boss told him that he was leaving for three weeks to visit all the regional sales managers, and while he was gone Dan—as the senior person in the department—would be in charge.

Dan had developed a new idea to provide sales incentives for distributors. He was convinced his plan would blow the socks off top management. The plan had been ready a month before, but Dan had waited for his boss's tour, just so he could have all three weeks alone with them. He knew his boss probably wouldn't be overjoyed about having been left out of the loop, but it wouldn't matter. By the time his boss returned it would be a done deal. Using his temporary authority, he set up a meeting of the executive committee and made his surprise presentation.

It surprised them all right, but Dan was a lot more surprised by the committee's long stony silence. His proposal was a disaster. He had totally missed a critical point, so the idea was unworkable. Dan was devastated. After the executive committee left the room he sat alone at the long dark conference table and pondered his cataclysm. He knew he had just lost the game. His boss (and everyone else) would hear about what had happened and his boss would lower the boom on him, hard.

For days Dan cringed as he thought about the disaster and waited for his boss's return. Finally, just before his scheduled arrival, Dan pulled himself together. He decided he wouldn't wait for his boss to come to him. He would go to see his boss as soon as he got back to the office and get it over with.

Standing, not sitting, before his boss's desk, Dan felt like someone about to be court-martialed. Dan said there was something he had to tell him. His boss gazed up at him from an expressionless face. "I rode back from the airport with one of the VPs," his boss said. "I already heard about your special meeting."

"I suppose you'll want me to transfer to another department," Dan said. He was hoping he wouldn't be fired outright.

"Why should I want to inflict you on someone else?" his boss replied. His face was still impassive.

Dan swallowed hard and asked if his boss wanted him to resign.

Dan's boss rose from his chair and walked deliberately to the window. Dan couldn't see his face. Then suddenly he turned toward him, and Dan could see the small track of a smile. "No," he said, "I want you to stay on the job."

Dan could hardly believe he had heard the words. He was all at once relieved, elated, and grateful. After thanking his boss profusely for the second chance, he quickly and insistently reassured him that he would never do anything like that again.

"I'm sure you won't," Dan's boss grinned even more broadly. "You're too smart to make the same mistake twice. I'm sure your next venture will be even more creative."

One of the guys at our table shook his head and said he didn't know whether that boss was a fool, a saint, or just awfully confident in himself. Maybe all three, someone else said. ❖

67

Many will say my thoughts are too unpredictable to capture, too innocent for this subtle world, too inconstant for these analytic times. In fact, it is their unpredictability, innocence, and inconstancy that animate my thoughts. To the extent my thoughts are predictable, subtle, and constant they become arid.

If my thoughts cannot be well defined, what then do I mean to say? What then do I value? One thing is kindness that arises not from duty and extends without intention. A second is freedom from that clinging grip on status and extravagance that holds so many captive. The third, and most important, thing I value is recognizing the limitless extent of Tao. And fourth, I value patience.

68

Against force, yield and twist away.

Against anger, cultivate calm.

Against opposition, seek victory without warfare.

Against rebellion, unearth grievances.

When strife can be avoided, that is best. When it cannot be, endeavor to quiet your opponent's force rather than to beat it down. A minimum of contention is the guide.

69

The military strategy of Tao says, avoid preemptive strikes. Respond to attack as required and do minimum damage to your opponent. When you hold superior strength, take care to display no aggressive intent. Possessing superior strength, accommodate your opponent generously.

Taking no precipitous action, one demonstrates the action of peace. Speaking without threat, one disarms the opposition. Earnestly asserting, without enmity, one disallows an enemy's existence.

It is a serious mistake to engage in needless battles. Damage must result for all. But when battles must be fought, take care that kindness should survive.

70

These words I speak about the way are not hard to understand, nor are they hard to follow. If the way were complex, or a passing fad of words that required only moving one's lips, it would be popular. But the way requires action, and action carries risk and portent. Once set in motion, who can tell the consequence of action?

The one who hacks his way most quickly dulls himself

If fewer people choose the way, does that make it lesser? Only where words' and actions' empty selves begin is there revealed, so wondrously, the gem that gleams within.

71

Behold the important person:

She displays her scholarship and pretends
to know.

Behold the one beside her:

She speaks little, but when she does, all listen.

That one knows how little she knows.

Recognize the symptoms of self-importance
promptly. For quick relief, take two aspirins of
humor (a laugh at yourself is preferable) and
continue. For long-lasting correction, burst
your own games, burn your own covers. Clear
seeing is the cure.

72

The way bestows great sight and
so frees people from the apprehensions of the
day. Freed from daily apprehensions, some are
frightened or worried by the world's indifference. But if great sight yields serenity in
peaceful times and courage in times of battle,
why should it not also yield them in times of
indifference?

The great seer does not present herself, nor is she proud of her accomplishments. She has been freed of daily apprehensions and her fear of the world's indifference. She claims no credit.

73

Those who follow the way are no more noble than those who do not. Who can say that those who do not follow the way are not following the way?

Life's process produces paradoxes large and small, yet does so in an orderly way; is questioned repeatedly, yet gives answers without limit; tolerates diverse points of view, yet insists on change; articulates no goal, yet gets its way.

Life's system is wide open, yet no one escapes it.

74

Punishment is not a cure.

Many no longer fear punishment; why threaten them with it? If punishment served its purpose, crime and error would have left us long ago.

If there is to be punishment, let it be the inevitable consequence of the deed performed. If a person takes on the responsibility for punishing others it is like an unskilled laborer taking on the task of a master carver—he can hardly help but cut his own hand.

75

When people are too long exploited they become resentful.

Therefore, resentment's roots are planted in the excesses of those who hold power. People too long dominated rebel. Rebellion's roots are planted in the excesses of those who hold authority.

When people become irresponsible, uninterested in their organization's welfare, uncaring of their work, the branches of their irresponsibility, disinterest, and uncaring grow upon the tree of unfeeling leadership.

A sound leader knows how to value others.

THE PAULSON SAGA

TOM ARRIVED AT LUNCH just after his boss had given him what he called "the reaming of his life." Tom said she was one tough lady and all the people in the department tried to stay out of her way, but this time she had caught him in a massive blunder. After we heard about his chewing-out in all its gory detail, other people began to reminisce about working for tyrants they had known. When Bill's turn came he told us about Paulson.

Paulson had a reputation as a smart businessman who played hardball. He was a shrewd negotiator and his division was a money maker. Not many of his peers cared for his belligerence, but his profits did get grudging admiration, and he was well rewarded for his quarterly results. The company focus was on short-term profit at the time, and that was what Paulson did best. His division had a hot new product, and he was exploiting it to the maximum. Paulson was a maximizer by nature, and he maximized by pushing and squeezing. He pushed his customers for maximum profit and squeezed his employees and suppliers for maximum yield.

120

Working for Paulson was primitive and basic. People in his division strove to survive. Those who were natural predators worked to attain maximum ferocity, and those who were not ferocious by nature tried to hide in the deepest holes they could find or dig. Ferocity and hiding were the main occupations in Paulson's organization.

For as long as they could, the hiders spent their energy avoiding responsibility for anything at all that might go wrong and, whenever possible, shifting responsibility elsewhere. To avoid blame they hid lost sales, customer complaints, and all bad news. But gradually, as Paulson relentlessly pursued them for results, almost all their hiding places were discovered. So people became hopeless and resentful. Feeling that doom was inevitable and fast approaching anyway, the hiders turned their efforts toward spite and subversion. They gossiped critically with their customers. They leaked pricing plans to their competition. They whispered detrimental secrets to friends in other divisions. And so, in a shorter time than usual, the problems and slippages in Paulson's business came to the attention of his boss.

During this same period, Paulson's customers and suppliers were also growing increasingly resentful of his methods. Among them were some who were at least as predatory as Paulson and had in their own times squeezed just as hard, but that made them no more lenient.

Within a year, two competitive companies caught up with Paulson's technology and his customers switched their orders in droves. The division lost money, and early the following year Paulson's boss suggested that he resign. Paulson pointed out that in the next six months his division would bring its newest product on line. He asked for just a little while longer to turn up the revenue curve. His request was denied.

A year after Paulson left, his replacement received credit for the new product and got a big raise with stock options. Paulson, after a short job search, was hired as the head of operations at another company with hot technology and ambitions for lavish profits. There he repeated his previous pattern including its finale: After four years he was again fired. ❖

When one is
on fire with
words, reality
becomes
obscured by
smoke

76

In life a body is soft and vulnerable; in death a body stiffens. It is the same for plants—the delicate and fragile grow, the rigid and brittle break or decay.

When organizations are permeable and flexible they thrive. When they stiffen they lose their vigor and resilience. When the planks of party platforms dry out they crack.

What is stiff and brittle fails. What is pliable and sensitive rises.

77

Like a bell-shaped curve distributes populations, nature arranges its most esteemed designs. Highness is moved toward low. Lowness is moved toward high. Nature, over time, always moves toward leveling.

The courses chosen by some seem opposite; to take from those who have little, and to add more to those who have much.

What can be offered to those who have so much? What will they treasure? Only the Tao offers richer rewards. Only Tao can help lighten obsession with gain, can quiet compulsion for renown, can demonstrate the equality of all achievement. The person of Tao is thus made free.

78

Water is soft and fluid, yet it will wear down stone that is hard and heavy. This shows the truth that, in time, the most intractable things and persons submit to the weakest. Most people know this, but cannot find use for it in their lives. That is because they think that "in time" they will be dead and beyond caring.

Since most people find no use for this truth, they produce leaders. For leaders provide them with scapegoats. People must have leaders so that someone other than themselves will be responsible for their fate.

Those who would lead must accept these conditions.

Those who are followers could change them.

79

When a man ends a negotiation by imposing his will upon another, resentment is the residue. A sound man pays generously for what he gets, and allows generously for an unsound man who may not.

A sound man may receive no recognition at all for his generosity, nor any reciprocity, nor even credit in heaven. Still he follows his way and his way remains with him.

80

In the heartland people work. They are the heart of the country and would not choose to be its mind even if they could. In the heartland there is space between places, and people's labors provide what they need. Here people live simply and have small use for show, might, or the newest baubles of technology and fashion. Although other places can be reached easily, people in the heartland prefer to stay at home.

81

Words that express truth are simple and few. Subtle expressions may render art but not truth.

The person who is confident need not argue to convince others or herself. The person bent on making convincing arguments, delivered in an elaborate manner, is unlikely to be confident.

The one who knows the fact, need not expound the theory. She does not sow or harvest words. She gives kindness to others and herself feels grateful. She shares her gifts with others and is not diminished. She lives a life in which her achievements are many, and she claims no credit.

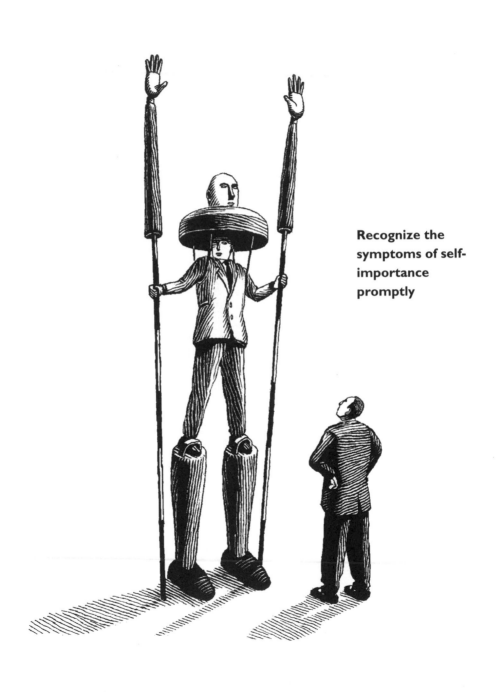

Recognize the symptoms of self-importance promptly

TRAPS OF WORDS

JUST BEFORE HE RETIRED, Bill told his next-to-last story. We were having a small, farewell luncheon for him. Several of the people in the group said they wanted Bill to know he would be missed. Jennifer said Bill's words and stories had meant a lot to her—the one about Beejay's elephant had been especially meaningful to her own personal development. Bill seemed to think about that for a minute, then said he had one more story about the elephant he wanted to tell.

Alice worked in the same department as Beejay and was a close friend. Beejay told her about her elephant and Alice was intrigued. She said she wished more than anything that she had an elephant of her own. She had come to the conclusion, she said, that Beejay's elephant was enlightened and self-actualized. These were ideals Alice had admired for years. In fact, Alice had been studying enlightenment devotedly. She was an avid reader of theories about the new sciences. She knew about chaos theory, holography, and brain-wave healing. She understood synchronicity and new paradigms. She had read about both Eastern and Western religions. She had studied and compared the philosophies of the Tao and Zen, of Mahayana and Hinayana Buddhism. Alice had also taken a number of psychological inventories and tests to understand herself better, and she joined a group dedicated to advancing "an enlightened point of view."

Alice researched these topics so thoroughly she became known as something of an authority on the subject of enlightenment. She was called upon sometimes to give talks at local conferences. After a time Alice was officially honored by an invitation to participate as a panelist at a national conference in Washington, D.C. Alice was both excited and nervous in front of what seemed to her a huge audience. Her nervousness grew as she glanced sideways at the other two panelists. They were leading authorities. Alice participated in the panel's discussions, but when she compared in her mind what she said with what she considered the more sophisticated and erudite views of the other panelists, she felt discouraged.

Then, during the question-and-answer segment of the session, a young woman asked the panel, "Can a person become enlightened gradually, or does it have to happen suddenly?" It was Alice's turn to give the first response; she had never been asked that question before. For the life of her, she could not recall what the authorities she had read and heard had to say about it, especially the two with whom she now shared the podium. After an uncomfortably long hesitation, she finally replied that it could occur both ways; but, embarrassingly, she couldn't think of anything else to say to support her position. Then she listened to the responses of the other panelists. While they seemed politely vague, Alice was convinced they were contradictions of her answer. Nor did she discover any support for her view when she looked out to the audience. For the remainder of the session, Alice thought about and blamed herself for what she considered her lack of information.

Afterward, feeling depressed and not in a mood for company, Alice walked the several blocks back to her hotel. In her room she continued to be troubled. All she could do was wish that she had someone like Beejay's elephant to talk with. Soon dusk came, and when the darkening sky dimmed the room Alice turned on a small light atop the hotel desk. There beneath the light, gleaming in its sudden illumination, was Beejay's elephant. Alice knew it despite its new disguise as three sheets of hotel stationery.

Beejay's elephant invited Alice to sit at the desk and write her troubles down. Alice picked up her pen and wrote: My reputation is ruined. I'll never be able to hold my head up at a conference again. I was so inadequate.

I just wasn't able to make any case at all, and I'm sure I seemed a perfect fool to both the panelists and the audience.

"There are," said the elephant, "three perspectives to consider. If you are confident you need not win arguments. If you are less confident you must convince others in order to shore up your confidence. If you are ambitious you must make an elaborate case to brace your ego. Simple words are closer to the bone, but no words can reach the marrow, only you yourself can.

"As for the audience," continued Beejay's elephant, "neither Jesus, Buddha, Moses, nor Muhammad received enlightenment from the consensus of an audience—no more than from the philosophies of the experts of their day. Each of us must travel his own journey and return to where he started, which of course by then has somehow changed.

"Live your life each day, and from time to time recall that the views you see before you and the ideas imagined in your mind are only momentary versions of the world. While dancing to the music of your nature, recall that the distinctions you make between one concept and another are like toys and games, wonders for your diversion. Do not sink beneath them. Avoid, when you can, too long or intense pondering. Instead allow your quick wisdom to carry you forward. Recall that every cause is an effect, every effect is a cause. There is no absolute way to figure out why anything happens. Just take care of business and be kind.

"Now, I must go," the elephant said. "Elephants must always move along." ❖

People must have leaders so that someone other than themselves will be responsible for their fate

About the Author

STANLEY M. HERMAN is the author of The People Specialists *(1968),* Authentic Management *(1977, with M. Korenich), and* A Force of Ones *(1994). He has also written scores of articles for management publications and columns for newspapers and magazines, and he has appeared in management films and videos. Herman has held positions with the General Electric Company and TRW as human resource director and director of training and organization development. He has taught at the University of Southern California; the University of Richmond; the University of California, Los Angeles; Pepperdine University's Master of Science in Organization Development Program; the Federal Executive Institute; and other professional development programs.*

A Survey of Syntax
in the
Hebrew Old Testament

A Survey of Syntax
in the
Hebrew Old Testament

by

J. Wash Watts

Professor of Old Testament Interpretation
New Orleans Baptist Theological Seminary

WILLIAM B. EERDMANS PUBLISHING COMPANY
GRAND RAPIDS, MICHIGAN

PHOTOLITHOPRINTED BY GRAND RAPIDS BOOK MANUFACTURERS, INC.
GRAND RAPIDS, MICHIGAN
PRINTED IN THE UNITED STATES OF AMERICA

Preface to the Revised Edition

The original form of this work was published in 1951. In the thirteen years since that time no serious effort has been made to contradict its interpretation of the distinctive meanings in Hebrew verb forms and syntactical constructions. Some deficiencies have been pointed out by friendly critics; strong words of commendation have also been received. These developments have stimulated my desire to apply these interpretations in translation and in exegesis. One result has been the publication of *A Distinctive Translation of Genesis* in May, 1963, by Wm. B. Eerdmans Publishing Co. Similar works based upon this treatment of syntax are in progress.

Comparison of the treatment of Hebrew imperfects in the present work with the use of imperfects in Arabic has greatly strengthened my confidence concerning crucial features of the interpretation here given. I was able to make such comparison while teaching in Lebanon in 1961-62 and enjoying special opportunity for consideration of Arabic. This led to additions to the treatment of imperfects, the completion of the treatment of conditional sentences, extended treatment of dependent clauses, and many rearrangements intended to aid the study of all features by others.

Consideration of the following list of special features in this work should help a student to understand that the whole work is intended to give him keys to the interpretation of biblical Hebrew not found anywhere else:

(1) Distinctive translations for all perfects, which leave no need for the old theory that Hebrew used a *waw* consecutive with perfects at times.

(2) Distinctive translations for all imperfects, which leave no need for the old theory that *waw* consecutive makes the imperfect to which it is attached to receive the force of a preceding perfect or some other verb form. (This included a very important comparison with the use in Arabic of imperfects in past time and a consequent explanation of Exodus 3:14.)

(3) Distinctive translations for all participles, which leave no need for translation of any participle as though it were some other verb form.

(4) An interpretation of subjunctives so as to explain the combination of perfects with certain particles in conditional sentences and the combination of perfects with an interrogative pronoun in rhetorical questions

5

as furnishing expressions which are subjunctive in the sense of being contrary-to-fact.

(5) Distinctive translations for all types of cohortatives and jussives, which leave no occasion for failure to translate these forms according to their own nature.

(6) The addition of jussives of acquiescence to the various types of jussives previously described and consequent interpretations of Genesis 49:16-18; Isaiah 6:9-10, which should receive searching consideration in connection with our interpretation of predestination.

(7) Distinctive translations for all infinitives, which leave no need for interpreting an infinitive absolute as a substitute for an imperative, and which include this translation for Exodus 20:8: Remembering the sabbath day in order to keep it holy, *six days* you shall labor and do all your work.

(8) A treatment of all uses of *waw* conjunctive and *waw* consecutive so as to indicate a basic distinction between the two.

(9) A treatment of *waw* conjunctive with a perfect as having a correlative force in all cases.

(10) Explanation of *waw* consecutive as characteristic of narrative and of *waw* correlative as characteristic of prophecy.

(11) Detailed explanation and translation of relative clauses so as to illustrate the use of the relative particle and the pronouns used to introduce them.

(12) A new and consistent treatment of conditional sentences which makes it possible to remove subjective and inconsistent expressions in the translation of them. This treatment is applicable to all the legal ordinances stated in conditional form. Accordingly, a full translation of Exodus 21:2-14 is offered as proof of the claim made concerning this treatment.

The author owes a great debt of gratitude for aid and for use of his work on syntax by fellow workers in the department of Old Testament at the New Orleans Baptist Theological Seminary. These men are Dr. J. Hardee Kennedy, now Dean of the School of Theology, Dr. John Olen Strange, Dr. Thomas J. Delaughter, and Dr. George W. Harrison.

Dr. John D. W. Watts, who has taught Old Testament and Hebrew at the Baptist Theological Seminary, Ruschlikon-Zurich, Switzerland, since 1949, and who is now President, has likewise contributed much helpful criticism and suggestion.

Dr. H. Leo Eddleman, who has been a teacher of Hebrew through many years, and who is now President of the New Orleans Baptist Theological Seminary, has been most helpful and encouraging through more than thirty years.

—J. WASH WATTS

New Orleans, Louisiana

Contents

Preface   5
Introductory Explanations   9
Abbreviations   10

Chapter One:
SENTENCE STRUCTURE IN SIMPLE SENTENCES   13
    I The Verb   13
    II Subjects   16
    III Accusatives   18
    IV Adverbial Phrases   22
    V Negatives   23
    VI Interrogatives   24
    VII Exclamations and Optative Expressions   24
    VIII Means of Expressing Special Emphasis   25

Chapter Two:
INTRODUCTORY MATTERS CONCERNING VERBS   28
    I State   29
    II Time   30
    III Mood   31
    IV Conclusion: Distinctive Translations   32

Chapter Three:
INDICATIVE PERFECTS   35
    I Simple Perfects   36
    II Previous Perfects   44
    III Characteristic Perfects   46
    IV Correlative Perfects   47

Chapter Four:
INDICATIVE IMPERFECTS   55
    I Frequentative Imperfects   56
    II Progressive Imperfects   58
    III Characteristic Imperfects   60
    IV Consecutive Imperfects   60

Chapter Five:
PARTICIPLES   70

Chapter Six:

SUBJUNCTIVES   74
    I Contrary-to-Fact Subjunctives   74
    II Potential Subjunctives   76
    III Optative Subjunctives   77

Chapter Seven:

IMPERATIVES   88
    I Imperative Imperfects   88
    II Imperatives Using the Special Form   89
    III Imperatives with *h* Added   90

Chapter Eight:

INFINITIVES   91
    I Infinitives Absolute   91
    II Infinitives Construct   94

Chapter Nine:

MEANS OF INTRODUCING INDEPENDENT CLAUSES   100
    I Use of the Conjunction *Waw* apart from Verbs   100
    II Co-ordinating Conjunctions in Comparative,
        Disjunctive, and Adversative Clauses   101
    III Uses of *Waw* with Verbs   103

Chapter Ten:

MEANS OF INTRODUCING DEPENDENT CLAUSES   118
    I In Subject and Object Clauses   118
    II In Relative Clauses   119
    III In Cause and Reason Clauses   126
    IV In Purpose and Result Clauses   129
    V In Circumstantial Clauses   130
    VI Types of Conditional Sentences   133
    VII Verbal Sequences in Conditional Sentences   134
    VIII A Comparison of Conditional Sentences in Exodus
        21:2-14   143
    IX Mixed Forms in Conditional Sentences   147

Selected Bibliography   151
Index of Biblical References   157

Introductory Explanations

Syntax (*syntaxis* in Latin; *suntaxis* in Greek; from *suntassein,* to put together in order) is "connected system or order."[1] With reference to language, it means the due arrangement of words in sentences and their agreement. This book is a survey of syntax in the Hebrew Old Testament. The arrangement of the book is as follows:

(1) In simple sentences, the basic facts concerning sentence structure are illustrated. Therefore a brief study of structure in simple sentences will be undertaken first.

(2) In compound sentences, the independent clauses are linked together by conjunctions. Old Testament usage gives a significance to these conjunctions that appears to be unique in the field of language. This significance depends in large measure upon the nature of the verbs with which they are used. It is necessary, therefore, to undertake an extensive, thorough, and sharply defined appraisal of the distinctive meanings in these verbs before the compound sentences as a whole are treated. When they are finally examined completely, the distinctive meanings of the conjunctions can also be defined.

(3) In complex sentences, the dependent clauses come into view. In the dependent clauses, the relations between conjunctions and prepositions on the one hand and the moods of verbs on the other involve many complex arrangements of words and clauses that are dependent for their meaning upon comparison with their use in independent clauses. The study of these complex arrangements must come last.

---

1 *Webster's New International Dictionary of the English Language,* (2nd ed.; Springfield: G. & C. Merriam Company, 1944), p. 2560.

9

Abbreviations

(Periods are omitted for the sake of brevity)

GENERAL

ASV — American Standard Version

AT — An American Translation

AV — Authorized Version

BDB — Brown, Driver, and Briggs

DV — Douay Version

ERV — English Revised Version

Eng — English

Heb — Hebrew

MNT — Moffatt's New Translation

RSV — Revised Standard Version

TECHNICAL

Note: The chief purpose of these abbreviations is to make possible the syntactical summaries given at the close of discussion concerning each construction mentioned. Another purpose is to facilitate the use of footnotes. These abbreviations may also be used in class work by teachers or pupils to summarize rapidly their own conclusions concerning the syntax of any construction. Standing alone, many of them appear ambiguous; but in the combinations in which they appear, the proper meaning is obvious because of the context.

abs — absolute

acc — accusative

acq — acquiescence

act — active

adj — adjective

adv — adverb

app — apposition

art — article

ass — asseverative

cau — cause, causal

cer — certainty

ch — characteristic

cir — circumstance, circumstantial

cl — clause

coh — cohortative

10

com — complete, completeness, command, common
comp — compulsory, complement, comparison
con — confidence, contrary-to-fact, consent, construct
cond — condition, conditional
conj — conjunction, conjunctive
cons — consecutive
cont — continuous, continuance, contrast
co-or — co-ordinate
cor — correlative
dat — dative
dec — decree
dem — demonstrative
dep — dependent
des — desire
det — determination
dir — direct
dis — discourse
em — emphatic
ell — elliptical
exc — exclamation
exh — exhortation
fre — frequentative
fut — future
gen — genitive
imp — imperfect
imv — imperative
inc — incomplete, incipient
ind — indicative, indirect, indefinite, independent
inf — infinitive
int — interrogative, intensity, introducing
jus — jussive
lim — limitation
lit — literally
log — logical
man — manner

n — noun
nar — narrative
nat — nature
nec — necessity
neg — negative
obj — object
opt — optative
pa — past
pas — passive
per — permission, personal
pet — petition
pf — perfect
phr — phrase
pl — place
plu — plural
pos — possibility
pot — potential
pre — present
prev — previous
pred — predicate
prep — preposition
priv — privative
pro — prophetic, pronoun, probable
prog — progressive
pt — participle
pur — purpose
rea — reason
rel — relative
req — request
res — result, responsibility
rhe — rhetorical
sen — sentence
seq — sequence
sing — singular
sp — specific, special
sub — subject, subsequent, subordinate
subj — subjunctive
suf — suffix

sug — suggestion
sum — summary
syn — syntax, syntactical
tem — temporal

tran — translation, translated
und — understood
vb — verb
wil — willingness

Chapter One

Sentence Structure in Simple Sentences

In the study of simple sentences we need to summarize many scattered facts arising out of previous studies of grammar. Here and there some of the more intricate details need to be added.

Following normal word order, verbs are treated first, then subjects with modifiers, then objects with modifiers. In case there are two objects, it is understood that the more important comes first.

I

THE VERB

In a simple sentence only one verb is in question, for each Hebrew verb makes a clause of its own. In translation we may compress several separate clauses into one; but in the original, except in rare uses of participles, they are separate by reason of the fact that each Hebrew verb carries its subject with it. Thus we deal here with the relation of a single verb to its subject or subjects.

1. The connection between subject and predicate is expressed in the following:
> (1) A regular verb:
>> Gen. 1:1— . . . God *created* . . . .
>> Gen. 1:2a — and the earth *was* waste and void.
> (2) The verb "to be" understood:
>> Gen. 1:2b — And darkness (*was*) upon the face of the deep.
>> Gen. 28:13, 15 — . . . I (am) Yahweh . . . . And behold, I (am) with you.

The verb is written in parentheses in these translations to show that it was not in the Hebrew. No verb of any kind appeared in the original written statement. Yet there was undoubtedly an unexpressed idea signified by the placing of two substantives, two nouns or a pronoun and a noun, together in this way. Contexts make it clear that such a statement was understood as a declaration or a denial that the two substantives are identified. The Hebrew seemingly felt no need for further expression in making such a statement. Thus we have what some grammarians have called a substantive or nominative sentence. It may be easier for some to think of these expressions as implying the verb "to be" in some form. In such cases we can say that the verb "to be" is understood, i.e., contained in the author's thought but not expressed in a word.

A somewhat similar expression appears at times when users of English are making introductions. The statement "Mr. Jones, — Mr. Smith!" means, of course, Mr. Jones, this is Mr. Smith. Even as the demonstrative pronoun "this" is omitted in the first sentence, so one of the substantive forms is often omitted in the Hebrew sentences. Thus, "I (am) with you" in Gen. 28:15 means "I am the one with you," or else "I am one who is for you, at hand and on your side."

These expressions are used frequently in Hebrew, and they should be considered quite normal. Perhaps the uses of "to be" in past or present time that have an emphatic word before them are the ones to be considered unusual. The description of the earth in Gen. 1:2a as a thing that was "waste and void" is an example, for "earth" was placed emphatically, i.e., before the verb. Unless the verb was written, one could not tell that the author was expressing emphasis. The author used this verb "to be" in an unusual way in order to emphasize its subject.

In future time, the Hebrew authors wrote out the verb "to be." The purpose appeared to be that of using it as a specific expression of frequentative or progressive action. Therefore, Jacob, when reflecting upon the promises Yahweh made to him at Bethel, said, "Seeing that Yahweh *will continue to be* with me . . ." (Gen. 28:20). Therefore, two of the great promises contained in the initial statement of Yahweh's covenant with Israel were written thus: " . . . and as for you, *you will become* for me a kingdom of priests and a holy nation"

(Ex. 19:6). Such use of "to be" in future time likewise reflects the fact that omission of "to be" is the normal usage in past and present time.

(3) A personal pronoun in the third person, no matter what the person of the subject:

Deut. 12:23 — For the blood (3rd per) *it* is the life; or, For the blood is the life.

II Sam. 7:28 — Thou (2nd per) art *he,* The (One True) God; or, Thou art The (One True) God.

Zech. 4:5 — Do you know what *they,* even these, are? or, Do you know what these are?

(4) The following particles:

yesh, there is

Job 11:18 — *There is* hope.

'en, there is not

Ex. 5:16 — Straw *is not* given.

hinneh, behold

Gen. 18:19 — *Behold,* in the tent!

2. Agreement of subject and verb appears as follows:

(1) A verb that precedes its subject may agree with it in gender and number, or appear in the third masculine singular without regard for the gender and number of the subject:

Isa. 47:1 — Yea, *there shall come* (3rd mas sing) *evil* (fem sing).

Mic. 2:6 — *Reproaches* (fem plu and written last in Heb) *will not depart* (3rd mas sing).

Ps. 119:137 — *Right are* (3rd mas sing) *thy judgments* (mas plu).

(2) A verb that follows its subject agrees with it in gender and number, as a rule:

Gen. 1:2a — *The earth* (fem sing) *was* (fem sing) waste . . . .

(3) A verb with a dual subject is usually in the plural but occasionally in the feminine singular, because there is no dual form of the verb:

Isa. 1:15 — *Your hands are full* (com plu) of blood.

I Sam. 4:15 — And *his eyes were dim* (fem sing).

(4) When any word, even a pronominal suffix, comes between the verb and the subject, the question of agreement is frequently disregarded. Examples are found in I Sam. 4:15;

Joel 1:20; Isa. 34:13; Ps. 103:5. (This practice has been pointed out in recent years by G. R. Driver.)

(5) A verb with a compound subject including a genitive used in connection with *kol,* all, agrees with that genitive; it may do so with a genitive used in connection with *qol,* voice; and it may do so in poetry whenever the author desires to emphasize the genitive:

> Gen. 5:5 — And all (nom) of the days (gen) of Adam came to be (plu) nine hundred and thirty years.
>
> Gen. 37:35 — And all his sons and all his daughters rose up (plu) to comfort him.
>
> Gen. 4:10 — The voice of thy brother's blood (lit, bloods) is crying out (plu).
>
> I Sam. 2:4 — A bow of mighty men is broken (plu).

(6) A verb with two or more subjects joined by *waw* may agree with one and be understood with the other, or it may be in the plural to express agreement with them taken together:

> Num. 12:1 — Then proceeded to speak (sing) Miriam and Aaron.
>
> I Sam. 31:7 — Saul and his sons died (plu).

(7) A verb with a collective noun may be singular or plural, although the plural is more frequent. An author may switch back and forth in the same passage:

> Ex. 33:8-11 — *All the people proceeded to stand* (plu), and *they took their stations* (plu), each at the door of his tent; . . . and *all the people saw* (sing) the pillar of cloud; . . . and *all the people rose up* (sing), and they worshipped (plu), each at the door of his tent.

(8) A verb with a plural subject denoting a group, each member of which is characterized by a certain action, may be in the singular to make the predicate apply to each member. Cf. Num. 24:9; Ex. 31:14. Hebrew authors shift in various ways from general to individual subjects or from individual to general ones. Sometimes this occurs several times in one sentence, apparently for variety.

II

Subjects

1. An ordinary subject is represented by the following:
    (1) A noun:

Gen. 2:6 — And *a mist* proceeded to go up.
(2) A pronoun or pronominal suffix joined to a particle:
    II Sam. 7:28 — *Thou* art God.
    Gen. 6:13 — And *behold I* am bringing destruction on
    them.
(3) An adjective used as a noun:
    Ps. 4:7; 4:6 in Eng — *Many are saying,* Who can show
    us any good?
(4) An adverb that assumes the force of a noun:
    II Sam. 1:4 — *Many* of the people have fallen.
"Many" represents the Hebrew word *harbeh,* which is
regularly used as an adverb meaning greatly or exceedingly.
Here, however, as in Jer. 42:2 and a few other instances, it is
construed as a noun. The possibility of such a change arises
out of the fact that this adverb originated as an infinite absolute,
which may serve both as an adverb and a noun.
(5) A prepositional phrase modifying an indefinite subject:
    Ex. 16:27 — *Some* of the people went out.
A literal translation in this case would be, "They from
the people went out." "From the people" is not an adverbial
phrase modifying "went out"; rather, it is a restrictive phrase
modifying "they." The persons indicated by "they" are not
identified in any other way by the context. "From the people"
is therefore so identified with "they" as to be an essential part
of the subject.

2. An indefinite subject may be represented by the following:
    (1) A verb in the third person, masculine, singular or plural:
        Ps. 126:2 — Then *they said* among the nations . . . .
        Isa. 9:5, 9:6 in Eng — And *one* (or *men*) will call his
        name . . . .
    (2) A verb with a participle from its root for a subject:
        Deut. 22:8 — If *any man should fall* from thence (lit,
        if *one* falling *should fall* from thence), . . .
    (3) The pronoun of the second person singular:
        Gen. 13:10 — Like the land of Egypt when *you come* to
        Zoar.

3. An impersonal subject is represented by a verb in the third
person. When reference to nature is made, the verb is always
feminine. Otherwise, the verb is usually masculine; and if passive,

always masculine. Our neuter pronoun "it" is used for translation
in these cases:

Amos 4:7 — On one piece *it rained* (fem).

Job 3:13 — If I had slept [the sleep of death], then *it had been*
rest to me.

Isa. 53:5 — By reason of his stripes *there shall be healing* for us
(lit, *it shall be healed* for us).

III

ACCUSATIVES

Any noun in the predicate governed by the verb rather than
a preposition must be construed by us as an accusative. In
translation, however, it is necessary to put with many of these
nouns such prepositions as English uses with genitives, datives, or
accusatives. The history of many Hebrew words shows that
Hebrew usage has varied in its use of prepositions with these
words, sometimes using one, sometimes not doing so. Accordingly, our addition of prepositions for the sake of English minds is
not contrary to Hebrew thought, but it renders explicit what is
implicit in the Hebrew.

II Kings 8:13 furnishes an instructive example. Translated
literally it reads this way: Yahweh has caused me to see you
king. "Me" is the object of the causative action of the verb;
"you" is object of "see," the root idea of the verb; and "king"
is an adverbial accusative, describing the condition in which
"you" is seen. When we translate thus: "Yahweh has shown you
to me as king"; we leave "you" as a direct object, not needing
a preposition; we turn "me" into an indirect object and therefore put "to" with it; and we put "as" with "king," making it into
an adverbial phrase.

These accusatives may be classified mainly by their service as
direct objects of the verb or as adverbial accusatives that specify
some particular aspect of the verbal state. Among double accusatives and cognate accusatives both types are found.

1. Object accusatives:

Gen. 1:1 — God created *the heavens and the earth.*

Gen. 6:2 — And they proceeded to take *for themselves wives.*

II Kings 8:13 — Yahweh has shown *to me you* as king, or
Yahweh has given *to me a vision of you* as king.

A variation in the use of prepositions with the object accusatives needs to be observed carefully. A direct object, like "heavens" in Gen. 1:1, does not need a preposition. An indirect object, however, may or may not receive one in Hebrew. In Gen. 6:2 "for" is written in Hebrew with "themselves," but in II Kings 8:13 no preposition is written with "me."

Omission of prepositions is regular in Hebrew composition when any other type of adverbial accusative is used. Accusatives of specification of all kinds and also cognate accusatives are thus written. Accusatives of specification, however, do require prepositions in English. The translator, therefore, must take care to discern the preposition that fits the context.

2. Accusatives of specification:

These accusatives are called accusatives of specification because each one specifies the particular reference of the verbal action or state in its sentence. That reference may be to place, time, limitation, condition, manner, means, or result. The context must be relied upon for indicating what kind of reference is specified, and the translator must supply the preposition that helps to make it clear.

(1) Specifying place:

Gen. 45:25 — And they proceeded to come *into the land* of Canaan.

Gen. 33:18 — And he proceeded to camp *before the city*.

Gen. 18:1 — And he was sitting *at the entrance* to the tent.

I Kings 18:32 — And he proceeded to build the stones (dir obj) *into an altar* (adv acc of pl whither).

Ps. 3:8 — Thou shalt smite all my enemies (dir obj) *on the cheek-bone* (adv acc of pl where).

Prepositions answering to the question, Whither? include to, into, out of, and the like. Prepositions answering to the question, Where? include before, at, in, on, by, beside, and the like.

(2) Specifying time:

Ps. 1:2 — He meditates *day and night*.

Gen. 5:3 — And Adam continued to live *for a hundred and thirty years*.

Concise wording may omit prepositions, as in Ps. 1:2, but it is possible to add them, saying, "by day and by night."

(3) Specifying limitation of distance, number, place, and so forth:

Gen. 7:20 — *Fifteen cubits above* them . . . the waters prevailed.

Amos 5:3 — The city going forth *up to a thousand* will leave a remnant *up to a hundred,* and the one going forth *up to a hundred* will leave a remnant *up to ten.*

(4) Specifying condition:

Amos 2:16 — *As one stripped naked* will he flee in that day.

I Sam. 15:32 — And Agag proceeded to go to him *with confidence.*

Gen. 37:35 — I shall go down to my son *in mourning.*

(5) Specifying manner:

Ps. 56:3 — Many are fighting against me *in pride.*

Gen. 46:2 — And they proceeded to bow down to him *with their faces to the ground.*

Gen. 32:31 — I have seen God *face to face.*

Prov. 22:23 — And he shall spoil those spoiling them (dir obj) *as to the soul* (adv acc of man).

(6) Specifying means:

Isa. 1:20 — *By the sword* you will be devoured.

Ps. 139:14 — *For by wonders* am I distinguished.

Gen. 2:7 — And Yahweh proceeded to form the man (dir obj) *out of dust* (adv acc of means).

Ex. 6:3 — *By means of my name Yahweh* I did not make myself known to them.

(7) Specifying result:

Zech. 14:4   And the mount of Olives shall be split *so as to be a great valley.*

I Sam. 5:9 — And the hand of Yahweh began to be upon the city *so as to be a very great confusion.*

Hag. 2:11 — Ask the priests (dir obj) *for instruction* [*so as to get instruction*] (adv acc of res).

3. Cognate accusatives:

Ex. 29:9 — And you shall gird them (dir obj) *with girdles* (cog acc, also acc of means).

A noun from the same root as its verb is frequently put with that verb as a cognate accusative. This appears to be done in order to give a concrete example of the verbal action or added information

about it. Thus these cognate accusatives are essentially adverbial accusatives.

The translation of these cognate accusatives requires care because users of English dislike such repetition. Usually a word that is cognate in significance but not in stem can be found to represent the accusative. In Gen. 1:29 we may translate thus: "an herb producing seed," rather than saying: "an herb seeding seed." At times, as in Zech. 8:2 and II Sam. 19:5, Hebrew itself uses accusatives which are cognate in significance only. We may easily make this practice general. Oftentimes a suitable preposition must be added. Cf. Gen. 37:5; II Sam. 7:7; 13:36; Jer. 22:19.

4. Use of *'eth* with accusatives:

When it is desired to point to a word as specially important, *'eth* is used before the thing defined. Thus it is used in the following ways:

(1) Generally before a direct object if it is definite (Cf. Gen. 1:4. Particularly is this true when the direct object is placed before the verb.)

(2) Before words which by nature specify definite things

a. The following pronouns:

'asher, who, which, or what (Gen. 9:24).

Strictly speaking, this word is the particle of relation, but it serves as a pronoun.

zeh, this (Lev. 11:4)

mi, who (Isa. 6:8)

The fact that *'eth* never appears before *mah,* what, emphasizes the fact that it is used to mark that which is definite. Whereas *mi* is used to identify persons and is always definite, *mah* is used to refer to the nature of things and is indefinite.

b. Certain words which at times are used to specify individuals:

kol, when meaning each (Deut. 2:34)

'asher, other (Jer. 16:13)

'echadh, one (I Sam. 9:3)

c. A noun or a singular pronoun unaccompanied by an article and used to typify a group (Ex. 21:28; Isa. 41:7; 50:4).

d. Designations of particular time (Ex. 13:7) or place (Judg. 19:18).

e. Adverbial accusatives that locate a verbal state (I Kings 15:23; 17:25).

(3) Before words that identify the subject or object more clearly or fully (Gen. 27:42; Judg. 20:44; I Sam. 26:16; II Sam. 11:15; Ezek. 17:21).

IV

Adverbial Phrases

1. Adverbial phrases introduced by a preposition:

In addition to any phrase composed of an ordinary noun with a preposition and used to modify a noun, adjective, or adverb, there must be included here those phrases composed of infinitives construct with prepositions. These occur very frequently in Hebrew, and in English they are usually turned into various kinds of clauses. So far as construction is concerned, they are adverbial phrases.

2. Adverbial phrases expressing comparative or superlative degree:

The comparative degree is expressed by use of the preposition *min,* from, prefixed to the second word involved in the comparison, as in Gen. 29:30. The superlative degree is expressed in the following ways:

(1) By use of the phrase *mikkol,* from all, as in Gen. 3:1 and Job 1:3.

(2) By use of the preposition *be,* among, with the second of the nouns compared, as in Song of Sol. 1:8.

(3) By emphatic use of the positive accompanied by the article, as in the clause "David was the smallest" (I Sam. 17:14); or by emphatic use of the positive with another noun in construct relation, as in the expression "the three oldest" (I Sam. 17:14); or by emphatic use of the positive with a pronominal suffix attached (Jonah 3:5).

(4) By ordinary use of nouns in construct relation, when the first is the singular and the latter the plural of the same noun, as in Gen. 9:25; or when there is a partitive relation between the nouns, as in Jonah 3:5.

3. Adverbial phrases using *h* directive to indicate the place whither an action leads (Gen. 14:10) or the place where it happens (I Kings 4:14).

V

Negatives

Negative particles appear immediately before the words they negate. Even the verb is preceded by its negative, for negatives are emphatic by nature.

1. *lo'*, not, is strongly declarative and with the imperative imperfect is prohibitory. It is widely used with verbs. Occasionally it appears before a noun or an adjective (Deut. 32:6, 21), giving a meaning like the prefixes un-, in-, and im-. Perhaps the Hebrews thought of it in these situations as followed by the verb to be. In Num. 16:29 we may use the verb to be after *lo'* and the relative pronoun after *YHWH*.

2. *'al,* do not, is contingent in nature and is used with cohortatives and jussives.

3. *terem,* not yet, is used with verbs only (Gen. 2:5).

4. *lebhilti,* in order that . . . not, is the regular negative with infinitives (Gen. 4:15; Deut. 17:19, 20). Rarely is it used with other forms, and the relative pronoun is to be understood as being with it in such cases (Ex. 20:20). When used with nouns it is sometimes equivalent to "without" (Isa. 14:6).

5. *'en,* there is not, is the construct form of *'ayin,* nothing. It is used regularly with nouns and participles and occasionaly with infinitives. When a participle needs a negative, *'en* is nearly always used. When it appears with an infinitive, the infinitive is a noun (Ps. 40:6). With a noun it is equivalent to "without" (Joel 1:6).

6. *beli,* 'not,' and its short form *bal* are used like *lo'*. *bal* occurs only in poetry. *beli* with nouns is equivalent to without (Job 8:12).

7. *belo',* without, is practically always with nouns (Isa. 55:1). Once, in Num. 35:23, it occurs with an infinitive, the particle serving as a preposition and the infinitive as a noun.

8. Combinations of these particles (I Kings 10:21; II Kings 1:3; Isa. 5:9).

9. A negative combined with *kol*, all, or *'ish*, each one, to express the idea of nothing or no one (Ps. 49:18; I Sam. 11:13).

VI

INTERROGATIVES

Interrogatives, like negatives, come first in Hebrew sentences.

1. Interrogative Particles:
   (1) *ha*, which does not imply an answer (Gen. 4:9; 8:8; 24:58).
   (2) *halo'*, which does imply an affirmative answer (Ex. 14:12).

2. Interrogative Pronouns:
   (1) *mi*, who?, always refers to the identification of persons (II Sam. 23:15; Ps. 24:10). Any noun with this interrogative, which is not directly personal, will be found to refer to a name or other identification of a person (Gen. 33:8; Judg. 13:7).
   (2) *mah*, what?, always refers to the nature of a person or thing (Zech. 1:9). It is used in the sense of wherefore to express reproach (Ex. 17:2); in the sense of how to express objection or doubt (Job 9:2); with *le* and the first person to deny connection with something (I Kings 12:16); with *le* and the second person to express condemnation (Isa. 3:15).
   (3) *'ezeh*, which?, also refers to things (I Kings 13:12).

3. Interrogative Adverbs:
   (1) *mathay*, when? (Gen. 30:30).
   (2) *'ekhah*, how?, inquires as to manner (Deut. 18:21).
   (3) *kammah*, how much?, how long? (Gen. 47:8).
   (4) *lammah*, wherefore?, why?, inquires as to purpose (Ex. 2:13).
   (5) *maddua'*, why?, inquires as to cause (Isa. 5:4).
   (6) Combinations of various kinds (Gen. 16:8; Jer. 5:7).

VII

EXCLAMATIONS AND OPTATIVE EXPRESSIONS

Exclamations are of course emphatic. There is no verb for them to precede, but they do precede whatever else there may be in the

phrase (I Sam. 23:20; Gen. 43:20; Isa. 5:20; Joel 1:15; Gen. 43:23; Num. 14:28; Gen. 18:25).

Among the optative expressions are the following: the particle *lu* (Gen. 17:18; 23:13; Num. 14:2); the particle *'im* (Ps. 139:19); and the pronoun *mi* with an imperfect, especially in the expression *mi yitten,* who would give? (II Sam. 23:15; Ex. 16:3).

VIII

MEANS OF EXPRESSING SPECIAL EMPHASIS

In addition to expressions that are by nature emphatic, i.e., negative, interrogative, and exclamatory expressions, the following ways of expressing special emphasis are used:

1. Unusual word order:

Gen. 1:2a — And *the earth* was waste and void.

In this case Hebrew indicates the emphasis by placing the subject before the verb. English composition can do the same thing by means of underscores in a manuscript and italics in print.

Gen. 3:10 — *Your voice* I heard in the garden.

Here the direct object is before the verb.

Gen. 4:6 — Therefore Yahweh proceeded to say *to Cain,* "For what reason are you angry?"

The indirect object is before the direct object, which is the entire statement in quotation marks. All indirect objects placed before direct objects are emphatic in some degree. In this case we see a method used quite frequently with quotations by which attention is called to the person addressed in the quotation.

Gen. 4:7 — *At the very door* sin is lying in wait.

Here an adverbial phrase is placed in a position of strong emphasis.

Gen. 3:14 — *Because you have done this, cursed* are you.

The reason clause is placed ahead of the main clause. It places strong emphasis, therefore, upon the fact that God's judgment was based upon the deeds of the Serpent, not merely upon his possibilities or tendencies.

"Cursed" appears in a substantive expression, one with the verb "to be" understood. Since there is no written verb to mark the position of other words as regular or irregular, the question of emphasis faces circumstances for which previous observations have

not prepared us.   They need to be studiously observed wherever they appear.

The ordinary statement in this case would be: "You are cursed." The whole statement is addressed to the Serpent, so the ordinary statement would start with the personal pronoun referring to him. Whenever the normal order of the two substantives in such a statement is reversed, the purpose appears to be emphasis upon the one placed first.

Gen. 9:26 — *Blessed* is Yahweh, the God of Shem.

"Blessed" is a participle.   Since participles are inflected like nouns, they often serve as predicate complements.   In such cases they are one of the two substantives in a substantive sentence, and the verb "to be" understood links the two as in any other substantive sentence.   Moreover, reversal of normal word order indicates emphasis.   Normal order in this instance would put Yahweh before the verbal form.   The reverse order puts the emphasis on "blessed."

2. Repetition:

(1) Repetition of a noun, like Yahweh in Ex. 34:6 or earth in Jer. 22:29.

(2) Repetition of verb forms, using an infinitive absolute with the finite verb, usually an infinitive absolute of the same root and stem.

If the infinitive absolute precedes the verb, as in Ex. 19:5, it emphasizes the certainty of the verbal action or state.   The conditional clause, therefore, means this: "If you will *indeed* harken, . . ."   If the infinitive absolute follows the verb, as in Isa. 6:9, it emphasizes continuance or the like.   The word of the prophet, therefore, was to be this: "Hear you, *keeping on hearing,* but do not understand."

(3) Repetition of the reference to a distant antecedent by placing a noun in apposition with a personal pronoun that refers to it:

Ex. 2:6 — Then she proceeded to open (it) and to see *him, even the child.*   (The antecedent is "son" in v. 5)

(4) Repetition of the reference to an emphatic antecedent by means of the demonstrative pronoun "these, i.e., the same."

Gen. 6:4 — *The Nephilim* were in the earth in those days . . . , *the same* were the mighty men that were of old.

(5) Repetition of a pronoun, either as a separate pronoun, or a pronominal suffix, as in Job 1:15; II Sam. 17:5; Ps. 27:2:

Job 1:15 — And *I* only escaped, *even I alone,* to tell you.

(6) Placing a word or phrase independently at the beginning of the sentence, without grammatical connection with what follows, and resuming reference to it later by one of the following means:

  a. *Waw* used as a demonstrative adverb:

  Isa. 6:1 — *In the year that king Uzziah died, then* I began to see the Lord.

  b. Both *waw* and a pronoun:

  Gen. 22:24 — *And his concubine,* whose name was Reumah, *even she also,* proceeded to bear Tebah.

3. The pronoun *hu'*, referring to a subject already stated, as in Lev. 17:11 and Isa. 7:14:

Isa. 7:14 — Therefore the Lord *himself* will give you a sign.

This use of *hu'* is to be distinguished from that of *hahu'*, which means that, or, the same.

4. Use of a pronoun with the preposition *le* after verbs. This usage indicates that the action of the verb refers in particular to one specified by the pronoun as in Gen. 12:1 and Isa. 31:8:

Gen. 12:1 — Get *yourself* out from your land, from your kinsfolk, and from your father's household. . . .

5. Identification with a specially important thing or person, marked by addition of the definite article:

I Kings 18:17 — Is it *you, the one troubling* Israel?

Isa. 37:16 — Thou art *God* (lit, Thou art *he, The* [One True] *God.*)

The substantive sentence is used for identification. There is, however, no inverted word order. The great significance of the words put in apposition with the pronoun arises out of the context, and the article or other expression of definiteness calls special attention to it.

Chapter Two

Introductory Matters Concerning Verbs

The position of the verb in the Hebrew sentence is an indication of its importance in syntax as well as in the more fundamental parts of grammar. In the study of etymology and accidence the verb is given a major portion of our attention, not merely because its construction is difficult for those unfamiliar with Semitic thought-forms, but because the understanding of its significance is essential to an understanding of its sentence. Therefore, we also put it first in syntax, and afterwards we turn to sentence structure as a whole.

The syntax of Hebrew verbs is dominated by the following factors: (1) state, (2) time, (3) mood, (4) voice.

Voice is so clearly associated in introductory grammar with the stems of the verb that there is doubtless no need for further treatment. The other three characteristics, however, must be more carefully examined.

The sources of evidence in this examination may be broadly distinguished as follows: (1) evidence of the state appears usually in the grammatical construction of the verb alone, but at times additional evidence is in the context; (2) evidence of the time appears in the context only; (3) evidence of the mood appears as a rule in the verb and the context.

Definitions of state, time, and mood must be sharply drawn in the light of this evidence if translation is to be accurate. Furthermore, it appears advisable to define each point in terms that will enable the reader to judge it separately from each other point because one's choice of translation will often depend upon a separate judgment concerning each point. First of all, therefore, general definitions will be undertaken; then the varied developments can be examined.

28

I

STATE

State, as used at present and generally in this work, means condition of action, mind, body, or event. Let this use of the word "state" be carefully observed. Occasionally it will be necessary to distinguish certain actions and states, setting them in contrast with each other, as in the comparison of stative and active verbs. Here the word "state" is much broader. It applies to the condition indicated by any verb, active or stative, and describes that condition in a general sense as complete, incomplete, or continuous.

In formulating our judgments concerning state, we observe first of all these simple facts: a perfect indicates a complete state, i.e., one that is finished or established; an imperfect indicates an incomplete state, i.e., one that is not finished and so in beginning, or is not established and so subject to interruptions and repetitions; a participle indicates a continuous state, i.e., one in progress but not subject to interruptions. Inasmuch as imperatives have the same ground form as imperfects, they also indicate incomplete states.

After this preliminary observation about state, we proceed to examine time and mood in turn. Certain evidence as to time helps us to decide concerning mood. For instance, if a perfect is in future time and also in an interrogative sentence, this combination indicates a subjunctive mood. Likewise, certain evidence concerning time and mood helps us to make a more precise appraisal of the state. For instance, if a perfect is in past time and there is with it a particle indicating a subjunctive mood, we know that the state, though viewed as complete, is contrary to fact. In connection with all subjunctives and imperatives, the state contemplated by the author is merely a mental state, not yet realized in any sense; therefore, state and mood are inevitably linked together as two sides of the same thing. In view of this identification of state and mood, we can observe that perfects indicate contrary-to-fact states, imperfects indicate potential states or states that are optative in the sense of being desired, and imperatives indicate states that are imperative in the sense of being compulsory.

Infinitives are not mentioned because they are never really verbs. They develop as verb forms and partake of certain verbal characteristics, but their true nature is nominal or adverbial. They will be treated later as adverbs and gerunds.

The state of the verb is generally, but not always, indicated by

its grammatical form.   A perfect standing alone, as it nearly always does, indicates a completed state; but with certain particles it indicates the opposite extreme, a contrary-to-fact state.   Under ordinary circumstances an imperfect indicates an incomplete state; however, circumstances appearing in the context may indicate that the state is not actually begun but merely potential; likewise, other circumstances may indicate that its state is optative.   A participle indicates a continuous state.   An imperative indicates a compulsory state.

II

TIME

The time of the Hebrew verb must be judged in the light of its context.   There are no obvious markers in grammatical formation or syntactical arrangement.   The reader must view the context as a whole, whether it be a sentence, a paragraph, a passage, a book, or a sphere of knowledge, and discern the time that fits.

Time, as used here, is that which distinguishes the state of the verb as before, now, or after.

A time which is related to a single time viewpoint, i.e., before, now, or after the time of the author, and not also before or after some other time, will be designated by a single or simple name, as a past, a present, or a future:

Gen. 1:1 — In the beginning God *created* (a pa) the heavens and the earth.

Gen. 4:10 — The voice of your brother's blood *is crying* (a pre) unto me.

Gen. 4:14 — And from thy face *I shall be hid* (a fut).

A time which is related both to the time of the author and to another time will be designated by a compound name, as previous present or subsequent past.   Let it be observed that both parts of these names indicate time.   Names like present perfect and future perfect are not used in the designation of time because they mix the idea of state with that of time.   It is desired that each point of syntax be judged separately.

A previous past is a past time previous to another past time, as in the following:

Gen. 2:2 — And he rested (a pa) on the seventh day from all the work which *he had made* (a prev pa).

A previous present is a present time which is previous to another present time, as in the following:

Isa. 1:4 — Ah, sinful nation . . . children dealing (a pre) cor-
ruptly! *They have forsaken* (a prev pre) Yahweh.

A previous future is a future time which is thought of as previous
to another future time, as in the following:

I Sam. 20:22 — Go (a fut), for Yahweh *will have sent* (a prev
fut) you.

A subsequent past is a past time which was subsequent to another past time, as in the following:

Jer. 52:7 — Then a breach was made (a pa) in the city, and
all the men of war *proceeded to flee* (a sub pa).

A subsequent present is a present time which is subsequent to
another present time, as in the following:

I Sam. 21:15; 21:14 in Eng — You begin to see (a pre) a man
going mad. Wherefore do you *proceed to bring* (a sub pre)
him unto me?

A subsequent future is a future time which will be subsequent
to another future time, as in the following:

Isa. 10:3, 4 — And what will you do (a fut) for the day of
visitation? . . . Without me they shall bow down (a fut) under the prisoners, and under the slain they *will proceed to fall*
(a sub fut).

III

MOOD

Mood originally meant mind, feeling, or heart. It is used now to
describe one's spirit, attitude, or temper. In grammar mood describes the subject's manner of feeling or thinking concerning the
state of the verb.

The mood is indicative when the state is thought of as a fact;
subjunctive when it is considered contrary-to-fact, potential, or
optative; imperative when one commands the doing or acceptance
of it.

The indicative mood, because it views that state as a fact,
naturally accords with the nature of the perfect and of the participle. Any perfect standing alone, i.e., apart from the particles
used to mark a contrary-to-fact idea, is indicative. Likewise, any
participle standing alone is indicative. Imperfects may be either
indicative or subjunctive, being indicative when the context shows
that the author expected the state of the verb to be realized.

The subjunctive mood, because it views the state as unreal or
uncertain, naturally accords with the nature of the imperfect. To

indicate that an idea is possible, a simple imperfect is used, and the context alone is depended upon to show that it is a potential subjunctive.   To indicate that a possibility is also the desire of the author, special forms of the imperfect are used; a special suffix or an internal vowel change is depended upon to show that they are optative subjunctives.   The only way the subjunctive can use perfects or participles is by placing before them particles which indicate that a statement is contrary-to-fact.   The combination uses their established nature to establish the unreality of the statement in which they appear.

The cohortative and the jussive belong to the same mood.   Both express desire, urgency, i.e., an optative mood.   Both appear with forms of the imperfect, the cohortative regularly with forms in the first person, and the jussive regularly with forms in the second or third person.   The two supply what is known in English as optative subjunctives.

The cohortative is indicated by the addition of the letter *h* to the verb form or by a vowel change, and, when negative, by the use of the negative particle *'al*.

The jussive is indicated sometimes by the use of the negative particle *'al*, sometimes by a vowel change, and sometimes by the context alone.

The imperative is sometimes indicated by its own special form, sometimes by the use of an imperfect in the second person with the negative particle *lo'*, and sometimes by the context alone.

The special form of the imperative is used to express positive commands only (cf. Ex. 20:12).

The imperfect in the second person may also be used to express prohibitions (cf. Ex. 20:10).

The imperfect in the second person may also be used to express a positive command.   In such a case the context alone is relied upon to indicate the imperative idea (cf. Ex. 20:9).

CONCLUSION: DISTINCTIVE TRANSLATIONS

When the three foregoing points of syntax have been determined, their combination furnishes a guide to the translation.   In existing translations the lack of uniformity in the handling of these points causes a serious loss of clarity and vividness.   Many have concluded that uniformity in the determination and translation of these points is impossible.   Nevertheless, the present suggestions con-

cerning them grow out of a belief that the Hebrew authors did work upon uniform principles in their use of them and that an attempt to regain the force of the original is worthy of the best of our efforts.

The table that follows suggests a distinctive translation for each combination of syntactical points.   Only active verbs in the active voice are used.   However, the parallels for stative verbs and for the passive forms of active verbs may be worked out easily.   These distinctive translations seek to express the essential idea in each combination in such a way that it may be clearly distinguished from all others.   The exact wording of the distinctive translations cannot be rigidly emulated in every translation, but the essential idea can be maintained.

The examples given in the treatment of varied developments following the table of distinctive translations are intended to demonstrate the possibility of maintaining the essential idea of the verb amid all the variations of translations.   The wording of existing translations, preferably that of the American Standard Version, is used wherever it appears to be true to the essential idea; but a new wording is offered where existing translations seem to fail to make that idea clear.   With each group of illustrations the combination of syntactical points is indicated so that comparison with the table of distinctive translations may be made.

A TABLE OF DISTINCTIVE TRANSLATIONS

STATE	TIME	MOOD	TRANSLATION
1. Com	Pa	Ind	He killed.
2. Com	Pre	Ind	He kills, he does kill.
3. Com	Fut	Ind	He shall kill.
4. Com	Prev pa	Ind	He had killed.
5. Com	Prev pre	Ind	He has killed.
6. Com	Prev fut	Ind	He will have killed. He shall have killed
7. Inc	Pa	Ind	He repeatedly killed.
8. Inc	Pre	Ind	He repeatedly kills.
9. Inc	Fut	Ind	He will repeatedly kill.
10. Inc	Sub pa	Ind	He began to kill. He proceeded to kill.
11. Inc	Sup pre	Ind	He begins to kill. He proceeds to kill.
12. Inc	Sub fut	Ind	He will begin to kill. He will proceed to kill.
13. Cont	Pa	Ind	He was killing.
14. Cont	Pre	Ind	He is killing.
15. Cont	Fut	Ind	He will be killing.
16. Com	Pa	Con subj	If he had killed.
17. Com	Fut	Con subj	Who can kill?
18. Inc	Fut	Pot subj	He could kill. He would kill. He should kill.
19. Inc	Fut	Opt subj (Coh)	I (or we) will kill. Let me (or us) kill. I am willing to kill.
20. Inc	Fut	Opt subj (Jus)	Do thou kill. Let him kill.
21. Inc	Fut	Imv (Imp)	Thou shalt kill.
22. Inc	Fut	Imv	Kill thou.
23. Inc	Fut	Imv & Jus	Kill thou—oh do kill!

Chapter Three

Indicative Perfects

All indicative perfects describe completed states. They are single, finished, and certain. In other words, a perfect looks at one thing, sees it as a whole, and thinks of it as certain.

The fact of fundamental importance is that a perfect is single. Whereas an imperfect may describe a state as the first in a series, implying a relation to others of its kind, a perfect pictures it alone, not bearing within itself any indication of relation to other states. There may be others, the context may indicate a relation, but a perfect does not link itself to another verb in any way. "Created" in Gen. 1:1 describes the one act of creation performed "in the beginning" and gives no hint concerning the other acts of creation.

(This view of the perfect is contrary to the generally accepted interpretation of the perfect when it is accompanied by the conjunction *waw*. According to Gesenius, Driver, Muller, Harper, and apparently all other authors who have dealt with the subject, the perfect with *waw* may receive the force of a frequentative imperfect. If so, Hebrew fails to maintain in its use of the perfect and imperfect a distinctive meaning for each, one that is always true to the fundamental nature of its own form. It is intended in this work to take issue with that kind of interpretation. In the treatment below of correlative perfects, further discussion of the matter will be found.)

The single state described by a perfect is also finished. An imperfect may describe the beginning of development of a state, but a perfect sees its conclusion and perfected character. The "was" of Gen. 1:2 asserts that the "waste and void" or unorganized state of original matter existed at the time it was created. A translation

35

like "came to be" would be contrary to the nature of the perfect. On the other hand, many imperfects are used in Gen. 1:3-19 to describe those developments through which law and order emerged in the material universe.

The single whole described by a perfect is also considered as certain. An imperfect may picture a state as possible or desired or expected, but a perfect sees it as actual, real, and sure. The "let us make" of Gen. 1:26 expresses God's desire that the formation of man should proceed, implying that it did not exist at the time of the speaking. The "he had made" of Gen. 1:31 refers to it as already accomplished.

It is helpful to note that each perfect bears all of these three general characteristics. Let us emphasize the *and* as we say that a perfect state is single, *and* finished, *and* certain.

In addition to these general characteristics, various groups of perfects manifest some characteristics peculiar to themselves. To facilitate study of these, the following classifications are suggested.

I

SIMPLE PERFECTS

The great majority of perfects are simple in *all* their relations, and it is this simplicity which distinguishes them from other perfects. While all perfects are simple in the sense of being singular, simple perfects are also uncomplicated by relationships indicated by the context. Some perfects are so related within the context as to show one of the following facts: (1) that their time is previous to another time; (2) that their state is characteristic of a life or period of time; (3) that the facts they describe are correlatives of another fact. Simple perfects, however, remain entirely unrelated to other verbs. They are uncomplicated within or without.

These simple perfects include both active and stative verbs. There is no difference between the two as far as the foregoing is concerned. The following examples, however, will reveal slight differences in other ways.

1. Simple Actions:

A simple action belongs to an exact point or period of time. A period, therefore, serves well as a graph for it (.).

(1) A past time (Combination 1):

Gen. 1:1 — In the beginning God *created* the heavens . . . .

The state is complete, for the verb is a perfect standing alone. The time is past, for it describes the beginning of creation. The mood is indicative, for it is part of a narrative. Translation should not involve difficulties here. AV, ASV, and RSV give it according to the accepted text. When MNT and AT amend this sentence, making it a time clause dependent on verse 2, they obscure the leading statement of a great story. Hebrew narrative under normal circumstances, i.e., when there is no context to indicate the contrary, begins with a perfect.

Syntactical summary: com-pa-ind (nar)

Gen. 6:9 — Noah *walked* with God.

The state is complete, for the verb is a perfect standing alone. It describes Noah's life as a whole, not at various times. The time is past, for it is the time of Noah. The mood is indicative, for it is part of a narrative. Translation is again a simple matter. AV, ASV, RSV, MNT, and AT, all agree in rendering it. MNT paraphrases the meaning of the verb but does not differ as to syntax.

Syntactical summary: com-pa-ind (nar)

Gen. 36:2 — Esau *took* his wives of the daughters of Canaan.

A frequentative imperfect could have been used, but the author's choice of a perfect indicates that he looked at the one fact of Esau's taking heathen wives, not the separate instances of such conduct. Translation is easy in this case also. AT paraphrases the meaning but is true to the syntax.

Syntactical summary: com-pa-ind (nar)

All the verbs above are narrative perfects. Being in past time where completeness is obvious, they exhibit plainly the normal characteristics of a perfect. It is helpful, therefore, to realize that past time is the most natural atmosphere for a perfect and that any appearance in another time needs to be carefully observed. Whenever a perfect appears in present or future time, it takes on a special significance.

(2) In present time (Combination 2):

II Sam. 24:23 — All this, O king, *does* Araunah *give* to the king.

The time is present, for these words are the conclusion of Araunah's offer to give (cf. 24:22), not a statement that he did give. David did not permit him to give. These facts are missed

by AV but recognized by ASV, RSV, MNT, and AT. The mood is indicative, for Araunah is stating as positively as possible that so far as willingness can go he does give everything to David. Translation needs to bring out the emphasis of Araunah, and also to distinguish between such emphasis upon an isolated fact and the use of a perfect to mark a fact as characteristic of a life. The translation of RSV, MNT, and AT, because they lack emphatic auxiliaries, do not do this. Therefore, the translation of ASV is chosen, except that "doth" is changed to "does" according to a modern English trend.

Syntactical summary: com-pre-ind (em)

I Kings 1:11 — Have you not heard that Adonijah . . . *does reign.*

Apparently we have here another simple present, as recognized by AV and ASV. MNT, AT, and RSV have substituted a previous present by paraphrasing the meaning of the verb. When we stick to its real meaning, it is an emphatic affirmation of the fact that Adonijah reigns which fits the context.

Syntactical summary: Com-pre-ind (em)

Gen. 14:22 — I *do lift up* my hand to Yahweh.

The time appears to be present, despite the fact that AV, ASV, RSV, and AT have interpreted it as previous present. MNT interprets it as present. Both a past (I lifted up) and a previous present (I have lifted up) appear to be ruled out by the fact that the lifting up of the hand signified an oath, and there had been no occasion for it prior to the suggestion in 14:21 that Abram take the spoil for himself. That suggestion apparently provoked the oath then and there. The mood is indicative because Abram was affirming the taking of an oath. The translation needs to reflect the emphatic positiveness of Abram in taking this oath. As stated in 14:23, Abram's desire was to prevent the king of Sodom from saying, "I have made Abram rich." This desire evidently provoked his emphatic use of the perfect in affirming his oath. Accordingly, we use the emphatic auxiliary "do" to reflect the strength of his mood.

Syntactical summary: com-pre-ind (em)

I Kings 1:35 — And him I *do appoint* to be prince.

The time appears to be present, because the verb describes actual installation and there had been no such act previously. The mood is indicative, for David was affirming the appoint-

ment as shown by 1:33-35a. The translation must needs make obvious the emphatic switch from an ordinary indicative imperfect in future time (1:35a) to this emphatic perfect in present time (1:35b); therefore, the emphatic auxiliary is used again.

Syntactical summary: com-pre-ind (em)

All verbs in this group may well be called emphatic perfects. The effect of any simple perfect in present time is emphatic, and it may be reflected in translation by the use of emphatic auxiliaries. They should be carefully distinguished from previous-present perfects and characteristic perfects, which are also in present time.

(3) In future time (Combination 3):

The effect of any simple perfect in future time is an emphasis upon the assurance felt by the speaker concerning the fulfilment of his words. In all cases there is unwavering assurance, but the reasons for that assurance vary. Further classification of these expressions is suggested as a means of helping us recognize these various reasons. Every such expression is a matter of unusual importance in Scripture, and we should not fail to recognize one when we meet it.

    a. Perfects of Confidence:

        Gen. 17:16 — And moreover *I will give* you a son of her.

    All translations recognize the assurance expressed by this perfect in future time, and they reflect it by the use of the auxiliary "will" with the first person.

Syntactical summary: com-fut-ind (con)

        Gen. 30:13 — The daughters *shall* surely *call* me blessed.

    AV, ASV, RSV, and MNT make no attempt to reflect the force of this perfect in future time. They handle it exactly as they handle an imperfect interpreted as a pure future. AT makes an attempt by introducing the adverb "certainly." No objection need be raised to this or similar adverbs. But why not add a simple step corresponding to the use of "will" with the first person, as seen in Gen. 17:16, and use the auxiliary "shall" with the second or third person?

Syntactical summary: com-fut-ind (con)

        Num. 17:27; 17:12 in Eng — We *will die,* we *will perish,* all of us *will perish.*

All translations put these verbs in the present. Apparently they interpret them as emphatic or characteristic perfects. Two separate statements in the verse following, however, show that the perishing and dying is viewed as future. That being true, the perfects that are used should be interpreted as perfects of confidence. They express the certainty the speakers felt about an event that was future to them. This sense of certainty arose from their own thinking, not from revelation. Perfects of certainty reflect both of these facts.

Syntactical summary: com-fut-ind (con)

The name perfect of confidence fits these verbs better than perfect of certainty, which has been generally used. The idea of certainty applies in some sense to all perfects in future time, but it does not distinguish one group from another. The basis of assurance in this group is self-assurance or confidence, no matter whether it be proper self-reliance or unwarranted cocksureness. God's assurance in Gen. 17:16 was of course warranted. Leah's in Genesis 30:13 was probably so, but that of the Israelites in Num. 17:27 was a case of jumping to conclusions. In all cases there is that feeling of certainty that grows out of confidence on the part of the speaker, but there may be no certainty otherwise concerning fulfilment of the speaker's words.

b. Prophetic Perfects:

Isa. 11:8 — And upon the den of an adder a weaned child *shall put* his hand.

AV, ASV, and RSV have used "shall" here. "Shall" in such cases is used also by W. R. Harper.[1] MNT uses a paraphrase which gives no place for either "shall" or "will," thus obscuring one of the most prominent features of the language. AT uses "will," and in doing so it apparently develops an inconsistency in its own usage. From 10:33 to this verse it interprets a series of perfects with *waw* as receiving the force of a pure future imperfect in third person as found in 10:33 and uses "will" with each one. Since it accepts "will" as the characteristic for the future imperfects and for perfects linked to it by *waw,* what can there be even in its own premises to justify the handling of a perfect sepa-

---

1. W. R. Harper, *Elements of Hebrew Syntax* (New York: Charles Scribner's Sons, 1888), p. 57.

rated from *waw* as though it were another imperfect? Such failures to maintain the distinctions of the Hebrew ought to arouse us to see the urgent need of adopting methods of translation that will maintain those distinctions. Prophetic perfects were used by the prophets with fine discrimination, to give climactic touches of power to their perorations, and we are throwing away jewels of prophetic teaching when we allow the muddy waters of indistinct translations to obscure them.

Syntactical summary: com-fut-ind (pro)

> Isa. 9:5; 9:6 in Eng — For to us a child *shall be born,* a son *shall be given* to us.

All the translations have used present time here: AV, ASV, RSV, and AT the simple present, MNT a previous present. This is not done because they consider these verbs as describing the actual present. Instead they are applying an interpretation which is stated by S. R. Driver as follows: ". . . continually the series of perfects is interspersed with the simple future forms, as the prophet shifts his point of view, at one moment contemplating the events he is describing from the *real standpoint* of the present, at another moment looking back upon them as accomplished and done and so viewing them from an *ideal position* in the future."[2] Such supposed shifting of viewpoint is very confusing, even to the student of the Hebrew text. It leaves the reader of the English hopelessly lost. Moreover, this supposition is not necessary. Adoption of "shall" as a characteristic of the perfect in second or third person and in future time would mark it clearly as future, as distinguished from the pure future imperfect using "will," and as indicating the dramatic certainty of the prophetic perfect.

Syntactical summary: com-fut-ind (pro)

> Num. 24:17 — There *shall come forth* a star out of Jacob.

Again the "shall come" of AV, ASV, and RSV is clear, and the "has come" of MNT and AT is confusing. The reference is unquestionably to the future, as shown by the first part of the verse. Then let that reference be clear and strong.

2. S. R. Driver, *A Treatise on the Use of the Tenses in Hebrew* (3rd ed.; Oxford: The Clarendon Press, 1892), p. 19.

Syntactical summary: com-fut-ind (pro)

Other examples appear in Isa. 5:13;   8:8;   9:1;   10:28; 28:2;   53:12;   Hos. 4:6;   Amos 5:2;   Ps. 67:7;   110:5.

The basis for assurance in these cases is a revelation from God on one hand and faith on the other.   This faith is always warranted because it is based on God.   Though the prophet prove to be unworthy, as did Balaam, the speaker of Num. 24:17, the prophetic word never will prove unworthy, for its author and finisher is God.

If a question arises as to whether a verb be a perfect of confidence (word of the author) or a prophetic perfect (word received by the author from God), the determinative question must be, Does the Scripture passage represent it as a word received from God?   This question need not trouble us greatly in translation, for we translate the same way in both cases; but it helps to clarify the meaning of these idioms.

The faith expressed in these perfects is identified with the prophets, and the name prophetic perfect fits them well.

It is very important to note that all perfects of confidence and prophetic perfects appear apart from conjunctions.   This fact sharply distinguishes them from the correlative perfects which will be described later.

It is also very important to observe that the auxiliary of the verb, the "shall" or the "will," is the reverse of the one ordinarily used.   We ought to utilize every means at our command to retain in our translations the force of these peculiarly important idioms, and there appears to be no way in English to do this except through rigid observance of the distinctions between "shall" and "will."   With the first person "will" is used here to indicate the positiveness of these perfects, because "shall" in these cases would make a mild statement.   With the second and third persons "shall" is used here to indicate the positiveness of these perfects, because "will" in these cases would make a mild statement.

In addition to making it possible for a discerning reader of the English text, even though he lack a knowledge of Hebrew, to take note of prophetic perfects, this method of translation would eliminate from English translations much confusing fluctuation in the handling of the English future tense. Any extensive comparison of AV, ERV, ASV, RSV, MNT, and AT will reveal the fact that this fluctuation is widespread.

It is doubtless due in large measure to the problems involved in interpreting the so-called *waw* consecutive with perfects. These cannot be dealt with until we have gone further in our study of perfects and of the conjunction *waw*. We may observe even here, however, that the suggestions made above are in accord with the highest literary standards. George O. Curme says, concerning a pure future in English: "Shall in the first person, singular and plural, is the standard usage in England, though not uniformly observed, and is still the preferred form in the higher grades of literary language in America, though now not so uniformly used as it once was."[3] Accordingly, he says concerning the modal use of "shall" in the second and third persons: "As a modal auxiliary it indicates the will of someone other than its subject, representing its subject as standing under the will of another who commands him, promises or assures him something, wishes something to be arranged to suit him, threatens him, resolves to do something for his benefit or injury, or it represents the speaker as determined to bring something about or prevent it. . . . It represents the speaker as proclaiming the will of God or destiny in a prophetic or oracular announcement of something that shall take place."[4]

2. Simple states:

Some stative verbs describe intellectual, emotional, or volitional states: know, remember, hate, love, refuse, trust, and rejoice. Some of them describe pure states of being: be righteous, be high, be full, be old, be beautiful, be weary, and be great. In all cases there is no real action, only a condition of body, mind, or spirit.

A simple state is like a simple action in that it stands as a unit, singular, finished, and certain. It is different, however, in that it is indefinitely extended beyond the time of completion. One knows and keeps on knowing. The fitting graph is a short line (⸺⸺⸺).

    (1) In past time (Combination 1):
        Gen. 40:23 — But the chief butler *remembered* not.
        Ex. 1:7 — And the children of Israel *were fruitful.*

3. George O. Curme, *A Grammar of the English Language* (Boston: D. C. Heath and Company, 1935), III, p. 363.
4. *Ibid.,* pp. 364, 365.

Ps. 31:15; 31:14 in Eng — But I *trusted* in Thee, O Yahweh.

Syntactical summary: com-pa-ind (nar)

These are narrative perfects as truly as are the simple active verbs in past time.

(2) In present time (Combination 2):

Ex. 3:19 — And as for me I *indeed know*.

Job 34:5 — I *am surely righteous*.

Ps. 31:7; 31:6 in Eng — But as for me in Yahweh *do I trust*.

Syntactical summary: com-pre-ind (em)

These are emphatic perfects. The use of adverbs and auxiliaries to bring out the emphatic force in the English needs to be carefully observed.

(3) In future time (Combination 3):

Isa. 11:9 — For the earth *shall be full* of the knowledge of Yahweh.

Isa. 15:9 — For the waters of Dimon *shall be full* of blood.

Isa. 53:10 — And Yahweh *shall be pleased* with the bruising of him.

Syntactical summary: com-fut-ind (pro)

These are prophetic perfects. Again "shall" with the third person is used to indicate that the state described is determined and absolutely certain.

II

Previous Perfects

One of the complications into which a perfect is brought by its context is that of previous completion. When it is written in Gen. 2:2, "And he rested on the seventh day from all his work which he had done," it is evident that God's work was completed before he rested. The fact that the state described is previous to another distinguishes a large group of verbs and gives occasion for the name previous perfect.

There is a combination of active and stative ideas always associated with a previous perfect. From Gen. 2:2 it is evident that the state resulting from God's work continued until he began to rest. The graph that fits this situation is a horizontal line

extended up to a perpendicular line representing the point of time
it precedes (————————▎).

    (1) In past time (Combination 4):

        Gen. 2:8 — And he put there the man whom *he had*
          formed.

        I Sam. 28:20 — And there was no strength in him, for
          he had not eaten bread.

        I Kings 7:8 — Solomon made also a house for Pharaoh's
          daughter whom *he had taken* to wife.

    All translations agree here.

Syntactical summary: com-pa-ind (prev)

    (2) In present time (Combination 5):

        Isa. 1:3-4 — Israel does not know . . . they *have forsaken*
          Yahweh.

        Gen. 32:11; 32:10 in Eng — I am not worthy of the least
          of all the loving-kindnesses which thou *hast done* for
          thy servant.

        I Sam. 12:3 — Here I am: witness against me . . . whose
          ox *have I taken?*

    Again all translations agree.

Syntactical summary: com-pre-ind (prev)

    (3) In future time (Combination 6):

        Isa. 4:3-4 — And it shall come to pass that he that is
          left in Zion . . . will be called holy, . . . when the
          Lord *shall have washed away* the filth of the daughters
          of Zion.

    AV, ASV, and RSV use "shall have" here, and this previous
perfect in future time is clearly distinguished by it. When
MNT and AT shift back to a previous present, they muddle
the question of time in the same way they do when translating
prophetic perfects.

Syntactical summary: com-fut-ind (prev)

        II Sam. 5:24 — And let it be . . . that then you will bestir
          yourself; for then Yahweh *shall have gone forth* before
          you . . . .

    AV appears to have interpreted this as a prophetic perfect,
disregarding the previous relation. ASV and AT shift to present time, RSV to previous present time. Only MNT gives it
as a previous future. It uses "will have" instead of "shall have";
but the difference between these two is not great, and it seems

reasonable to accept either in translating previous relation in future time. "Shall" makes the statement a prophetic declaration, "will" makes it a simple affirmation, and it is impossible when previous relationship exists to tell how the author intended it.

Syntactical summary: com-fut-ind (prev)

>   I Sam. 14:10 — Then we will go up, for Yahweh *shall have put* them in our hand.

AV, ASV, RSV, and AT use the previous present, and MNT the simple present. Yet their going up is of course future, and the time of Yahweh's putting their enemies into their hand is related to that. Putting into their hand refers to Yahweh's answer to their prayer, his overruling their test so as to give a sign of his will; and that answer had not been given at the moment Jonathan spoke.

Syntactical summary: com-fut-ind (prev)

All previous states are described by perfects, and all subsequent ones by imperfects. Thus it appears that the name previous perfect is fitting because of the obvious contrast with the subsequent nature of those imperfects usually called Progressives.

III

CHARACTERISTIC PERFECTS

Another complication into which a perfect is occasionally brought by its context is that of characteristic or typical significance. A single act or state is made to typify the character of a person or thing. This relation gives occasion for the name characteristic perfect.

When it is said in Isa. 1:3, "An ox knows his master . . . , Israel does not know," we understand that recognition of his master is a distinguishing trait or characteristic of an ox but not of Israel. We know this because the whole chapter is devoted to a description of the moral character of Israel. When the contrast between an ox and Israel is drawn in the midst of this characterization of Israel, it is obvious that Isaiah is characterizing both, telling not merely what they know at some particular moment, but what kind of knowledge distinguishes one from the other.

The fitting graph for this characteristic perfect is a period with-

in a circle, a single act or state corresponding to a larger but similar sphere (⊙).

Job 7:9 — A cloud *is temporary* and proceeds to go away.

Isa. 40:7 — Grass *withers,* a flower *fades.*

Ps. 1:1 — Blessed is the man who *walks* not in the counsel of the wicked, and in the way of the sinners he *stands* not, and in the seat of the scoffers he *sits* not.

In Job 7:9 and Isa. 40:7 all translations agree, giving clear recognition to this kind of perfect. Ps. 1:1 is handled the same way in AV, ASV, and RSV, but MNT gives its verbs what appears to be an emphatic interpretation, and AT makes them previous presents. Emphasis must be admitted as a possible interpretation, but there is no clear ground for a previous relation. In many cases, as in Ps. 119:113, the possibility of more than one interpretation must be admitted, and each interpreter left to his choice.

All characteristic perfects appear to be in present time. Their extended application to a sphere of life or being accords with such usage, their present being a broad unrestricted present without any specific limitations as to time. In other words, that which is asserted to be true now is generally true of the subject.

Syntactical summary: com-pre-ind (ch)

The three perfects in present time need to be clearly distinguished. These three kinds are: (1) emphatic; (2) previous; (3) characteristic. The emphatic ones stress the fact that a certain state does exist; the previous ones indicate that the state occurred before another; and the characteristic ones make the state typical of some life or thing. In translation the emphatic ones may be marked by emphatic auxiliaries or adverbs; the previous ones by the auxiliaries "had," "has" (or have), and "shall have" accompanying the participle; and the characteristic ones by absence of these auxiliaries.

IV

CORRELATIVE PERFECTS

Another complication for a perfect develops when it is linked by the conjunction *waw* to a preceding expression so as to indicate a correlative relationship. As the word "father" and the word "son" imply each other, or as a whole and its parts imply each other, so a perfect with *waw* attached and its antecedent imply each

other. This relationship is correlative and gives occasion for the name correlative perfect.

A circle, representing the antecedent, divided into segments, which are its correlatives, will furnish a graph (⊕).

The visible mark of correlative perfects is their immediate connection with the conjunction. It is always attached to them, but never to other perfects.

The translation of correlative perfects need not differ from that of other perfects except for the immediate connection with the conjunction. Scrupulous care should be exercised to maintain the connection with correlatives and to avoid it with others. Sometimes it may be necessary to let the subject come between the conjunction and verb in order to make a natural sentence in English, but the close connection between conjunction and verb ought to be made as obvious as possible in all cases.

Students need to realize that the interpretation of the conjunction *waw* is a matter of far-reaching significance in Hebrew. A separate study of it will be undertaken after all verb forms have been studied and in connection with sentence structure.

In each case there are two verbs to be considered: the perfect with *waw,* and whatever verb precedes it, which will be called its antecedent. In Gen. 2:10, for instance, "was as it were four heads" represents the perfect with *waw,* and "began to be divided" represents its antecedent.

When these two verbs are alike, both being perfects, all translators agree in making them co-ordinate. Inasmuch as correlation includes co-ordination, differing from ordinary co-ordination merely in the fact that its co-ordination is inherent and permanent, the translation works out well in all cases.

When the two verbs are different, however, translations differ in all sorts of ways. In Gen. 2:10, where the antecedent is an imperfect, AV, ASV, and RSV translate that imperfect like a perfect and the perfect with *waw* like an imperfect, while MNT and AT avoid the problem by paraphrasing in ways that disregard the original text. In Deut. 11:10, where the antecedent is also an imperfect, AV, ASV, RSV, and MNT translate both as perfects, while AT translates both as imperfects. And this confusion appears in the very places where the old theory of *waw* consecutive with the perfect is supposed to apply regularly, i.e., in narratives begun with an imperfect and continued by perfects with *waw*. (Cf. Pars. 49-3 and Par. 112 of *Gesenius' Hebrew*

Grammar; Chapter VII of *The Use of the Tenses in Hebrew* by
S. R. Driver; pp. 17ff. of *Hebrew Syntax* by August Muller; Par.
25 of *Elements of Hebrew Syntax* by W. R. Harper.)

The explanation of perfects with *waw* as correlatives offers one
explanation for all of them and a way out of this confusion in
translation. According to it, correlative perfects may follow
any kind of antecedent and yet be translated as perfects, the
correlative relation being indicated by the attachment of the perfect to the conjunction.

1. In past time (Combination 1):

Gen. 2:10 — And a river was going out from Eden, . . . and
from there it began to be divided *and was as it were four
heads* (lit, *for four heads*).

As the delta land of the garden of Eden made the river divide,
its four divisions were like the separate headwaters of a great
stream. "Began to be divided" and "was as it were four heads"
are different descriptions of the same thing.

Josh. 6:8, 9 — Then it proceeded to be so, that . . . seven
priests passed over, bearing seven rams' horns as trumpets
before Yahweh, *and they blew* upon the trumpets. The
armed men were going before the priests who blew upon the
trumpets, and the rear portion [of the priests] was going after
the ark, going on steadily and blowing continuously.

These two verses together make it quite obvious that the
passing over did not occur separately from the blowing of the
trumpets. The passing over and the blowing were two phases
of one general movement. Thus the perfect "and they blew" at
the end of 6:8 furnishes an excellent example of a correlative
perfect. The absence of sequence is obvious. The inseparable
relation of the two actions as parts of one general movement,
actions that combined the military and the religious warning to
the enemy, is likewise clear.

Deut. 2:30 — Yahweh your God hardened his spirit *and made
strong* his heart.

Hardening and making strong (or obstinate) are obviously
different descriptions of the same thing. Thus they are correlative
ideas.

Deut. 11:10 — Where you were accustomed to sow your seed,
and you watered with your foot as the garden of herbs.

Watering with the foot is a part of the process of sowing seed, as it is done in an irrigated land.   A toe is used to break a ridge and let water from an adjoining furrow flow over the seed that has just been dropped.   These likewise are correlative ideas.

Ps. 27:2 — They stumbled *and fell.*

Stumbling and falling are parts of such a downfall or destruction of enemies as the context contemplates.   Being parts of the same whole, they too are correlative ideas.

In past time correlative perfects are translated like narrative perfects.   Their connection with the conjunction, however, distinguishes them, for Hebrew usage does not permit ordinary narrative perfects to be linked together by *waw.*

Syntactical summary: com-pa-ind (cor)

2. In present time (Combination 2 or 3):

Isa. 1:2 — Children I have made great *and have exalted.*

Hos. 4:3 — The land mourns continually, *and is faint* every inhabitant of it.

Jer. 12:3 — And thou, O Yahweh, dost know me, thou seest me continually, *and dost test me.*

Syntactical Summary: com-pa-ind (cor)

In other translations the same sort of confusion is found as was seen above.   In Isa. 1:2 there is agreement, for the verbs are both perfects.   In Hos. 4:3, where the antecedent is an imperfect, AV and ARV treat both as prophetic perfects, while MNT, AT, and RSV put both in present time.   In Jer. 12:3, where the antecedent is also an imperfect, AV treats both like previous perfects, while ASV, RSV, and AT apparently, but not clearly, treat both as imperfects, and MNT paraphrases.   In all three cases the two verbs describe parts of the same thing and thus are correlated.

As the above examples show, correlatives in present time may be translated like a previous present perfect, a characteristic perfect, or an emphatic perfect.   Still they are distinguished by the connection with *waw,* for Hebrew usage does not permit any other perfect to be linked with *waw.*

3. In future time (Combination 3):

Gen. 17:20 — Behold, I will bless him (pf of con), yea *I will make him fruitful,* and *I will multiply him* exceedingly.

Gen. 40:13 — Within three days Pharaoh will lift up your head

and shall restore you to your office, *and you shall put* the cup of Pharaoh into his hand.

Isa. 2:2 — The house of Yahweh will be established at the head of the mountains, *and shall be exalted* above hills, *and shall flow* to it all the nations.

Ex. 19:10-13 — *Go* to the people, *and you shall sanctify* them . . . *and they shall wash* their garments, *and they shall be ready* . . . *and you 'shall set* bounds.

Syntactical summary: com-fut-ind   (cor)

The translations often put a terrific strain on subjective judgment in deciding what interpretations to give to the perfects with *waw*.   In Gen. 17:20, where the antecedent is another perfect, they are made co-ordinate; and the translation works out well. In Gen. 40:13 and Isa. 2:2, where the antecedents are imperfects, they are made imperfects.   In Ex. 19:10-13, where the antecedent is an imperative, two are made imperatives, but one is made a jussive imperfect, and another is made a potential subjunctive.   In other words, the imperative antecedent is considered, for the purpose of the old theory, the equivalent of an imperfect in its effect on the perfects that follow; then the *waw* with the perfects is supposed to give to the perfects the force of an imperfect, but that imperfect may be any kind of imperfect; and the translator switches around from one to another with no apparent guidance other than his own subjective judgment.   This kind of thing is done quite frequently.   If the translations always made these perfects to receive the force of their antecedents, at least the application of their theory would be clear.   But alas! the fact that they do so most of the time and the results in those instances happen to be what we are accustomed to in English gives a plausibility to their theory that lulls us into forgetting the strange logic of it.   When we take time, however, to examine the many instances in which it fails to lead to any justifiable interpretation of the text, we are faced with the conclusion that it is inadequate.

In AT many efforts to attain more distinctive translations have been made, and some of them appear here.   In all cases the antecedents and their attached perfects are kept in the same time. In Gen. 17:20, the prophetic perfect used as an antecedent is put in future time and marked by an emphatic adverb.   In Isa. 2:2, the imperfect used as an antecedent is clearly treated as an

imperfect. These efforts are a tremendous improvement over many unjustified paraphrases by which MNT avoided the problems which all students of the subject knew to exist in previous works. While AT has not escaped the confusion entirely, it has at least tried to stick to the text and to interpret it.

The correlative relations in these examples appear as follows: in Gen. 17:20, making fruitful and multiplying are parts of the blessing; in Gen. 40:13, restoration to office and performance of one of its functions by putting Pharaoh's cup in his hand are parts of the lifting up of the chief butler's head; in Isa. 2:2, exaltation above hills (little powers) and the coming of the nations like a stream are parts of the same great restoration of Israel to which belongs establishment at the head of the mountains (big powers); and in Ex. 19:10-13, Moses' sanctifying the people, their washing their garments, their getting ready, and Moses' setting of bounds are all details of the situation which Moses was expected to put in order, thus being correlated in the mind of the speaker with the command to go.

The translations of these correlatives may be handled exactly like perfects of confidence and prophetic perfects, except for the connection with the conjunction.

It is helpful to observe that these perfects with *waw* are very common in future time. At some points in the future they pile up, any number being used in a series. After imperatives the details of the command are customarily given by them. Also they are used constantly in lengthy descriptions of the future. In prophetic utterances several chapters may be tied together by them. This frequent use in future time is in sharp contrast with a decidedly infrequent use in past and present time. Thus their frequent use in future time becomes a feature of the language, that verb whose natural element is the past being shifted to the future when attached to the conjunction.

A corresponding peculiarity of the imperfect must be kept in mind while studying this situation. Whereas the natural element of the imperfect is future time, when attached to *waw* consecutive it appears almost always in the past.

Examining all these evidences, we realize that these idioms are very peculiar, very closely related to each other, and very important.

The freedom with which we link English perfects in past time after this fashion, "They ran and they skipped and they played,"

and English imperfects in future time after this fashion, "They will run and skip and play," is that which makes the Hebrew idiom so strange to us. Hebrew never uses either of these ways of expression. Moreover, when we take into account the fact that "the other Semitic languages do not exhibit this peculiarity, excepting occasionally the Phoenician, the most closely related to Hebrew, and of course the Moabitish dialect of the *Mesa* inscription, which is practically identical with Old Hebrew,"[5] we know that probably we must look to Biblical Hebrew alone for evidence bearing on an explanation.

This shift of both perfects and imperfects to the natural time of the other when they are attached to certain forms of *waw* indicates that the fundamental characteristics of each pertain to the state represented and in no sense to time. In these relations, therefore, we have excellent oportunity for comparison and marking essential distinctions.

The importance of these idioms in Hebrew is indicated by the fact that few passages omit the use of one or the other. Moreover, the meaning of highly important passages depends upon their interpretation. Their use is so important as to color more or less the whole language.

Therefore, let the foregoing observations concerning the nature of the Hebrew perfect be accepted as evidence to be weighed in connection with the nature of the imperfect and the various forms of the conjunction *waw*. As tentative steps in this study the following suggestions may be kept in mind:

1. The correlative nature of the perfect with *waw* fitted it for the account of details in extended descriptions of the future. When looking into the future, it is impossible for human understanding to grasp much of the sequence of things. This remains true even when the mind of man is illumined by the light of prophecy. One may become conscious of many circumstances of revealed truths, yet remain unaware of their temporal and logical order, seeing only their inherent connections with some central fact. It is understandable, therefore, that prophecy should multiply correlative perfects and minimize consecutive imperfects.

5. E. Kautzsch, *Gesenius' Hebrew Grammar* (28th ed.; Oxford; The Clarendon Press, 1910), p. 132.

2. The progressive nature of the imperfect with *waw* consecutive fitted it for tracing the sequences of history. When telling stories and narrating history, human interest usually looks for chains of development which lead steadily onward to a goal. Repetitions and details may be added when wanted, but the times when they are wanted are comparatively few. It is understandable, therefore, that all narratives should multiply consecutive imperfects and minimize correlative perfects.

A SUMMARY OF INDICATIVE PERFECTS AND IMPERFECTS

Perfects (Single and finished and certain)		Imperfects (Partial)	
Name and Graph	*Distinctive Features*	*Name and Graph*	*Distinctive Features*
1. Simple	Unrelated	1. Frequentative	Part of a series
2. Previous ⌐	Effective up to another time	2. Progressive or Subsequent ∟	Developing from another time
3. Characteristic ⊙	Typical of an individual	3. Characteristic ⊙	Typical of a group
4. Correlative ⊕	Coexistent and related logically by inherent and permanent co-ordination	4. Consecutive ⌇⌇⌇⌇	Successive and linked by temporal or logical sequence

Chapter Four

Indicative Imperfects

All imperfects represent incomplete states. They are either repeated (fre), or developing (pro), or contingent (subj). In other words, they are either part of a series, or partially developed, or partially assured. In all cases they are partial in some sense, i.e., incomplete.

The state described by an imperfect is partial when it is frequentative, because it is part of a series of repetitions of the same act or condition. No one of these repetitions is seen as established and abiding. When Ps. 1:2 says, "And in his law he meditates day and night," the imperfect verb alone expresses the idea that the man meditates frequently. The words "day and night" carry out this idea more explicitly. The repeated meditations may produce development, but no one is seen as producing a fixed and permanent state of meditation such as a perfect would represent.

The state described by an imperfect is partial when it is progressive, because the progress described is only a part of its total development. One act or condition is described, but it is also true that only a part of it is described. In Ex. 15:1 such an imperfect, standing alone, suddenly appears in a historical account characterized by narrative perfects and imperfects with *waw* consecutive. If we translate after the fashion of the AV, saying, "Then sang Moses," we show utter disregard for the introduction of this imperfect apart from *waw* consecutive. W. R. Harper caught the force of it when he translated it thus, "Then Moses . . . proceeded to sing."[1]

1. W. R. Harper, *Elements of Hebrew Syntax* (New York: Charles Scribner's Sons, 1888, p. 59.

55

The state described by an imperfect is partial when it is subjunctive, because the assurance of its fulfillment is contingent upon the fulfilment of other matters. A possibility is indicated but not a certainity. Gen. 4:7, as translated by Moffatt, "Yet you ought to master it," indicates that it is possible for Cain to master sin but not certain that he will.

It is helpful to note that each imperfect bears only one of these three general characteristics. Let us emphasize the *or* as we say that an imperfect is frequentative *or* progressive *or* subjunctive.

To facilitate further study of these characteristics, the following classifications are suggested. We include here only the indicative ones, both frequentatives and progressives.

I

Frequentative Imperfects

The distinctive feature of frequentative imperfects is repetition. The fitting graph will be a series of dots, representing a repeated action, or a series of short lines, representing a repeated state (. . . . or - - - -). No effort will be made, in citing examples, to separate active and stative verbs.

Translation of this idea of repetition into English cannot as a rule be accomplished by English verbs standing alone. Some sort of adverbial modifier must be added. If the Hebrew text does not provide one like the "day and night" of Ps. 1:2, it is necessary to add to the English verb an adverb like frequently, repeatedly, regularly, customarily, habitually, or always. A paraphrase that says one is accustomed to do so and so has the same effect.

1. In past time (Combination 7):
    I Sam. 1:7 — And so he *did regularly year by year*. (Or) And so he *was accustomed to do year by year*.
    Judg. 21:25 — Each man *was accustomed to do* that which was right in his own eyes.
    Judg. 14:10 — For this the young men *were accustomed to do*.
    Ps. 55:15; 55:14 in Eng — We *were accustomed to take sweet counsel* together; in the house of God *we were accustomed to walk* in a throng.

Syntactical summary: inc-pa-ind (fre)

This interpretation has been coming into the translations

gradually. AV and ASV have it only in Judg. 14:10; MNT in I Sam. 1:7 and Judg. 14:10; AT in Judg. 21:25 and 14:10; RSV in I Sam. 1:7; Judg. 14:10; Ps. 55:14a.

2. In present time (Combination 8):

I Sam. 16:7 — For man *is accustomed to consider* according to the eyes, but God *is accustomed to consider* according to the heart.

Isa. 1:11 — For what to me is the multitude of your sacrifices? *constantly says* Yahweh.

Prov. 8:17 — As for me, the one who loves me I *always love,* and the one who diligently seeks me *always finds* me.

Syntactical summary: inc-pre-ind (fre)

The translations put nearly all of these verbs in present time, but they make no distinction between them and characteristic or emphatic perfects. The adverbs are needed to mark that distinction.

3. In future time (Combination 9):

Ex. 4:16 — He *will be* to you for a mouth.

Gen. 24:19 — I *shall draw* water for your camels.

Hos. 14:5, 14:4 in Eng — I *shall heal* . . . I *shall love* them freely. (Or) I *shall always love* them freely.

Syntactical summary: inc-fut-ind (fre)

Through some unexplained influence all translations have been led to put a modal interpretation on these verbs like a jussive of decree or cohortative of determination. Yet outward signs of the jussive or cohortative are lacking, and there appears to be nothing in the contexts to require such interpretation. One can see reasons why the authors might have used a jussive or cohortative, but when evidence of the use of either of these comes from the context alone, it ought to be decisive.

In future time the use of adverbs to bring out the frequentative force is not so urgent as in other times. Some form of incompleteness is obvious in any simple future statement. Whether that incompleteness be due to a frequentative or a progressive idea can be judged from the context. The only distinction that will matter greatly will be that between perfects and imperfects in future time, and it can be handled by strict observance of the suggestions concerning "shall" and "will." We may exercise our choice, therefore,

concerning the use of adverbs according to our judgment as to what makes the smoothest and most effective translation.

II
Progressive Imperfects

The distinctive feature of progressive imperfects is development or progress. Whereas frequentatives indicate repeated occurrences, progressives describe a single occurrence while in progress. Whereas perfects describe one thing as complete, progressives describe one thing as being in a process of development.

In all cases of progress there is a starting point, for progress is a movement onward from some point. Even when the point of departure is not specified, it is understood to exist. With progressives in past time it is usually obvious. With those in present and future time it is frequently obscure, yet it must be taken for granted. Therefore, there is always a double reference to time, and the time of the verb is always subsequent to another time mentioned or implied by the context. For this reason progressives might fittingly be called subsequent imperfects. The fitting graph is a horizontal line, representing the act or condition described, proceeding away from a perpendicular line, which represents the time from which is proceeds (⌊_____).

The development of progressives, like the repetition of frequentatives, cannot as a rule be represented by the corresponding English verbs standing alone. If their progress is in beginning, its incipiency can be expressed by a combination of "begin" with the infinitive of the English verb. If mere progress without reference to its beginning is indicated, the progressive force may be expressed by a combination of "proceed" with the infinitive of the English verb.

1. In past time (Combination 10):
   Judg. 2:1 — I *proceeded to bring* you up from Egypt.
   I Kings 3:16 — Then *proceeded to come* two women, harlots, to the king.
   I Kings 8:1 — Then Solomon *proceeded to assemble* the elders of Israel.

Syntactical summary: inc-pa-ind (prog)

No recognition has been given these imperfects in past time by the translations. Nevertheless, they stand out in the midst

of historical narratives as clearly as the one pointed out by W. R. Harper in Ex. 15:1. They mark the fact that development started at a certain time, growing out of a situation just described. Thus the coming of the women of I Kings 3:16 happened immediately after God's promise to give Solomon wisdom. Their case came as a test and proof of his wisdom, and we miss part of the significance of this passage if we fail to see that.

2. In present time (Combination 11):

I Sam. 21:15; 21:14 in Eng — Behold you *begin to see a* man going crazy; wherefore do you *proceed to bring* him to me.

Num. 24:17 — I *begin to see* him but not now: I *begin to behold* him but not near.

Jer. 6:4 — The day has turned, and the shadows of evening *begin to lengthen.*

Syntactical summary: inc-pre-ind (prog or inc-prog)

Perhaps there is no profit in continuing to point out the vagaries of translations in each case. Our main purpose is to seek consistency for our own translation, and we may do so here from the basis of our previous definitions.

Ordinary progressives, those whose beginnings are not definitely marked by the context, and incipient progressives, those whose beginnings are definitely marked, are left in one category because their nature is essentially the same. Both are characterized by progress.

3. In future time (Combination 12):

Ex. 9:5 — Tomorrow Yahweh *will do* this thing. (Or) Tomorrow Yahweh *will proceed to do* this thing.

I Sam. 10:5 — After that you *will come* to the hill of God. (Or) After that you *will go on* to the hill of God.

I Sam. 20:21 — And, behold, I *shall send* the lad.

Syntactical summary: inc-fut-ind (prog)

In future time the need for the addition of auxiliaries like begin and proceed to bring out the progressive force is not nearly so strong. When it is said in I Sam. 24:21, "I know that you will surely be king," we understand this as meaning: "I know that you will surely become (or proceed to be) king." These verbs furnish the pure futures of English more naturally than any others,

and as a rule it is doubtless well to let them be stated as simply as possible.

III

Characteristic Imperfects

Now and then the frequentative force of an imperfect is used to characterize an individual as a member of a group or species. Whereas a characteristic perfect designates a state which is typical of the whole life or character of an individual, a characteristic imperfect designates a state which marks one as a member of a certain group, because it is repeated in each member of that group. When Isa. 51:12 speaks of "a man that dies," it uses a word for man that means a mortal being, and the verb "dies" indicates that all mortals die. A graph may be made by making a circle, representing the characteristic act or condition, and enclosing a series of dots, which represent the members of the group. (   )

Gen. 49:27 — A wolf that *ravens.*

Isa. 62:1 — A lamp that *burns.*

Ps. 17:12 — A lion that *is greedy* of his prey.

Syntactical summary: inc-pre-ind (ch)

In translation a characteristic imperfect can hardly be distinguished from a characteristic perfect without resorting to cumbersome paraphrase. Both appear only in present time, and both need to be distinguished from emphatic perfects by avoiding emphatic auxiliaries. It appears best, therefore, to make no difference in the translation of the verbs themselves, leaving the reader to detect the imperfects by the fact that their subjects are typical of groups rather than isolated individuals. There are only a very few clear cases of the characteristic imperfect, and all of them appear in relative clauses introduced by "that"; so the problem of recognizing them is a small one after all.

IV

Consecutive Imperfects

Progressive imperfects are very frequently linked together so as to form a chain of sequences. A special form of the conjunction "and," a *waw* with *pathah* followed by *daghesh-forte,* is used with each verb in such a chain. This is the only use made of this special conjunction; so it appears to have been in-

tended to mark the consecutive relationship of these imperfects. The name *"waw* consecutive" has been widely used for this conjunction and is quite appropriate. Likewise, the word "consecutive" may aptly be used to describe the imperfect which always accompanies a *waw* consecutive.

Occasionally a frequentative imperfect is introduced into the chains of progressive imperfects in the same way as a progressive. The frequentative bears no outward mark to distinguish it from the progressives. It depends upon its context or other sources bearing upon its context for evidences concerning its force as a frequentative. If there is evidence that its action or state was repeated, it is a frequentative. An example appears in Gen. 5:4 (Cf. discussion under 1. below). If there is evidence that the verb's action or state occurred only once, the verb is a progressive. An example appears in Gen. 5:3 (Cf. discussion under 1. below). If there is no clear evidence, it is probably best to consider the verb progressive.

The importance of the distinction between progressive and frequentative force can be seen in Gen. 2:19. If a reader sees Gen. 1:1-2:3 and Gen. 2:4-25 as narratives used by an author or editor who combined them harmoniously, then each is in the context of the other. Accordingly, the fact that the first describes the creation of animals prior to the creation of mankind is occasion for giving to the consecutive imperfect at the beginning of Gen. 2:19 a frequentative force. The translation which says that God continued to form animals after he made man leaves no ground for a charge that the two narratives contradict each other at this point. This charge, which has been made often by reputable expositors of Genesis, is a result of the old method of interpreting *waw* consecutive. *Waw* consecutive was interpreted at this point as making the imperfect a consequence or an equivalent of a preceding perfect. That preceding perfect, which translators probably considered the starting point of the chain of imperfects with *waw* consecutive in 2:4-25, appears in 2:5. The concluding clause, "And *as for a man,* there was not one to till the ground," contained the negative for a substantive clause with the verb "to be" understood. That verb, if it had been written, would have been a perfect. Following it, imperfects with *waw* consecutive appear in verses 6, 7, 8, 9, 15, 16, 17, 18, 19 to tie together the narrative. Following the old interpretation of *waw* consecutive, translators have rendered the imperfect at the beginning of

verse 19 as "formed," which is the translation for a perfect. The distinctive force of the imperfect is lost completely. Thus occasion has been given for the charge that the two narratives contradict each other.

The starting point of these chains may be marked in many ways. Preceding perfects frequently serve to do so. Other imperfects, participles, infinitives, and even nouns are so used. Sometimes there is no preceding word. Maybe it was not the author's desire in such cases to fix the starting point except as being somewhere in the past. The word for "and it came to pass" is the one most commonly used in this way, and it is comparable to the English phrase "once upon a time."

A graph may be made by linking the graphs of several consecutives. The upright lines, shaped as braces, will stand for the conjunctions which link the verbs to their starting points as well as the starting points themselves. (} } } } } } }).

1. In past time (Combination 10):
Gen. 5:3 — . . . then *he proceeded to beget* a son.

Since only one child is involved, the verb is a progressive imperfect. The interpretation of the verb as progressive is reflected by the auxiliary "proceeded."

Gen. 5:4 — . . . and *he continued to beget* sons and daughters.

The imperfect with *waw* consecutive is written exactly as in Gen. 5:3; the context, however, shows that the action occurred repeatedly. The auxiliary "continued" reflects the frequentative force.

The contrast observed here appears again in the following verses: Genesis 5:6 and 7; 9 and 10; 12 and 13; 15 and 16; 18 and 19; 21 and 22; 25 and 26; 28 and 30. Similar contrasts are scattered through Gen. 11:10-24.

These contrasts appear to have been introduced quite deliberately. They show, therefore, that progressive and frequentative imperfects were distinguished from perfects in all cases and also distinguished each from the other.

Gen. 12:1 — And Yahweh *continued to say* to Abram, . . .

The frequentative interpretation in this case may be seriously questioned by some. For that reason the evidence will be examined at length. This evidence does not give ground for a dogmatic opinion, but it does indicate a strong probability. This

probability can be seen only by meticulous examination of the evidence.

That part of the context which provides evidence in this case includes these words from the latter part of the verse: "your country," "your kindred," and "your father's house."

"From your land" in Gen. 12:1 uses the word land separately from the word "kindred," which appears in the phrase immediately after this one. The word "land" standing alone can be applied to any land. The word "kindred" standing alone is used to describe things in general which are related to a person by that person's birth. Its most usual application is to one's kin in general. In Gen. 43:7 it is made to include brothers as well as a father. When the two words are tied together in a genitival relation, as in Gen. 11:28, each word restricts the other. The land becomes the land of one's birth or nativity, as in Haran's case. Other instances appear in Gen. 24:7; 31:13; Jer. 22:10; 46:16; Ezek. 23:15; Ruth 2:11. The kin referred to become those who gave one birth in that land — one's forefathers, one's ancestors — rather than kin in general. In Biblical usage at least the words are thus restricted when linked together.

When Abram, according to Gen. 24:4, called Charran "my land," he used "land" separately in accord with the usage described. When he, according to Gen. 24:7, referred to the land of his birth, he used "land" and kindred (forefathers) together.

Our immediate interest is in the fact that Abram had known both Ur and Charran as his land before he moved on into Canaan. Therefore, the words "from your land" could have applied to Ur at one time and to Charran at another. "From your kindred" was likewise applicable to the kindred in Ur and to the kindred in Charran. "From your father's household" also was applicable in Ur as well as in Charran.

Since all evidence observed thus far leaves the question open, it is worthwhile to take note of the fact that Jewish tradition has persistently clung to the conviction that there was a call in Ur. At least it is the oldest tradition. We ought to hesitate before we conclude there was no ground whatever for it.

Stephen, according to Acts 7:2, 3, said, "The God of glory appeared unto our father Abraham, when he was in Mesopotamia, before he dwelt in Haran, and said unto him, 'Get thee out of thy land . . . .' " (ASV). Stephen was also dogmatic. He was, however, preaching at the time he made this dogmatic statement,

not writing a commentary. Probably he felt no need before his audience in Jerusalem for supporting this statement about Abraham. He seems to have taken for granted that he was voicing an established conviction about a well-known matter. Certainly he believed there was evidence to sustain his statement. He could, of course, have cited what has been presented here, but his positiveness makes it likely that he knew more than this.

These scattered and in some cases unsubstantiated bits of evidence cannot be said to be conclusive. Nevertheless, their cumulative effect is to create a probability. Accordingly, such searchers for truth as Martin Luther, John Peter Lange, Robert S. Candlish, Marcus Dods, and H. C. Leupold have been strongly inclined to accept this probability as the most probable conclusion indicated by the evidence as a whole. Lange stated his conclusion this way: "*Out of thy country* — the fatherland. The land of Mesopotamia as it embraced both Ur of the Chaldees and Haran."[2] In accord with this conclusion, A. Gosman, who translated Lange's Commentary on Chapters XII-XXXVI, added this note of his own:

> There is no improbability in the supposition that the call was repeated. And this supposition would not only reconcile the words of Stephen and Moses, but may explain the fifth verse: "And they went forth to go into the land of Canaan, and into the land of Canaan they came." Abram had left his home in obedience to the original call of God, but had not reached the land in which he was to dwell. Now, upon the second call, he not only sets forth, but continues in his migrations until he reaches Canaan, to which he was directed.[3]

In accord with the probability that exists concerning the call of Abraham, the first imperfect in Gen. 12:1 is credited with a frequentative force.

Gen. 25:34 — Then Jacob gave to Esau bread and lentil soup, *and he proceeded to eat* and *to drink* and *to arise* and *to go his way,* and thus Esau *proceeded to despise* the birthright.

When there is only one consecutive, "and he proceeded" indicates movement and sequence in an attractive way; but when there is a chain of them, it becomes repetitious and cumbersome. If the

2. John Peter Lange, *Genesis in Commentary on the Holy Scriptures,* Philip Schaff, ed., reprint by Zondervan Publishing House (n.d.), p. 391.
3. In Lange, *op. cit.,* p. 393.

consecutives are close together, as in Gen. 25:34, this may be avoided by the use of "proceeded" in the first case, and infinitives in the others, leaving "proceeded" to be understood but not written. Otherwise synonyms of "proceed" and varied expressions conveying the idea of sequence will be needed.

Sentences, or parts of them, and even paragraphs, may intervene between the verbs in a series of consecutives. No matter how far one may be separated from others, its progress starts from some link in its own chain. Nearly always its progress starts from the link immediately preceding it, and all links form one chain. Once in a while it starts from some link further back, making two chains to start from a common source. For instance, the last verb in the example above states a logical consequence which parallels all of the preceding chain. The despising started with or before the eating and runs concurrently with the eating, the drinking, the arising, and the going.

Syntactical summary: inc-pa-ind (cons)

There are, of course, able translators who consider the translation of Hebrew imperfects in past time as perfects to be a small matter. The contrary opinion is insisted upon in what follows for the sake of those who wish to consider the matter thoroughly.

Insistence upon a distinctive meaning for any imperfect in past time is strongly supported by the use of imperfects in Arabic. Arabic is very close to Hebrew in its alphabet, vocabulary, grammar, and syntax. Its maintenance of distinctive meanings both for perfects and imperfects is, therefore, evidence that carries great weight in the interpretation of the basic ideas in these verb forms. There is probably no evidence outside the Bible itself that supports this insistence upon distinctive translations for these imperfects so strongly. This statement is not intended to say that Arabic uses imperfects everywhere that Hebrew uses them. Nevertheless, it does use them with meanings that parallel closely the Hebrew meanings which we cite. Moreover, such explanations as Arabic grammarians sometimes give in the words, "the equivalent of a perfect," are not intended to say that the two forms are the same. They do say that Arabic uses imperfects in senses equivalent to certain Latin or English perfects. A triangle and a rectangle can be equivalent, i.e., equivalent in space, yet they are not the same thing.

During the period 1941-1961, Dr. Jochanan Kapliwatsky of Jerusalem prepared a series of studies for English speaking students who are beginners in the study of Arabic. The series is entitled *Arabic Language and Grammar,* and it contains four parts with grammatical facts richly illustrated by reading exercises. Because this work is for beginners, syntactical explanations are stated as simply as possible, and repetitions involving progressive and additional explanations are scattered through the series. For that very reason they furnish very helpful guidance in consideration of this matter.

The first statement is as follows:

> The Arabic verb has two main tenses which, however, are not real tenses in their European sense. These two main tenses are generally known as Perfect and Imperfect.
>
> The Perfect denotes a finished action, most often referring to the *past,* and the Imperfect denotes an unfinished action, most often referring to the *present* or *future.*[4]

Another explanation is as follows:

> The imperfect denotes an unfinished action most often referring to the present or future. In reality, however, the time of action is expressed by an adverb, or particle.[5]

Kapliwatsky's statement amounts to the same as saying that the Arabic imperfect maintains its distinctive force at all times, and that those speaking Arabic have accommodated this verb form to ideas of tense and time by adding adverbs and particles.

Another statement is this (This is given in contrast to several dealing with the perfect and demonstrating its maintenance of a distinctive meaning in any time.):

> *Kad* followed by an Imperfect means 'sometimes' or 'perhaps,' e.g. *huwa kad yarjihu,* 'he sometimes returns' or 'perhaps he will return.'[6]

This explanation shows that, even in future time, the imperfect carries a frequentative or subjunctive force, not the singular and indicative force of the Perfect.

Yet another statement appears in this:

> To express "he used to," the perfect of *kana*[7] is used before

4. Jochanan Kapliwatsky, *Arabic Language and Grammar,* (Jerusalem, Palestine, Part I, Rubin Mass, 1941; fourth edition, Hamaarav Press, 1959), p. 48.
5. *Ibid.,* Part II, p. 19.
6. *Ibid.,* Part III, p. 71.
7. The pf 3rd mass sing of the verb, "to be" in Arabic.

the Imperfect of another verb, e.g. "he used to ride (out) every day three times";[8] "she used to open the door twice every day"; "and there used to be in the city a commander with a thousand men."[9]

This explanation clinches the assertion that Arabic imperfects in past time, as well as imperfects in present or future time, are used with a force as truly distinctive as those of any other verb form.

In the last sentence used to demonstrate this usage there is another feature that the student ought to take care to understand. The perfect of the verb "to be" is used before the imperfect of the same verb. The perfect emphasizes the time as past; the imperfect emphasizes the action as frequentative. This construction with the perfect and the imperfect of the same verb is quite unusual. Nevertheless, it is grammatically possible and proper. It drives home this distinctive force of the imperfect in a powerful way. The apparent parallel between this and one of the Hebrew imperfects in Ex. 3:14 is thrillingly interesting. The argument that has continued for two millenniums over the translation of that verse in the Septuagint and over the part it has played in the English translation "I am what I am" or "I am that I am" has surely confirmed the charge that "I am" is not a proper translation for a Hebrew imperfect. That translation could fit a substantive sentence with the verb "to be" understood or a characteristic perfect but not an imperfect. The first of the two imperfects of the verb "to be" in this verse could be interpreted quite fittingly as a repetition of the identical form found two verses before this one. In that case, it refers to the future. In view of the strong emphasis in the early verses of the chapter upon Yahweh's keeping of his promises to Abraham, Isaac, and Jacob, the second imperfect could be a repetition of this great truth. In such case, it is past. Translated in keeping with the example given above, the statement becomes this: "I shall continue to be what I used to be" or "I shall continue to be what I have always been." This rendering is cryptic but understandable, unusual but powerful, simple yet crowning its context with a statement of Yahweh's faithfulness so brief as to be amazing and so meaningful as to be inspiring.

8. Arabic sentences accompanying these translations have been omitted.
9. Kapliwatsky, *op. cit.,* Part IV, p. 48.

2. In present time (Combination 11):

Isa. 44:12 — He forges (ch pf) iron as an axe, and he works (another ch pf) with coals, and with hammers *he proceeds to fashion it,* and *thus he proceeds to work* it with the arm of his strength; also he is hungry (another ch pf) and has no strength, he drinks (another ch pf) no water; and *so he becomes faint.*

These are rare, and they follow the same pattern in translation as those in past time.

Syntactical summary: inc-pre-ind (cons)

3. In future time (Combination 12):

Isa. 9:5; 9:6 in Eng — For a child shall be born (a pro pf) to us, a son shall be given (another pro pf) to us, and *will come to be* the rule upon his shoulder, and one *will proceed to call* his name Wonderful Counsellor, Mighty God, Everlasting Father, Prince of Peace.

These likewise are rare and constitute no new problem in translation.

Syntactical summary: inc-fut-ind (cons)

The interpretation of *waw* consecutive will be discussed further when conjunctions are dealt with. It is good to observe even now, however, that the way to a new interpretation of *waw* consecutive is opened by recognition of a distinctive character in all perfects and all imperfects. If every perfect is interpreted as having a force peculiar to perfects and every imperfect a force peculiar to imperfects, old ideas about the influence of *waw* consecutive upon them are out of place.

Consecutive imperfects are characteristic of all types of narratives. A chain of these consecutive imperfects is the thread by which all the parts of a narrative are tied together. Even as a very large portion of the Old Testament is composed mainly of narrative, so the interpretation of consecutive imperfects is a very important part of Old Testament translation and Old Testament interpretation.

Within a narrative an author may introduce other types of composition. The series of jussives in the story of creation, Gen. 1:1-2:3, is interwoven with the consecutive imperfects to define with precision the author's teaching concerning Yahweh's development of created things. A mixture of participles, incipient

imperfects, and substantive clauses may be used, as in Gen. 2:10-14, for the sake of accurate and vivid description. A series of correlative perfects may be added, as in Ex. 33:8-11, to make many details of a great scene stand out in the reader's mind as actions that occurred at one and the same time. These same correlative perfects may be the author's means of presenting an extensive prophecy, as in Isa. 11:1-12:6, as a unit. When the narrative is resumed, however, a consecutive imperfect signifies the movement, the progress, the sequence of it.

To lose sight of the distinctions involved in these various types of composition leads to the loss of many clues to interpretation, at a great many places. Yet our translations have persisted in applying theories that have made the translation of consecutive imperfects and correlative perfects to be alike. For example, they have translated Gen. 1:3 this way, "And God said, Let there be light . . .," instead of saying, "And God proceeded to say, Let there be light . . .," or "Afterwards God proceeded to say, Let there be light . . . ." As a result we have been left in the dark as to what was the first act of creation affirmed by this story. Expositors have differed and disputed and left us more in the dark than ever.

English readers feel no loss as a rule, because they have been accustomed from childhood to the type of narrative used by the translators, and because they have never known any other type of composition in narrative.

Nevertheless, there is a tremendous loss!

Chapter Five

Participles

All participles are in the indicative mood. It is expedient, therefore, to consider them before turning to subjunctive imperfects and perfects in subjunctive combinations.

Participles partake of the nature of verbs and of nouns. This fact accounts for a list of peculiarities, as follows:

(1) Participles serve both as verbs and as nouns. The same form can mean "is killing" or "the one who is killing."

(2) Verbal participles are inflected like nouns. Their endings signify number and gender but not person. Therefore, their subjects must be written, there being nothing in the participle itself to indicate a pronominal subject.

(3) Verbal participles always retain the nature of a predicate complement. Evidence of this appears in the following:

a. The subject is regularly written before the participle. If a copulative verb is thought of as linking the two, as is always possible, that is the natural order. In such case the participle is a predicate complement.

b. Some form of the verb to be is occasionally put with the participle after the fashion of a periphrastic conjugation (cf. Ex. 3:1). This puts into words what is merely understood in other cases.

(4) The regular negative with a participle is *'en,* the construct state of *'ayin,* nothing. It negates the idea of being or existence, meaning is not, are not, was not, were not, etc. Obviously, then, a participle with *'en* is a noun.

(5) Passive participles serve as gerunds. Examples: *nora',* one to be feared; *nekhbadh,* one honored, or an honorable one.

All participles represent continuous states. Even in the noun there is a continuous manifestation of the state described by the verb.

This continuous state of the participle needs to be clearly distinguished from the continual state of a frequentative imperfect. A telephone line is continuous like a participle, but its poles are continual like a frequentative. Thus the graph of a participle is a long line (——————).

The difference between participles and progressive imperfects lies in their implications as to limits. Participles indicate no limitations, no point for beginning or ending, while progressives proceed from some point.

1. In past time (Combination 13):

Gen. 18:1 — And he *was sitting* at the door of the tent.

Gen. 37:7 — We *were binding* sheaves.

Judg. 7:13 — And behold, there *was* a man *telling* to his comrade a dream.

Syntactical summary: cont-pa-ind

The translations suggested here are characterized by continuous aspect, as Curme describes it,[1] or by the progressive conjugation, as Opdycke describes it.[2] It is formed by adding the present participle to various forms of the verb to be when the verb is active and the past participle to progressive forms of the verb to be (i.e., I was being seen, etc.) when the verb is passive. The continuous force of the Hebrew participle is thus clearly reproduced.

English translators have been very lax in their handling of these participles. They frequently substitute for them translations which belong to other verb forms. In Gen. 18:1, AV, ASV, RSV, and MNT give us the translation of a narrative perfect, only AT handling it like a participle. In Gen. 37:7, all of them handle the participle as a participle. In Judg 7:13, all except AV do so. Why they so frequently fail to do so in other cases is hard to understand.

It is interesting to observe that in Judg. 7:13 the participle

---

1. George O. Curme, *A Grammar of the English Language* (Boston: A. C. Heath and Company, 1935), III, p. 373.

2. Opdycke, John B., *Harper's English Grammar* (New York: Harper and Brothers, 1941), p. 173.

is handled as the abridgment of a relative clause, *Who was telling to his comrade a dream.* ASV handles it this way, and this way is the exact form of the Hebrew sentence.

2. In present time (Combination 14):
   Gen. 4:10 — Your brother's blood *is crying* out to me.
   Deut. 4:1 — I *am teaching* you.
   Isa. 1:7 — Strangers *are devouring* your land.
Syntactical summary: cont-pre-ind

The present progressive clearly distinguishes these present participles from all perfects and imperfects in present time. The translations constantly use a simple present, AV and ASV doing so in Gen. 4:10; AV, ASV, RSV, and MNT in Deut. 4:1; and all of them in Isa. 1:7. What interpretation they intend to put upon their simple present is uncertain, but at least it is not distinctive. In doing so they lose much of the animation and vividness of the Hebrew. It appears possible to retain the continuous movement of the participle in all cases, and faithful efforts ought to be made to do so.

3. In future time (Combination 15):

In future time a remarkable use is often made of the continuous idea of the participle. The progress appears to start in the present and to stretch into the future. This is a mental feat which creates a vivid and dramatic effect. It is as when one says, "I am coming," though the actual start has not yet been made, and he means, "I will indeed be coming," or "I will be coming immediately." Emphasis is thus laid on one or the other of the following thoughts: (1) The decision is being effected; and, in mind at least, progress is already under way. (2) The actual start will follow immediately.

Occasionally, circumstances in the context show that the time is entirely future. Then we need a strictly future translation. Otherwise, we need the present-future combination to give the dramatic assurance of certainty or immediate beginning.
   Gen. 6:17 — Behold, I *am bringing* the flood, even water, upon the earth.
   Gen. 7:4 — For after seven days I *will be causing it to rain* upon the earth forty days and forty nights.

I Sam. 19:11 — If you are not delivering your life tonight, tomorrow, you will be a dead man (lit. one made to die).

II Sam. 12:23 — I *am going* to him, but he cannot return to me.

II Sam. 20:21 — And the woman said to Joab, Behold, his head *is being thrown* to you over the wall.

Syntactical summary: cont-fut or pre + fut-ind

Again the progressive conjugation appears to be the only expression capable of carrying the force of the participle. MNT uses it in Gen. 6:17 and II Sam. 12:23. AT uses several interesting paraphrases for it, seemingly intended to express the present-future force described above. These are "am about to bring" in Gen. 6:17, "am going to make it rain" in Gen. 7:4, and "expect to go" in II Sam. 12:23. Something of this sort is doubtless good in Gen. 7:4, where we have a pure future, but elsewhere they seem weak. "I am about to come" is a weak expression as compared with "I am coming," when someone is waiting for you. Translations with "about" in them cannot adequately represent participles in present-future time. The woman talking to Joab in II Sam. 20:21 and saying, "His head is being thrown to you over the wall," was not making a promise about the future time but giving a vivid picture of immediate action. Likewise, David speaking of his dead child in II Sam. 12:23 was not putting off his progress toward a reunion into the indefinite future but saying, as it were, "From this moment I am on my way to join him."

Chapter Six

Subjunctives

Whereas *indicatives* represent ideas as *realities* (cf. p. 32), *subjunctives* represent them as *mental conceptions,* ideas apprehended by reason or imagination only. In Hebrew three main types of subjunctives appear: (1) contrary-to-fact, (2) potential, (3) optative. The contrary-to-fact type combines perfects and participles with certain particles to show that the unreality of an idea is fixed and permanent, i.e., it is impossible. The potential uses the imperfect to indicate that something is possible. The optative uses the imperfect, usually with additions or changes to mark its special force, to show that something is not merely possible but also desired by the author.

I

CONTRARY-TO-FACT SUBJUNCTIVES

Occasionally a perfect or a participle is brought into a combination which associates it with a subjunctive idea. This at first seems very strange, and we must observe closely the particles with which it is combined to understand the effect. The verb itself is never actually subjunctive, for it retains the full force of its certainty; the combination, however, indicates a contrary-to-fact idea and is thus subjunctive. This is true in contrary-to-fact conditional sentences and in rhetorical questions.

1. Conditions with *lu* or *lule* (Combination 16):
   Judg. 8:19 — *If* you *had kept* them *alive, I would not have slain* you.

74

Isa. 1:9 — *Except* Yahweh of hosts *had left* us a very small remnant, as Sodom had we been.

Ps. 81:14-15; 81:13-14 in Eng — *If* my *people* were *listening* to me . . . I *would soon subdue* their enemies.

Syntactical summary: com-pre-con subj

In these contrary-to-fact conditional sentences a special introductory particle, either *lu* or *lule,* is used to indicate that the condition is contrary-to-fact.   After it a perfect may be used both in the protasis and apodosis.   The perfect in the protasis appears to indicate that the condition stated in such a clause is non-existent and impossible.   The perfect in the apodosis appears to indicate that the conclusion based upon the contrary-to-fact condition is as fixed in impossibility as the condition itself.   The effect of the particle upon each of these verbs, though the particle appears only before the first, conveys ideas called by us subjunctive.   This is true because we call all imaginary or contrary-to-fact ideas subjunctive.   Nevertheless, these perfects are still single, finished, and certain; and they should not be identified with the Hebrew subjunctive imperfects which are subjunctive by reason of their own nature.   It is the combination, not the perfect alone, that approximates our English subjunctive.   This forcing of contingency and certainty into the same statement is very rarely done, but it furnishes a peculiarly dramatic expression which creates an impression of unavoidable obligation or inescapable necessity.

Only in Num. 22:33 does any other particle than *lu* or *lule* appear with a perfect in these conditions.   Moreover, the appearance there of *'ulay,* perhaps, does not make sense.   So the following bit of advice appears to be correct: "Read *lu* for *'ulay* in Numbers 22:33."[1]   These facts make it easy to detect the use of such conditions by the presence of *lu* or *lule.*

When imperfects appear in these contrary-to-fact conditional sentences, nothing strange or peculiar is involved.   *Lu* or *lule* provides a context that signifies the subjunctive mood.

2. Rhetorical questions (Combination 17):

Num. 23:10 — *Who can count* the dust of Jacob?

Isa. 53:1 — *Who can believe* our report; and, as for the arm of Yahweh, upon whom *can it be revealed?*

---

1. Brown, Driver, and Briggs, *A Hebrew and English Lexicon of the Old Testament* (New York: Houghton Mifflin Co., 1906), p. 530.

Jer. 30:21 — For *who* is there that *could be security* for his own heart in order to come near to me?

Syntactical summary: com-fut-con subj

These questions are distinguished by the fact that they apply to future time and use a perfect with *mi, who?*.   An imperfect with *mi* in future time would ask an ordinary, open question like this: "Who will go for us?" (Isa. 6:8).   A perfect with *mi* in past time would also ask an open question like this: "Who told you that you were naked?" (Gen. 3:11).   In the rhetorical question, the perfect nullifies the normal implications of the interrogative, showing that it is not truly an interrogative but is put there merely for rhetorical effect; and the interrogative nullifies the normal implications of the perfect, showing that it is not a mark of reality but is put there to establish the certainty of a negative answer.

The perfect with *mi* in Gen. 21:7 has generally been interpreted as subjunctive.   Because the reference is apparently to the past, the following interpretation is preferred:

Gen. 21:7 — And she went on to say, *Who spoke* a word to Abraham, (saying), Sarah shall suckle children?   Yet indeed I have borne him a son in his old age.

II

POTENTIAL SUBJUNCTIVES

The partially assured, tentative aspect of the imperfect is utilized in a potential subjunctive.   *lu* may be added in some cases, but as a rule only the context is relied upon to mark it as subjunctive rather than indicative.   Those evidences out of the context which mark its state as possible rather than real may be classified as follows: (1) those indicating or questioning the mere possibility of it;   (2) those indicating or questioning desire concerning it;   (3) those indicating or questioning responsibility for doing it.   Any such indication or question reflects the fact that a thing does not already exist but is merely possible.

1. Subjunctives of mere possibility (Combination 18):
    Gen. 13:16 — If a man *could be able* to number the dust of the earth, also your seed *could be numbered.*
    Deut. 1:12 — How *can I bear* alone your cumbrance?
    Isa. 1:18 — Though your sins *be* as scarlet, they *may be* made white as snow.

Psa. 24:3 — Who *may ascend* into the hill of Yahweh?

Syntactical summary: inc-fut-pot subj (pos)

2. Subjunctives of desire (Combination 18):

I Kings 13:8 — If you *would give* me half your house, I could not go in with you.

The subjunctives of desire are distinguished from the optative subjunctives by the fact that desire in the potentials arises from some other source than the author while desire in optatives does arise from the author.

Ruth 1:13 — *Would* you therefore *tarry* till they were grown?

Syntactical summary: inc-fut-pot subj (des)

3. Subjunctives of responsibility (Combination 18):

Ex. 3:11 — Who am I that I *should go* to Pharaoh?

I Chron. 12:33, 12:32 in Eng — To know what Israel *ought to do.*

Syntactical summary: inc-fut-pot subj (res)

All of these subjunctive imperfects are in future time, and this fact helps to mark them.

Translation needs to vary only so much as is necessary to express the ideas of mere possibility, desire, or responsibility.

III

OPTATIVE SUBJUNCTIVES

Two modified forms of the imperfect are used to express an author's desire, urge, or feeling. The first person is used to express an exhortation or cohortation affecting the speaker or a group of which he is a part; so this form is called cohortative. The second or third person is used to enjoin another or others; so these forms are called jussives.

External marks are generally used to identify these two forms beyond question. On the other hand, it is evident from many texts that an imperfect without any mark other than its relation to the context may bear the optative force, especially as a jussive. In rare instances (cf. Deut. 33:16; Isa. 5:19; and Ps. 20:4) the sign of the cohortative appears on a jussive. On the other hand, the internal vowel change customary with the jussive appears in some of those cohortatives to which cohortative *h* could not be added. These facts seem to indicate that these two forms of the optative subjunctive were considered so much alike

in nature that the usual mark of either could be used with the other if there was likelihood of its not being recognized for lack of an external mark.   In any case the extensive efforts made to mark these two forms lays upon us an obligation to respect their peculiar force wherever it can be discerned and likewise to avoid construing an imperfect without marks as an optative unless the evidence from the context appears to be decisive.

1. Cohortatives:

Cohortatives express the author's desire, urge, or feeling concerning himself and do so by direct reference to himself, using pronouns in the first person.   When the speaker refers to himself alone, the cohortative may express determination, request, or willingness; when he is free, determination; when he is entreating another for permission, request; when he is yielding agreeably to inevitable consequences, willingness.   If the speaker includes others, the cohortative expresses exhortation.

(1) Determination (Combination 19):

Deut. 17:14 — *I will set* a king over me. (Or) *I am determined to set* a king over me.

Gen. 17:2 — And *I will make* my covenant between me and you that I may increase you exceedingly.   (Or) For *I am determined* to make (set or establish) my covenant between me and you that I may increase you exceedingly.

Ex. 3:3 — *I will turn aside* now that I may see this great sight.   (Or) *I am determined to turn aside* now that I may see this great sight.

Hos. 13:14 — *I will be* your plagues, O death; *I will be* your destruction, O Sheol.   (Or) *I am determined to be* your plagues, O death; *I am determined to be* your destruction, O Sheol.

Syntactical summary: inc-fut-opt subj (coh of det)

If the auxiliary "will" is used with cohortatives, we have the problem of distinguishing them from perfects of confidence in the first person.   The problem can be solved in either of two ways: (1) using emphatic auxiliaries with perfects of confidence and will with cohortatives;   (2) using "will" with perfects of confidence in first person and using "determined," "intend," and the like with infinitives to express the force of cohortatives.   Perhaps the latter is best.

Because translators have often interpreted as cohortatives verbs not marked as such in the Hebrew and, on the other hand, have failed to interpret as cohortatives some that are marked as such in Hebrew, we need to note with care the marks that are used. In the foregoing a cohortative *h* is added to the verb in Deut. 17:14; Gen. 17:2; Ex. 3:3; while in Hos. 13:14 there is a shift of accent and consequent vowel change. This shift of accent and vowel change are the same changes that occur frequently in jussives. Both in cohortatives and jussives these changes are due to an added stress in pronunciation, which is produced by the urgency of the mood and pulls the accent backward. They are rare in cohortatives, and this is probably due to the fact that the cohortative *h* can be added in the great majority of them. In Hos. 13:14 *h* could not be added because the verb itself ended in *h*. As seen in Judg. 18:4, the same change with the same verb is produced by *waw* consecutive, for it also draws the accent backward; but the two forms found here, without any conjunction, can be explained only as cohortatives or errors.

In this same connection it is exceedingly interesting to observe in Gen. 17:2 and Ex. 3:3 that the second verb is a *l-h* verb in both cases, attached to a simple *waw,* and without a shift of accent or a vowel change. The absence of all external marks leads to the conclusion that these are not cohortatives, as all the translations have made them, but parts of subordinate, subjunctive clauses. (Cf. Purpose and Result Clauses, the treatment of which comes later.)

On the other hand, the obvious marks of an optative in both verbs cited in Hos. 13:14, plus the fact that a cohortative interpretation fits the context, lead to the conclusion that those are cohortatives. Only AV and a note in ASV and RSV recognized them. Nevertheless the evidence appears incontestable. Moreover, neglect of them, and the neglect of many other optatives, appears to be one of the very serious failures of our translations.

The fitness of these two cohortatives is strongly indicated by all parts of the chapter in which they appear. Verse 14 makes this quite obvious when translated thus:

> From the power of Sheol, I shall ransom them;
> from death, I shall redeem them;
> *I am determined to be* your plagues, O death;
> I am determined to be your destruction, O Sheol;
> any change of mind will be hidden from mine eyes.

The importance of this interpretation is seen when we observe this word as a messianic prophecy and link it with two preceding ones in Hosea and with those that follow in Isaiah. Hos. 3:5 identifies the Yahweh who promises to save Israel, despite all her terrible sins, with David their king (the Second David). Hos. 11:9 calls this Saviour "The Holy One in the midst of thee," the transcendent one who makes himself immanent in Israel. Hosea's description prepares the way for Isaiah's marvelous use of "the Holy One of Israel" as a means of tying together all his pictures of Messiah as the God-man. This same verse stresses the assurance that the Holy One will not come in wrath. Thus it prepares the way for the assurance of Hos. 13:14 and for the incomparable picture of the Messiah who dies in Israel's stead given in Isa. 52:13-53:12. What a tragedy it is to have one of the links in this golden chain lost by unfaithful translations!

(2) Request (Combination 19):

Gen. 50:5 — *Let me go up,* I pray.

Ex. 3:18 — And now *let us go,* we pray.

Deut. 2:27 — *Let me pass through* your land.

Ps. 25:2 — *Let me* not *be ashamed.*

Syntactical summary: inc-fut-opt subj (coh of req)

The negative *'al* (cf. Ps. 25:2) is another of the special marks of an optative. The particle of entreaty (I pray! or, please!) is in accord with the urge of an optative; but it also appears frequently with imperatives, and it is not a characteristic of either.

(3) Willingness (Combination 19):

Gen. 46:30 — *I am willing to die* at this time.

Isa. 38:10 — *I am willing to go* into the gates of Sheol.

Ps. 4:9; 4:8 in Eng — In peace *I am ready both to lie down and to sleep.*

Syntactical summary: inc-fut-opt subj (coh of will)

The "let me die" of AV, ASV, RSV, and MNT, in Gen. 46:30, — AT does not recognize the cohortative — does not appear to be the best translation. It is the language of request, and a request should be addressed to the one exercising control over it. The apparent intent of the cohortative in this case is to express mere willingness.

In Isa. 38:10 both MNT and AT seek to give a special force to the cohortative, but they make it a potential rather than an optative subjunctive. The interpretation given by BDB to the preced-

ing phrase, in connection with the *domi* (cessation), helps to clarify the fitness of the interpretation given here.[2]

In Ps. 4:8, AV, ASV, RSV, and AT recognize the jussive but seem to interpret it as expressing determination. Perhaps David did not feel at the time that rest and sleep were under his control.

(4) Exhortation (Combination 19):

Ps. 2:3 — *Let us break asunder* their bands and *let us cast away* their cords from us.

Gen. 24:57 — And *let us inquire* at her mouth.

Isa. 1:18 — Come now and *let us prove* each other.

Jonah 1:7 — And *let us cast lots*.

Syntactical summary: inc-fut-opt subj (coh of exh)

2. Jussives:

Jussives express the author's desire, urge, or feeling concerning other things than himself. The author may use a jussive to express a wish that actually applies to himself; but, in doing so, he uses the third person as though speaking of another, and only the context reveals the fact that he is thinking of himself.

When the jussive refers to persons or matters over which the author exercises authority, it may express a polite command, a decree, or a permission. Otherwise, it may express a petition, a suggestion, a wish, or mere acquiescence.

(1) Polite command (Combination 20):

Prov. 3:7 — *Do* not *be wise* in your own eyes.

Deut. 15:3 — *Let* your hand *release* it.

I Kings 20:8 — *Do* not *listen*.

Syntactical summary: inc-fut-opt subj (jus of com)

In these instances the author expresses his will concerning the person to whom he is speaking and over whom he assumes control.

Signs appear as follows: in Prov. 3:7, the negative and a shift of accent followed by apocopation; in Deut. 15:3, a vowel change; and in I Kings 20:8, the negative *'al*.

(2) Permission (Combination 20):

Ezra 1:3 — *Let him go up* and *let him build*.

I Kings 13:33 — Whoever was willing (lit, the willing one), to him he proceeded to give authority, (saying), Yea, *let him be* among the priests of the high places.

Isa. 45:21 — Yea, *let them take counsel* together.

2. *Ibid.*, p. 198.

Syntactical summary: inc-fut-opt subj (jus of per)

In these instances the author expresses his will concerning a person or persons to whom he is not speaking, but over whom he assumes control.

The signs appear as follows: in Ezra 1:3 and I Kings 13:33, a shift of accent and vowel change; in Isa. 45:21 the context alone is depended upon, the command to declare which opens the verse making an indicative out of place and an optative the expression that fits.

In I Kings 13:33 we have one of many instances in which grammarians claim that there is a copyist's error[3] or else the jussive has lost its force and should be handled as an ordinary perfect.[4] Driver claims that this construction is in past time and therefore turns it into a purpose clause.[5] All of these arguments are obviated by understanding that we have here a quotation of the permission Jeroboam issued to anyone willing to serve in his new priesthood. As a quotation the time becomes future. As a quotation the jussive fits, for it is synonymous with the preceding statement, "he proceeded to give authority" (lit, he proceeded to fill his hand; or, he proceeded to make full his power.) Omission of the word "saying" was not strange in Hebrew. Isa. 45:14 furnishes another instance of its omission before a quotation. Moreover, a jussive or cohortative with a *waw* conjunctive that relates it to a person other than its subject seems to have been understood as evidence of a quotation. Hos. 11:4 furnishes a good example: With cords of a man I proceeded to draw them, with bands of love; and so I became to them as one lifting a yoke off their jaws (saying), Yea, I will set food before them.

(3) Decree (Combination 20):

Gen. 1:3 — *Let* there *be* light.

Gen. 1:9 — *Let* the waters *be collected* . . . and *let* the dry land *be seen.*

Esther 7:2 — What is your request, Queen Esther? Yea, *let it be granted* you.

---

3. E. Kautzsch, *Gesenius' Hebrew Grammar,* 28th ed. (Oxford: The Clarendon Press, 1910), p. 322f.

4. *Ibid.,* p. 323.

5. S. R. Driver, *A Treatise on the Use of the Tenses in Hebrew,* (3rd ed., Oxford: The Clarendon Press, 1892). p. 67, sec. 63.

Syntactical summary: inc-fut-opt subj (jus of dec)

In these instances the author expresses his will concerning an event or condition over which he assumes control but without speaking to a particular person. In Esther 7:2, the king is speaking in Esther's presence and for her benefit, but he is not addressing his decree to her.

In Gen. 1:9, the context alone indicates a jussive, the organization of the story of creation being such as to indicate that the verb is part of a series of divine decrees, beginning in 1:3 and 1:6 with forms that are unmistakably jussives. In Esther 7:2, the apocopation of the *l-h* verb marks the jussive, though the fact that it is in pause has prevented its accent from shifting.

(4) Petition (Combination 20):
Gen. 44:33 — *Let* your servant *remain,* I pray.
I Kings 8:26 — And now, O God of Israel, *let* your word *be fulfilled,* I pray.
Gen. 19:20 — And *let* my soul *live.*
Gen. 18:30 — O *let* not the Lord *be angry.*

Syntactical summary: inc-fut-opt subj (jus of pet)

In these instances the author is expressing his will concerning himself to another person who has control over him. He does so by the indirect method of referring to himself in the third person.

The usual signs appear in all cases. In I Kings 8:26, the ultima has a *metheg* to insure pronunciation of its vowel, but the *mehuppakh* on the penult marks the main accent and the shift that has taken place.

(5) Suggestion (Combination 20):
Gen. 41:33 — *Let* Pharaoh *look out* a man.
I Kings 1:2 — *Let* there *be sought* . . . a young woman.
I Kings 22:8 — *Let* not the king *say* so.

Syntactical summary: inc-fut-opt subj (jus of sug)

In these instances the author is expressing his will concerning another person over whom he does not assume control.

In I Kings 1:2 only the context marks the jussive. It introduces a proposition which cannot be a command because it is spoken by servants to their king. It is shown by the preceding verse to be an expression of will concerning another person over whom these servants do not have control.

(6) Wish (Combination 20):
I Sam. 1:23 — Only *let* Yahweh *establish* his word.

> Ps. 14:7 — O that the salvation of Israel *would come out* of Zion.
>
> Gen. 30:34 — Behold! Would that (it were so)! *Let it be* according to your word.

Syntactical summary: inc-fut-opt subj (jus of wish)

In these instances the author expresses his will concerning events or conditions over which he does not assume control but whose fulfillment he does desire.

In each of these cases the jussive is either part of or preceded by an exclamation that helps to mark it. In I Sam. 1:23 it is *'akh*, only!; in Ps. 14:7, it is the idiomatic expression *mi yitten*, Who will give? — Would that!; in Gen. 30:34, *lu*, Would that! Translations have made this *lu* of Gen. 30:34 a part of the expression that follows it, but the massoretic text handles it as an exclamation, separate from the jussive that follows.

(7) Acquiescence (Combination 20):

> Gen. 49:17 — *Let* Dan *be* a serpent by the way.
>
> Mic. 1:2 — *Let* the Lord Yahweh *be* a witness against you.
>
> Eccles. 12:6 — (Saying) Yea, *let* the pitcher *be broken* at the fountain.
>
> Isa. 6:9 — Hear, keeping on hearing, but *do not perceive*.

An author uses a jussive at times to express his state of mind concerning events or conditions which he neither controls nor wishes but does accept as inevitable because they are the will of God. The jussive alone deals with the immediate situation. The context may indicate a hope of change later, as in Gen. 49:17, 18, or the lack of such hope, as in Isa. 6:9, 10, but the jussive alone does not reflect anything concerning the author's thought about a change. It expresses mere acquiescence in, submission to, or resignation to the will of God. This type of jussive, therefore, may be called quite appropriately a jussive of acquiescence.

In Eccles. 12:6, all translations have reduced the jussive to the level of a long line of imperfects preceding it which are not marked as jussives. In doing so they lose the climactic stroke of a surpassingly beautiful word picture, in which the aged one resigns himself to the inevitable approach of death.

In Mic. 1:2 all translations except MNT have recognized the jussive in an acceptable way. When Moffatt translates this way,

"The Eternal has a warning for you," he merely paraphrases. The fact that he resorted to paraphrase reflects his recognition of a problem. Instead of solving it, he alters the text.

We need to realize that this jussive is in the third person. It is not, therefore, a mere continuation of the imperatives used just before and thus a plea to the people that they permit Yahweh to bear his witness. They were commanded immediately before to listen to it, for it was a matter of deepest concern to them. This jussive, however, adds something different from a command. It is recognition of a moral necessity that Yahweh's witness against Samaria and Jerusalem be heard among the peoples of the earth as a justification of the terrible punishment to be brought upon them. This witness is a witness which condemns his people, shuts them up to judgment, and leaves them subject to the punishment of captivity. Certainly the prophet did not request or suggest or wish for this terrible punishment of his people. He did, however, express his acquiescence in it, realizing that the sin of his people on the one hand and the justice of God on the other required it. Accordingly, the prophet uses cohortatives of willingness in verses 8, 9 below, crying out, "I am ready to lament and wail, I am ready to go stripped and naked, . . . for her wounds are incurable. . . ."

Gen. 49:17 is part of a statement that includes Gen. 49:18, as follows:

Let Dan *continue* as a snake in the grass. . . . For thy salvation do I wait, O Yahweh.

In this case AV, ASV, RSV have handled the jussive of verse 17 like a prophetic perfect. MNT has handled it like a characteristic perfect. AT does recognize the presence of a jussive but handles it like a wish. None of these is accurate, for Jacob does not wish Dan to be like a snake, nor does he expect him to continue so forever. Recognizing that he is so at the time, he acquiesces in the expectation of his continuing that way until God works a change. His anticipation of that change is revealed by the verse that follows, "*For thy salvation* do I wait, O Yahweh."

Isa. 6:9 is part of a command that includes Isa. 6:10, as follows:

Then he said, "Go, and you shall say to this people, 'Hear, keeping on hearing, but *do not perceive* [the meaning]; yea see, keeping on seeing, but *do not understand* [the message].' " Cause the heart of this people to be fat, and their ears heavy, and their eyes shut, That it may not be possible for their eyes to see, and for their ears to hear, and for their heart to

understand, and that they shall repent, and that there shall be healing for them.

In this case, two special points of syntax are involved. The first applies to the adverbial phrases following the imperatives in verse 9, and the second applies to the jussives themselves indicated by the "do not" of the translation.

The adverbial phrases, "keeping on hearing" and "keeping on seeing," represent infinitives absolute that follow the imperatives, "hear" and "see." If they had preceded, they would have signified certainty, but in that they follow they signify continuance. AV and ASV first rendered them as expressing certainty but added notes afterwards to signify continuance. DV, MNT, AT, and RSV have used various expressions but definitely agree in signifying continuance. This is important for the reason that continuance of hearing without understanding at any point is that which dulls the spiritual senses to the point of finally killing those senses. In other words, these adverbs of continuance describe the experience of the people that would result in spiritual insensibility, and the jussives describe acquiescence on the part of the prophet in that inevitable fact.

The jussives have been ignored, or at least obscured, by all of these translations except RSV. They make these jussives to appear exactly like imperatives. The point of acquiescence, with its deep sense of regret accompanied by unequivocal resignation, is lacking. These failures are doubtless due to recognition of a very difficult problem that appears here without adequate appreciation of the solution.

At first glance the jussives signified by the negative "do not" seem to involve an enigma which defies understanding. The command to hear and the command to see appear to be mockery in view of the urge not to perceive the meaning and the urge not to understand the message. Since the message of a prophet was supposed to be delivered in sincerity, thus a command to hear to be accompanied by a desire that those hearing should hear with understanding, the explanation that follows it to the effect that hearing would be impossible presents quite a puzzle.

First of all, the distinction made between the message the prophet was to deliver and the effect of that message needs to be carefully observed. The two commands in verse 9, "hear" and "see," followed by the two jussives, "do not perceive" and "do not understand," are the message. The description of its effect begins with

the word "cause" in verse 10 and includes everything which follows. This distinction is recognized in AT and RSV.

The two jussives were intended to signify the prophet's realization of the people's failure to receive or understand his message. This would be contrary to a prophet's normal hope, but it would also be a correct observation of the results. He would be forced to acquiesce in this fact. Evidently, Yahweh taught his prophet to use these jussives in order to prepare him to expect this denial of his normal hope and to steel his heart against the bitterness of disappointment. He could know at least that he had been obedient and that he had done his best.

The Lord's command in verse 10 that his prophet should cause ears to be heavy, eyes to be shut, and so on, was a command to keep on prophesying even though the prophesying would produce this effect in hearts that would not heed. Because the people would not receive the message, their hearts would be hardened by it. Their refusal to heed would result in complete loss of spiritual sensitivity or capacity for understanding. Thus the very same message that would bring salvation to believers would bring spiritual blindness and damnation to those who would harden their hearts against it. According to this last verse there was no hope for a change in the masses of the people of Isaiah's day. The difference between them and Dan was that a fixed state of mind and heart, a loss of the capacity for spiritual perception, would ultimately be involved in their case, while only habits of life were involved in Dan's case. As long as spiritual perception is possible, a change of mind and heart is possible; thus a change of life and destiny is possible.

Syntactical summary: inc-fut-opt subj (jus of acq)

Chapter Seven

Imperatives

In dealing with imperatives it needs to be remembered that they have the same ground form as the imperfect. This signifies that the two are closely similar in nature, and it helps to explain the fact that both the imperfect and the special form of the imperative are used as imperatives. Furthermore, we observe the following: (1) imperative imperfects are used both in positive and negative commands; (2) the special imperative form is used in positive commands only; (3) the *h* which is added regularly to cohortative imperfects is occasionally added to the special form of the imperative. This gives us three types of imperatives to consider.

It has been customary to disregard the question of state in connection with all imperatives. This is natural in view of the fact that mood is so prominent. Nevertheless, there is a contemplated state in connection with any imperative as surely as there is with any potential subjunctive, cohortative, or jussive. In all these cases the state is a mental conception, but in this subjective sense their states do exist.

I

IMPERATIVE IMPERFECTS
(Combination 21)

Gen. 3:14 — Upon your belly *you shall go* and dust *you shall eat.*

Ex. 7:2 — As for you, *you shall speak* all that I command you.

Josh. 8:7 — Then, as for you, *you shall arise* from the ambush.

Ex. 20:9 — Six days *shall you labor.*

Gen. 2:17 — But from the tree of the knowledge of good and evil *you shall* not *eat*.

Ex. 20:3 — *You shall* not *have* other gods before me.

Ex. 20:15 — *You shall* not *steal*.

Syntactical summary: inc-fut-imv (imp)

The emphases, which seem to accompany all imperative imperfects, may be the key to choices between imperative imperfects and special forms of the imperative. The imperfects place preformatives for person, number, and gender ahead of the verbal idea and then permit emphatic words, including the negative, to be used ahead of the preformatives. It is also true that they are always used for negative imperatives. The special forms of the imperative, on the other hand, put the verbal idea first and never associate with a negative. These facts point toward two conclusions: (1) Negative imperatives always use the imperfect because it is the only one that permits emphasis upon the negative. (2) Positive imperatives use the imperfect when there is an emphasis upon something other than the verbal idea, and the special form when the emphasis is to be upon the verbal idea itself.

The following distinctions between prohibitions expressed by the imperfect and prohibitions expressed by the jussive are very helpful. "In prohibition, (1) in the second person, the ordinary imperfect takes *lo'* and means *thou shalt not*, the jussive takes *'al* and means *do not*; (2) in the third person, the ordinary imperfect takes *lo'* and means *he shall not*, the jussive takes *'al* and means *let him not*."[1]

There is very little conflict in the use of "shall" between imperative imperfects and prophetic perfects because imperative imperfects are necessarily in the second person and prophetic perfects nearly always in the third person.

II

IMPERATIVES USING THE SPECIAL FORM
(Combination 22)

Ex. 6:11 — *Go in, speak* to Pharaoh.

Ex. 4:7 — *Return* your hand into your bosom.

---

1. W. R. Harper, *Elements of Hebrew Syntax* (New York: Charles Scribner's Sons, 1888), p. 67.

Ex. 20:12 — *Honour* your father and your mother.
Syntactical summary: inc-fut-imv

In order to retain clearly the distinctions between the special forms and the imperfects, translators should keep the verbal idea first. Whereas the imperative imperfect of "kill" says, "You shall kill," the special imperative says, "Kill."

III

IMPERATIVES WITH *h* ADDED
(Combination 23)

Ex. 3:10 — *Come now — please!* — that I may send you.
Ps. 44:27; 44:26 in Eng — *Arise, O do arise!* To our help!
Ps. 51:14; 51:12 in Eng — *Restore* unto me — *I beg of thee* — the joy of my salvation.
Syntactical summary: inc-fut-imv + jus

The addition of the jussive idea emphasizes the earnestness of the command, indicating that the author not merely commands but also urgently pleads for compliance. To render these forms as mere imperatives, as our translations usually do, is to ignore some of the heart throbs of the Bible.

Since imperatives are always in the second person, it is obvious that the *h* is used with them to indicate a jussive force. This is another evidence that the cohortative and jussive are so identified that their external marks can be switched from one to the other.

Chapter Eight

Infinitives

Infinitives are verb forms but not verbs. Essentially they are nominal in their nature, naming the state of the verb. At the same time they retain certain verbal characteristics.

Infinitives manifest the character of a noun in the following ways: (1) they serve as subjects; (2) they serve as objects; (3) they are put in construct relations (genitive relations) with other nouns.

Infinitives retain verbal characteristics but never serve as verbs. Like a verb they may have an object when they stand in phrases or clauses. At times they are used where we expect imperatives or other forms. Grammarians have reasoned that they are the equivalent of various other forms.[1] However, there appears to be no sufficient reason for doing so. (Cf. Ex. 20:8; II Kings 5:10; Isa. 7:11 below.)

Infinitives absolute and infinitives construct are distinguished in meaning as well as form. The infinitives absolute name the state of the verb in an absolute or unrelated sense; so they cannot be tied into the sentence by prepositions, possessive pronouns, or the construct relation. The infinitives construct, on the other hand, do relate themselves to the sentence by means of prepositions, possessive pronouns, and construct relation.

I

INFINITIVES ABSOLUTE

Infinitives absolute may serve as nouns (gerunds), adverbs, or governing words in adverbial phrases.

---

1. E. Kautzsch, *Gesenius' Hebrew Grammar*, (28th ed., Oxford: The Charendon Press, 1910), p. 345.

1. Gerunds:
    (1) Serving as subjects:
        II Kings 4:43 — *Eating* and *leaving* over [will there be].
        I Kings 22:30 — *Disguising* and *coming* into the battle [will it be for me]; but, as for you, put on your [kingly] garments.
        II Kings 5:10 — *Going on* [shall there be], and you shall wash seven times in the Jordan.

Syntactical summary: inf abs as sub

(Descriptions of state, time, and mood are omitted, because we no longer deal with verbs.)

As a noun, the infinitive absolute is a strong, independent, striking expression used for dramatic effect. No matter whether it serves as a subject or as an object, this is true. As a subject, it often has no written verb, the verb "to be" being understood, of course, but the word standing dramatically alone.

Such paraphrases as are used by our translations do not do much harm in these cases. However, they do obscure the fact that an infinitive absolute is used, and the habit of changing the form of expression chosen by the author leads to serious loss in other places. In II Kings 5:10, we easily conclude that the infinitive has the force of an imperative. Still, it is true that the infinitive puts emphasis upon the fact that going on is a necessity rather than upon the idea that the prophet is merely commanding Naaman to go on.

    (2) Serving as objects:
        Jer. 23:14 — I see *committing adultery* and *walking* in lies.
        Isa. 22:13 — Behold *slaying* oxen and *killing* sheep, *eating* flesh and *drinking* wine;
        Isa. 1:16, 17 — Cease *doing* evil; learn *doing* good.

Syntactical summary: inf abs as obj

The power of the infinitive to control an object of its own, even while the two together serve as the object of the verb, appears clearly here. This power is a retention of verbal nature.

2. Adverbs:

As an adverb, the infinitive absolute sometimes comes into common use with any verb, but generally it is reserved for use with perfects and imperfects from its own root. In the latter sense it may emphasize the intensity or the certainty, the continuance or the completeness of the verbal action it modifies. When emphasizing

intensity or certainty, it regularly precedes its verb. When emphasizing continuance or completeness, it follows its verb. Sometimes it is accompanied by *halokh,* going on, or a similar form, to magnify continuance yet more.

(1) Common adverbs:

Deut. 9:21 — I took the calf . . . and stamped it, *grinding thoroughly.*

Mic. 6:8 — And walking *humbly* with your God.

Neh. 2:2 — And so I became *very much* afraid.

Syntactical summary: inf abs as adv

(2) Emphatic adverbs signifying intensity or certainty:

Gen. 2:17 — You will *surely* die (lit, *dying,* you will die).

Ex. 21:28 — The ox should *certainly* be stoned.

I Sam. 20:6 — It was *urgently* requested of me.

Syntactical summary: inf abs as adv (cer or int)

(3) Adverbs signifying continuance or completeness:

Gen. 8:7 — And it proceeded to go forth, *continually* going to and fro.

II Sam. 3:16 — And he went on, *weeping more and more.*

II Sam. 3:24 — And he proceeded to go, *going completely away.*

Gen. 26:13 — And the man became great and continued to go forward, *becoming greater and greater.*

Syntactical summary: inf abs as adv (cont or com)

3. Governing Words in Adverbial Phrases:

Gen. 12:9 — And Abram journeyed, *going on* and *traveling* toward the south.

Ex. 20:8, 9 — *Remembering* the sabbath day in order to keep it holy, six days you shall labor.

Isa. 7:11 — Ask for yourself a sign from Yahweh your God, *making* it deep to Sheol or *making* it high to heaven.

Syntactical summary: inf abs in adv phr

In Ex. 20:8, 9 we see the damage done by turning the infinitive absolute into an imperative. As an imperative it makes verse 8 to stand alone. When all of verse 8 is seen as an adverbial phrase, it cannot stand alone. It modifies the verb of verse 9, "you shall labor," and explains the emphasis upon the "six days" of that service. In other words, the two verbs together command us to work

six days with a view to consecration of the seventh to rest and worship.

In Isa. 7:11, the first form may be either imperative or infinitive absolute, while the second is definitely an infinitive absolute. Because the first is parallel to the second, each citing an extreme in a context calling for extremes, exegesis seems to require that it be interpreted as an infinitive absolute. As such it must govern the word following. That word by itself could be interpreted as "ask it — please!" or "to Sheol." As an imperative that word is repetitious at a moment calling for utmost brevity and force; and it destroys the striking description of extremes, which were evidently intended to furnish climatic force to the prophet's statement. With the infinitive absolute as a governing word, "to Sheol" is the only meaning that fits the second word. Thus interpreted the power of the prophet's words is tremendous.

II

INFINITIVES CONSTRUCT

Infinitives construct serve only as nouns. They may be subjects of verbs, objects of verbs, genitives of other nouns, or objects of prepositions.

1. Subjects of verbs:
   Gen. 2:18 — Man's *being* alone is not good.
   I Sam. 18:23 — Is it a small thing *to make one's self* a son-in-law to a king?
   Isa. 7:13 — Is the *wearying* of men a small thing to you?
Syntactical summary: inf con as sub

2. Objects of verbs:
   I Kings 3:7 — I know not *to go out* or *to come in*.
   Num. 20:21 — And Edom refused *to give* Israel *passage* through his border.
   Isa. 37:28 — I know your *dwelling,* your *going out,* your *coming in,* yea, your *raging* against me.
Syntactical summary: inf con as obj

3. The Genitive of Another Noun:
   Gen. 2:4 — In the day of Yahweh-God's *making* of heaven and earth.

Eccles. 3:4 — A time of *mourning* and a time of *dancing*.
II Chron. 24:14 — Vessels of *serving*.
Syntactical summary: inf con as gen

In these instances translations use infinitives and gerunds to represent the infinitive construct. The ease with which English interchanges the two forms, often without apparent distinction in meaning, makes this a fitting thing to do.

4. Objects of Prepositions:
    (1) With the preposition *le* (to):
    le is used with infinitives construct very frequently. The variety of its meanings in these cases is such as to require painstaking discriminations.

    In some cases *le* has lost its force as a preposition, as the English preposition "to" does in sayings like this, "To err is human, but to forgive is divine." The fact that we can say, "Erring is human, but forgiving is divine," shows that "to" has lost its force in this statement. In these cases *le* serves as a part of the infinitive itself.

    In cases where *le* retains its force as a preposition, meanings like direction, specification, and relationship prevail. The idea common to all its meanings appears to be that of relation. It relates a verbal state to another fact that signifies its specific nature; it relates it to a purpose, result, or time toward which it is directed; or it relates it to a necessity toward which it tends, is intended, or is obligated.

    a. As a part of the infinitive itself:
        Gen. 4:2 — And she continued *bearing* (lit, to bear), even Abel, his brother.
        Gen. 6:1 — When men began *to multiply* (or, multiplying) upon the face of the ground.
        Gen. 11:18 — And so they gradually ceased *building* (lit, to build) the city.
Syntactical summary: inf con + *le* (obj of vb)

    In translation it matters little whether we maintain the infinitive form or use a gerund. Frequently the two forms of expression are interchangeable in English without loss of meaning. Even when the infinitive form is maintained, we must look upon it as the object or subject of the verb; so it

serves in the same way as the gerund. Therefore, these forms
are grammatically the same as those under 1. and 2. above.

    b. To show the specific nature of the verbal state:

        I Sam. 12:17 — Your evil is great which you did . . . *in
asking* (or, *in respect to asking, with regard to asking*) a king for yourselves.

        I Sam. 14:33 — Behold the people are sinning *in eating*
with the blood.

        Isa. 55:7 — For he will abundantly *pardon* (lit, deal
abundantly *with respect to pardoning*).

Syntactical summary: inf con + *le* (sp nat of vb)

    c. To show the relation of the verbal state to a *purpose
toward which it is directed*:

        I Sam. 1:3 — He went up *in order to worship*.

        Gen. 1:17-18 — And so God proceeded to put them
in the expanse of the heavens *to give light* . . . and
to rule . . . and *to divide.* . . .

        Gen. 2:3 — Which God created *for making* (or, for the
purpose of making, i.e., for development).

Syntactical summary: inf con + *le* (pur of vb)

"To" gives a neat expression of purpose when the context
clearly indicates purpose. However, it is also used to express
result. Because of this ambiguity, "to" is the fitting expression in many instances, inasmuch as it is impossible for us
to know whether the author intended his infinitive to express
purpose or result. When purpose is clearly intended, we can
bring it out by using "in order to."

In Gen. 2:3, there is difference of opinion as to whether
purpose or result was intended. BDB favors result.[2] Purpose
is the interpretation given here, for the following reasons: (1)
The whole story of creation is skillfully arranged from beginning to end to show that the process of making, i.e., development, was the will of God for all created things. (2) The infinitives in Gen. 1:17 which are selected by BDB as expressions for purpose,[3] appear to be parts of the long series of
jussives and infinitives expressing this will or purpose of God.
(3) This series of expressions signifying purpose is summed

2. Brown, Driver, and Briggs, *A Hebrew and English Lexicon of the
Old Testament* (New York: Houghton Mifflin Co., 1906), p. 517.

3. *Ibid.*

up in these final words of 2:3, and thus it makes an adroitly drawn introduction to the "generations" or developments which follow, showing that sin was a violation of God's purpose for the moral development of mankind and that faith in God's purpose is essential to the salvation of the race.

d. To show the relation of the verbal state to an end or result toward which it is directed:

> I Kings 2:3 — And you shall keep the charge of Yahweh your God *so as to walk* in his ways, *so as to keep* his statutes.
>
> Judg. 5:18 — Who despised their life *to the point of dying*.
>
> II Kings 20:1 — Hezekiah was sick, *even to the point of dying*.

Syntactical summary: inf con + *le* (res of vb)

"So as to" is the most exact expression of result. In many cases, however, "to" and other variations will be suggested by the context.

e. To serve as a sign of direct discourse:

> Ex. 6:10 — And Yahweh proceeded to speak to Moses, *saying,* Go in, speak to Pharaoh.

After verbs of speaking, swearing, declaring, and the like, frequent use is made of the infinitive of *'amar,* to say, with *le* to mark direct discourse. The most probable explanation of this usage is that it originated as an indication of the result of the verb. However, it appears to be thought of usually as a mere sign of direct discourse.

Syntactical summary: inf con + *le* (sign of dir dis)

f. To show the relation of the verbal state to a necessity toward which it tends, is intended, or is obligated:

> Esther 8:8 — For the writing written in the king's name and sealed with the king's seal is not *to be reversed*.
>
> Isa. 6:13 — And if there remain in it a tenth, indeed it shall again be *for burning*.
>
> Prov. 19:8 — The one keeping understanding is *bound to find good*.

Syntactical summary: inf con + *le* (nec of vb)

g. To show the relation of the verbal state to a time approached by it:

Gen. 15:12 — The sun was *about to set* (near the time of setting).

I Kings 2:1 — And the days of David gradually drew near *to the time of dying*.

I Kings 18:29 — Then they continued to prophesy *until the time of offering* the evening sacrifice.

Syntactical summary: inf con + *le* (time of vb)

(2) With other prepositions related to time:

Josh. 3:14-16 — And it came to pass *during (be) the moving* of the people from their tents, *just before (le) passing over* the Jordan . . . and *at (ke) the coming* of the bearers of the ark to the Jordan . . . then the waters going down from above came to a halt.

I Kings 3:1 — And he proceeded to bring her to the city of David *until ('adh) finishing* the building of his house and the house of Yahweh.

Hos. 7:4 — Who is accustomed to cease stirring [the fire] *from the time (min) of kneading* dough *until the time of ('adh) being leavened*.

Syntactical summary: inf con + a prep (time of vb)

While many other prepositions appear with infinitives construct, there are no such problems in other cases as with *le*. Nevertheless, it is necessary to observe the distinctions between *le, be, ke, 'adh,* and *min* in reference to time. *be* indicates that the verbal state occurred in or during the period of time indicated by the infinitive; *ke* that it occurred at the point of time indicated by the infinitive; *le* that it occurred at a time before and near to, i.e., approaching the time indicated by the infinitive; and *min* that it continued from the time indicated by the infinitive.

Oftentimes it is fitting in translation to turn the adverbial phrases formed by these combinations into temporal clauses, substituting a conjunction for the preposition. Thus in Gen. 2:4, instead of saying, "in their being created," we may say, "when they were created."

(3) With *be* in a causal sense:

Ex. 33:16 — Is it not *by reason of your going* with us?

Ps. 46:3; 46:2 in Eng — Therefore we shall not fear *because of the upheaval* of the earth.

Syntactical summary: inf con + *be* (cau of vb)

(4) With *ke* in a comparative sense:
    II Sam. 3:34 — *Like falling* before children of iniquity did
    you fall.
Syntactical summary: inf con + *ke* (comp of vb)

(5) With *min* in a causal sense:
    II Sam. 3:11 — And he was not able any more to answer
    Abner a single word, *because he feared* him (lit, *on
    account of his fearing* him).
Syntactical summary: inf con + *min* (cau of vb)

(6) With *min* in a privative sense:
    Isa. 5:6 — And I shall charge the clouds *not to rain*
    (lit, *from raining*) upon it.
In such cases the privative force of the preposition is equiva-
lent to a negative.
Syntactical summary: inf con + *min* (priv of vb)

(7) With inf con + *ba'abhur* as an expression of purpose:
    Ex. 9:16 — I have made you to stand *in order that I may
    show* you my power (lit, *for the sake of showing* you
    my power).
Syntactical summary: inf con + ba'abhur (pur of vb)

Chapter Nine

Means of Introducing Independent Clauses

The conjunction *waw* is the most commonly used means of introducing independent clauses. Its relation to these clauses needs careful interpretation. This interpretation needs to distinguish its use apart from verbs from its use with verbs. Certain other conjunctions used in comparative, disjunctive, and adversative clauses also need to be noted. *Waw,* however, is the only one whose use constitutes a problem.

The frequent use of *waw* where English prefers variety was not due to a lack of other conjunctions. The following observation concerning other conjunctions is quite pertinent: "Their frequent use was felt instinctively to be inconsistent with the lightness and grace of movement which the Hebrew ear loved . . . ."[1] The result of this instinctive feeling was the constant use of *waw* where English prefers variety and makes use of conjunctions like but, then, so, thus, therefore, that, and many others.

Only uses of *waw* as a copulative conjunction belong here. Instances in which it serves as a demonstrative adverb, meaning then and pointing to a specified time, do not belong here.

I

USE OF THE CONJUNCTION *Waw* APART FROM VERBS

There is an important distinction between the use of the conjunction *waw* to co-ordinate verbs and its use to co-ordinate clauses without being immediately related to the verbs by attach-

1. Brown, Driver, and Briggs, *A Hebrew and English Lexicon of the Old Testament* (New York: Houghton Mifflin Co., 1906), p. 252.

ment to one of them.   In co-ordinating verbs it never draws an exclusive antithesis, but in co-ordinating clauses it may reflect an antithesis inherent in the clauses themselves.

In this connection BDB makes the following comment, "In such cases prominence is usually given to the contrasted idea by its being placed immediately after the conjunction."[2]   As a result the conjunction is separated from the verb.   No explanation of apparent exceptions is offered by BDB.   It appears, however, that all exceptions can be removed, and rightly so, by translating *waw* as "and."   Lev. 26:45 furnishes an example, as follows: *And* (usually translated "but") I will for their sakes remember the covenant of their ancestors.   This verse appears to be correlated with the last statement of the preceding verse, "For I am Jehovah their God."   If so, the meaning is *"and"* rather than *"but,"* and there is no antithesis.   If the conjunction with correlative perfects is always handled as "and," then there are apparently no exceptions.

When we consider only those cases in which clauses, not verbs, are co-ordinated, we do find cases of sharp contrast, as in Gen. 2:17; 4:2.   In these the meaning is "but."   At times, as in Judg. 14:16, it introduces a contrast so as to suggest a question.

As seen in Isa. 46:4 and I Sam. 25:43, *waw* apart from verbs has an additive force as it does with them.   In these cases the meaning is "and" or "and also."

Examples:

Isa. 46:4 — I made, *and* I will bear, *yea* I will carry so as to deliver.

I Sam. 25:43 — *And* also David took Ahinoam.

Gen. 2:17 — *But* from the tree of the knowledge of good and evil you may not eat.

Gen. 4:2 — *But* Cain was a tiller of the ground.

Judg. 14:16 — I told it not to my father or my mother, *and* shall I tell it to you?

II

CO-ORDINATING CONJUNCTIONS IN COMPARATIVE, DISJUNCTIVE, AND ADVERSATIVE CLAUSES

Comparison may be observed in clauses linked by *waw* conjunctive, as in Job 5:7.   However, it is revealed in such cases by

2. *Ibid.*, p. 252, 1, e.

the obvious nature of the comparison, not by the conjunction. This fact is emphasized by the appearance of comparison in some cases when there is no conjunction, as in Job 24:19. It is permissable for us to make the comparison stand out by using correlative conjunctions like "as . . . so," but we should realize that we are imposing on the Hebrew sentence an addition to its original form and on the conjunction a meaning it could not have in the original form of the sentence.

When the Hebrew authors desired to cast a sentence in comparative form, they usually made use of *ka'asher* followed by *ken* as in the following:

Isa. 52:14, 15 — *Just as* many shall be astonished at thee —
So marred more than that of any man his appearance,
And his form more than that of the sons of men —
So shall he startle many nations.

At times *'asher* is used with the same force as *ka'asher* in these comparisons (cf. Ex. 10:6; 14:13; 34:18). Sometimes *ken* is used without its correlative conjunction being written, as in Isa. 55:1 and Jer. 3:20. In Eccles. 5:15, *kol-'umath she-*(in all points as) is used to indicate a complete parallel.

In disjunctive clauses the following are found:

Job 34:29 — *Whether* (*waw*) it is to a nation or (*waw*) to a man . . . .

Lev. 5:2-4 — *Or* (*'o*) if . . . *or* (*'o*) if . . . *or* (*'o*) if . . . .

Ex. 19:13 — No hand shall touch it . . . indeed he shall surely be stoned *or* (*'o*) shot through, *whether* (*'im*) it be beast *or* (*'im*) man.

Josh. 17:16 — *Both to* (*la-*) those who are in Bethshean *and to* (*wela-*) those who are in the valley of Jezreel.

Gen. 24:44 — *Both* (*gam*) drink thou, *and also* (*wegam*) for thy camels I shall draw.

Gen. 21:26 — *Neither* (*wegam . . . lo'*, lit, and also . . . not) did you tell me, *nor* (*wegam . . . lo'*) did I hear of it except today.

These examples show that *'o*, or, is the conjunctive naturally adapted to an exclusive antithesis.

In adversative statements the following are found:

I Sam. 8:19 — So they proceeded to say, No! *but* (*ki'im*) there will be a king over us.

Gen. 18:15 — So he proceeded to say, No! *but* (*ki*, without *'im*) you did laugh.

III

USES OF *Waw* WITH VERBS

The meaning of the conjunction *waw,* when attached to verbs, is very closely related to the meaning of the verbs themselves, particularly in the case of perfects and imperfects. Superficial evidence appears in the great frequency with which this conjunction is attached to verbs, the different forms it assumes with verbs, and the effect of the combinations on the sentence. Our preceding studies of verbs have laid a foundation for the study of this relationship, and here the combinations will be considered.

There are two forms of *waw* as a conjunction with verbs. The simple form, usually written with *shewa,* is called *waw* conjunctive. The special form, usually written with *pathah* and followed by *daghesh forte,* is called *waw* consecutive.

The relation of *waw* conjunctive and *waw* consecutive to the verbs to which they are attached is so close that there appears to be a very sharp distinction between the combinations using *waw* conjunctive and the combinations using *waw* consecutive. When considered from the viewpoint of the distinctive character of perfects and imperfects, these combinations become the major problem in the syntax of biblical Hebrew.

As a fundamental distinction between *waw* conjunctive and *waw* consecutive, the following interpretations are offered:

(1) *Waw* conjunctive appears always to indicate a parallel. It is the only form of *waw* used with correlative perfects, and this usage magnifies the parallel. With imperfects the relation may be co-ordinate or collateral, but it is still parallel. A subordinate reason clause is collateral. A graph may be formed by parallel lines with a brace at their ends to represent the conjunction. (════════════}).

(2) *Waw* consecutive appears always to indicate a sequence. It is the only form of *waw* used with consecutive imperfects. The relation between the imperfects linked by it may be temporal sequence, logical consequence, logical cause, or logical contrast. In all cases there is a sequence. A graph may be formed by consecutive lines with a brace at their juncture to represent the conjunction (──── } ────).

The exact contrast in meaning between these two forms of *waw* suggests that the difference in form was intentionally conceived as a means of indicating the difference in meaning.

Theories concerning the use and meaning of *waw* consecutive have differed from the interpretations given in this work at so many vital points that it will be necessary to examine these theories thoroughly. Then it will be possible to give a treatment of *waw* consecutive in accord with the treatment of indicative imperfects given previously in this work. Because a special feature of *waw* conjunctive is its use with correlative perfects, and because correlative perfects can be understood best in light of their contrast with consecutive imperfects, all combinations using *waw* conjunctive will be treated after treatment of those using *waw* consecutive.

1. Former Theories of *Waw* Consecutive:

The distinction between *waw* conjunctive and *waw* consecutive drawn above contradicts former interpretations in several ways. It is well, therefore, to note these contradictions and also the primary reasons for objecting to the old theories. Afterwards the positive interpretations of *waw* will furnish the fundamental argument against the old theories, inasmuch as they leave no place for the old theories.

The points of contradiction are as follows: (1) Whereas the old theories have said that there is a *waw* consecutive with perfects, this interpretation sees no such thing; (2) whereas the old theories have said that *waw* consecutive with perfects made those perfects the consequence of a preceding imperfect or its equivalent, this interpretation sees in every perfect a distinctive meaning arising from the fundamental character of all perfects; (3) whereas the old theories have suggested that the shift of accent on some perfects when *waw* is attached is a sign that the *waw* is a *waw* consecutive, this interpretation suggests that these shifts of accent are due to the grouping of words and syllables rather than changes of meaning; (4) whereas the old theories have said that *waw* consecutive with imperfects made those imperfects the consequence of a preceding perfect, giving them the force of perfects and virtually turning them into perfects, this interpretation sees in every imperfect a distinctive meaning arising from the fundamental character of all imperfects.

Primary reasons for objecting to the old theories are as follows:

(1) The theory that perfects are used with the force of imperfects and *vice versa* is contrary to all reasonable expectations. Normal and correct developments in all other languages tend

toward a discriminating usage that forbids substitution of one verb form for another.

(2) The fact that no special form of the conjunction appears with the perfect as it does with the imperfect is ground for doubt that a change in the fundamental meaning of the conjunction with the perfect was ever intended by the Hebrew authors.

(3) The theory that "the external indication" of a *waw* consecutive with a perfect "is to be found in the *alteration of the tone* which constantly attends and accompanies it"[3] is not supported by sufficient evidence.   In explaining his conclusion, Driver describes it as a "conjecture."[4]   In his discussion of the theory Harper makes this comment: "As a matter of fact, the cases in which there is no change of tone are as numerous as those in which there does occur change."[5]   We may add that this great number of exceptions is not peculiar to parts of the Bible or certain authors but typical of all.   If the one "external evidence" is lacking in approximately half the alleged cases, is not the burden put upon the subjective interpretation of the reader an overwhelming one?

(4) Advocates of the theory admit that there are constructions with *waw* for which the theory offers no explanation. Driver says, "The instances which occur must simply be recorded as *isolated irregularities,* of which no entirely adequate explanation can be offered."[6]   In a footnote on the same page he adds ". . . in view of the number of instances it can scarcely be maintained with Stade that all examples found in preexilic passages are due to corruption of the text."[7]

(5) The theory defines no clear method of determining the force of the verb with *waw*. Driver says, "Whatever . . . be the shade of meaning borne by the first or 'dominant verb,' the perfect following . . . assumes it too: be the dominant verb a jussive, frequentative, or subjunctive, the perfect is virtually the same."[8]   The word *virtually,* however, is made to cover a

3. S. R. Driver, *Hebrew,* (3rd ed., Oxford: The Clarendon Press, 1892), p. 115.

4. *Ibid.,* p. 118.

5. W.R. Harper, *Elements of Hebrew* (New and Revised Edition by J. M. Powis Smith. New York: Charles Scribner's Sons, 1921), p. 104.

6. S. R. Driver, *op. cit.,* p. 161.

7. *Ibid.*

8. *Ibid.,* p. 118.

strange mass of tangled ideas. It is true, of course, that in most cases translation can make the perfect with *waw* appear virtually the same as the dominant verb, but there are many in which it cannot. Harper cites perfects following imperfects with *waw* consecutive and gives to the perfects the force of a "frequentative imperfect." He cites other perfects following perfects and gives to them the force of "an ordinary future imperfect." He cites other perfects following perfects and makes the latter ones "imperatives." He cites other perfects in conditional sentences following "a participle, an infinitive, a finite verb (Perf. or Impf.), or a noun"[9] and makes them into imperatives. Where then is there a standard that can be consistently followed? Comparison of current English translations, the AV (1611), the ERV (1885), the ASV (1901), Moffatt's NT (1922), the Smith-Goodspeed AT (1939), and the RSV (1952), will show that the authors had not found one. Examples have been given in the preceding study of verbs.

(6) The confusion that prevails in the minds of students of the old theory is evidence that its logic is not merely so baffling as to overwhelm the majority of students but actually unsound. The most zealous ones, those who try to apply the theory to the Old Testament text as a whole, find themselves constantly vexed by confusing inconsistencies to which an application of the theory leads in translation. The distaste for Hebrew among theological students, growing largely out of an impression that it cannot really be understood, and leading 90 percent or more to drop it as soon as school requirements are met, appears to be attributable to the confusion arising from this theory more than any other single factor in the problem.

(7) The uncertainty persisting in the minds of the chief advocates of the theory is yet stronger evidence that their conclusions were based on weak foundations.

The unending search for a satisfactory explanation of this special function of *waw* has stood for more than a century as evidence of this uncertainty. It has been steadily pressed but not concluded ever since Bottcher in 1827 suggested that *waw* consecutive would be a better description of this special function than *waw* conversive. *Waw* conversive or *waw hippukh*

9. W. R. Harper, *Elements of Hebrew Syntax* (New York: Charles Scribner's Sons, 1888), p. 78.

had been inherited from Jewish grammarians of the tenth century and handed on without critical examination by Christian grammarians like Johan Reuchlin (1506), John Buxtorf (1615), and N. G. Schroeder (1792). Schroeder did suggest the need for interpretation by describing an imperfect with the special *waw* as *futurum relativum*, thereby suggesting that it was future by reason of its relation to something else. Since then the possibilities of this special function of *waw* have been examined at length by such men as Wilhelm Gesenius (1815), Heinrich Ewald (1827), A. B. Davidson (1878), August Muller)1882), W. R. Harper (1888), S. R. Driver (1892), and E. Kautzsch (1909). Nevertheless, their own words reveal again and again that they themselves remained conscious of serious questions left unanswered. A typical example is this statement of E. Kautzsch:

> It is difficult to give a proper explanation of this phenomenon . . . when we have given up the theory of a special *waw conversivum* in the unscientific sense mentioned in 49 b, note, at the end, and if we accept the fact that the *perfect* and *imperfect consecutive* cannot possibly be used in a way which contradicts their fundamental character as described in Pars. 106 and 107 . . . . The simplest view is to suppose that the use of the *perfect consecutive* originated from those cases in which it had to express the conclusion (or final consequence) of an action which was continued (or repeated) *in past time,* and that this use was afterwards extended to other cases, in which it had to represent the temporal or logical consequence of action, etc., still in progress, and thus in the end a regular interchange of the two tenses became recognized.[10]

The fact that Jewish scholars have remained as much in doubt about this matter as Gentile scholars has been shown by Dr. H. Leo Eddleman. Dr. Eddleman learned modern Hebrew in Palestine among Hebrew-speaking Jews; and he says, "In modern Palestinian Hebrew practically all scholars, influenced largely by their Occidental background, call *waw* consecutive *waw hammehappecheth,* which is equivalent to *waw hippukh* (*waw* conversive). Typical of these is Dr. Menahem Naor of the Hebrew University, Jerusalem, who says, 'There is [the method] whereby in our speaking of several actions, which occurred in the past, we put the first verb only in the past tense

---

10. E. Kautzsch, *Gesenius' Hebrew Grammer* (28th ed., Oxford: The Clarendon Press, 1910), p. 330, footnote.

and the verbs coming after it we put in the future tense, however, we join to them the *Waw* which changes them from future to past.' These grammarians do not, however, apply this same function of *Waw* to the case of a series of Perfects with when following an Imperfect."[11]

The reference of Dr. Eddleman to a difference made by modern Jewish grammarians in their interpretation of the function of *waw* with perfects and imperfects indicates a struggle in their minds over the very problems magnified in this work. While as far as we know no treatment of the whole matter has been produced by them, the evidence of an effort in that direction is significant. It indicates a sense of need in minds most conversant with Hebrew for a more adequate explanation of the ancient usage than has hitherto been given.

2. Uses of Waw Consecutive in Co-ordination:

In the case of *waw* consecutive and any imperfect to which it is attached, it is well to look at the relationship from the viewpoint of the verb. Thus viewed, the relationship is that of temporal sequence, logical result, logical cause, or logical contrast, i.e., the *waw* makes the verb to which it is attached to be a temporal sequence, a logical result, a logical cause, or a logical contrast of the verb preceding. Sometimes, as in Gen. 22:7, there are sequences parallel to each other. However, these follow a common antecedent and each is a sequent of that antecedent.

Waw consecutive is used only with indicative imperfects. Thus the sequence of *waw* consecutive and the progressive or frequentative force of the imperfect form a combination especially adapted to the description of lineal relationship. This idiom is thus distinguished at all times from those using *waw* conjunctive and describing parallel relationship.

Examples show that consecutive imperfects are not dependent upon any particular kind of antecedent. They abound in past time, and they frequently follow perfects; but this is not necessarily so even in narrative, as Gen. 2:6, 7; Ex. 15:1; I Kings 3:16; 8:1, 2 will show. (Evidence of consecution arises solely out of the combination of the imperfect with *waw* consecutive.) Thus the imper-

---

11. H. Leo Eddleman, "*Waw* Consecutive and the Consecution of Tenses as Reflected by Eighth Century Hebrew" (unpublished manuscript, Southern Baptist Theological Seminary, Louisville, Kentucky), p. 25.

fect with *waw* consecutive forms an idiom as independent and meaningful as the perfect with *waw* conjunctive.

Translation of the *waw,* however, must depend upon the logical relation of the constructions it links together. This is true with all forms of *waw;* it is particularly so with *waw* consecutive because the distinctions are many and sharp. Hebrew minds preferred to leave more to the interpretation of the reader than we do. In English we must insist upon translations of *waw* consecutive like the following:

Temporal sequence: also, and, likewise, then, afterwards.

Logical result: so, therefore, thus, hence, accordingly, consequently.

Logical cause: for, because, since, inasmuch.

Logical contrast: but, yet however, nevertheless, still.

(1) To indicate a temporal sequence:

Gen. 1:1-3 — In the beginning God created the heavens and the earth. . . . *Afterwards* God *proceeded to say,* "Let light come into existence"; so light began to be [i.e., on the earth. cf. v. 2].

Gen. 6:9, 10 — Noah was (nar pf) a righteous man; perfect was he (nar pf) among his contemporaries; with God Noah walked (nar pf). *And* Noah *proceeded to beget* three sons.

Gen. 2:6, 7 — And a mist proceeded to go up from the earth (prog imp), and it watered (cor pf) all the face of the ground, *then* Yahweh *proceeded to form* the man of dust from the ground, *then to breathe* into his nostrils the fulness of the breath of life.

(2) To indicate a logical result:

Gen. 2:7b — . . . then to breathe into his nostrils the fulness of the breath of life; *so* the man *became* a living creature.

Gen. 3:6-16 — Then the woman began to observe that the tree was good for good, and . . ., and . . . ; *so she proceeded to take* some of its fruit, *and to eat, and to give* also to her husband with her, *and he to eat. Thus came to be open* the eyes of both of them, *and they to know* that they were naked, *and to sew* together fig leaves, *and to make* for themselves girdles. Then (tem seq) they began to hear the voice of Yahweh God walking in the

garden at the breezy time of the day; *so they proceeded to conceal themselves,* the man and his wife, from the face of Yahweh God in the midst of the trees of the garden. And (tem seq) Yahweh God continued to call to the man and (tem seq) to say, Where are you? *So he proceeded to say,* Your voice I heard in the garden; *therefore I became afraid,* for naked was I; *so I proceeded to conceal myself.*

(3) To indicate a logical cause:

(Use of *waw* consecutive to introduce a cause or reason clause is subordination rather than co-ordination. Section (3), however, is included here to give the student opportunity to observe the similarity in construction. See Cause and Reason Clauses later.)

II Sam. 14:5 — Of a truth *I am a widow, for* my husband *passed away.*

Ex. 2:10 — And she *began to call* his name Moses, *because she was in the habit of saying,* Indeed from the water I drew him.

Isa. 53:1, 2 — *Who* can *believe* our report? . . . *for he will grow up as a tender plant* before him.

(4) To indicate a logical contrast:

I Sam. 10:27 — And *the children of Belial* [worthless ones] *said,* How can this one save us?; so they proceeded to despise him, *and they did not bring* him *a gift; but he continued to be as a dumb man.*

Deut. 4:33 — Has a people *heard the voice of God* speaking out of the midst of the fire, as you heard it, *yet continued to live?*

Isa. 5:2 —And (tem seq) he proceeded to dig it and (tem seq) to gather its stones and (tem seq) to plant it with choice vines and (tem seq) to build a tower in the midst of it, and even a winepress he chiseled out (nar pf) in it, for he began to anticipate (log cau) the production of grapes: *nevertheless it brought forth rotten fruit* (lit, stinking things).

(Conclusion) Characteristic of Narrative:

Waw consecutive is the characteristic feature of all narrative. The narrative will begin, as a rule, with a perfect, as in Gen. 1:1, then shift to an imperfect with *waw* consecutive, as in

Gen. 1:3, in order to indicate a sequence between the verbal states. It may at any time, for emphasis, thrust words between the conjunction and a certain verb, letting that verb return to the perfect state. Soon, however, it will return to the *waw* consecutive with an imperfect in order to pick up the chain of sequences. Within the sentences introduced by *waw* consecutive, all kinds of varying constructions may appear, but always the narrative will return to *waw* consecutive to indicate movement from one event to another, one state to another, and so on and on so long as it is the wish of the author to continue his narrative. No matter whether the narrative be history, parable, story, legend, myth, or some other type of literary narrative, this is the manner of its composition.

Waw consecutive, therefore, is a major feature of Hebrew syntax. Accordingly, its recognition, its interpretation, and its distinction from all other conjunctive forms are exceedingly important.

3. Use of *Waw* Conjunctive in Co-ordination:

In order to maintain the same viewpoint at all times, we look at the relationship indicated by *waw* conjunctive from the viewpoint of the verb which follows it. Thus viewed the relationship is co-ordinate, correlative, or subordinate; i.e., the *waw* co-ordinates, correlates, or subordinates the verb to which it is attached with or to the verb preceding.

At times the relation is merely temporal, indicating simultaneous existence; at times it is also logical, indicating synonymous meaning; and in both cases there is a co-ordinate parallel, the two verbal states being made for the time being to enjoy equal rank and order.

As a rule imperfects, participles, and imperatives are co-ordinated with others of their own kind, with state, time, and mood being the same. The only variation that appears is the linking of cohortatives and jussives expressing polite commands and suggestions with imperatives expressing out-and-out commands. The co-ordination of clauses wherein verbs are separate from *waw* and assume wide dissimilarity, as in Isa. 46:4, is not in question here. Thus it appears that similarity of state, time, and mood is essential to such close co-ordination of verbs as is indicated by the attachment of *waw* to one of them.

The translation "and" seems to fit all cases, except those in

which repetition in the verbal idea calls for the strengthening of "and" by the asseverative force of "yea."

    (1) To co-ordinate indicative imperfects:

        Isa. 40:30 — Even youths *will faint and be weary,* and young men will utterly fall.

    (2) To co-ordinate participles:

        I Kings 3:3 — . . ., except that he *was sacrificing and burning incense* in the high places.

    (3) To co-ordinate subjunctive imperfects:

        Jer. 31:37 — If the heavens above *can be measured and* the foundations of the earth beneath *can be searched out,* . . .

    (4) To co-ordinate cohortative imperfects:

        Gen. 50:50 — Now therefore *let me go up, I* pray, and *let me bury* my father, . . .

    (5) To co-ordinate jussive imperfects:

        Gen. 1:6 — *Let there be* an expanse in the midst of the waters, yea *let there be* a dividing of the waters . . . .

    (6) To co-ordinate imperatives:

        Amos 5:15 — *Hate* evil *and love* good *and establish* justice.

    (7) To co-ordinate different states

        I Sam. 28:22 — Now therefore, *hearken* (imv), I pray, to the voice of your handmaid, and *let me put* (coh of req) before you a morsel of bread; *yea eat* (imv), *and let there be* (jus of sug) strength in you when you go in the way.

(Perfects do not appear in this list because the co-ordination that is indicated in their usage is a stronger type of co-ordination than that indicated in the case of other verbs. They are linked by *waw* conjunctive to imperatives to show the details of the command, to the protases of conditions taken for granted or sure to occur in general experience, and to central statements in prophetic utterances to explain and expand what the prophet says God will do for his people. Thus they introduce features of a preceding statement that are counterparts of it, related to it logically by inherent and permanent co-ordination. This is correlation, and it will be observed in the next section.

Combinations using *waw* conjunctive to subordinate one sentence to another do not belong in this treatment of independent clauses. A treatment of them will be found under Purpose and Result Clauses.)

4. Use of *Waw* Conjunctive in Correlation:

In all examples of correlation the conjunction retains the same parallel significance it has with co-ordinates. The verb, however, does not depend upon similarity to its antecedent for evidence of correlation. The antecedent may vary widely. The evidence of correlation appears to arise solely out of the combination of a perfect with *waw* conjunctive.

The parallel significance of *waw* conjunctive and the fixed nature of the perfect make a combination fitted to indicate that one state is a counterpart of another. The antecedent may present a general idea, while correlatives supply the details; it may give only a part, while correlatives describe other parts. In any case correlatives designate a state as a fixed part of a larger unit. The unity of the whole is the fundamental concept of this relationship. No matter whether the antecedent appear in a statement of fact, a conditional statement, a command, or an exhortation, details presented by this idiom fill out the picture and appear as fixed parts of it.

When a perfect is correlated with a frequentative imperfect, we naturally ask, "Is not the action of the perfect repeated as surely as the action of the imperfect?" For instance, if Gen. 2:6 is translated thus: "But a mist went up continually from the earth, and it watered the whole face of the ground," is it not indicated that the watering occurred frequently, even as the rising of the mist? Yes, it is so indicated, because the perfect with *waw* correlates watering with the frequent rising of the mist. Frequency is indicated by the imperfect, correlation by the perfect with *waw*.

An illustration in Ex. 6:6-8 is an outstanding example of this. There the statement, "I am Yahweh," is used like a sermon text. It is given in the beginning as the antecedent of all that follows, then repeated for emphasis in the middle and at the end. It is given as an assurance that God will fulfil his promise to bring Israel out of Egypt and back to the Promised Land. Accordingly, seven carefully correlated steps are itemized. In their midst an eighth correlative assures Moses that the people themselves will eventually

realize that their God is Yahweh. Moreover, all of these steps are characterized as fulfilments which God will inevitably bring to pass by reason of the fact that he is Yahweh, God of faithfulness, righteousness, and redeeming love, able and determined to keep his covenants.

Another excellent illustration is that in Isa. 28:13b. There the prophet indicates that it is the purpose of Yahweh, in dealing with stubborn sinners who refuse all the aid of his merciful providence, to give them providential occasion for going on and on in their rebellion till they reap inevitable correlatives of reprobate character — falling backward, being broken, snared, and captured.

This idiom is so peculiar, yet its use so general and its interpretation so important in exegesis, that it challenges our best efforts to understand it. Careful comparison with the one which uses *waw* consecutive with the imperfect will help. In both cases a peculiar force is developed by reason of the combination of a conjunction and a verb with natures peculiarly adapted to each other.

Translation of the conjunction should accord with states that are counterparts of each other. "And" will give the mildest possible description of this close relationship; "then," "so," and similar translations will bring out the logical connection more forcefully. In most cases there is doubtless no occasion for stress; but in the apodosis of a conditional sentence, "then" is certainly needed.

Translation of the perfect should accord with its antecedent in time and mood. In the future, where the overwhelming majority of cases occurs, the auxiliaries "shall" and "will" need to be used always as an indication of the certainty expressed by the perfect.

Translators of the perfect have not hitherto recognized or stressed this relationship. Therefore, conflicting ideas such as contradiction have been unnecessarily read into it at times. In Gen. 47:30 a "but" has been put with the first correlative. Evidently this was done to make a contrast with the closing word of 47:29. That is unnecessary, because the closing word of 47:29 can be treated as a parenthetical statement. Moreover, the change has led to an artificial reconstruction of 47:30, adding "when" to the first clause and eliminating the conjunction in the second. If all correlatives in the two verses are treated as correlatives of the oath Joseph was asked to take, the Hebrew is clear. Another case of similar confusion occurs in Ex. 21:18-19. In all such cases we must look for a better translation, for contra-

diction does not accord with the nature of this idiom as seen above.

Such contrast as is expressed by "yet" or "still" does fit this idiom in many contexts. In these cases the conjunction indicates that, though a preceding statement is true, the one following is also true. This example in I Kings 8:27-28 is a good illustration:

Is it indeed true that God will dwell upon the earth? Behold, the heavens and the heaven of heavens *cannot contain* thee; how then this house which I have built: *Yet, thou shalt have regard* unto the prayer of thy servant . . . so as to hearken unto the prayer which thy servant is praying before thee this day.

(1) To correlate a perfect with a narrative perfect:

Eccles. 1:16 — Lo, *I magnified and increased* wisdom more than any one before me in Jerusalem.

(2) To correlate a perfect with an emphatic perfect:

Isa. 49:6 — *It is indeed too light* a thing for you to be my servant for raising up the tribes of Israel . . . *yea, I indeed give thee* as a light of nations, to be my salvation to the ends of the earth.

(3) To correlate a perfect with a previous-present perfect:

Isa. 1:2 — Children *I have made great and have exalted.*

(4) To correlate a perfect with a characteristic perfect:

Ex. 6:6-8 — *I am* [verb "to be" understood here, which would be *hayah* if written] *Yahweh, and I will bring you out* from under the burden of the Egyptians, *and I will rid you* of their bondage, *and I will redeem you* with an outstretched arm and with great judgments, *and I will take* you to me for a people, *and I will be* God to you, *and you shall know* that I am Yahweh your God, the one bringing you out from the burdens of the Egyptians, *and I will bring* you to the land which I sware to give to Abraham, Isaac, and Jacob, *and I will give* it to you as an inheritance: I am Yahweh.

(5) To correlate a perfect with a perfect of confidence:

Gen. 9:13-16 — My bow *will I surely set* in the cloud, *and it shall be* for a sign of the covenant between me and the earth; *and it shall be,* when I am bringing a cloud over the earth, then shall the bow be seen (pf + *waw* as a dem adv) in the cloud, *and I will remember*

my covenant . . .; *yea,* the bow *shall be* in the cloud, *and I will look upon* it so as to remember the everlasting covenant.

(6) To correlate a perfect with an indicative imperfect:

Gen. 24:7 — *He will send* his angel before you, *and you shalt take* a wife for my son from there.

(7) To correlate a perfect with a participle:

Isa. 8:7 — Behold the Lord *is bringing up* against you the waters of the river, mighty and great, even the king of Assyria and all his glory, *and it shall go* up over all its banks.

(8) To correlate a perfect with a prophetic perfect:

Isa. 8:8 — And it shall sweep onward (cor pf) into Judah. *It shall overflow, and shall pass through;* to the neck it will reach (prog imp), and the spreading out of its wings shall be (cor pf) the fullness of the breadth of thy land, O Immanuel.

(9) To correlate a perfect with a subjunctive imperfect:

Isa. 28:13 – That *they may go on and shall fall backward and shall be broken and shall be snared and shall be captured.*

(10) To correlate a perfect with an imperative:

Ex. 3:16 — *Go and thou shalt gather* the elders of Israel, *and thou shalt say* to them, Yahweh the God of your fathers hath appeared to me.

(11) To correlate a perfect with a jussive:

Gen. 41:34 — *Let* Pharaoh *do* this, *and let* him *appoint* overseers over the land, *and he shall take* a fifth part of the land of Egypt during the seven years of plenty.

(12) To correlate a perfect with an infinitive absolute:

Isa. 5:5b — . . . *removing* its hedge *so that it shall be* for consumption and *breaking down* its wall *so that it shall be* for trampling.

(13) To correlate a perfect with a conditional statement:

Gen. 18:26 — *If I shall find in Sodom fifty righteous persons . . ., then I will spare* all the place for their sakes.

(Conclusion) Characteristic of Prophecy and Similarly Unified Composition:

Waw correlative is an outstanding characteristic of the composition used in prophetic utterance.   Whereas narrative with

waw consecutive attached to imperfects deals with the past, prophecy with *waw* correlative attached to perfects deals with the future. Whereas the consecutive imperfects in narrative trace a series of sequences, the correlative perfects in prophecy describe the various details, or parts, or features of one central fact. Whereas consecutives state facts of experience, correlatives state facts of faith. This unique idiom is used in other important ways, but each one reflects the same characteristic feature seen in prophecy, i.e., unity with an antecedent.

After an imperative an author may use any number of correlative perfects to break down the original command into details. If the author desires to issue an entirely different command, he continues with the imperative.

In dramatic portrayal of various phases of a scene, all occurring at the same time, an author uses these correlatives. See Ex. 33:8-11. Within the sentences introduced by them, imperfects are used to describe movement and progress. The several correlatives, however, present different aspects of one scene.

In conditional sentences correlatives appear in protasis and apodosis. Always they are united with an antecedent. In the apodosis, the entire protasis is the antecedent.

The vital significance of these correlatives in prophecy lies in the fact that they describe logical, not chronological relations. They provide no ground for chronological charts that attempt to reveal the time order of eschatological events. They merely tie the great assurances of prophecy with the revelations, the promises, and the covenants of Yahweh God.

Chapter Ten

Means of Introducing Dependent Clauses

The types of dependent clauses are many. Because their natures vary so widely, the means of introducing them are many.

I

IN SUBJECT AND OBJECT CLAUSES

1. Subject Clauses:

Ruth 2:22 — It is good . . . *that (ki) you should go with his maidens.*

Eccles. 5:4 — It is better *that ('asher) you should not vow.*

In subject clauses it is customary to use *ki* or *'asher* as an introductory particle, *ki* usually, *'asher* less frequently. Even when serving thus as conjunctions, these particles appear to retain something of an old pronominal force. This is readily seen in *'asher* because it is regularly used as a substitute for a relative pronoun. Likewise *ki,* judged by synonymous particles in cognate languages, is thought to have originated as a demonstrative pronoun. These facts help us to understand that these particles sum up the meaning of their clauses, standing as it were in apposition to them, and thus they relate their clauses to the main verb exactly as a simple noun or pronoun used for a subject is related to the main verb.

2. Object Clauses:

Gen. 3:11 — Who told you *that (ki) you were naked?*

I Sam. 10:19 — . . . for you proceeded to say to him, *(ki) "A king shall you put over us."*

118

I Sam. 15:20 — And Saul proceeded to say to Samuel, (*'asher*) *"I have hearkened to the voice of Yahweh."*

Ex. 7:9 — If Pharaoh should speak to you, saying (*le'mor*), *"Present a sign on your behalf."*

Gen. 41:15 — I have heard concerning you, (*le'mor*), *"You can hear a dream so as to interpret it."*

Ex. 7:9 — And you shall say to Aaron, *"Take your staff."*

Ps. 9:21; 9:20 in Eng — Let the nations know *they are men.*

In object clauses *ki* and *'asher* are used as in subject clauses, except that they make their clauses objects rather than subjects of the main verb.   In direct discourse they lose their force as conjunctions.   They may retain the old force as a pronoun in apposition with the statement that follows, becoming equivalent to quotation marks, as in I Sam. 10:19, 15:20; but they are omitted at times, as in Ex. 7:9 and Ps. 9:21.   Doubtless because of their omission, *le'mor* is used at times as another means of indicating a quotation.   In some cases, like Gen. 41:15, we feel no need for translating it, leaving it as a mere sign of quotation.

II

IN RELATIVE CLAUSES

A relative clause is always related to some noun, either written or implied, in the main clause.   Thus it partakes of the nature of an adjective, and the question of agreement with its noun is important.   The relative particle *'asher* is nearly always used to introduce it, and sometimes the demonstrative pronoun *zeh* or *zu,* this.   Since *'asher* is now a mere particle signifying relation, not a relative pronoun, a personal pronoun is usually brought into the relative clause to show agreement with the antecedent in person, number, and gender.   The fact that the particle suffers no inflection at all makes it impossible for it to reflect such agreement. With the introduction of the personal pronoun, three essential points become involved in this indication of relation: (1) the antecedent, (2) the relative particle, (3) the personal pronoun.

In many cases, however, one or more of these essential points is not expressed, being merely implied.   The translator must be prepared to fill in where English cannot bear similar abbreviation.   In such cases, the identification of each of the three essential points

with the other two becomes the key to the problem, as shown in the examples that follow.

1. With the relative clause written fully:
   Gen. 9:3 — Every moving thing *that is alive* . . . (lit, every moving thing which it is a living thing. . .).

The three essential points are as follows: (1) "moving thing" represents the antecedent; (2) "that" or "which" represents the relative particle (either English word may serve, since the antecedent is not a person); and (3) "it" in the literal translation of the original represents the personal pronoun.

The relative clause is composed like a substantive sentence; therefore, it has "is" for its verb, though the verb is not written in the original.

The personal pronoun is in the third person masculine singular; thus it indicates agreement with the antecedent. At the same time its apposition with the relative particle, which is the subject of the relative clause, marks the identification of the three and applies the description of the predicate "is alive" to all three. The identification is so close that it becomes unnecessary to carry the personal pronoun into the translation. The relative pronoun of the English, when substituted for the relative particle of the original, is quite sufficient to indicate the agreement. Retention of the personal pronoun would make the translation awkward.

An interesting fact appears in the translation of this relative clause into Arabic. It is reduced to one word in Arabic, and that word is an adjective. This interpretation reflects correctly the adjectival character of relative clauses.

   Gen. 24:15 — Rebekah *who was born to Bethuel* (lit, Rebekah who she was born to Bethuel).

The student needs to observe that the "who" of the literal translation stands for the relative particle of the original, while the "who" of the final translation is an English relative pronoun. Also let it be observed that the personal pronoun of the original, i.e., "she," is contained in the verb.

"She," being third person feminine singular, agrees with "Rebekah." It serves the same purpose as "it" in Gen. 9:3. When the relative particle of the original is replaced by the relative pronoun of the English, the need for "she" disappears.

   Jer. 28:9 — As for the prophet *who continually prophesies*

peace (lit, who he continually prophesies peace), by means of the coming to pass of the word of the prophet will the prophet *whom Yahweh has really sent* be known (lit, . . . whom Yahweh sent him in truth).

In the first of these relative clauses, the personal pronoun is contained in the verb of the original. It is necessary, therefore, to understand as in Gen. 24:15 that the relative particle of the original becomes a relative pronoun in translation. Its inflection as a nominative third person masculine singular agrees with "prophet" and with "he." When this is understood, "he" is no longer necessary, for "who" becomes the subject of the clause.

In the second relative clause, the relative particle of the original is not identified with the subject of the relative clause, i.e., "Yahweh," as in clauses already examined. It is identified with the direct object of the original, i.e., "him." When the relative pronoun of the translation is put in the objective case to agree with "him," "him" has served its purpose and may be omitted.

Ruth 2:12 — . . . Yahweh, the God of Israel, *under whose wings you have come to take refuge* (lit, who you have come to take refuge under the wings of him).

In this clause the relative particle is not identified with the subject or the direct object, since the antecedent, "Yahweh," does not serve as either of these. The phrase "of him," however, says that the wings mentioned in the relative clause are his wings. This phrase represents as construct, i.e., genitive, the relation between "wings" and "him." In the English this genitive relation can be indicated by the possessive case of the relative pronoun. When the relative pronoun in the possessive case is substituted for the relative particle of the original, "of him" is no longer needed.

Isa. 49:3 — . . . Israel *in whom I shall glorify myself* (lit, whom in you I shall glorify myself).

Again the relative particle refers to an antecedent that is neither subject or object in the relative clause. The antecedent, "Israel," is brought into the relative clause by the adverbial phrase "in you," with "you" as object of the preposition "in." When this preposition is put before the relative pronoun and the phrase "in whom" substituted for the relative particle of the original, the need for the phrase "in you" ceases.

In all these examples, the relative pronoun of the translation takes the case the relative particle of the original would have if it

were a pronoun. For this reason it is necessary for the student, when reworking the composition of these clauses, to work out a literal translation including both the relative particle and the relative pronoun before he tries to put the translation in a finished form.

2. With the personal pronoun omitted:

Gen. 1:7 — . . . between the waters *which were under the expanse* (lit, which underneath with reference to the expanse). If the personal pronoun is added to this literal translation, the whole construction reads thus: between the waters which *they* were under the expanse.

As soon as the relative particle, "which," in the original is understood to have become the relative pronoun, "which," in the translation, it is not necessary to retain the personal pronoun, "they." All relations are clear without it. "Which," as subject of the relative clause is nominative. It does not change form as an objective identified with the antecedent, "waters," which is object after a preposition.

Gen. 2:8 — . . . the man *whom he had formed* (lit, which he had formed). Written with the personal pronoun added to the relative clause, the whole construction reads thus: the man which he had formed *him*.

Since the antecedent, "man," is the direct object of its verb, the personal pronoun, "him," is made the object of its verb. Then it is obvious that the relative pronoun to be substituted for the relative particle must be in the objective case; so we get "whom." "Him" is no longer necessary.

Gen. 35:13 — . . . in the place *where he had spoken with him* (lit, which he had spoken with him). Written with the personal pronoun added, the relative clause of the original reads thus: which he had spoken with him *in it*.

In the complete relative clause, the personal pronoun which is added, i.e., "it," is tied in by the preposition "in," so that the phrase "in it" indicates the place where the speaking took place. It also harmonizes with the phrase "in the place," of the main clause. When the phrase "in which" is substituted for the relative particle, it may be used as it is or turned into the conjunctive adverb "where."

Jer. 7:12 — . . . my place, *which is in Shiloh, where I made my name to dwell in the beginning* (lit, which in Shiloh, which I

made my name to dwell there in the beginning). When a personal pronoun is written into each of these clauses, they read thus: which *it* is in Shiloh, which *in it* I made my name to dwell there in the beginning.

In the first of these clauses, all relations are settled like those in Gen. 1:7.

The second is almost exactly like that in Gen. 35:13. One difference appears in the fact that this one includes the adverb "there" in its original form. Therefore, when the phrase "in which" is substituted for the relative particle, it is natural to turn it into the conjunctive adverb "where" and to drop the adverb "there."

I Kings 8:47 — . . . in the land *whither they have been carried captive* (lit, which they have been carried captive there). With the personal pronoun added, the literal form reads thus: which *into it* they have been carried captive there.

The only difference between this and the preceding example is the fact that the verb in this case involves motion into or whither. Therefore, the conjunctive adverb that fits all relations is "whither" rather than "where."

Gen. 10:14 — . . . and the Casluhim, *from whom the Philistines went out* (lit, which from there the Philistines went out).

In this case the relative particle refers to "Casluhim," a people, while the phrase "from there" refers to the place of their abode. If both ideas are expressed fully, the clause will read like this: which *from the place of them* the Philistines went out.

"From whom" in the suggested translation uses the preposition "from" to signify a place and a going out from it. This phrase also uses "whom" to represent the relative particle turned into a relative pronoun and put into the objective case after the preposition.

In all these cases, due to the absence of the personal pronoun, the translator must deal with the relative particle as the representative of both. As a first step, he must observe the way the personal pronoun would fit into the clause, if used. Then he may transfer this personal pronoun or its entire phrase to the place of the relative particle. At the same time, he must substitute a relative pronoun for the relative particle and use its inflection as a means of integrating and abbreviating the whole construction.

3. With the relative particle, perhaps the personal pronoun also, omitted:

Gen. 15:13 — . . . sojourners will your descendants be *in a land*

that is not theirs (lit, in a land not belonging to them). With
relative particle and personal pronoun written, this literal
form would be thus: in a land *which it* will not be theirs.

The relative particle "which" is turned into the relative pronoun
"that." "It" is then unnecessary.

Isa. 42:1 — Behold my servant *whom I uphold continually* (lit,
Behold my servant — I uphold him continually). With the
relative particle inserted this reads thus: Behold my servant
which I uphold him continually.

"Which" is turned into a relative pronoun and put into the objective case, in agreement with "servant" and with "him." "Him"
becomes unnecessary.

Job 1:1 — There was a man . . . *whose name was Job* (lit, *Job
his name*). With relative particle and personal pronoun added the clause reads thus: who the name of him was Job.

The relative pronoun, "who," can replace the personal pronoun,
"him," if put in the objective case as object of the preposition, "of."
The construct relation in "the name of whom" can then be expressed by "whose name," with the pronoun in the possessive case.

Ps. 16:3 — . . . even the excellent ones *in whom is all my delight* (lit, even the excellent ones — all my delight is in them).
With relative particle added, the relative clause reads thus:
which in them is all my delight.

"Which" becomes "whom" when made a relative pronoun and
put in the place of "them." Then the phrase "in whom" is moved
to the place of the relative particle.

4. With the antecedent included in the relative particle:

II Kings 10:5 — Therefore *he that was over the household* and
he that was over the city . . . proceeded to send to Jehu (lit,
who over the household and who over the city). With antecedent and relative pronoun written separately, these clauses
read this way: he who over the household and he who over
the city.

In both clauses, "who" as a relative particle becomes a relative
pronoun in the nominative case, because it serves as subject of its
clause. Then the verb "to be" understood needs to be written.
Likewise "he," in agreement with this "who," is written into the
main clause as subject of the verb "proceeded to send."

I Sam. 16:3 — . . . and you shall anoint for me *him whom I shall* name for you (lit, who I shall speak to you). When the antecedent and the relative particle are written separately, this clause reads this way: him who I shall speak to you.

When "who" is made a relative pronoun and put in the objective case as object of the verb "name," "him" is needed in the main clause as object of the verb "anoint." "Name for you" is a modern idiom equivalent in this context to "speak to you."

Gen. 43:16 — . . . then he proceeded to say *to him who was over his household* . . . (lit, say to who over his household). With antecedent and relative particle written separately this clause becomes: *to him who* over his household.

When "who" is made a relative pronoun, it serves as subject of its clause, and its verb needs to be written. Then "to him" is needed in the main clause to make all relations clear.

5. With antecedent, relative particle, and personal pronoun omitted:

When all points ordinarily involved in the indication of relation are omitted, it will be found that something in the main clause implies the antecedent. With the antecedent in mind other points can be discerned as in the examples under 3. In other words, the ways of indicating relation seen in examples under 1. are thought of as either written or implied in all cases, no matter how many omissions there are.

Ex. 4:13 — . . . send, I pray, by the hand of whomever *you will* (lit, by the hand of — you will send). With antecedent, relative particle, and personal pronoun written in, this entire statement reads this way: . . . send, I pray, by the hand of *him who you will send him.*

When "who" becomes a relative pronoun, it is put in the objective case to agree with the "him" of the relative clause. Then "him" is needed to complete the main clause and keep all relations clear. Since the use of "him" as both antecedent and personal pronoun makes its reference indefinite, it can unite with "who" in "whomever."

Job 18:21 — . . . and this is the place of him who *does not know God* (lit, and this is the place of — does not know God). Written fully this becomes: and this is the place of *him who he* does not know God.

When "who" becomes a relative pronoun, it is in the nominative case as an appositive of "he" and subject of the clause. "He" is no longer needed in the relative clause, but "him" is needed to complete the construct (gen) relation of "place" in the main clause. The relative particle with its entire clause served this purpose previously.

> Isa. 65:1 — I will let myself be consulted *by those who have not asked;* I will let myself be found *by those who have not sought me* (lit, have not asked; — have not sought me). Written fully and with the implication of the previous present verbs brought out, these clauses read this way: *by those* who they have not asked previously; by those who they have not sought me previously.

When the "who" in each clause becomes a relative pronoun, it is in the nominative case, being in apposition with "they" and the subject of its clause. "They" is no longer needed, but "by those" is needed in the main clause.

III

In Cause and Reason Clauses

Reason clauses usually cite facts already known to exist, as explanations of other facts. In these cases they point to actual causes. In other cases they cite definitely anticipated actions or situations, as ground for a warning or an exhortation. In these cases they point to strongly recommended reasons for actions, attitudes, or decisions. In all cases, the causes mentioned are thought of as definite and certain; so the verbs used are indicatives: perfects wherever the causes have already occurred or exist at the time of writing, imperfects if they are yet to occur.

The particles used to introduce these clauses accord with their nature. Some describe the cause or reason as that on which another fact is logically placed. These are: *'al,* on, upon, on account of; and *be,* in, on, by means of. Some describe the cause or reason as that from which the other fact proceeds as a consequence, a substitute, or an end. These are: *min,* from, as a result of; *tahath,* instead of, in return for; and *'eqebh,* as a consequence of, as an end of, due to. Some describe the logical accord or correspondence between the cause or reason and its consequence. These are: *ya'an,* answering to, corresponding to; and those combinations in which it appears with *ki* and *'asher. ki* and *'asher* are

the particles whose origin was probably pronominal and which are used in a nominal sense to stand in apposition with the whole clause that follows.   The pronominal particles follow the others when they are combined, and this usage is probably due to the fact that the others are thought of as prepositional in character.   Sometimes *ki* and *'asher* stand alone in these clauses.   They appear at such times to carry the meaning of the other particles with which they are often combined rather than a distinct meaning of their own.   *Waw* consecutive, likewise, when attached to an imperfect describing a cause rather than a consequence as is usual with this combination, takes on the force of these characteristically causative particles.   Thus it means *because* or *for*.

Ps. 119:136 — Streams of water run down from my eyes, *because ('al) they do not keep thy law.*

Amos 1:3 — (cf. 1:6, 9, etc.) For *('al) three transgressions, yea, for ('al) four,* I shall not turn it (i.e., the punishment) away, *even because of their threshing instruments of iron* (i.e., because they have threshed. . .).

Phrases with an infinitive and *'al* are frequently used to express a reason.   They may well be expanded, as in this case, into clauses in the translation.

Deut. 31:17 — Are not these troubles come upon me, *on account of the fact that ('al 'ki) my God is not in my* innermost being.

II Sam. 3:30 — . . . so Joab and Abishai . . . killed Abner, *because of the fact that ('al 'asher) he had slain* Asahel.

Deut. 23:4, 5; 23:3, 4 in the Eng — An Ammonite or a Moabite shall not enter into the assembly of Yahweh, *because of the affair in which they did not meet you with bread and water ('al debhar 'asher).*

Jer. 3:8 — . . . *on account of all the causes in which ('al kol 'odhoth 'asher) a backslider, even Israel, had played the harlot,* I sent her away.

Gen. 39:9 — . . . neither has he kept back anything from me but you, *on account of the fact that (ba'asher) you are his wife.*

Isa. 43:3, 4 — *Because (ki) I am Yahweh your God, the Holy One of Israel, your Savior,* I give Egypt as your ransom, Ethiopia and Seba in your stead.   *Since (me'asher, i.e., due to the fact that) you are precious in my eyes,* you are honorable and

I love you, and I continually give men in your stead and nations instead of your life.

Deut. 8:20 — . . . *so will you perish, because* ('*eqebh*) *you will
not hearken.*

Amos 4:12 — *As a consequence of the fact that* ('*eqebh ki*) *I
shall do this to you,* prepare to meet your God. . . .

I Sam. 26:21 — . . . I shall no more do you harm, *in return for
the fact that* (*tahath 'asher*) *my life was precious in your eyes
this day.* . . .

Prov. 1:28, 29 — Then they will call upon me, but I will not
answer . . . *due to the fact that* (*tahath ki*) *they hated knowledge, and the fear of Yahweh they did not choose.*

Num. 20:12 — *Because* (*ya'an*) *you did not put your trust in
me so as to sanctify me in the eyes of the children of Israel,*
therefore you will not bring this congregation into the land.

Isa. 3:16 — *In answer to the fact that* (*ya'an ki*) *the daughters
of Zion are haughty,* the Lord will smite. . . .

Deut. 1:36 — . . . *to him I shall give the land* . . . *in answer to
the fact that* (*ya'an 'asher*) *he has wholly followed Yahweh.*

Gen. 3:14 — *Because* (*ki, in answer to the fact that*) *you have
done this,* cursed are you.

Gen. 30:18 — *Because* ('*asher, in answer to the fact that*) *I
have given my maid,* God has given me my hire.

Isa. 53:1, 2 — Who can believe our message? and to whom can
the arm of Yahweh be revealed? for (*waw, waw consecutive
of a logical cause*) *he will grow up before him as a tender
plant* (lit, a little sucker, or a dependent plant) *and as a root
out of dry ground.*

At times it is natural for us to take a co-ordinate clause introduced by *waw* conjunctive, as in Gen. 6:17; 22:12; Ex. 23:9; Job
22:12, and turn it into a reason clause with "for" as a conjunction.
In these cases the clause introduced by *waw* states a fact that can
be causally related to the first clause. The fact that the author
used *waw* conjunctive means that he chose to leave discernment
of the causal relation to the mind of the reader. If, however, the
causal relation is clear, we do no violence to the text in substituting
a causal conjunction and letting the clause be dependent. An instance in which the need for this interpretation is compelling is this:

Isa. 3:7 — I shall not be a binder up, *for* (*waw*) *in my house
there is neither bread nor clothing.*

IV

IN PURPOSE AND RESULT CLAUSES

When an imperfect is linked with an imperative or cohortative by *waw* conjunctive, its mood appears always to be subjunctive and its relation subordinate. The same is generally true when an imperfect is linked with any perfect or imperfect in the indicative. The only exceptions are rare. For instance, in Isa. 46:4, where the last three verbs are imperfects in the first person singular and in future time, "I" is written emphatically with the first two; but with the third, even though it is expressing the same general idea, the emphatic "I" is dropped, and the verb is attached to *waw* conjunctive. The explanation, apparently, is an intention to let the third express the purpose of the second.

This construction is used to express purpose or result. In Hebrew, as in English, it is often impossible to distinguish between purpose and result. If the preceding verb is an imperative or cohortative, purpose appears clearly, the voluntative force of the first calling for purpose in the second. If the preceding verb is an indicative, it is hard to distinguish at times between purpose and result, but the prevailing effect appears to be result.

Translation should be varied according to the occasion for making the idea of purpose or result explicit. When there is no occasion for making a distinction, "that" serves for the conjunction; when purpose is clear, "in order that" is better; and when result is clear, "so that" is the best expression. In all cases the auxiliary of the subjunctive verb is "may" or "might," for past time, "may" to express stronger possibility in the present and future, "might" to express remote possibility in the present and future.

Examples:

Ex. 3:10 — And now *come,* I pray, *that I may send you.*

Ex. 4:18 — . . . yea, *let me return* to my brothers who are in Egypt *that I may see* if they are yet alive.

Lam. 1:19 — My priests and my elders perished in the city when *they sought food in order that they might sustain* their lives.

Num. 23:19 — God *is not* a man, *so that he may lie.*

Jonah 1:11 — What *shall we do* to thee, *so that* the sea may be calm for us?

In all cases cited *waw* conjunctive has served as an introductory particle. Other conjunctions that serve this same purpose appear in the following:

Gen. 12:13 — *Say,* I pray, that you are my sister, *in order that* (*lemay'an,* to the end that) *it may be well* for me.

Gen. 27:4 — And *make* for me tasty things . . . *so that* (*ba'ab-hur,* for the sake of) my soul *may bless* you before I die.

Either of the conjunctions in these last two verses is followed at times by *'asher,* that. Occasionally *'asher* alone occurs as the connecting word. In Eccles. 7:14, the phrase *'al dibhrath,* to the end that, serves the same purpose.

Infinitives construct with the preposition "to" (*le*) are used quite frequently to express purpose or result. The meaning is so very close to that of a purpose or result clause that it is expedient oftentimes to turn the phrase into a clause, making the infinitive to be a finite verb. The only suggestion concerning the distinction in meaning between the phrase and the clause is that the phrase is related to the antecedent verb in particular while the clause is related to the whole of its antecedent clause.

V

In Circumstantial Clauses

Circumstantial clauses describe circumstances which qualify, modify, or limit the verbal action or state. These circumstances specify the time, the place, the means, the manner, the limitation, or some other condition of the action or state described by the verb of the main clause. It is obvious, therefore, that they are related to their main clauses in the same way that adverbial accusatives and their phrases are related to simple sentences. All of them are adverbial. Thus the Hebrew naturally makes use of adverbs to introduce time clauses. The Hebrew usually omits all introductory words when using the other circumstantial clauses. This may be due to the fact that other statements concerning circumstances almost always employ an adverbial phrase rather than an adverbial clause. Apparently the only departures from this practice occur when *he* and *'odh* are combined to express continuance or *min* and *'odh* are combined for the same purpose. Since such words point to time as well as other circumstances, it is natural that full clauses be formed with them as with other conjunctive adverbs expressing

time. Elsewhere, however, the introductory words are omitted, and it is necessary for English translation to supply those that fit the circumstances.

The conjunctive adverbs commonly used in the time clauses may be observed in the following:

Josh. 3:1 — . . . and they proceeded to journey from Shittim, to come to the Jordan, . . . and to lodge there *before (terem) they proceeded to pass over.*

Gen. 38:11 — . . . Remain a widow *until ('adh) Shelah my son will be grown up. . . .*

Deut. 2:14 — And the days . . ., *until ('adh 'asher) we passed over the brook Zered,* were thirty and eight years. . . .

'asher sums up the clause that follows as in various other kinds of clauses, but it does not appear to add to the meaning of *'adh.*

Lev. 14:43, 44 — And if the plague come again . . . *after ('ahar) he has taken out the stones,* then the priest shall come and look.

Ezek. 40:1 — . . . *in the fourteenth year after ('ahar 'asher) the city was smitten* . . . the hand of Yahweh was upon me.

Again *'asher* does not add to the meaning of the conjunctive adverb. Accordingly, English translations have ceased to add "that" to represent it.

Ex. 5:23 — . . . *since (me'az) I came to Pharaoh to speak in thy name,* he has dealt ill with this people.

Ps. 32:3 — . . . *when (ki) I kept silence,* my bones wasted away.

Isa. 28:4 — . . . *while yet (be'odh) it is in his hand,* he proceeds to eat it.

Num. 22:30 — . . . upon which you have ridden *ever since (meodh) you existed until this day.*

When circumstantial clauses appear without a conjunction, there may be some uncertainty concerning the exact nature of the circumstance. The two examples that follow will illustrate this fact.

II Sam. 18:14 — And he took three darts . . . and thrust them through the heart of Absalom, *(while) he was yet alive in the midst of the oak.*

"While" is not a part of the Hebrew text; therefore, the choice of it is a matter of interpretation. It is apt to be understood as indicating mere time, while the author may have omitted the conjunction to avoid that implication. He may have been thinking of the

ruthlessness and cruelty of Joab and intending to emphasize the manner of this killing as another murder like that of Abner.   To bring out this phase of the matter one could translate thus: *with him still alive.*

Isa. 5:11 — Woe unto them that tarry late in the evening (*while*) *wine inflames them.*

Time is almost certainly involved here.   Either "while" or "til" may be used to express it.

The widespread use of phrases to describe verbal circumstances gives occasion oftentimes for the translator to expand these phrases into clauses.   The vividness of them may be more forcefully portrayed where it is possible to employ more words.   The following passage as a whole furnished an occasion for such expansion in certain phrases.   The phrases in question are these: "in the moving of the people from their tents" and "at the coming of the bearers of the ark to the Jordan."

Josh. 3:14-17 — And it came to pass, *during the time that the people moved from their tents for the purpose of passing over Jordan,* that the priests bearing the ark of the covenant were before the people.   *And at the moment when the bearers of the ark came to the Jordan,* then the feet of the priests bearing the ark were dipped in the edge of the waters, for the Jordan is full, over all its banks, all the days of Harvest.   However, the waters coming down from above proceeded to come to a standstill, they rose up in one heap, a great way off, in (a place called) Adam . . ., and the waters going down to the Salt Sea (the Dead Sea) were exhausted, they were cut off, and the people passed over opposite Jericho.   Therefore, the priests bearing the ark of the covenant of Yahweh continued to stand on dry ground in the midst of the Jordan, even securely, *while* (*waw*) *all Israel was passing over on dry ground, until* (*'adh 'asher*) *all the nation had finished passing over the Jordan.*

In verse 17 of the passage just quoted, in the clause introduced by "while," the Hebrew uses *waw* conjunctive, and the original clause is independent, co-ordinate.   Nevertheless, the clause describes a circumstance like the others observed in this section, and it is expedient to turn it into a dependent time clause.   Such occasion arises often.

It is also true that oftentimes an independent clause introduced by *waw* consecutive can be turned quite fittingly into a time clause.

An occasion of this kind arises whenever the first of two clauses, both introduced by *waw* consecutive, is used for the sole purpose of describing conditions pertaining to the time of the second.   Students need to remember that *waw* consecutive does not necessarily link its clause to the clause immediately before it.   The two clauses may be linked to a common source.   Thus Gen. 4:8 may be rendered this way:

Gen. 4:8 — . . . *while they were in the field,* Cain proceeded to rise up against Abel his brother and to slay him.

The first clause, translated literally, reads thus: . . . and it came to pass, in their being in the field, . . . Each of these clauses has the first clause of verse 8 as its starting point.   Thus the first is used for the sole purpose of describing circumstances prevailing in the second.

This kind of construction occurs often in Hebrew, and the English translation is made much more attractive by the change, without any loss of meaning.

VI

Types of Conditional Sentences

No sort of unanimity has existed among students of Hebrew concerning classification of conditional sentences. Perhaps this has been largely due to lack of unanimity of opinion as to the nature of perfects, imperfects, and the conjunction *waw*.

In accord with preceding interpretations in this work four main types appear.   These four main types are comparable to the four that appear in other languages. This is doubtless due to the fact that the distinctions are rooted in logic rather than the idioms of any particular language.   These four main types are as follows:

(1) A condition *taken for granted,* i.e., one whose fulfilment is thought of as having already occurred.

(2) A condition *contrary to fact,* i.e., one whose fulfilment is considered impossible.

(3) A *more probable* condition, i.e., one whose possibility of fulfilment is taken for granted but whose actual fulfilment, in the case of an individual, is uncertain.

(4) A *less probable* condition, i..e, one whose possibility of fulfilment in any case and whose actual fulfilment are both uncertain.

VII

Verbal Sequences in Conditional Sentences

Type	Verb in Protasis	Verb in Apodosis
1. Taken-for-granted	Pf or pt Pre, prev pre, or prev fut Ind	Imp, pt, pf, or pf + waw Pre or fut Ind
2. Contrary-to-fact	Pf or pt with *lu* or *lule* Con subj Prev pa or pre	Pf or imp (with the force of *lu* or *lule* brought forward) Con subj Prev pa or fut
3. More Probable	Imp or pt Pre or fut Ind	Imp or pf + waw Pre or fut Ind
4. Less Probable	Imp Pre or fut Subj	Imp Fut Subj

Since each type uses particles and verbs which are signs of its own logical character, the particles and verbs of each type will be discussed separately. At the same time, there is a logical relation between protasis and apodosis in each type that calls for a careful consideration of their own relation in each type.

Type 1: Taken-for-granted:

(1) Verbs and Particles in the Protasis:

The condition stated by the protasis is expressed almost always by an indicative perfect, and occasionally by a participle, which is also indicative. Such verbs in previous present or previous future time present the condition as occurring previous to the time of speaking or previous to the time of the verb in the apodosis. Thus, for the sake of logical reasoning, they assume the occurrence of the condition, i.e., they take it for granted.

The particle used most often to introduce these conditions is *'im,* if. Occasionally, when the context shows that there is no uncertainty about fulfilment of the condition, this particle may be rendered seeing that, or when.

Another particle that appears quite frequently is *ki,* meaning

if, in case that, supposing that, when, or though (when an adversative idea is expressed.)

Ki 'im, but if, or except, is used to present emphatically an exception to or limitation upon a statement already made. Cf. Gen. 32:27. (When the *'im* of this combination loses its force, as in Gen. 32:29, and its clause contradicts rather than limits the preceding clause, so that the resultant meaning is only a strong "but," its clause is co-ordinate rather than conditional. Cases in which the two particles are to be translated separately, as in I Sam. 14:45, also do not belong under this heading.)

Hen and *hinneh,* lo! and behold!, also appear occasionally. Practically they are the equivalent of *'im.* Cf. Gen. 4:14; Ex. 6:12; II Kings 5:20.

The particle of relation, *'asher,* in case that, or when, appears occasionally. Practically it is the equivalent of *ki.* Cf. Ex. 21:13.

In exceptional cases, the conjunction *waw* serves to introduce the condition. In these cases the conjunction is *waw* correlative, being attached to a perfect, and it ties into the clause it introduces the conditions stated in the antecedent clause. Cf. Gen. 33:13b; 44:22b.

It is possible for an author to depend upon juxtaposition and logical relation of protasis and apodosis to indicate what is the protasis. In such a case no introductory particle is written. Cf. Prov. 25:16.

(2) Examples:

Job 10:14 — If (*'im*) I indeed sin (pf in pre time), then thou dost mark me (pf + *waw* in pre time).

Ex. 1:16 — . . . if (*'im*) it is (pf of vb "to be" und but not written, in pre time) a son, then you shall kill (pf + *waw* cor in fut time) him.

Ps. 41:7a; 41:6a in Eng — And if (*'im*) he does come (pf in pre time) to see [me], he speaks falsehood continually (imp in pre time).

Job 7: 13-14 — When (*ki*) I say (pf in pre time), "My bed will comfort me . . .," thou dost frighten me (pf + *waw* cor in pre time) with dreams.

Ex. 8:17; 8:21 in Eng — But if (*ki'im*) you are not sending away (pt in pre-fut time) my people, behold, I will be sending (pt in fut time) upon you, and upon your

servants, and upon your people, and into your houses swarms of flies.

II Kings 5:20 — . . . Behold (*hinneh*), my master has spared (pf in prev pre time) this Naaman the Syrian, in not receiving at his hand that which he brought; as Yahweh lives, most assuredly I will run after him, and I will take (pf + *waw* cor in fut time) something from him.

Gen. 44:22b — . . . The lad could not afford to leave his father; for if he shall leave (pf + *waw* cor in fut time) his father, then he [his father] shall die (pf + *waw* cor in fut time).

(3) Verbal Sequence:

The relation between protasis and apodosis appears to be strictly logical in all cases. *Waw* consecutive is never used; thus temporal sequence is ruled out. As a rule no conjunction appears in the apodosis; thus the very purpose of a conditional sentence to link a condition and a conclusion in a consistent statement is relied upon as a rule to indicate the logical relation. An imperfect in the indicative mood asserts the conclusion in the simplest possible way. A perfect in the indicative adds force to the assertion; a participle adds vividness. A perfect with a conjunction attached to it, in other words a correlative perfect, likewise adds force by use of the perfect, and in addition it makes explicit reference to the assertion by use of the correlative *waw*. This reference can be felt strongly, even in the "then" of English translations.

The verbal sequence involved in this expression of logical relation varies the state and time of the verbs but not the mood. An indicative in the protasis is followed by an indicative in the apodosis. Thus we observe that an indicative which asserts something as taken for granted in the condition calls for an indicative which does the same thing in the conclusion.

Type 2: Contrary-to-fact:

(1) Verbs and Particles in the Protasis:

Type 2, like Type 1, uses as its verb a perfect or a participle, usually a perfect, occasionally a participle. Unlike Type 1, however, it always uses an introductory particle. That introductory particle is either *lu* or *lule*.

Lu with a perfect or participle, as in this type, introduces a

condition which the author knows has not occurred or which he thinks cannot occur. This particle with subjunctive imperfects carries an optative force in Type 4 but does not do so here. Here it marks its conditions as contrary to fact. It is translated if, but its meaning amounts to this: "If that which has not happened had happened, then the statement that follows would be true."

Lule', if not, except, or unless, is the opposite of *lu*. It is a combination of *lu* with the negative *lo'*, not. Through usage *lo'* has come to be pronounced as *le'*. It introduces a condition which the author knows has occurred, but which his statement describes, for the sake of logical reasoning, as not having occurred. This particle also marks its condition as contrary to fact.

It is essential to our understanding of these sentences to observe that it is the combination of the verb and its particle, not the verb alone, that indicates the contrary-to-fact nature of the condition. Alone these verbs would be indicative, asserting facts. The combination requires a classification of its mood as subjunctive, because it describes its condition as contrary-to-fact. The idea expressed is contingent, being dependent upon the thinking of the author for whatever reality it possesses. Thus it is subjunctive.

(2) Examples:

Judg. 13:23 — . . . if (*lu*) Yahweh had desired (con subj pf in prev pa time) to kill us, he would not have taken (con subj pf in prev pa time) from our hand a burnt-offering and a meal-offering.

Isa. 1:9 — Except (*lule'*, if not) Yahweh had left (con subj pf in prev pa time) for us a very small remnant, as Sodom had we been (con subj pf in prev pa time).

Deut. 32:27, 29 — Had it not (*lule'*) been (con subj pf of vb "to be," und but not written, in prev pa time) that I continually dreaded an enemy's provocation, lest their enemies should judge amiss, lest they should say, "our hand is exalted," then Yahweh had not done (con subj pf in prev pa time) this. If (*lu*) they had been wise (con subj pf in prev pa time), they would have proceeded to understand (con subj imp in prev pa time) this, they would have proceeded to look with discernment (con subj imp in prev pa time) to their latter end.

In verse 27a translators face a baffling puzzle unless they recognize the contrary-to-fact perfect of the verb "to be," which is understood as being there although it is not written, after the familiar pattern of simple sentences which use no written verb in asserting the existence of something.   Without that verb "to be," the main verb in the protasis would be the indicative imperfect "I continually dreaded."   That situation would violate all known usage in this type of condition.   Recognition of the verb "to be" places a contrary-to-fact subjunctive perfect in the protasis, corresponding to another in the apodosis, found in verse 27d.

Another point of interest appears in verse 29.   Imperfects are used in each of the two apodoses, as contrary-to-fact subjunctive imperfects.

>Ps. 81:14, 15; 81:13, 14 in Eng — If (*lu*) my people were hearkening (con subj pt in pre time) to me, Israel would walk continually (con subj imp in fut time) in my ways, in a little while I could subdue (con subj imp in fut time) their enemies, yea, upon their adversaries I would turn (con subj imp in fut time) my hand.

The participle in the protasis is a striking feature here. Again we find imperfects in the apodoses, three of them.

(3) Verbal sequence:

The logical relation of protasis and apodosis remains logically consistent.   Though *lu* or *lule'* is not repeated in the apodosis, the purpose of a conditional sentence to link a condition and a conclusion in a consistent and unified statement is relied upon to show that the contrary-to-fact character of the protasis is carried over into the apodosis.   A perfect in the apodosis states the conclusion in terms of one fixed action or state.   An imperfect states the conclusion of progress or frequency.   In either case the sentence as a whole indicates that the conclusion is contrary to fact.

The verbal sequence makes a contrary-to-fact subjunctive to follow a contrary-to-fact subjunctive.   Verbal state and time varies, as in Type 1, but not the mood.

Type 3: More Probable:

(1) Verbs and Particles in the Protasis

Imperfects and participles appear in the protasis, imperfects regularly, participles very rarely.   The perfect is not used, and

this fact shows that this type passes from the fixed conditions of Types 1 and 2 into the realm of probability.

Both *'im* and *ki* are used regularly as introductory particles. *'Akh 'im,* but if, or if, however, occurs rarely with an adversative force. All of these introduce conditions whose possibility of fulfilment in many cases is not questioned, but whose actual fulfilment in an individual case is uncertain. Thus their conditions may fittingly be called more probable. They are certainly more probable than those of Type 4, in which both possibility and actual fulfilment are uncertain.

In a series of conditions which employs both *ki* and *'im,* perhaps *'akh 'im* and the like, *ki* introduces a situation or factor common to all, while *'im* or any other introduces details and variations. Thus *ki,* as a rule, introduces conditions more likely to occur than those introduced by *'im.* Nevertheless, the context may add to the normal force of *'im* and make it to introduce a condition concerning which no uncertainty is expressed. Thus Jacob, in Gen. 28:20-22, was accepting the promise Yahweh had just made to him. Moreover, he was promising in turn to accept Yahweh as his God and also to pay tithes to him. The promise about tithing was not bargaining, for Yahweh had already made his promise. Jacob's promise was a response of gratitude and a promise of obedience. Therefore, in this passage *'im* means "seeing that." Likewise, in Num. 36:4, Isa. 4:4; 24:13; 28:25, *'im* means "when."

(2) Examples:

Mal. 2:2 — If (*'im*) you will not hear (ind imp in fut time), and if (*'im*) you will not lay it (ind imp in fut time) to heart, to give glory to my name . . ., then I will send (ind pf + *waw* cor in fut time) the curse upon you, yea, I will curse (ind pf + *waw* cor in fut time) your blessings.

Isa. 1:19, 20 — If (*'im*) you will be willing (ind imp in fut time) and shall hearken (ind pf + *waw* cor in fut time, adding to the description of the condition), the good of the land you will eat (ind imp in fut time). But if you will be unwilling (ind imp in fut time) and shall rebel (ind pf + *waw* cor, adding to the condition), by the sword you will be devoured (ind imp in fut time).

Gen. 44:32 — . . . if (*'im*) I shall not bring him (ind imp

in fut time) to you, then I will have sinned (ind pf +
waw cor in prev fut time) against my father forever.

Comparison of this verse with Gen. 43:9 is highly instructive.
In Gen. 43:9 Judah, while speaking to his father, anticipates the
same situation he does here, while speaking to Joseph. However, in 43:9, he uses a condition taken for granted, while here
he uses a more probable condition. In speaking to his father he
wanted him to think of the return of Benjamin as an event
taken for granted, so that he would let Benjamin go to Egypt.
In speaking to Joseph, whom he knew only as premier of Egypt,
he could not afford to take the condition for granted, yet he
desired desperately to impress him with the terrible effect a
failure on his part to assure the return of Benjamin would have
on his father. For Joseph's sake he needed to picture that
failure as probable but not as taken for granted. When he
went on to offer himself as a substitute for Benjamin, he indeed made a tremendous impression on Joseph. In other words,
Judah recognized the fine distinction he made, and he felt the
force of it very deeply. It was an exceedingly important matter
to him.

Ex. 21:2, 5, 6, 7, 11 — When (*ki*) you buy (ind imp in
pre time) as a slave a Hebrew man, six years will he
serve (ind imp in fut time); and in the seventh, he may
go out free . . . . But if (*'im* with the conjunction "but")
the servant says (ind imp in pre time) positively, "I
love my master, my wife, and my children; I shall not
go free," then his master shall bring him (ind pf + *waw*
cor in fut time) to The [One True] God, yea, he shall
bring him (ind pf + *waw* in fut time) to the door, or
the door-post, and his master shall bore (ind pf + *waw*
cor in fut time) his ear through with an awl, and he
shall serve him (ind pf + *waw* cor in fut time) forever.

And when (*ki*) a man sells (ind imp in pre time),
his daughter as a house-hold slave, she will not go out
as the male-slaves go out. . . . And unless (*'im* + the
negative) he does (ind imp in fut time) these three
things for her, then she shall go out (ind pf + *waw* cor
in fut time) for nothing, without money

(Verses 3, 4, 8, 9, 10 are omitted here because their conditions belong to Types 1 and 4. The last sentence in verse 2
is included because it prepares the way for the contrasting state-

ment in verse 5. Compare the treatment of the whole passage
below under Type 4)
   (3) Verbal Sequence:
   In type 3, indicatives in the protasis are followed by indicatives in the apodosis. This is like the sequence in Type 1.
Moreover, the indicative in the apodosis may be an imperfect
or a perfect with *waw* correlative. So far as Type 3 construction in the apodosis goes, it is exactly like that in Type 1.

Type 4: Less probable:
   (1) Verbs and Particles in the Protasis:
   Imperfects only are used in the protasis. Moreover, the conditions are described in ways that raise questions concerning
the possibility of fulfilment. Therefore, these verbs are subjunctive. They not only express uncertainty about fulfilment in
an individual case, but in any case.
   'Im appears as the only introductory particle. In all cases
it means if, or though, never when, or seeing that, as it does
occasionally in Type 1 and Type 3.
   (2) Examples:
      Gen. 13:16 — . . . if (*'im*) a man could be able to count
         (subj imp in fut time) the dust [particles] of the earth,
         also your seed [descendants] could be counted (subj
         imp in fut time).
      Jer. 31:36, 37 — "If (*'im*) these ordinances could depart
         (subj imp in fut time) from before me," is the express
         utterance of Yahweh, "also the seed of Israel could cease
         from being a nation before me forever." Thus doth say
         Yahweh: " 'If (*'im*) the heavens above could be mea-
         sured (subj imp in fut time), and the foundations of
         the earth could be searched out (subj imp in fut time),
         also I could cast off (subj imp in fut time) all the seed of
         Israel, because of all that they have done,' is the ex-
         press utterance of Yahweh."
      Jer. 33:20, 21 — If (*'im*) you could break (subj imp in
         fut time) my covenant with the day and my covenant
         with the night, so that day and night would not be in
         their time, also my covenant with David could be broken
         (subj imp in fut time), so that there would not be a son
         of his reigning upon his throne — and with the Leviti-
         cal priests my ministers.

Isa. 1:18 — Though (*'im*) your sins may be (subj imp in pre time) as scarlet, they may be made white (subj imp in fut time) as snow: though they may be red (subj imp in pre time) like crimson, they may become (subj imp in fut time) like wool.

(3) Verbal Sequence:

In the translations given above, subjunctive imperfects in the protases are followed by subjunctive imperfects in the apodoses. This feature of verbal sequence is thus presented as the essential characteristic of Type 4 conditional sentences. As indicatives follow indicatives in Type 1, that in the protasis being a perfect or participle; as contrary-to-fact subjunctives in Type 2 follow contrary-to-fact subjunctives, that in the protasis being a perfect or participle preceded by *lu* or *lule'*; as indicatives follow indicatives in Type 3, that in the protasis being an indicative imperfect; so subjunctives follow subjunctives in Type 4, that in the protasis being a subjunctive imperfect. The mere fact that there appears to be a pattern here that can relieve translations of a high degree of subjectivity is enough to challenge every student of the subject to examine this apparent pattern very, very carefully.

On the other hand, there is much, much variation from this suggested pattern in existing translations. This, likewise, demands examination.

As stated in the introduction to this treatment of conditional sentences, "no sort of unanimity has existed among students of Hebrew concerning classification of conditional sentences." This fact has been obvious and very disturbing. In view of the earnest effort throughout this survey to find a distinctive meaning for all verb forms, all conjunctions, all combinations of these, and all types of sentence structure, it follows therefore that another comment in the introduction is pertinent here: "Perhaps, this has been largely due to lack of unanimity of opinion as to the nature of perfects, imperfects, and the conjunction *waw*."

Accordingly, an attempt will be made in the section that follows to apply all previous conclusions to this exceedingly complex matter. An extensive passage, filled with conditional sentences from end to end, will be used as a basis for this examination.

VIII

A Comparison of Conditional Sentences in
Exodus 21:2-14

In the following passage conditions belonging to Type 1 and Type 3 are included along with those belonging to Type 4. This gives an excellent opportunity for comparison and for drawing certain important conclusions concerning the syntactical construction used for these sentences. Only in the conditions of Type 4 will a description of the verbs be included. This will be done to mark these conditions as belonging to Type 4 and to invite comparison with the other types in this passage.

Exodus 21:2-14:

2. When (*ki*) you buy as a slave a Hebrew man, six years will he serve; and in the seventh he may go out free, without paying anything. 3. If (*'im*) by himself he should come in (subj imp in fut time), by himself he may go out (subj imp in fut time); if (*'im*) he is married, then his wife shall go out with him. 4. If (*'im*) his master should give (subj imp in fut time) him a wife, and she shall bear (pf + *waw* cor, which merely adds to the condition a detail which assumes the same conditional force as the preceding verb) him sons or daughters, the wife and her children should belong (sub imp in fut time) to her master, but he may go out (subj imp in fut time) by himself. 5. But if (*'im*) the servant says positively, "I love my master, my wife, and my children; I shall not go out free," 6. then his master shall bring him to The [One True] God,[1] yea, he shall bring him to the door, or to the door-post, and his master shall bore his ear through with an awl, and he shall serve him forever.

7. When (*ki*) a man sells his daughter as a household-slave, she will not go out as the male-slaves go out. 8. If (*'im*) she is not pleasing in the eyes of her master, who has espoused her to himself,[2] then he shall cause her to be redeemed: to a foreign people he will not have power to sell her, because of his dealing deceitfully with her. 9. And if (*'im*) he should espouse her (subj imp in fut time) to his son, according to the judgment for daughters he should deal

1. Or, the judges.
2. Some mss. read thus: so that he has not espoused her.

(subj imp in fut time) with her. 10. If (*'im*) he should take (subj imp in fut time) for himself another [wife], her food, her clothing, and her duty of marriage he should not diminish (subj imp in fut time). 11. And if (*'im*) he does not do these three things for her, then she shall go out for nothing, without money.

12. One who smites a man, and he dies, may surely be put to death. 13. But in case (*'asher*) he did not lie in wait, but The [One True] God delivered [his enemy] into his hand, then I will appoint for you a place to which he may flee. 14. But when (*ki*) a man acts with premeditation against his neighbor to slay him with guile, from my altar you will take him that he may die.

Frequently in this passage and in similar passages wherever the ordinances are recited, other translations use a subjunctive in the protasis and an indicative in the apodosis. Ex. 21:3 furnishes a good example: "If by himself he comes in, by himself he shall go out." Imperfects appear in both in the Hebrew, and the translations make one subjunctive, the other indicative.

In searching for reasons why this has been done, a situation in the immediate context should be noted. At the end of verse 2 there is a statement that introduces all the conditional sentences that follow from verse 2 through verse 6. That final sentence is not a condition. If the author had intended to put the statement in a conditional sentence, it would have served as conclusion rather than condition after this fashion: and if he should desire to go out free, he may do so. As written it is merely a statement, preliminary to the several conditional sentences that follow.

In view of the logical relation between that preceding statement and the varying choices stated afterwards, it is not logically consistent to say "he shall go out free." Various possibilities are stated below, and wherever an alternative choice is stated consistency requires an introductory statement that says "he may go out free." The lack of logical integrity, when verse 2 says that the slave shall go out and verse 6 says that he shall remain forever, smites the mind of a thoughtful reader.

Since the verb in this introductory statement is an imperfect, it may be interpreted as subjunctive. Then its auxiliary must be "may," not "shall." (Even if it were interpreted as an indicative, it would not take "shall." Only a perfect could do that.)

With the introductory statement in the subjunctive, a subjunctive statement of varied details given in protases is consistent. Apodoses in the subjunctive are likewise consistent. The logical consistency of these can be recognized easily in verses 3a and 4. Similar interpretations are called for in verses 9 and 10.

Instructive contrasts appear in verses 2a, 7, and 14. Imperfects are used in protasis and apodosis to describe basic legal practices. Apparently, this is indicated by the use of *ki* as the introductory particle. Thus "when" is required in translation. Thus the imperfects are indicatives, and the sentence is Type 3.

Other instructive contrasts appear in verses 5, 6 and 11. Imperfects are used in the protasis to describe particular situations in which the condition is so stated as to eliminate all alternative conditions. Naturally that imperfect is indicative. Then the apodoses use perfects with *waw*. Thus they not only give a positive, i.e., indicative, statement to the only conclusion allowed by law in that case but they state it as forcefully as possible.

Conditions using perfects or participles, but not with *lu* or *lule'* before them, fall into Type 1. After these conditions taken for granted, the use of a perfect with *waw* correlative in the apodosis is quite consistent. One example appears in verse 13.

Conditions with the same composition as substantive sentences, i.e., without a written verb but with the verb "to be" understood, imply such a verb in the indicative perfect. Thus they also belong to Type 1. Examples appear in verses 3b and 8a. In both cases a perfect with *waw* correlative is used in the apodosis. This usage emphasizes the sequence which requires the same mood in protasis and apodosis.

A correlative construction correlated with a subjunctive antecedent, as in the protasis of verse 4, assumes the conditional force of its antecedent, since it states a detail of that antecedent. It is then consistent with a subjunctive conclusion. In all cases where a correlative appears in an apodosis, as in verses 3b, 6 (four instances), 8a, 11, and 13, that correlative has an indicative in the protasis as its antecedent. All this magnifies the interpretations of verbal sequence as requiring the same mood in protasis and apodosis.

The use of perfects with *waw* in the apodoses of these sentences presents a body of evidence that is vital to our entire treatment

of Hebrew syntax.   The following points require this evaluation of its importance:

(1) The interpretation of these perfects with *waw* contains the same problem involved in perfects with *waw* anywhere else. Our survey has revealed no variation in the essential idea expressed by this construction, i.e., unity with its antecedent. Therefore, any variation in this situation is expected to be in the context of this particular construction, not in the construction itself.

(2) The interpretation of these perfects with *waw* has been baffling, even to the very best scholars in the field, and to a degree that is almost unbelievable until one examines the mass of conflicting interpretations given to conditional sentences in works on Hebrew syntax. Men who have been unable to accept the theory that the *waw* with these perfects is *waw* consecutive, and that it brings to these perfects the force of the verb in the protasis, in many cases an imperfect, have been forced into silence with little or nohing to relieve their confusion.   Men who have accepted this theory have continued through centuries of effort to turn out translations with a woeful lack of consistency in them.   The same inconsistencies noted above in the discussion of Ex. 21:2-14 appear in AV, ASV, MNT, AT, RSV, and in all commentaries, so far as the author is aware of them.

(3) The translation of Exodus 21:2-14 gives an excellent opportunity for weighing the force of perfects with *waw,* because conditional sentences of Types 1, 3, and 4 appear together with many occasions for comparison.

In verse 3b the first instance occurs, in these words, "and his wife shall go out with him."   Since this conclusion deals with the wife in case of her husband choosing to go free, the one conclusion allowed by the law is stated very positively by this construction.

In verse 4a, this construction is in the protasis following a main verb, and it assumes the time and mood of that main verb. This fact illustrates the unity it expresses, but it affects the sentence as a whole in no other way than the addition of a detail to the condition.

In verses 5 and 6, which are parts of one sentence, the apodosis uses four of these constructions to describe the one conclusion allowed by the law.   Again they do so with force, naturally so.

Verse 8a, like 3b, uses this construction in the apodosis to state very positively the point required by the law.

In verse 11, the protasis eliminates all conditions other than its own, then the apodosis uses this construction to emphasize the one conclusion allowed by the law.

Verse 13 is like 3b, with the same need for force in statement of the one conclusion allowed by law.

This translation uses the auxiliary "shall" to express the force of these perfects with *waw* wherever they appear in apodoses, and it does not use it in any other case.   This distinction makes these perfects with *waw* to stand out, even as the logical consistency of all these sentences requires.   This then becomes crucial evidence in resolving our problem.

In view of the consistency brought to this passage by consistent interpretation of its verbs, and in view of conviction that similar interpretation brings consistency to all passages listing ordinances, the pattern of verbal sequences described above is believed to be confirmed.

IX

MIXED FORMS IN CONDITIONAL SENTENCES

The sentences discussed in the foregoing have belonged to regular types.   Conditional sentences are not always so regular by any means.

At times a condition belonging to one type is combined in the protasis with a condition of another type, as follows:

Isa. 4:4 — When (*'im*) the Lord shall have washed away (ind pf in prev fut time) the filth of the daughters of Zion, and the bloodguiltiness of Jerusalem he will proceed to purge (ind imp in fut time) from her midst by the spirit of justice and the spirit of burning, then Yahweh shall create (ind pf + *waw* in fut time) over each dwelling in Mount Zion and over her assembly a cloud by day, even a smoke-cloud, and a brightness of a flame of fire by night . . . .

The first condition belongs to Type 1, and the second to Type 3.   The apodosis, however, which employs an indicative perfect with *waw*, fits both of them.

Conditions are frequently mixed with clauses that are not conclusions of a normal type.   Frequently interrogative, imperative, cohortative, or jussive clauses appear in place of the normal

statements we have observed.   It is impossible to reduce such sentences to a system.   The essential thing to remember in these cases is that each part of the sentence must be judged by the standards for its type of clause.

Oaths and imprecations belong to this group.   Occasionally these are written fully, as in Ruth 1:17, but frequently the apodosis is omitted, no expression of any kind appearing in its place, as in II Sam. 11:11.   Often a formal expression indicating an oath, like *chay Yahweh*, as lives Yahweh, will accompany the condition, but it does not furnish the apodosis.   Probably the apodosis is understood to be in all cases the equivalent of that which is sometimes written: "The Lord do so to me and more also."   The effect of such expressions is to convey the strongest possible impression that the thing in question will or will not be done.   If the particle used is *'im* or *ki,* supposing the doing of it, the effect is to affirm that it will not be done, as in I Sam. 14:45.   If the particle used is *'im lo,* if not, supposing that the thing not be done, the effect is to affirm the doing of it, as in Gen. 24:38.   For the sake of clarity, the translation must often render the effect rather than the literal expression.

For the sake of clarifying some of these interpretations, certain examples will be examined more closely:

Ruth 1:17 — . . . so let Yahweh do (a jussive imp), yea, let him add [to it, i.e., destroy me], if (*ki*) death itself (lit, the death) can divide (subj imp in fut time) between me and you.

The condition is stated last.   Ruth's words appear to express conviction that death itself cannot put an actual or permanent barrier between them.   There is no word like "only" or "aught but" among her words.

II Sam. 11:11 — . . . as you live, and as your soul lives, [let Yahweh destroy me, an unexpressed jus imp, serving as the apodosis], if (*'im*) I shall do (ind imp in fut time) this thing.

The clauses "as you live" and "as your soul lives" were idioms that signified the taking of an oath.   They did not state the conclusion, but they prepared the mind of the hearer to realize that the customary conclusion was desired by the speaker as surely as if it had been spoken.

I Sam. 14:45 — . . . as Yahweh lives, [let Yahweh destroy us, a jus imp expressing the conclusion] if (*'im*) one hair of

his head (lit, from the hair of his head) will fall (ind imp in fut time) to the ground.

The effect of this dramatic oath is to swear that no hair of his head will fall to the ground.

Gen. 24:38 — If not (*'im lo'*) to the house of my father you will go, and to my family, and you shall take (cor pf in fut time, adding to the condition), [let Yahweh destroy me].

The effect of this is to swear that, as Yahweh lives, the servant will succeed by the help of Yahweh in securing a wife for Isaac from among Abraham's own people.

Selected Bibliography

I. HEBREW GRAMMAR AND SYNTAX

Alting, Jacob, *Fundamenta Punctationis Lingua Sancta.*
Frankfort-on-the-Main: Knochi & Eslingei, 1746.

Baer and Strack, *Die Dikduke ha-teamim des Ahron ben Moschek ben Ascher.*
Leipzig: 1879.

Blake, Frank Ringgold, *A Resurvey of Hebrew Tenses.*
Rome: Pontificium Institutum Biblicum, 1951.

Bush, George, *A Grammar of the Hebrew Language.*
New York: Leavitt, Lord & Company, 1835.

Carlson, E. Leslie, *Elementary Hebrew.*
Kansas City: Central Seminary Press, 1945.

Davidson, A. B., *An Introductory Grammar.*
Edinburgh: T. & T. Clark, 1900.

Davidson, A. B., *Hebrew Syntax.*
Edinburgh: T. & T. Clark, 1894.

Driver, G. R., *Problems of the Hebrew Verbal System.*
Edinburgh: T. & T. Clark, 1936.

Driver, S. R., *A Treatise on the Use of the Tenses in Hebrew.*
Oxford: The Clarendon Press, ed. 3, 1892.

Evans, D. Tyssil, *The Principles of Hebrew Grammar.*
London: Luzac and Company, 1912.

Ewald, Heinrich, *Syntax of the Hebrew Language.*
Edinburgh: T. & T. Clark (translated by James Kennedy), 1879.

Gray, George Buchanan, *The Forms of Hebrew Poetry.*
London: Hodder and Stoughton, 1915.

Green, Samuel C., *A Handbook of Old Testament Hebrew.*
London: The Religious Tract Society, 1921.

Green, William Henry, *A Grammar of the Hebrew Language.*
New York: John Wiley & Sons, revised ed., 1892.

151

Harper, William R., *Elements of Hebrew.*
New York: Charles Scribner's Sons, 1921.
Harper, William R., *Elements of Hebrew Syntax.*
New York: Charles Scribner's Sons, 1888.
Hurwitz, Hyman, *A Grammar of the Hebrew Language.*
London: John Taylor, ed. 2, 1835.

Kautzsch, E., editor and reviser, *Gesenius' Hebrew Grammar.*
Oxford: The Clarendon Press, ed. 28, 1910 (The first ed. appeared at Halle, Germany in 1813. Twelve more editions were made by W. Gesenius himself; ed. 14 to ed. 21 by E. Rödiger, ed. 22 to ed. 28 by E. Kautzsch; translated by A. E. Cowley).

Lee, S., *A Grammar of the Hebrew Language.*
London: James Duncan, 1827.

Mannheimer, S., *Hebrew Reader and Grammar.*
New York: Bloch Publishing Company, ed. 15, 1892.
Martin, Malachi, *The Scribal Character of the Dead Sea Scrolls.*
Louvain: Publications Universitaires, 1958.
Muller, August, *Outlines of Hebrew Syntax.*
Glasgow: James Maclehose and Sons (translated and edited by James Robertson), 1882.

Naor, Menahem, *Iquare Hadiqduq Haivree,* (in Hebrew).
Haifa: Beth Sefer Hareali Maivree, 1937.

Ostborn, Gunnar, *Tora in the Old Testament* (a semantic study).
Lund: Hakan Ohlssons boktr., 1945.

Palache, Jehuda Leon, *Semantic Notes on the Hebrew Lexicon.*
Leiden: E. J. Brill (translated from the Dutch by R. J. Zwi Werblowsky), 1959.

Qimhi, D., *Hebraicum Institutionem,* libri IV.
Paris: Robert Stephanus, 1549.

Reuchlin, Johann, *Rudimenta Linguae Hebraicae.*
Pforzheim: 1506.
Robinson, Theodore Henry, *The Poetry of the Old Testament.*
London: Duckworth, 1947.

Schroeder, N. G., *Institutiones ad Fundamenta Linguae Hebraicae.*
Stettiniana: In officina Librar, 1792.
Segal, M. H., *A Grammar of Mishnaic Hebrew.*
Oxford: The Clarendon Press, 1927.
Stuart, Moses, *A Grammar of the Hebrew Language.*
Andover: Flagg & Gould, 1831.

Weingreen, Jacob, *A Practical Grammar for Classical Hebrew.*
Oxford: The Clarendon Press, 1952.

Wickes, William, *A Treatise on the Accentuation of the Three So-Called Poetical Books of the Old Testament.*
Oxford: Clarendon Press, 1881.

Wood, C. T., and Lanchester, H. C. O., *A Hebrew Grammar.*
London: Kegan, Paul, Trench, Trubner & Co., Ltd., 1920.

Yates, Kyle M., *Essentials of Biblical Hebrew.*
New York: Harper and Brothers, ed. 4, 1938.

Yoder, Sanford Calvin, *Poetry of the Old Testament.*
Scottdale, Pa.: Herald Press, 1952.

Young, George Douglas, *Grammar of the Hebrew Language.*
Grand Rapids: Zondervan Publishing House, 1951.

II. HEBREW LEXICOGRAPHY AND CONCORDANCE

Brown, Driver and Briggs, *A Hebrew and English Lexicon of the Old Testament* (Based on the Lexicon of Wilhelm Gesenius as translated by Edward Robinson).
New York: Houghton Mifflin Company, 1906.

Buxtorf, John (the elder), *Thesaurus Grammaticus Linguae Sanctae Hebraicae.*
Basel: 1615.

Davidson, A. B., *A Concordance of the Hebrew and Chaldee Scriptures.*
London: Samuel Bagster and Sons (revised and corrected), 1876.

Furst, Julius, *A Hebrew & Chaldee Lexicon.*
Leipzig: Bernhardi Tauchnitz, ed. 3, (translated by S. Davidson), 1867.

Gesenius, Wilhelm, *Hebräisch-deutsches Handwörterbuch des Alten Testaments.*
Leipzig: 1810-1812.

Gesenius, Wilhelm, *Hebrew and Chaldee Lexicon to the Old Testament Scriptures.*
Grand Rapids: reprint, Wm. B. Eerdmans Publishing Co., translated and edited by Samuel Prideaux Tregelles, 1846-1857.

Gesenius, Wilhelm, *A Hebrew and English Lexicon of the Old Testament.*
Boston: Crocker and Brewster, (translated by Edward Robinson), 1836-1854.

Gesenius, Wilhelm, *Neues Hebräisches-deutsches Handwörterbuch.*
Leipzig: 1815-1828.

Gesenius, Wilhelm, *Thesaurus Philologicus Criticus Linguae Hebraeae et Chaldaeae Veteris Testamenti.*
Leipzig: 1829-1842.

Grossman and Segal, *Compendious Hebrew-English Dictionary.*
(Comprising a Complete Vocabulary of Biblical, Mishnaic, Medieval and Modern Hebrew.)
Tel Aviv: Dvir Publishing Co., 1946.

Koehler, Ludwig, *Lexicon In Veteris Testamenti Libros.*
Vols. 1 & 2; Aramaic portions by Walter Baumgartner). Grand Rapids: Wm. B. Eerdmans Publishing Co., 1953.

Mandelkern, Solomon, *Veteris Testamenti Concordantiae.*
Leipzig: Veit et Comp., 1896.

Parkhurst, John, *Hebrew and English Lexicon.*
London: William Baynes and Son, (a new ed., corrected, enlarged and improved), 1923.

Roy, W. L., *A Complete Hebrew and English Critical and Pronouncing Dictionary.*
New York: John F. Trow & Company, 1846.

Yehuda, Ben, *A Complete Dictionary of Ancient and Modern Classical Hebrew.*
New York: Thomas Yoseloff, 1960.

Zorell, Franciscus, *Lexicon Hebraicum et Aramaicum Veteris Testamenti.*
Rome: Pontificum Institutum Biblicum, 1951.

III. ENGLISH GRAMMAR, SYNTAX AND LEXICOGRAPHY

Curme, George O., *Syntax* (Vol. III of *A Grammar of the English Language*).
New York: D. C. Heath and Company, 1931.

Opdycke, John B., *Harper's English Grammar.*
New York: Harper & Brothers, 1941.

Webster's New International Dictionary of the English Language.
(Harris, W. T., Editor-in-Chief; Allen, F. Sturges, General Editor.)
Springfield: G. & C. Merriam Co., 1932.

IV. MASORETIC TEXT

Baer, Seligman, *Biblia Hebraica.*
Leipzig: Bernhardi Tauchnitz, 1879.

Ginsberg, C. David, *Hebrew Bible.* (with text and critical apparatus based upon the Bomberg Bible.)
London: Trinitarian Bible Society, 1894.

Ginsberg, C. David, *Introduction to the Hebrew Bible.*
London: Trinitarian Bible Society, 1897.

Kittel, Rud., *Biblia Hebraica.* (With masoretic text provided by
P. Kahle.)
Stuttgart: Priv. Württ. Bibelanstlat, ed. 7, 1951.

Letteris, Maier Halevy, ...
London: British and Foreign Bible Society, 1890(?)-1937.

Simonis, Johannis, *Biblia Hebraica.*
Halle: ed. 4, 1828.

Van der Hooght, Everadi, *Biblia Hebraica.*
Leipzig: Bernhardi Tauchnitz, ed. 3, 1833.

V. TRANSLATIONS

American Standard Version.
Published in America in 1901 A.D.

An American Translation.
Made by J. M. Powis Smith and a group of scholars,
Chicago: University of Chicago Press, 1927.

Authorized Version.
Published in England in 1611 A.D.

Die Heilige Schrift.
Made by Emil Kautzsch and a group of scholars,
Elbefeld: R. Brochhaus, 1907.

Douay Version.
Published in England in 1609 A.D.
New York: P. K. Kenedy & Sons, 1941.

English Revised Version.
Published in England in 1885 A.D.

The Holy Bible from Ancient Eastern Manuscripts.
Containing Old & New Testaments.
Translated from the Peshitta, the Authorized Bible of the
Church of the East, by George M. Lamsa.
Philadelphia: A. J. Holman Company, 1957.

The Holy Bible in Modern English.
Written by Ferrar Fenton.
London: Adam & Charles Black, 1903.

*The Holy Scriptures According to the Masoretic Text,
A New Translation.*
Made by Jewish Scholars in America,
Philadelphia: The Jewish Publication Society of America, 1917.

The New English Bible.
Oxford University Press;
Cambridge University Press, 1963.

A New Translation.
Made by James Moffatt,
New York and London: Harper & Brothers, 1922.

New World Translation of the Hebrew Scriptures.
Made by New World Translation Committee.
Brooklyn: Watchtower Bible and Tract Society, 1953-1960.

Revised Standard Version.
New York: Thomas Nelson & Sons, 1952.

The Septuagint.
Made by Jews in Egypt about 275-150 B.C.
Edited by Henry Barclay Swete.
Cambridge: University Press, 1887-1934.

The Vulgate
Made by Jerome in Palestine about 390-405 A.D.
Contained in the Triglot Bible,
London: Richard D. Dickinson, 1890.

Index of Biblical References

(The following references are given primarily with reference to the Hebrew Bible. If a reference in parentheses is given, it refers to English translations.)

Verses	Page Numbers	Verses	Page Numbers
	Genesis	2:19	61, 62
1:1	13, 18, 19, 30, 35, 36	3:1	22
1:1-3	109	3:6-16	109
1:2	13, 14, 15, 25, 35	3:10	25
1:3	82, 83, 111	3:11	76, 118
1:3-19	36	3:14	25, 88, 128
1:4	21	4:2	95, 101
1:6	83, 112	4:6	25
1:6-9, 15-19	61	4:7	25, 56
1:7	122, 123	4:8	133
1:9	82, 83	4:9	24
1:17, 18	96	4:10	16, 30, 72
1:26	36	4:14	30, 135
1:29	21	5:3	19, 61, 62
1:31	36	5:4	61, 62
1:1—2:3	61	5:5	16
2:2	30	5:6, 7, 9, 10, 12	
2:3	96	13, 15, 16, 18,	
2:4	94	19, 21, 22, 25,	
2:4-25	61	26, 28, 30	62
2:5	23, 61	6:1	95
2:6	17	6:2	18, 19
2:6-9, 15-19	61	6:4	26
2:6, 7	108, 109	6:9	37
2:7	20	6:9, 10	109
2:8	45, 122	6:13	17
2:10	48, 49	6:17	72, 73, 128
2:10-14	68	7:4	72, 73
2:15	23	7:20	20
2:17	89, 93, 101	8:7	93
2:18	94	8:8	24

VERSES	PAGE NUMBERS	VERSES	PAGE NUMBERS
9:3	120	27:4	130
9:13-16	115	28:42	22
9:24	21	28:13, 15	13, 15
9:25	22	28:20	14
9:26	26	28:20-22	139
10:14	123	29:30	22
11:18	95	30:13	39, 40
11:10-24	62	30:18	128
11:28	63	30:30	24
12:1	27, 62, 63, 64	30:34	84
12:9	93	31:13	63
12:13	130	32:11 (32:10)	45
13:10	17	32:27, 29	135
13:16	76, 141	32:31	20
14:10	22	33:8	24
14:21-23	38	33:13	135
15:12	98	33:18	19
15:13	123	35:13	122, 123
16:8	24	36:2	37
17:2	78, 79	37:5	21
17:16	39, 40	37:7	71
17:18	25	37:35	16, 20
17:20	50, 51, 52	38:11	131
18:1	19, 71	39:9	127
18:15	102	40:13	50, 51, 52
18:19	15	40:23	43
18:25	25	41:15	119
18:26	116	41:33	83
18:30	83	41:34	116
19:20	83	41:59	119
21:7	76	43:7	63
21:13	135	43:9	140
21:26	102	43:16	125
22:7	108	43:20, 23	25
22:12	128	44:22	135, 136
22:24	27	44:32	139
23:13	25	44:33	83
24:4	63	45:25	19
24:7	63, 116	46:2	20
24:15	120, 121	46:30	80
24:19	57	47:8	24
24:38	148, 149	47:29, 30	114
24:44	102	49:17, 18	84, 85
24:57	81	49:27	60
24:58	24	50:5	80
25:34	64, 65	50:50	112
26:13	93		

Verses	Page Numbers
Exodus	
1:7	43
1:16	135
2:6	26
2:10	110
2:13	24
3:1	70
3:3	78, 79
3:10	90, 129
3:11	77
3:14	67
3:16	116
3:18	80
3:19	44
4:7	89
4:13	125
4:16	57
4:18	129
5:16	15
5:23	131
6:3	20
6:6-8	113, 115
6:10	97
6:11	89
6:12	135
7:2	88
7:9	119
8:17 (8:21)	135
9:5	59
9:16	99
10:6	102
13:7	21
14:12	24
14:13	102
15:1	55, 59, 108
16:3	25
16:27	17
17:2	24
19:5	26
19:6	15
19:10-13	51, 52
19:13	102
20:3	89
20:8	91
20:8, 9	93
20:9	32, 88
20:10	32

Verses	Page Numbers
20:12	32, 90
20:15	89
20:20	23
21:2-6	144
21:2-11	140
21:5	141
21:2-14	143, 145, 146
21:3, 8	147
21:18, 19	114
21:28	21, 93
23:9	128
29:9	20
31:14	16
33:8-11	16, 68, 117
33:16	98
34:6	26
34:18	102
Leviticus	
5:2-4	102
11:4	21
14:43, 44	131
17:11	27
26:45	101
Numbers	
12:1	16
14:2, 28	25
16:29	23
17:27 (17:12)	39, 40
20:12	128
20:21	94
22:30	131
22:33	75
23:10	75
23:19	129
24:9	16
24:17	41, 42, 59
35:23	23
36:4	139
Deuteronomy	
1:12	76
1:36	128
2:14	131
2:27	80

160INDEX

VERSES	PAGE NUMBERS	VERSES	PAGE NUMBERS
2:30	49	**I SAMUEL**	
2:34	21	1:3	96
4:1	72	1:7	56, 57
4:33	110	1:23	83
8:20	128	2:4	16
9:21	93	4:15	15
11:10	48, 49	5:9	20
12:23	15	8:19	102
15:3	81	9:3	21
17:14	78, 79	10:5	59
17:19, 20	23	10:19	118, 119
18:21	24	10:27	110
22:8	17	11:13	24
23:4, 5 (23:3, 4)	127	12:3	45
31:17	127	12:17	96
32:6, 21	23	14:10	46
32:27-29	137, 138	14:33	96
33:16	77	14:45	135, 148
		15:20	119
JOSHUA		15:32	20
3:1	131	16:3	125
3:14-16	98	16:7	57
3:14-17	132	17:14	22
6:8, 9	49	18:23	94
8:7	88	19:11	72
17:16	102	20:6	93
		20:21	59
JUDGES		20:22	31
2:1	58	21:15 (21:14)	25, 31, 59
5:18	97	23:20	25
7:13	71	24:21	59
8:19	74	25:43	101
13:7	24	26:16	22
13:23	137	26:21	128
14:10	56, 57	28:20	45
14:16	101	28:22	112
18:4	79	31:7	16
19:18	21		
20:44	22	**II SAMUEL**	
21:25	56, 57	1:4	17
		3:11	99
RUTH		3:16, 24	93
1:13	77	3:30	127
1:17	148	3:34	99
2:11	63	5:24	45
2:12	121	7:7	21
2:22	118	7:28	15, 17

Verses	Page Numbers		Verses	Page Numbers
11:11	148		5:20	135, 136
11:15	22		8:13	18, 19
12:23	73		10:5	124
13:36	21		20:1	97
14:5	110			
17:5	27		I Chronicles	
18:14	131		12:33 (12:32)	77
19:5	21			
20:21	73		II Chronicles	
23:15	24		24:14	95
24:22, 23	37			

I Kings

Verses	Page Numbers
1:2	83
1:11	38
1:33-35	39
1:35	38, 39
2:1	98
2:3	97
3:1	98
3:3	112
3:7	94
3:16	58, 59 108
4:14	22
7:8	45
8:1	58
8:1, 2	108
8:26	83
8:27-28	115
8:47	123
10:21	23
12:16	24
13:8	77
13:33	81, 82
15:23	22
17:25	22
18:17	27
18:29	98
18:32	19
20:8	81
22:8	83
22:30	92

II Kings

Verses	Page Numbers
1:3	23
4:43	92
5:10	91, 92

Ezra

Verses	Page Numbers
1:3	81, 82

Nehemiah

Verses	Page Numbers
2:2	93

Esther

Verses	Page Numbers
7:2	82, 83
8:8	97

Job

Verses	Page Numbers
1:1	124
1:3	22
1:15	27
3:13	18
5:7	101
7:9	47
7:13-14	135
8:12	23
9:2	24
10:14	135
11:18	15
18:21	125
22:12	128
24:19	102
34:5	44
34:29	102

Psalms

Verses	Page Numbers
1:1	47
1:2	19, 55, 56
2:3	81
3:8	19
4:7 (4:6)	17

VERSES	PAGE NUMBERS	VERSES	PAGE NUMBERS
4:9 (4:8)	80, 81	SONG OF SONGS	
9:21 (9:20)	119	1:8	22
14:7	84		
16:3	124	ISAIAH	
17:12	60	1:2	50, 115
20:4	77	1:3	46
24:3	77	1:3-4	45
24:10	24	1:4	31
25:2	80	1:7	72
27:2	27, 40	1:9	75, 137
31:7 (31:6)	44	1:11	57
31:15 (31:14)	44	1:15	15
32:3	131	1:16, 17	92
40:6	23	1:18	76, 81, 142
41:7 (41:6)	135	1:19, 20	139
44:27 (44:26)	90	1:20	20
46:3 (46:2)	98	2:2	51, 52
49:18	24	3:7	128
51:14 (51:12)	57, 90	3:15	24
55:15 (55:14)	56	3:16	128
56:3	20	4:3-4	45
67:7	42	4:4	139, 147
81:14-15 (81:13-14)	75, 138	5:2	110
103:5	16	5:4	24
110:5	42	5:5	116
119:113	47	5:6	99
119:136	127	5:9	23
119:137	15	5:11	132
126:2	17	5:13	42
139:14	20	5:19	77
139:19	25	5:20	25
		6:1	27
PROVERBS		6:8	21, 76
1:28, 29	128	6:9	26, 84, 85, 86
3:7	81	6:9, 10	84, 85, 86
8:17	57	6:13	97
19:8	97	7:11	91, 93, 94
22:23	20	7:13	94
25:16	135	7:14	27
		8:7	116
ECCLESIASTES		8:8	42, 116
1:16	115	9:1	42
3:4	95	9:5 (9:6)	11, 68
5:4	118	9:6	17
5:15	102	10:3, 4	31
7:14	130	10:28	42
12:6	84		

VERSES	PAGE NUMBERS	VERSES	PAGE NUMBERS
10:33	40	5:7	24
11:1-12:6	69	6:4	59
11:8	40	7:12	122
11:9	44	12:3	50
14:6	23	16:13	21
15:9	44	22:10	63
22:13	92	22:19	21
24:13	139	22:29	25
28:2	42	23:14	92
28:4	131	28:9	120
28:13	113, 116	30:21	76
28:25	139	31:36, 37	141
31:8	27	31:37	112
34:13	16	33:20, 21	141
37:16	27	42:2	17
37:28	94	46:16	63
38:10	80	52:7	31
40:7	47		
40:30	112	**LAMENTATIONS**	
41:7	21		
42:1	124	1:19	129
43:3, 4	127		
44:12	68	**EZEKIEL**	
45:14	82		
45:21	81, 82	17:21	22
46:4	101, 111, 129	23:15	63
47:1	15	40:1	131
49:3	121		
49:6	115	**HOSEA**	
50:4	21	3:5	80
51:12	60	4:3	50
52:13-53:12	80	4:6	42
52:14, 15	102	7:4	98
53:1	75	11:4	82
53:1, 2	110, 128	11:9	80
53:5	18	13:14	78, 79, 80
53:10	44	14:5 (14:4)	57
53:12	42		
55:1	23, 102	**JOEL**	
55:7	96	1:6	23
62:1	60	1:15	25
65:1	126	1:20	16
JEREMIAH		**AMOS**	
3:8	127	1:3	127
3:20	102	2:16	20

DATE DUE

OCT 9 '67			
NOV 7 '67			
NOV 21 '67			
NOV 18 70			
DEC 1 70			
JUN 2 2 '82			
GAYLORD			PRINTED IN U.S.A.

Secrecy

Books by Daniel Patrick Moynihan

Miles to Go: A Personal History of Social Policy

Pandaemonium: Ethnicity in International Politics

On the Law of Nations

Came the Revolution: Argument in the Reagan Era

Family and Nation

Loyalties

Counting Our Blessings: Reflections on the Future of America

A Dangerous Place

Ethnicity: Theory and Experience (editor, with Nathan Glazer)

Coping: Essays on the Practice of Government

The Politics of a Guaranteed Income

On Equality of Educational Opportunity (editor, with Frederick Mosteller)

Toward a National Urban Policy (editor)

On Understanding Poverty: Perspectives from the Social Sciences (editor)

Maximum Feasible Misunderstanding: Community Action in the War on Poverty

The Defenses of Freedom: The Public Papers of Arthur J. Goldberg (editor)

Beyond the Melting Pot: The Negroes, Puerto Ricans, Jews, Italians, and Irish of New York City (with Nathan Glazer)

Books by Richard Gid Powers

The History of the FBI (forthcoming)

Not Without Honor: The History of American Anticommunism

Secrecy and Power: The Life of J. Edgar Hoover

G-Men: Hoover's FBI in American Popular Culture

Handbook of Japanese Popular Culture (editor, with Hidetoshi Kato)

DANIEL PATRICK MOYNIHAN

Secrecy

THE AMERICAN EXPERIENCE

Introduction by Richard Gid Powers

YALE UNIVERSITY PRESS   NEW HAVEN & LONDON

Published with assistance from the Kingsley Trust Association
Publication Fund established by the Scroll and Key Society of
Yale College.

Designed by James J. Johnson and set in New Aster Roman by
The Composing Room of Michigan, Inc.
Printed in the United States of America.

Library of Congress Cataloging-in-Publication Data

Moynihan, Daniel P. (Daniel Patrick), 1927–
    Secrecy : the American experience / Daniel Patrick Moynihan ;
introduction by Richard Gid Powers.
        p.   cm.
    Includes bibliographical references and index.
    ISBN 0-300-07756-4 (alk. paper)

    1. Official secrets—United States—History—20th century.
    2. Executive privilege (Government information)—United States—
History—20th century.   3. Security classification (Government
documents)—United States—History—20th century.   I. Title.
JK468.S4M68   1998
352.3'79—dc21   98-8144

A catalogue record for this book is available from the British Library.

The paper in this book meets the guidelines for permanence
and durability of the Committee on Production Guidelines
for Book Longevity of the Council on Library Resources.

10   9   8   7   6   5   4   3   2

For Irving and Bea Kristol

Contents

Acknowledgments   ix

Introduction, *by Richard Gid Powers*   1

CHAPTER 1. Secrecy as Regulation   59

CHAPTER 2. The Experience of World War I   81

CHAPTER 3. The Encounter with Communism   110

CHAPTER 4. The Experience of World War II   125

CHAPTER 5. The Bomb   135

CHAPTER 6. A Culture of Secrecy   154

CHAPTER 7. The Routinization of Secrecy   178

CHAPTER 8. A Culture of Openness   202

Notes   229

Index   255

Acknowledgments

This work would not have been possible without the un-precedented assistance provided by members of the intelligence community in all its many branches. I am particularly indebted to William P. Crowell and Robert Louis Benson of the National Security Agency, Michael Warner of the Center for the Study of Intelligence of the Central Intelligence Agency, and Kevin B. Wilkinson of the Federal Bureau of Investigation. Meredith Gardner, who on December 20, 1946, deciphered the Venona cable which first opened the whole world of Soviet espionage in the United States, was an inspiration throughout.

John Earl Haynes of the Library of Congress kept coming up with treasures from the archives. Robert A. Katzmann of the Brookings Institution and the Georgetown University Law Center was a counselor of gentle wisdom combined with relentless rigor.

Eric R. Biel, Michael J. Lostumbo, Richard F. Bland, Joshua A. Brook, and Margaret B. Sloane were endlessly supportive, as was, as ever, Eleanor Ann Suntum.

Introduction

Richard Gid Powers

Secrecy is the first essential in affairs of the State.
—Cardinal de Richelieu

Every thing secret degenerates, even the administration
of justice; nothing is safe that does not show how it can bear
discussion and publicity.
—Lord Acton

One more thing, adds Senator Daniel Patrick Moynihan: "Secrecy is for losers."

Americans, we are told, love and admire winners, hate and despise losers. That on no less an authority than general and historian George S. Patton, Hollywood revised spectacular version. Why, then, did the American government, the hands-down winner in the global battles of the twentieth century, draw the veil of official secrecy over a large measure of its Cold War deliberations and decisions? And why has it clung to that system of Cold War security long after the war ended, and ended in a victory far more complete than ever imagined, even by that confident first generation of cold warriors?

Senator Moynihan, bringing a lifetime of experience as statesman and social scientist to bear on the problem, has examined the origins, growth, and significance of secrecy in American government. In this remarkable book, he proposes that governmental secrecy may be seen as a dark thread connecting and explaining some of America's most disastrous Cold War policies. In tracing the history of the American security system, he shines a new light on some of the most familiar, even legendary, events of the Cold War and reveals the critical significance of others that deserve to be better known. Drawing on hitherto unavailable files of the FBI and on discussions with architects of American Cold War policies, he argues that the most baleful consequences of the Cold War—the fissure in American culture that developed during the McCarthy period and the fathomless debts accumulated during the arms buildup of the Reagan years—could have been avoided had it not been for the secrecy that concealed from the American people what the government knew and what it did not know.

How, then, did the United States of America stumble into the shadows of a secrecy system that still produces more than 6 million classified documents a year and that pokes and prods some 3 million individuals to certify their worthiness to be trusted with papers stamped Confidential, Secret, and Top Secret? It has been estimated (by Moynihan, in fact) that if every newspaper in the United States devoted its every page to printing the classified documents produced by the government on that day alone, there would be room for nothing else. "Dear Abby" would bite the dust, along with Doonesbury and the baseball scores.

How, Moynihan asks, has this pervasive system of secrecy affected America's efforts to protect its interests abroad and its democracy at home? And how can the country free itself from the Cold War legacy of a culture of secrecy that so obviously mocks any pretensions to self-government and an open society?

A manuscript does not often arrive in a bottle on the beach. Every book has its history, and the genesis of this one is particularly interesting.

Senator Moynihan's career in government could hardly have been better designed to equip him with the ideas and the experience he would need for this study. Most pertinent, of course, was his eight-year term (from February 1977 until January 1985) on the newly established Senate Select Committee on Intelligence, for the last four years as vice chairman. During those last years Moynihan was, along with committee chairman Barry Goldwater, among the few to whom Director of Central Intelligence William Casey was supposed to unveil his secrets. At one key moment during the Iran-Contra affair, Casey did not unveil, lied about mining the harbor of the Nicaraguan capital, and Moynihan resigned. (He returned when Casey apologized and promised to mend his ways.) On the gravity of the Iran-Contra crisis, as it darkened and deepened and spread, Moynihan agrees with Theodore Draper: "If ever the constitutional democracy of the United States is overthrown, we now have a better idea of how this is likely to be done."[1] It was a brush, almost a collision, with disaster, all brought on by the ability of the national security agencies (here the CIA and the National Security Council) to keep their activities secret—not from the enemy, which was well aware it was being mined, shot at, and otherwise discomforted, but from elected officials in the United States with the constitutional right and duty to know what was going on.

It is not to be thought that Moynihan entered (or left) the intelligence oversight committee an adversary of the secret agencies of national security. After his statutory term of eight years, he received the CIA's Agency Seal Medallion for having demonstrated, in the words of the award, "that effective oversight of intelligence can be realized in a democratic nation without risk to the intelligence process." Nevertheless, it can surely be said that Moynihan's term on the intelligence oversight committee deepened his already lively skepticism about the worth of secrecy in protecting national security and gave him an even livelier interest in the subject of secrecy as a problem in democratic government.

Moynihan recalls developing that skepticism during his days as ambassador to India (1973–75), when he was "incredulous at what the Soviets were getting away with in the 'developing' world."[2] In an article written for Norman Pod-horetz's *Commentary* at about the same time, he argued that what was needed was less reliance on gathering secret information and more on telling the truth about the open realities of life in the Soviet Union and its client states. The American spokesman "should come to be feared in international forums for the truths he might tell."[3] Moynihan put that idea to work as permanent American representative to the United Nations (1975–76), when, as he says, he "got into all manner of disputes with the Soviets *which they started* but which we and the West generally had come to take for granted."[4]

Now it must be remembered that Moynihan (always) was the quintessential liberal anti-Communist. His commitment to that cause survived the Vietnam ordeal, which burnt away the anti-Communism of more than one of his liberal colleagues. (One of the most important connotations of the "neo" in "neoliberal" and "neoconservative"—and Moynihan has been called both—is anti-Communism.) Nevertheless, he had become increasingly skeptical about official Washington's assessments of the Soviet Union that warned of the Soviets' ever-increasing military, political, and economic strength. Moynihan was one of the first prominent Americans to point out that the Soviet empire had no clothes, not to mention no shoes, butter, meat, living space, heat, telephones, or toilet paper. In his view the Soviet Union was so weak economically, as well as so divided ethnically, that it could not long survive. That is just what he wrote in January 1975, though he then thought that the USSR might still "have considerable time left before ethnicity breaks it up."[5] Four years later, but still ten years before the Soviet bloc and the Soviet Union fell apart, he wrote in *Newsweek*: "The Soviet empire is coming under tremendous strain. It could blow up."[6]

It was data available to anyone who wanted to look for it, data that Moynihan examined with the eye of the professor he had once been, that gave him the confidence to make these startling predictions. The Soviets had indeed enjoyed a prodigious growth rate in the fifties, he conceded, but since then the "infrastructure of the Soviet state [had] sickened." From the 1950s to the 1970s the Soviet growth rate had halved, as had the volume of investment. The growth in the workforce was coming to an end, and productivity growth had halted. They were running out of oil. And there was something else thought impossible in modern societies, even in semimodern societies: the Soviet mortality rate was increasing and life expectancy was decreasing, probably because of epidemic alcoholism. Infant mortality was also climbing. And while the economy was collapsing, rising ethnic consciousness was turning the Soviet Union into a tinderbox of nationalisms.[7]

The Soviet Union, Moynihan argued, was dying, but he warned that its death throes could be dangerous. "So long as the [Soviet] economy was growing, the system could put up with the waste of armaments," he argued, "but that time is past." Its leaders might make a lunge for territory in the oil-producing regions "to reverse the decline at home and preserve national unity."[8]

In 1984 Moynihan told graduates of New York University that America "should be less obsessed with the Soviets," because "the Soviet idea is spent—history is moving away from it with astounding speed. . . . It is as if the whole Marxist-Leninist ethos is hurtling into a black hole in the universe. . . . The historical outcome is certain if we can keep the nuclear peace and attend to our own arrangements in a manner that they continue to improve. . . . Our grand strategy should be to wait out the Soviet Union—its time is spent. . . . When the time comes, it will be clear that in the end freedom did prevail."[9] He began to wonder if the end might not actually be at hand. He visited Alexander Solzhenitsyn at the Russian exile's Vermont farm and asked him, "Do you think you'll ever go back?" The novelist replied, "I had assumed I would be back by now."[10]

But, and this is the crucial "but," while Moynihan and

Solzhenitsyn could see that the Soviet Union was flat on its economic back, the men who shaped foreign policy in Washington could not. In the 1980s Moynihan was an observer at the START talks in Geneva. He would question the American negotiators about the Soviet Union's staying power: "When you are through with the mind-boggling details of this treaty with the USSR, what makes you think there will still be a USSR?" He drew blank stares.[11] In 1991 the chief negotiator, Max Kampelman, sent Moynihan an unsolicited letter recalling those exchanges. Kampelman wrote, "Whenever I am asked whether I had predicted the breakup of the Soviet Union or knew anybody who did, I have uniformly stated that the one person who had fully understood and made the correct analysis was you."[12] In 1992 Moynihan remarked within earshot of Henry Kissinger that the government "had failed to see the coming collapse of the Soviets, although some of us did argue it. So let's do better next time." Kissinger went into his "most sarcastic" mode and jeered, "I knew no one, at least I knew no one before this morning, who had predicted the evolution in the Soviet Union."[13] When Moynihan politely sent Kissinger documentation, he received a nice reply. Kissinger stood corrected: "Your crystal ball was better than mine."[14]

One factor that freed Moynihan to see what the policymakers refused to notice may have been his anti-Communism. Moynihan had never believed in the stability of totalitarian states that tried to eradicate the human yearning for freedom. Anti-Communists like Moynihan believed that totalitarian regimes, because they were held together by brute force, were inherently unstable and destined to fall. This was the original rationale of the containment doctrine, although these first principles were forgotten as the Cold War settled into interminable routine. Thus Moynihan had no predisposition to reject evidence that seemed to show the Soviet Union as weak and getting weaker. It was just what he expected.

In contrast, American policy-makers after the 1960s, and perhaps even earlier, tended to be pragmatists who discounted the importance of hearts and minds and concentrated on the facts on the ground. (In the Vietnam era, this frame of mind reached tragically hubristic levels in Secretary of Defense Robert McNamara's use of body counts as an odometer during his drive toward the dark at the end of the tunnel—or was it the light?) Some pragmatic policy-makers were predisposed to believe that the Soviet Union was fundamentally strong: they assumed that centrally planned command economies, because they did not have to produce profits (which went down on the "waste" side of their ledger), were more rational than market economies, and that any setbacks must therefore be only temporary. Other policy-makers seem to have lacked any convictions at all about human nature or the good society, so they were impressed by the muscularity of regimes predicated on power. Or they may have been impressed by the superiority of a utilitarian regime (the greatest good for the greatest number) in harnessing social energies for social goals. For whatever reason, American policy-makers in the 1960s seemed to reject reflexively evidence that conflicted with their belief that the Soviet Union was fundamentally strong and destined to become only stronger.

Why did the presidents and their men get the Soviet economy so wrong, and why were they so confident that they were right? They supposedly had access to the best intelligence of all about the Soviets, that is, secret intelligence. The problem with this intelligence, Moynihan began to suspect, was precisely that it was secret.

Moynihan was onto something: secret information as a weakness in decision making. The CIA, the National Security Agency (NSA), and the other intelligence agencies relied on secret sources of information. Their assumptions, calculations, and ways of manipulating data were just as secret. How impressive. Surely their conclusions had to be more accurate than those of outsiders with no access to classified information. And thus when presidents, national security advisors, and secretaries of state announced that the Soviet economy was soon going to surpass ours, doubters had no opportunity to get their analytic meat hooks into the national security establishment's data and reasoning. Let it be mentioned that the president's Top Secret National Intelligence Estimate was claiming that the Soviet economy was more than 59 percent the size of America's, at a time when the true figure was closer to 33 percent.[15] That is an error of almost 100 percent. Or 50 percent, depending on how you look at it. In any case, as they say at the rifle range, not even on the paper.

Proceeding from these secret assessments of Soviet strength rather than from the openly available facts about the sorry state of the Soviet Union, the Carter and Reagan administrations went on history's greatest peacetime weapons spending spree, and in six years (1982–88) the United States transformed itself from the world's greatest creditor nation into the leading debtor. "While we're not disintegrating," Moynihan wrote in 1990, "we clearly blew an extraordinary economic lead."[16]

Why did American policy-makers make such monumental mistakes? Why did America, facing an adversary gasping out its last breaths, spend itself into debilitating debt, all the while expanding covert operations against Soviet client states until the secret wars recoiled upon us and precipitated a constitutional crisis? The culprit, Moynihan proposed, was secrecy itself. He wrote (in 1990):

> The national security state developed a vast secrecy system which basically hid from us our own miscalculations. The mistakes, you see, were secret, so they were not open to correction. My favorite is the presidential commission chaired by H. Rowen Gaither, a founder of the Rand Corporation, entitled "Deterrence and Survival in the Nuclear Age." It reached President Eisenhower a few weeks after

the launching of *Sputnik* in 1957. The report warned of a missile gap, concluded that the Soviets had surpassed the United States in terms of military effort, and projected a rate of growth for the Soviet economy which would have them passing the United States by 1993. (Their machine-tool production was asserted to be twice ours.) The document, replete with profound error, remained classified until 1973. This is what presidents in the grimmest years of the Cold War knew, and what they knew was mostly wrong.[17]

Like the rest of us, Moynihan likes to be proven right by events, but he could take scant pleasure in pointing out he had told us so: "We will be paying for those mistakes for a long while. We already are. Average weekly earnings in America today are lower than they were when Dwight D. Eisenhower was president. The least we can do is to start dismantling the system that got it so wrong. Dismantle the secrecy system; find honest work for the threat-analysis crowd. Pay a little heed to the needs of America."[18]

And so in January 1993, to find out how and why and at what cost America had moved so much of its government behind the curtain of secrecy, Moynihan introduced legislation for a bipartisan study of the problem. The result, on April 30, 1994, was Public Law 103–236, establishing the Commission on Protecting and Reducing Government Secrecy, with twelve members: half from government, half from private life, four each nominated by the president, the Senate, and the House. Moynihan was chairman of the commission, Representative Larry Combest of Texas, vice chairman.[19]

The commission held thirteen formal meetings and programs between January 10, 1995, and December 12, 1996. Members and staff made seventy-five visits and presentations where they gathered more information and spread the word about their study. They visited the Central Intelligence Agency, the National Security Agency, the Federal Bureau of

Investigation, the army, the air force, the Department of Defense Security Institute, the Department of State, the presidential libraries, the American Historical Association, and the national archives. They even interviewed convicted spies at the Lewisburg and Allenwood federal penitentiaries in Pennsylvania. All told, the commission interviewed more than ninety-six agencies, corporations, and organizations and more than three hundred individuals, among them some of the country's best-known historians, policy analysts, and journalists.

On March 3, 1997, the commission issued its report, endorsed by all its members. The commission had, it stated, fulfilled its statutory mandate, which was to propose reforms designed to reduce the volume of classified information, thereby strengthening the protection of information that had been legitimately classified, and to improve existing personnel security procedures. In designing these proposals it had sought to ensure both the guarding of information where there is a sound basis for its protection and the timely disclosure of the information where there is not, or where the cost of maintaining its secrecy outweighs the benefits.

The report declared, in its first sentence, "It is time for a new way of thinking about secrecy."[20] There followed, in the lively plain English that is supposed to be the standard in government documents but seldom is, a comprehensive analysis of the federal government's apparatus for designating documents as secret and providing security clearances for those authorized to read them. In large measure, the report was an institutional history of the security system: an analysis of the legislative acts and executive orders from which the security system evolved, the record of previous studies and commissions that had tried to reform the system, and an assessment of the effectiveness of the current system in its primary mission of protecting the nation's vital secrets.

The commission concluded that the government's security system was classifying far too many documents at every stage, at far too great a cost, and that vital secrets were not adequately protected because of the vast volume of needlessly classified materials. Secrecy also had intangible costs in the erosion of public confidence in government, because so much of the government secrecy served only to protect the careers and reputations of policy-makers, without any clear justification in terms of national security.

The report recommended that government classification and declassification programs be given, for the first time, a statutory basis that set up uniform classifying procedures across the government to weigh the public benefit gained by openness against any possible damage to national security. The commission also recommended that the current procedures for granting security clearances be brought up to date to reflect how American society has changed since the procedures were instituted and that those procedures be given a statutory basis to protect both the interests of government and the civil liberties of citizens. In short, the commission issued a plea for common sense in security matters by restricting secrecy to material that truly needed to be kept secret, while opening up all other government records to the public.

The commission made six formal recommendations.

- Information shall be classified only if there is a demonstrable need to protect the information in the interests of national security.
- The president shall establish procedures for the classification and declassification of information.
- In decisions about whether information should be classified, the benefit from public disclosure shall be weighed against the need for secrecy. Where there is significant doubt, the information shall not be classified.
- Information shall remain classified for no longer than ten years, unless the agency specifically recertifies the

need for continued secrecy. All information shall be de-classified after thirty years, unless it is shown that demonstrable harm will result.
- There shall be no authority to withhold information from Congress.
- A national declassification center shall be established to coordinate, implement, and oversee declassification.[21]

While the commission was still gathering its materials and Moynihan was searching for the most effective way of presenting the commission's findings, he was asked to write an introduction to a new edition of *The Torment of Secrecy,* the McCarthy-era classic by sociologist Edward Shils.[22] While rereading Shils's outraged description of how the modern security system was imposed at the beginning of the Cold War, Moynihan discovered not only the theme of the commission's report but also the germ of the book you hold now in hand.

As Moynihan read Shils's work, he began to think as a social scientist about the problem of secrecy. Moynihan has a Ph.D. in government from the Fletcher School of Law and Diplomacy at Tufts University and has taught the social sciences at a number of universities, including Harvard. *Beyond the Melting Pot,* which he wrote with Nathan Glazer, is a classic study of American ethnicity and, among sociological studies of American culture, the tenth best-selling sociology book in American publishing history.[23]

Moynihan realized how social scientific theory could provide a unifying perspective to organize the commission's extremely disparate findings. Drawing on Max Weber and Emile Durkheim, he saw how he could discuss secrecy as a form of regulation (Weber) that could often take a ritualistic form (Durkheim) in order to stigmatize outsiders and critics (as distinguished from the functional secrecy that seeks simply to keep critical information from the enemy). The influence of these ideas is immediately felt in the commission's published report. In Moynihan's foreword to

Shils's book, he wrote, "I would hold that secrecy is best understood as a form of regulation."[24] The commission report, after calling for a new way of thinking about secrecy, suggests that the solution might be to consider secrecy "a form of government regulation."[25]

As we have seen, Moynihan had long been thinking about why American policy-makers had been so wrong in their evaluations of Soviet society and the Soviet economy. Shils's analysis of the impact of secrecy on science made him wonder if therein might lie the answer not only to that question but to many other Cold War puzzles.

Although Shils was a social scientist, when he examined the impact of secrecy on the sciences, for the most part he discussed only the physical sciences. Moynihan's attention was drawn to Shils's impatient and even irritated insistence that there really were no scientific secrets to be protected from the enemy, that the statement of a problem—the order to build a nuclear bomb, for example—is in itself for the engineer or the scientist a statement of the solution. More than that: because scientific progress depends on the open exchange of ideas, secrecy in science actually is a debilitating handicap to those enmeshed in its webs.

Moynihan realized that the most pressing intelligence problems of the Cold War had really been questions for the social scientist. How dynamic was the Soviet Union? What was the strength of its economy? How stable was its social order and its ethnic structure? Here secrecy was an even greater obstacle to research than it was in the physical sciences. In fact, secrecy made scientific investigation of these problems impossible, since, in order to be scientific, analysis requires that information be available to all for criticism and reevaluation. By this time Moynihan was accumulating more examples of how American policy-makers had relied on information that could have been exposed at the time as ludicrously wrong. In 1986 the CIA had claimed that the East Germans had a greater per capita production than did the West Germans. He found a Swedish economist who wrote in 1988 that the CIA had been claiming that the Soviet Union's per capita national income was higher than Italy's: "Anyone who has visited both countries should be able to see for himself that such a statement is absurd."[26]

Moynihan's thinking about Shils shaped the commission's finding that "secrecy has significant consequences for the national interest when, as a result, policy-makers are not fully informed, government is not held accountable for its actions, and the public cannot engage in informed debate." Shils's essay also informed the committee's recommendation that the government should change its security procedures to weigh the benefits of openness against the needs of security: "Greater openness permits more public understanding of the government's actions and also makes it more possible for the government to respond to criticism and justify those actions. It makes free exchange of scientific information possible and encourages discoveries that foster economic growth. In addition, by allowing for a fuller understanding of the past, it provides opportunities to learn lessons from what has gone before—making it easier to resolve issues concerning the government's past actions and helping to prepare for the future."[27]

Many of the ideas that Moynihan developed while thinking about secrecy and the social sciences could be used to give shape and direction to the commission's work. Others clearly could not. He could now see, for example, that the government's security system and the top policy-makers' reliance on secret sources of information had made them the victims of bad science, the social scientific equivalent for Americans of the Lysenkoism that had made Stalin's biology a laughingstock. Moynihan was moving in the direction of a comprehensive study of official secrecy in America and its impact on modern American history, but this would have transcended the statutory purpose of the commission: to make concrete proposals to protect and reduce secrecy. And a narrative history of controversial events was not the sort of project often successfully accomplished by a committee, particularly a committee on its way, Moynihan hoped, to a unanimous report.

Shils had also started Moynihan thinking about another way secrecy had damaged the United States during the Cold War. Shils's book described and denounced America's exaggerated, even hysterical, reaction to postwar revelations about Soviet espionage. Shils analyzed McCarthyism and the loyalty programs of the Truman and Eisenhower administrations as populist, anti-intellectual rituals of symbolic secrecy. They were intended to stigmatize and silence an elite inconveniently skeptical about the threat of domestic Communism and opposed to the right-wing anti-Communist goal of repressing the radical Left. Moynihan, as a liberal anti-Communist, shared Shils's contempt for McCarthyism, but he also began to wonder about McCarthyism's flip side: the reaction against McCarthy that took the form of a modish anti-anti-Communism that considered impolite any discussion of the very real threat Communism posed to Western values and security. Might less secrecy have prevented the liberal overreaction to McCarthyism as well as McCarthyism itself?

For some time Moynihan had known about the Venona intercepts, the coded transmissions between Moscow and its espionage network in America during World War II, intercepted and decoded by the army's Signals Security Agency at Arlington Hall in northern Virginia. Moynihan had encouraged the CIA to release the intercepts, and he gave the speeches that opened and closed the 1996 conference marking the publication of the NSA-CIA history of the Venona project.[28]

The Venona intercepts contained overwhelming proof of the activities of the Soviet spy networks in America, complete with names, dates, places, and deeds. Moynihan thought about what might have happened after the war if the government had revealed all it knew about Soviet espionage and the complicity of the American Communist Party before the Communist issue degenerated into a controversy over civil liberties. Instead, the project had been kept secret to prevent the Russians from learning that we had broken their codes. (They already knew, thanks to a spy among the code-breakers and thanks also to Soviet spy Kim Philby, British intelligence's liaison to the American intelligence services, whom the proud code-breakers had invited to tour Arlington Hall.) "What if the American government had disclosed the Communist conspiracy when it first learned of it?" Moynihan asked. That might have "informed the legitimately patriotic American left that there was, indeed, a problem that the Federal Bureau of Investigation, for example, was legitimately trying to address. But this did not happen. Ignorant armies clashed by night."[29]

Here was something worth thinking about: how government secrecy had kept Americans from understanding the real (but limited) extent of Soviet espionage in America and had therefore left them at the mercy of charlatans like McCarthy, for whom ignorance was no impediment to passionate intensity. Add this to the previous question of how secrecy had kept us from recognizing the sorry state of Soviet society and its economy, beguiling us into a new and expensive arms race when watchful waiting would have accomplished the same end at much less cost: these were vital matters scarcely capable of being adequately discussed in a bipartisan committee report. And so Moynihan embarked on his own exploration of the origin and growth of the American secrecy system and its impact on Cold War America. The result was an eighty-six-page appendix to the commission report, "Secrecy: A Brief Account of the American Experience."

But that was not to be the end of the story. Moynihan's appendix to the commission report had given him a chance to trace the history of official secrecy from World War I to the end of the Cold War and how the secrecy system had had disastrous consequences for American society. But there were still unanswered questions. How much had the American government actually known about Soviet espionage at the outset of the Cold War? And why had President Truman not been informed about the Venona intercepts, when the information they contained might have kept him from ignoring the problem of Communist infiltration of the government and so handing the issue over to McCarthy and his gang? The answers were slow in coming from the FBI, but once they arrived, they were astounding. Moynihan now had all the pieces he needed to assemble the story of the American experience with secrecy in the twentieth century. This book is that story.

Secrecy and Memory

America's experience with secrecy during the Cold War was, as Moynihan amply demonstrates, catastrophic. Americans were needlessly diverted from responding sensibly to domestic and international challenges and were led into hysterical and profligate policies that tore the social fabric and the financial balance sheet. Secrecy ceded the issue of domestic Communism to demagogues, while presidents came to rely on estimates of Soviet strength cooked up by spooks protected by secrecy from skeptical questioning. But that story is part of a larger story. If official secrecy had a devastating impact on American history, its impact on Americans' understanding of that history was a collateral disaster.

People are fascinated by secrets. They always have been. Throughout history they have tried to nose out the secrets of the famous and the powerful, speculating that hidden patterns of dark conspiracies control the affairs of men and nations. Normally, these theories of secret conspiracies stay where they belong: on the pages of thrillers by writers with particularly extravagant imaginations; in the minds of individuals of paranoid disposition, usually solitary but sometimes organized into cultlike associations of like-minded confederates; or possibly in the remote regions of the lunatic fringe, where belief in conspiracy theories is expressed in mantralike chants blaming the chosen enemy for whatever ill winds blow.

The key word in the preceding paragraph is "normally." Moynihan has conjured up some of the abnormality of the twentieth century, when unprecedentedly dangerous totalitarianisms with universalistic ambitions provoked apocalyptic responses, responses that at times seemed more rational than the objections of those who protested that the sky was not falling down, at least not exactly or not quite yet.

During times like these, conspiracy theories of history, which feed on official secrecy, climb out of the vasty deeps of politics and jostle for attention like space aliens in the saloon in *Star Wars*. And because of official secrecy, historical writing about the Cold War, both popular and scholarly, came to be permeated with dark suspicions about secret forces concealed by official lies—suspicions that in more reasonable times would have led to challenges that the authors produce their evidence or hold their peace, to put up or shut up.

Moynihan and Shils both noticed how official secrecy during the Cold War took on the overtones of ritual, that is, a performance intended to demonstrate who was in and who was out, who could be trusted and who could not—in other words, who should have the power and who should be powerless. In the beginning the struggle had been along ethnic lines, and the fear was of German Americans and their possible disloyalty; then the fight took on an ideological dimension, as Soviet Russia's American sympathizers were suspected of even more dangerous disloyalties.

A remarkably charismatic triad of concepts—conspiracy, loyalty, and secrecy—had been invited into politics. Before they would be banished—if in fact they are banished, as Moynihan hopes—enormous harm was done to the soul of American politics and to Americans' understanding of their history.

Symbolic secrecy, in the ritualistic sense mentioned above, proclaims that there are those who can be trusted with secrets and those who cannot. As such, it is a powerful tool, enabling dominant groups in government to delegitimize their opponents. But because official secrecy is such an obvious affront to the democratic principle of open government, it takes no great rhetorical skill to turn the weapon of secrecy against those who use it and to insist that public leaders who conceal their deliberations can be up to no good—that they, and not their critics, are the real conspirators against the public weal.

In wartime there is normally no argument but that the enemy is dangerous. The enemy is, after all, shooting in our direction. But the Cold War *was* a cold war; it was possible to argue about how dangerous the enemy was—more or less than the government professed or perhaps not dangerous at all—or whether in fact the enemy was even an enemy. Did official secrets contain proof that the government was erring on the side of insouciance or of hysteria? Or had the government concocted the whole emergency for purposes carefully concealed from the nation?

Official secrecy with its rituals and symbols surged to the surface of American politics during the Cold War. On two momentous occasions, during the brief and deplorable reign of Senator Joseph McCarthy and during the Vietnam crisis, the issue of secrecy took control of political debate in America.

During the early Cold War years, the McCarthyite Right insisted that the government was deliberately concealing FBI files containing proof that Communists had in fact already infiltrated the federal government. McCarthyism would probably have been impossible except for the claim that official secrecy was keeping the American people from the truth about Communism. McCarthy's political demise, which had more to do with his personal character and irresponsible methods than his absurd ideas about conspiracies in high places, permanently discredited the right-wing conspiracy theory of Cold War history, at least within the political mainstream.

Secrecy surged onto the center stage of politics a second time during the late days of the Vietnam War and during the Watergate crisis. Politics in America is at times—maybe most times—a battle for public opinion, but that was particularly true at the height of the debate over the war in Southeast Asia. Secrecy—the insistence that the *real* explanation of events has been concealed from the public—raises the possibility of transforming public opinion by changing perceptions of reality, making the stone rejected (and hidden) by the builder the cornerstone of a new consensus. If the government has sold a policy to the public without disclosing all the policy-makers knew, particularly if what they knew contradicted what they said, then the public would have every reason to reject the official explanation of events and to embrace the alternative. And oh, yes, you may be sure there will be an alternative.

Here is where Cold War historiography came to be infected with the virus of secrecy. In an effort to overturn the official justifications of the Cold War, those protesting the Vietnam conflict produced new histories of the Cold War based not on the documentary history of the Soviet-American conflict, but on what the documents supposedly left out or, more precisely, based on documents kept secret by the security system. The fact of official secrecy became the central affidavit proving the government's guilty complicity in the Cold War. A hunt for official secrets now ensued, as tireless as a beagle's for a rabbit, and secrets became central to the "revisionist" history of the Cold War—the historical view that found Washington primarily responsible for the Cold War.

Moynihan has traced how the system of governmental secrecy developed during the twentieth century and how this secrecy blighted prudent policy making. The documents that he unearthed prove dramatically how secrecy changed the history of the Cold War, and changed it more lamentably than we had suspected.

How could official secrecy have exerted such power that

at key moments it shaped and even transformed American politics? Moynihan and Shils profitably suggest that secrecy's power has roots in the culture of secrecy, in the myths and symbols and rituals produced by decades of guerrilla warfare between conspiracy-minded groups contending on the outer margins of American politics. But there came a moment when the conspiracy theorists' obsession with secrets moved from the margins of politics to the center, and the mere fact that there were official secrets acquired the power to discredit those who made and kept the secrets of the Cold War. Americans began to view their history in a new and unhealthy light: official explanations of Cold War policies were rejected in the conviction that the real explanations were always secret, and secret policies were undemocratic and therefore illegitimate. Now the *revelation* of secrets became a ritual, and eventually this new ritual became as empty, meaningless, and banal as the old rituals of official secrecy.

But it is also a testament to the basic health of the American system that myths, symbols, and rituals will take you only so far. Sooner or later you must produce some facts. And eventually the facts *were* produced. In time, scholars began to examine the supposed secrets of the Cold War, to analyze their contents, instead of merely heaping them up as trophies in the victory of revisionism over Cold War orthodoxy. And when the secrets were unveiled, what surprises they revealed. But surprises should be unwrapped at the right time and the right place, and not before a writer has a chance to perpetuate a modest measure of suspense.

Patterns of Secrecy

Secrecy sells. If secrets aren't interesting, nothing is. Open a database on recently published books and search for titles that contain the word "secrets" or "secrecy," and you will find hundreds, even thousands. (In the interest of full disclosure: your present writer climbed on the secrecy bandwagon himself, with his biography of J. Edgar Hoover, *Secrecy and Power*. The mysterioso quality of the S-word probably accounted for whatever commercial success it enjoyed.)

The new power that secrecy acquired in the late twentieth century went far beyond its capacity to arouse and momentarily satisfy curiosity. Secrets took on a new significance. They came to be seen as the keys that unlocked the mysteries of history.

In order for secrets to attain such power there would have to be preexisting patterns of interpretation that could meld the individual secrets into a master theory of history. The half century of political strife that preceded secrecy's moment of power during the Cold War supplied those patterns.

The hunt for secret conspiracies to explain historical events is an American tradition of long standing. Readers can consult the writings of Richard Hofstadter, which Moynihan mentions, as well as the works of David Brion Davis.[30] To sample the real, bottled-in-bond article straight from the distiller, you can order a few samples from the John Birch Society backlist, available through a toll-free number. Modern conspiracy theorists are quite up to date, thriving on the Internet.

There had been a few instances before the twentieth century when conspiracies emerged as significant factors in American politics. During the Revolution, patriots worried that the British government was conspiring to abolish Americans' rights as Englishmen. During the anti-Catholic ferment over immigration in the 1840s, the Know-Nothings warned that Jesuits and nuns were planning to seize the government. Before the Civil War, the slave power conspiracy haunted the northern imagination; the South feared Yankees were contriving to encourage slaves to murder their masters in their sleep and to subject their mistresses to even worse fates in those same beds.

When the Communist Revolution swept Russia in November 1917, however, conspiracy theory entered a new phase. The patterns that began to develop prepared the way for secrecy's hold over the American imagination later in the century. It was enough to turn some patriots into paranoids when they learned that Germany had helped Lenin get to Russia and when they saw American radicals applaud as the Bolsheviks pulled Russia out of the war. When, in March 1919, Moscow set up the Communist International, an organization of Communist parties everywhere (the U.S. party included) that was dedicated to world revolution, some Americans decided that they knew then all they would ever need to know about the way the world worked. Anyone who tried to tip the American applecart must be following orders from Moscow.

Events during 1919 and 1920 crystallized the nebulous dread of worldwide revolution. Attorney General A. Mitchell Palmer responded to a wave of political bombings, including one that blasted his Washington, D.C., home, by appointing the twenty-four-year-old J. Edgar Hoover to head a new division at the Justice Department. Hoover's charge was to monitor and, where possible, prosecute political radicals.[31]

The industrious and ingenious Hoover, not content with simply rounding up Communists, organized a mass movement against them, issuing a blizzard of documents promoting the idea that the country faced the threat of a "Radical Network." This was supposed to be a secret conspiracy centering on the American Communist parties and the Bolsheviks' undercover operatives; they were allegedly linked to webs that entangled the entire American reform movement. Hoover reserved his special wrath for the "parlor pinks": wealthy individuals, among them some society ladies, who supposedly underwrote the costs of the revolution.

The grassroots anti-Communists began to produce imaginative charts—Red Webs—that diagrammed the radical movement, tracing the nefarious paths of Moscow's influence over the American Left.[32] But while the Comintern and the American Communists would have liked nothing more than to achieve the sort of power their enemies imagined, those Red Webs never existed except in the dreams and nightmares of Communists and anti-Communists. Nevertheless, the anti-Communists now had their theory and were convinced that government files held the secrets that would prove it. Thus the right wing's obsession with government secrecy.

The American Left simultaneously developed its own conspiracy theory. In the wake of Hoover's Red Scare raids, a group of prominent leftist, liberal, and civil libertarian lawyers associated with the National Civil Liberties Bureau (later the American Civil Liberties Union) published their *Report upon the Illegal Practices of the United States Department of Justice*. Citing the widespread and undeniable abuses of aliens' rights during the Red Scare raids, the lawyers charged that the Justice Department was the instrument of a conspiracy against the constitutional rights of all Americans.[33]

That document may be regarded as the blueprint for the Left's analog to the Red Web theory: that there existed a vast right-wing conspiracy against the Left, an unconstitutional, well-organized campaign that included big business, the police, the military, and right-wing civic groups, coordinated by J. Edgar Hoover and his antiradical division within the Justice Department. Because the Nazis would wear brown shirts, let us follow historian Leo Ribuffo and call it the Brown Web theory.[34]

When the ACLU persuaded Attorney General Harlan Stone in 1924 to order J. Edgar Hoover, now the newly appointed director of the Bureau of Investigation (after 1935 the FBI), to end surveillance of American Communists and radicals, right-wing countersubversives were convinced that the Red Web had extended its power into the White House and that the ACLU was the conspiracy's legal front.

During the 1930s historical events produced such rich fare for conspiracy theorists that they became almost giddy from too much food for thought, if such imaginings warrant the name of thought. First, the decade produced a political movement that looked to right-wing conspiracy theorists precisely like their image of the Red Web. After Hitler's triumph in Germany in 1933, followed by the liquidation of the German Communist Party (once the pride of the world movement), Stalin ordered Communist parties everywhere to ally themselves with anyone who would fight Hitler. The resulting Popular Front created an alliance between genuinely independent organizations in the arts, education, and the labor movement together with others claiming to be independent but actually controlled by the party.

Right-wing conspiracy theorists went gaga. Witness the fantastic Elizabeth Dilling's *The Red Network* and *The Roosevelt Red Record and Its Background* and J. B. Matthews's less fanciful but still extravagant *Odyssey of a Fellow Traveler*. The most authoritative evaluation of the Stalinist penetration of America was Eugene Lyons's *Red Decade*. Lyons's judgments about the considerable but not unlimited control that the party exerted over American culture and institutions during the 1930s were later extended, expanded, and confirmed by Daniel Aaron and William O'Neill.[35]

The Red Web theory was also promoted by the House Un-American Activities Committee (HUAC) under Texas congressman Martin Dies, Jr., whose hearings did provide some accurate information about Communist penetration of American institutions, but information so thoroughly mixed with the irresponsible maunderings of conspiracy theorists that the true and useful reports were discredited.

Whereas the Right uncritically absorbed the Dies committee's reports as incontrovertible evidence of Red Web conspiracies, HUAC's excesses caused other fair-minded Americans to regard any investigation of the Communist Party as Red-smearing intended to discredit progressive reform and the entire Roosevelt administration. Anti-Communism came in some quarters to be regarded as a fascist plot, the au courant term for the old Brown Web.

The Left's fear of fascist plots was fanned to a fever pitch after Hitler's invasion of Poland. President Roosevelt had Director Hoover announce that the FBI had once again begun to surveil Communists, Nazis, and other extremists. The Left snapped to attention: Hoover was on their trail again, the same Hoover who had indiscriminately Red-Webbed the entire Left during the Red Scare.

As Europe careened into world war and Americans debated whether the United States should come to the aid of Great Britain, the two conspiracy theories of the Red Web and the fascist plot chased each another like the gingham dog and the calico cat of the old nursery rhyme. Isolationists like Charles Lindbergh painted a menacing portrait: Jews, the British, and the Roosevelt administration were conspiring to pull America into the war. Interventionists, far more effectively, published "exposés," such as John Roy Carlson's *Undercover*, that construed contacts between isolationists and the Nazi propaganda machine as evidence that isolationism was a pro-Nazi, anti-Semitic conspiracy to turn America over to Hitler.[36]

Pearl Harbor did nothing to halt the conspiracy mongering. Isolationists attached themselves to the cause of Pearl Harbor commanders Admiral Husband E. Kimmel and General Walter C. Short, charging that Communists in the administration had maneuvered America into the war to rescue Stalin. The administration joined the interventionists in smearing critics of its war policies as Hitler sympathizers. In 1944 the Justice Department put a motley crew of prewar isolationists on trial for sedition, charging that they were part of an international Nazi conspiracy.[37]

As the Cold War began, then, two mirror-image conspiracy theories had sidled into American politics, the Red Web and the Brown, each with passionate adherents at the opposite extremes of the political spectrum. Informed opinion rejected them both as hallucinations induced by the sulfuric air of politics sealed off from the bracing oxygen of open debate, but these conspiracy theories lurked in the background of politics, awaiting political conditions when the public's attention would shift from the surface of government to its hidden secrets.

The first of these to reemerge was the Red Web. It was carried into the political mainstream by Senator Joseph McCarthy, whose brain was knocked so off kilter by the dazzling revelations of conspiracy theories that he could harangue an astounded Senate with the news that General George C. Marshall was a Communist traitor at the center of "a conspiracy so immense" as to dwarf any in history.

McCarthy would have been nothing without government secrecy. He was able to gain hearing for his fantastic charges only because he could claim that the evidence to support them was kept hidden by the executive branch. Every time he requested classified documents from the government and they turned out to discredit his charges, he simply moved on to new and even more fantastic allegations— the supply of secrets for him to exploit was inexhaustible.[38] Senator Moynihan has even suggested that McCarthyism might not have appeared had the security agencies revealed to the president, and the president to the country, the full and somewhat disappointing facts about the spy menace: that it existed, that it was small, that it had been thoroughly investigated by the FBI. A poignant thought.

McCarthy's run was brief but gaudy. His televised disgrace in 1954 permanently discredited the Red Web and its adherents. After McCarthy, right-wing conspiracy theories would lead a weird half life in American politics, kept alive by a few adherents on the lunatic fringe. In the future they would emerge into the public spotlight only when lugubriously dragged there by mainstream politicians intent on exploiting the public's fear of secret plots and conspiracies while posing as the public's moderate protectors against extremism.

Thus Senator Milton Young of North Dakota rose in 1961 to inform a startled nation that a mysterious figure named Robert Welch, head of an equally mysterious group called the John Birch Society, had written a bizarre biography of Dwight Eisenhower that contained an astounding charge: the war hero and president was a "conscious, dedicated agent of the Communist conspiracy."[39] In a flash the media threw itself into the sort of wild-eyed furor that would later be called a feeding frenzy. What kind of a menace was this maniac Welch? What kind of threat to the republic did this Birch Society represent? And how dangerous was this bizarre cult that, according to an investigation by the California attorney general, was made up of "wealthy businessmen, retired military officers, and little old ladies in tennis shoes"?[40] It certainly sounded bad.

Politicians now took advantage of the John Birch panic to launch an attack on extremism, by which they meant right-wing conspiracy theorists. The Kennedy and Johnson administrations argued that only moderates like themselves, not the conservative opposition (read "extremists"), should be trusted with nuclear weapons. Senator J. William Fulbright pressured Secretary of Defense Robert McNamara to abolish the military's anti-Communist indoctrination programs, which Fulbright charged were producing an army of extremists. Walter Reuther wrote a memo that appealed to the president for a government attack on the extremist Right.[41]

Hollywood pitched in with films like *Seven Days in May* and *Dr. Strangelove* (both 1964) that exploited the liberal nightmare of a nation helpless before malevolent right-wing extremists with a power base in the military. President Eisenhower's valedictory warning about the military-industrial complex, originally meant to caution against the weapons industry's undue influence in politics and culture, was reinterpreted as a revelation of a conspiracy by the military and the big industrialists to subvert democracy.

The fear of right-wing conspiracies was used with devastating effect against Barry Goldwater during his 1964 presidential campaign. Goldwater's opponents for the Republic nomination portrayed him as a tool of the extremists. Nelson Rockefeller called him a dupe and a puppet of sinister right-wing forces. When Goldwater vacationed in Germany before the Republican convention, CBS correspondent Daniel Schorr claimed that Goldwater was making a spiritual pilgrimage to "Hitler's onetime stamping ground" and that the "American and German right-wings are joining up." CBS News ran a documentary on Goldwater that called him the candidate of "the John Birch Society, the Minute Men, and other extremists."[42]

By the time the Johnson administration began to escalate the Vietnam War, many Americans, particularly liberals, had developed a vague dread of a danger on the Right—conspiracies and plots by powerful secret forces at the highest echelons of industry and the military. The moment had come when the rituals of secrecy could move into the center of political life.

The Moment of Secrecy

That moment arrived early Sunday morning, June 13, 1971, when the first in an explosive series of stories by Neil Sheehan appeared on the front page of the *New York Times*.[43]

In 1967 Secretary of Defense Robert McNamara had commissioned an official history of the Vietnam involvement, a massive project that would become known as the Pentagon Papers. The project was completed by members of the Pentagon's in-house task force, one of whom was a Harvard-educated former marine named Daniel Ellsberg. An enthusiastic supporter of the war during his tour of Vietnam in 1965 and 1966 as a State Department official serving with the legendary General Edward T. Lansdale, Ellsberg had undergone a conversion into an antiwar activist.

While working on the "Top Secret–Sensitive" Pentagon Papers, Ellsberg became convinced that the record of the government's actual policy making in Vietnam was so greatly at variance with the government's stated rationale that, if the public had a chance to read the Papers, it would demand an end to the war. Ellsberg made an unauthorized copy for himself and began to shop the Papers around to antiwar politicians in Washington.

Then Ellsberg learned that Sheehan, whom he had known in Vietnam, was writing a *New York Times* essay that reviewed thirty books about the war. The title was to be "Should We Have a War Crime Trial?" That got Ellsberg's attention. He brought the Papers to Sheehan. Since Sheehan was convinced the war was a crime, there had to be criminals somewhere. Now he had a massive collection of secret government documents that detailed the decisions leading to that criminal war. Logically, then, these documents should constitute the evidence of official crimes.

The *Times* realized that it had one of the greatest scoops in journalism history. Maintaining absolute secrecy, the newspaper's reporters and editors barricaded themselves in a hotel and began to digest and summarize the huge bulk of documents that Ellsberg had handed over. These were the stories that began to appear in daily installments in the *Times* that Sunday. Government secrets—not what they revealed, but the mere existence of government secrets—would now prove to have the power to change the public's mind about the most controversial political issue of the day.

How did secrets acquire that power? Certainly it was sensational for a major newspaper—or any newspaper—to publish classified documents. It was the height of the Vietnam War, and the secret information that they contained was certainly of enormous interest to the country. Americans could now read a behind-the-scenes, day-by-day account of how the nation's leaders had evaluated conflicting reports from the field, guessed at the best response to confusing battlefield situations, and then urged their policies on the country with a confidence that none of them felt in private. At a minimum, the Pentagon Papers dramatized the old saw that every political decision is a 51–49 proposition but has to be sold as 100 percent certainty.

But as controversy over the war reached a boiling point, minimal interpretations were not on the table. Sheehan's introduction to the edition of the Papers that the *Times* published as a book claimed, "To read the Pentagon Papers in their vast detail, is to step through the looking glass into a new and different world. This world has a set of values, a dynamic, a language, and a perspective quite distinct from the public world of the ordinary citizen and of the two other branches of the Republic—Congress and the judiciary."[44]

Sheehan described the war as something hatched by plotters in deepest secrecy: "The guarded world of the government insider and the public world are like two intersecting circles." Within the secret circle of power, the public and Congress are seen as "elements to be influenced" rather than as participants having a legitimate interest in knowing what the government is planning: "The Papers also make clear the deep-felt need of the government insider for secrecy in order to keep the machinery of state functioning smoothly and to maintain maximum ability to affect the public world."[45] Vietnam policies were made in secret and had to be kept secret from a public that might have questioned, even rejected, them.

Senator Mike Gravel of Alaska, in the introduction to his edition of the Papers, went even further: "The Pentagon Papers tell of the purposeful withholding and distortion of facts. . . . The Pentagon Papers show that we have created, in the last quarter-century, a new culture, a national security culture, protected from the influences of American life by the shield of secrecy."[46]

In a matter of days the Pentagon Papers became the touchstone for a new view of American history: the decisions that shaped the Cold War were secret, and secrecy had protected these policies from a (virtuous) public that would have struck down the miscreants had the truth been known.

This remarkable transformation in popular attitudes, let it be remembered, was caused by a work of forty-seven volumes (the original length of the classified report) that almost no one had read (then or later). This massive government study was then abridged and published first in the lengthy newspaper series, which, again, few people read from beginning to end; then in a 677-page book, the *New York Times* paperback, which almost nobody read in its entirety; and then, finally, in a six-volume set, published by the Government Printing Office, which it would be remarkable if anyone has ever read from cover to cover.

Was there ever a greater illustration of the medium (secrecy) being the message (conspiracy)? Almost none of the minds changed by the Pentagon Papers ever came into contact with the words that supposedly constituted the proof of the conspiracy. Amazing.

Such a miraculous conversion of so many Americans from skeptics about conspiracies to believers in them could have happened only if they were predisposed to be so converted and only if the conversion conferred immediate benefits, if only of the psychological variety. Namely, if they went along with the interpretation of the Pentagon Papers urged by Ellsberg and Sheehan, readers and nonreaders alike could claim that they were not involved in the Vietnam disaster, were not complicit, because they had been kept from full awareness of the facts by government secrecy.

The impact of the Pentagon Papers on the popular mind was reinforced by the Nixon administration's ham-handed effort to keep them secret. Nixon's immediate instinct had been to let the *Times* publish and be damned, since the misdeeds that the Papers revealed, if misdeeds they were, were the work of Democrats. But Henry Kissinger was engaged in negotiations with the Chinese and is said to have persuaded the president that the Chinese wouldn't continue their secret parleys if they saw that Washington couldn't keep *its* secrets.

The government's effort to suppress the Papers seemed to prove that Sheehan and Ellsberg were right: that the Papers revealed guilty secrets about a government conspiracy to lead the country into Vietnam, because otherwise the government would not have tried to stop their publication. Ellsberg was put on trial for illegally possessing and copying classified documents, but the case was dismissed when the White House "plumbers" broke into the office of Ellsberg's psychiatrist and rummaged around for incriminating information. The collapse of the case seemed equivalent to a guilty verdict against the government.

Ironically, it had been liberals like those in the Kennedy and Johnson administrations that had taught the public to fear militarists secretly conspiring to drag the country into apocalyptic military adventures. Now this propaganda recoiled on the liberal architects of the Vietnam War. The Pentagon Papers launched the theory that the war in Southeast Asia (and perhaps the entire Cold War) had been a conspiracy hatched in private by liberal cold warriors who had used governmental secrecy to hide their decisions from the public and to avoid constitutional checks and balances. In their political strategy of posing as the public's defenders against the danger on the Right, "moderates" had built a trap for "extremists" and had stumbled into it themselves.

Opponents of the war, many of them involved from the beginning in the Cold War containment policies that had led finally to Vietnam, now could absolve themselves of guilt: it had not been the constitutional government that had led the country into war, they could now say; it was the secret work of the hidden government. The public had been out of the loop. And so was born a new history of the Cold War. It had been a secret history, and secrecy had brought it into the open.

The Power of Secrecy

Secrecy could achieve such a powerful hold on the American imagination because it became part of a ritual that reapportioned blame for Vietnam and Watergate, absolving some while condemning others. In Washington and in the culture as a whole, there was a political tendency—perhaps a movement—that had an investment in revelations of governmental secrets. Its political power was based on the belief that the secret files concealed guilty secrets that explained the Vietnam disaster and perhaps even the entire course of the Cold War.

An interpretive pattern now existed that could fit isolated secrets into a grand—and chilling—vision of a covert government hiding behind official secrecy, manipulating policy, with nothing but contempt for the will of the electorate and the rules of the Constitution. Revelations of the government's secret activities during the Cold War now fell like hammer blows against the schoolbook image of a constitutional, representative American government. An obvious point, but one worth repeating: we fit facts to our assumptions more than we fit our assumptions to the facts. As American society disintegrated during the final stages of the Vietnam War and the government splintered during the Watergate crisis, secrecy came into its own as a judgment on America's role in the Cold War.

As the revelations proceeded, they became self-interpreting—the simple fact of government secrecy was seen as proof that the government was steered behind the scenes by unknown conspirators. And more revelations that seemed to confirm the conspiracies of a secret government were not long in coming.

On March 8, 1971, a group of antiwar activists (probably the Catholic East Coast Conspiracy to Save Lives) raided the FBI resident agency in Media, Pennsylvania, and made away with the agency's domestic security files. At the end of the month an eighty-two-page extract was printed in the pacifist-socialist journal *WIN*. The files revealed a wide range of FBI activities against the antiwar movement. Hoover's aide Mark Felt said that the raid was "the turning point in the FBI's image," because release of the files justified the New Left's "paranoid fear of the FBI, which it hysterically equated with the Soviet secret police"—a view, he added, that now "seeped into the press and found growing expression among the more bewitched and bothered opinion makers." Even so, the FBI probably could have ridden out the storm if one of the files had not carried the hitherto unknown caption "COINTELPRO." This caught the eye of NBC correspondent Carl Stern, who used the Freedom of Information Act (FOIA) to sue the FBI for all documents dealing with COINTELPRO.[47]

On December 6, 1973, Stern received those documents. He now had evidence of the FBI's most deeply buried secrets: its operations modeled on counterintelligence programs (hence the acronym, from COUNTERINTELLIGENCE PROGRAMS) that used unusual, invasive, and possibly illegal tactics to disrupt first the Communist Party; then the Ku Klux Klan, the Black Panther Party, and the Socialist Worker Party; and, finally, the antiwar movement, with special focus on the Students for a Democratic Society.

Each of these groups could now argue convincingly that its constitutional rights had been violated by the bureau and, less logically but still plausibly (at least to some), that democratic debate had been aborted because their voices had been stifled. In other words, dissent had been defeated, not because its arguments lacked merit, but because of secret and illegal government plots.

Further proof of the new power of secrecy as a force in history came with Richard Nixon's resignation from the presidency. The ultimate political prize had been wrested from the disgraced president because he had been unable to prevent the press and the Congress from exposing the "White House horrors" to public gaze.

The Watergate era saw the normal political process partially eclipsed by a frenzied search for political secrets that, properly handled, could destroy the opposition. The congressional elections of 1974 and 1976 and Jimmy Carter's victory over Gerald Ford in 1976—one of his campaign promises was the vow "never to lie to you"—brought to power politicians who owed their success to the pursuit of secrets and to the public's readiness to interpret secrecy as a pattern of illegal, conspiratorial activity. The hunt for secrets made national heroes and Hollywood stars out of the investigative reporters who dug out those secrets.

In 1975 both houses of Congress lent their authority to investigations based on the thesis that a secret government had been directing the affairs of state during the Cold War. The Senate and House each appointed select committees (under Senator Frank Church and Congressman Otis Pike) to investigate, in the words of the Senate resolution, "the conduct of domestic intelligence or counterintelligence operations against United States citizens" to see whether they threatened "the rights of citizens."[48]

Both committees, armed with the ultimate weapon of the congressional subpoena, tunneled through the files of the FBI, the CIA, and the other national security agencies. The Pike committee, the more aggressive of the two, stirred up so much controversy that its report was suppressed. The Church committee's report was published, however, and it placed an official stamp of legitimacy on the conspiracy theorist's history of the Cold War. The investigators wove together examples of illegal (or at least unsavory) malfeasance by the intelligence agencies, producing a narrative in which the historical context of the security agencies' sins receded and sank below the historical horizon, while the misdeeds themselves were pilloried in isolated ignominy as self-motivated, self-indicting, and self-condemning. The purpose of domestic anti-Communism, it could be said (and was said), was simply to attack the rights of anyone who stood in the way of the government's power elite and its clients. By extension, the purpose of the Cold War abroad was to obliterate those unlucky enough to stand in the way of that elite's global power.

The Church committee made the Vietnam era's antiwar movement represent all dissenting movements of the past. Just as government repression had contributed to the Vietnam disaster, the committee suggested, the repression of earlier dissent had probably contributed to the country's misguided Cold War policies. Arguing backward, the committee held that if the FBI's repression of Vietnam-era dissent was unnecessary and wrong, then so were the bureau's earlier domestic intelligence campaigns. The Church committee complained that "from today's perspective it is harder to understand the nature of the domestic threats to security which, along with foreign espionage, were the reasons for establishing the FBI's intelligence program in the 1930s."[49]

The committee devoted most of its energy to exposing the FBI's COINTELPROS. Dismissing bureau attempts to justify the programs, the select committee flatly stated that COINTELPRO was a "sophisticated vigilante program aimed squarely at preventing the exercise of First Amendment rights of speech and association, on the theory that preventing the growth of dangerous groups and the propagation of dangerous ideas would protect the national security and deter violence." The committee was able to produce ample evidence that Hoover had labored hard to keep these activities secret, and in the post-Watergate era, which saw a cover-up as an admission of guilt, that proved that they were wrong.[50]

The House committee located a disaffected ex-agent who provided the exactly the conclusion the new view of secrecy was driving toward: "The FBI now constitutes a degenerative dictatorship in which the structure still remains but from which public support is rapidly being withdrawn. I further submit that such a dictatorship is incompatible with the constitutional concepts upon which this Nation is founded. I feel that this can be historically paralleled with the ascension of other dictatorships throughout the world."[51] Years later, the definitive study of the Church and Pike committees would be titled *Challenging the Secret Government*.[52]

The CIA also contributed its share of guilty secrets to the cauldron of boiling paranoia. Reporter Daniel Schorr broke the story of CIA assassination plots against foreign leaders, among them Patrice Lumumba of the Congo. Throughout 1975 the *New York Times* and other newspapers followed up with more details on the assassination story: the targets included, besides Lumumba, Ngo Dinh Diem of Vietnam and Rafael Trujillo Molina of the Dominican Republic. There were rumors of plots against Sukarno of Indonesia and Duvalier of Haiti, along with reports on the CIA's involvement with the Mafia in plots against Castro. In none of these cases did proof emerge that the CIA's plans had gone beyond the contingency phase, but the stories indelibly imprinted on the public mind an image of the CIA as a secret murder squad.

In 1973 retired Air Force colonel Fletcher Prouty (Oliver Stone's model for Colonel X in the film *JFK*) published *The Secret Team: The CIA and Its Allies in Control of the United States and the World*. One of his charges was that Allen Dulles had "positioned CIA personnel and agency oriented disciples inconspicuously throughout the Government." Schorr put Prouty on the air to charge that Nixon aide Alexander Butterfield had been the CIA's spy in the White House. The story fell apart when Butterfield convincingly refuted the allegations, but again there seemed to be another glimpse into the secret government.[53]

The power and prestige of the secret as the key to understanding the history of the Cold War now created a new receptivity for Cold War studies that blamed America for the whole ungodly mess. A brilliant group of revisionist historians associated with the so-called Wisconsin school of William Appleman Williams had been charging that the United States had been the guilty party in the breakdown of the wartime alliance with the Soviet Union. Williams's own *Tragedy of American Diplomacy* (1959) had argued that American diplomacy was dominated by the search for commercial markets for American produce and products. Other revisionists followed Williams in discovering that motives far less lofty than altruistic Wilsonianism lay behind American policies at the beginning of the Cold War. Denna Fleming, in *The Cold War and Its Origins* (1961), argued that anti-Communists in the Roosevelt and Truman administrations had sabotaged Roosevelt's plan for friendly relations with the Soviet Union. Gabriel Kolko's *Politics of War: The World and United States Foreign Policy, 1943–1945* made America's anti-Soviet policies during World War II largely responsible for the breakdown of the Soviet-American alliance and the beginning of the Cold War. Lloyd C. Gardner's *Architects of Illusion: Men and Ideas in American Foreign Policy, 1941–1949* concluded that "responsibility for the way in which the Cold War developed, at least, belongs more to the United States." Gar Alperovitz's *Atomic Diplomacy: Hiroshima and Potsdam, the Use of the Atomic Bomb, and the American Confrontation with Soviet Power* argued that the bomb had been dropped on Japan to warn Stalin against interfering with American plans for world empire.[54]

David Horowitz, whose *Free World Colossus: A Critique of American Foreign Policy in the Cold War* (1965) turned the revisionist thesis into a blistering anti-Vietnam polemic, later explained that his book had become standard reading in college history courses because Vietnam had created a hunger for works that discredited the historical justifications for Vietnam. "Cold War revisionism," he said, "that is, accounts of post-war history significantly at variance with the State Department line, was still illegitimate [before 1965]: it had no status as serious scholarship inside or outside the university." But Vietnam and Watergate created an opportunity for "secret histories" of the Cold War to undermine the old Cold War verities by denying the reality of the Soviet threat and questioning the motives behind the containment doctrine.[55]

Anti-Communists mounted a furious attack on the revisionists, questioning their selection of sources and their assumptions about Stalin's intentions. In particular, they noted a "proof by lack of evidence" as a characteristic methodology in revisionist Cold War history.[56] In other words, the revisionists discounted the policy-makers' explanations of events as insincere and dishonest, while deriving their revisionist views from the assumption that the real design of American foreign policy was so discreditable that, if it appeared on paper at all, it did so only on documents kept secret from the American people.

The revisionist historians certainly believed in what they were saying, and they were often researchers who spent their lives combing archives for evidence to support their arguments. In retrospect, however, it can be seen that acceptance of their ideas was the unforeseen (but, naturally, welcome) consequence of the public's general rejection of official explanations around the time of the Pentagon Papers. Revisionism's thesis was hardly sustainable without the assumption that the real explanation of events is always hidden behind a wall of official secrecy.

It was more because of these circumstances than the intrinsic force of their arguments that the revisionists' critique of American policy emerged in the 1970s first as an alternative and then as the dominant view of the Cold War's origins. Anti-Communists were demoralized to see what they had always held to be unassailable truths—the evil and danger of Communism—were now scorned and rejected by some of the brightest, most idealistic minds of the rising generation.

Congress itself avidly pursued more secrets. Bella Abzug of New York hectored the late J. Edgar Hoover's aged secretary, trying to wring from her an admission that the files she destroyed after the director's death were Hoover's long-rumored secret blackmail files. In 1976 the House established the Select Committee on Assassinations. After two years and nearly $5.8 million, the committee was on the verge of concluding that the Warren commission had been basically correct about President Kennedy's assassination, when it received an acoustic interpretation of police radio transmission recordings seeming to indicate that a second gunman had fired shots near the grassy knoll. Chief Counsel G. Robert Blakey, a specialist on organized crime who later achieved fame as the father of the RICO statute, suggested that the assassination was a mob hit and speculated that Santo Traficante of Tampa or Carlos Marcello of New

Orleans, or both, were involved. This was as close as any official body has ever come to endorsing a conspiracy theory on the JFK assassination, but it was soon discovered that the recording was made after the shooting, so that whatever the sounds were, they were not of gunfire.[57]

By the late 1970s a veritable industry had been built on acquiring secret FBI files via the Freedom of Information and Privacy Act and interpreting them as revelations of a secret government in charge of the national destiny. To scholars like Athan Theoharis, who served on the staff of the House Select Committee on Intelligence, we owe much of what we know about the FBI's behind-the-scenes activities under Hoover. But like the Spanish explorers whose geographical discoveries were an unintended consequence of their quest for the chimerical city of El Dorado, the scholars who intended to map the activities of a secret government advanced our historical knowledge without ever locating that secret government. Most of their time was spent digging through the debris left by bureaucrats and politicians reluctant to let the public in on discussions that would have been highly embarrassing if discovered by political enemies.

In some quarters, and they included some influential precincts in the government, the universities, and the media, secrecy became the explanation for almost everything that ailed America: had it not been for their ability to keep their machinations secret, the powers of darkness would not have enjoyed so long a reign. Full disclosure would produce, if not lemonade springs, then at least a golden age of good government devoted to progressive causes, with the swords of the cold warriors morphed into plowshares designed for ecologically sustainable development. Ah, if things were only that simple.

The Banality of Secrecy

Things were not that simple. The election of 1980 brought an unabashed anti-Communist to the White House. The

Cold War was revived and then resolved in one of the most peculiar endgames in history. To extract an analogy from Senator Moynihan's analysis, it was as though two chess grand masters had pursued an interminable and highly sophisticated strategy of feint and counterfeint, not noticing that, for the past forty or fifty moves, one side not only has been in checkmate but has had his queen, rooks, bishops, and knights all taken from the board. Of course, one not inconsiderable detail—that both sides had nuclear weapons—kept the game from being completely boring.

And the secrecy industry rumbled on. The Freedom of Information Act allowed failed and forgotten political activists to validate their identities. The FBI had always been the far Left's excuse for its political failures. Now the FBI provided old radicals with one final service: supplying files that proved a radical movement had actually existed, present appearances to the contrary. They must have had some importance if the FBI had kept tabs on them. The FBI's FOIA office was transformed into a genealogy service for the old Left, and the bureau had to devote major resources to processing files for release. Individuals bragged that they had filed hundreds, thousands, tens of thousands of requests. Every few weeks the media breathlessly revealed that the FBI had been keeping a file on a leftist writer or artist or Hollywood star. Or an FOIA request had revealed that a conservative or sometimes a liberal celebrity had furnished information to the FBI. Horrors!

But the unending revelations of government secrets was beginning to seem forced, clichéd, even a bit pointless. True, we live in an age of hype, but the hype for the latest revelations of government secrets had soared far beyond anything that could be supported by what the files revealed. A collection of the FBI's files on American writers carried the subtitle *The FBI's War on Freedom of Expression*, although the book was a themeless hodgepodge of investigative files, clipping files, cross-reference files, and files established because writers were named during a related or unrelated investigation. Missing was any proof that the FBI had ever established files on writers simply because they were writers. William F. Buckley, Jr., in fact, was moved to protest mildly, "Some of us will stop short of saying that the FBI was engaged in a war against freedom of expression, while agreeing that if that had been Mr. Hoover's intention, he was off to an appropriate start."[58]

Another collection of FBI files on American writers was billed as a shocking account of "the fifty-year espionage campaign waged by the CIA, FBI, and other intelligence agencies against . . . famed American writers." That shock was undercut by the content of the dossiers, which included newspaper clippings lodged in files for want of anywhere else to put them. The documents were less dangerous than ineffectual and a little silly, particularly because for the most part nothing came of them. Most Americans today would deplore the bureau's having accumulated these files. But it is easy after the fact to discount the security agencies' worries about the pro-Soviet sympathies of American artists and intellectuals. At the time, the Soviet Union had been able to mobilize much of the world's intellectual and artistic community against the United States' efforts to contain Stalin, when the success of those efforts was very much in doubt. But even if no allowances are made for the historical emergency that caused the files to be gathered, the dossiers hardly constitute evidence of the claim made in the aforementioned book's subtitle: *The Secret War Against America's Greatest Authors*. Some war. Some secrets.[59]

The ritual of secrecy was running out of steam. The new revelations were falling short of spectacular because the historical crisis (Watergate and Vietnam) was now receding into the past. Because the times no longer provided the public with a way of interpreting secrets, the political significance intended to be drawn from them had to be explicitly provided, and that interpretation had an embarrassing resemblance to the old "fascist plot" conspiracy theory.

A collection of interviews with radicals of the 1930s and

1940s was titled *It Did Happen Here*. "It" was fascism, an allusion to Sinclair Lewis's antifascist novel *It Can't Happen Here*, implying that the Cold War had turned the United States into a fascist country and that this fascist repression had defeated the Left. The Left did not simply lose out in the marketplace of ideas because of the weight of its own errors or because of the affluence of the American working class. "It" could not have simply been that Americans understood and rejected the politics of the interviewees. The title of another oral history of the Cold War, *Memories of the American Inquisition*, insinuated the same charge: the Cold War was simply a pretext for eliminating radicals from American politics, a view echoed in the title of *J. Edgar Hoover and the American Inquisition*. A documentary history of the domestic Cold War was called *The Age of McCarthyism*, thus eliminating the possibility that America's response to Communism was anything except its worst excesses.[60]

Desperation seemed to push some writers into disclosing that their obsessive laceration of Cold War orthodoxy was motivated less by logical reason than by something approaching religious fervor. A history of the Cold War was titled *Losing Our Souls*, although it was pretty clear that by "our souls" the author meant "your souls," that is, the souls of the policy-makers he attacked: "Our Cold War policy, for all its success in dissolving the USSR, was so grievously flawed that the United States may never fully recover from its effects upon our values, our freedoms, our politics, our security, the conditions of our material life, the quality of our productive plant, and the very air we breathe."[61]

Now when headlines (in gradually diminishing type sizes) announced that an FOIA request had revealed that the FBI had maintained a file on someone famous, the press had a vague sense that such things ought to be newsworthy, but it was no longer sure exactly why. Flipping to the more yellowed cards in their Rolodexes, reporters had to depend on aging radicals to vent the appropriate outrage and tie the new revelation into a sweeping indictment of the FBI, the Cold War, or the whole damn country.

By the late 1980s it was becoming difficult to get a hearing for the old fascist-plot theory without hyping it up by linking it to the grand tradition of conspiracy theory. A 1988 edition of I. F. Stone's *Hidden History of the Korean War* strained to justify its republication by placing Stone in the context of conspiracy-minded Roman historians. Stone was praised for connecting secret events into a pattern of the "arcana imperii [imperial secrets]—empire and its method as a hidden thing, shrouded above all from the people it ruled." Stone, the foreword claimed, "described a war in which 'an ephemeral elective occupant' at home [Truman] jousted with an 'ambitious proconsular Caesar abroad' [MacArthur], already plotting to turn against the capital the armies with which he had been supplied to hold distant marches against barbarian hordes."[62] The ad writers for *Star Wars* could hardly have done better.

Secrecy was beginning to evolve from a theme in historical analysis to the status of an aesthetic formula and plot convention in popular entertainment. Most viewers and reviewers scoffed at Oliver Stone's pretensions as a historian, but few could resist the melodramatic excitement that Stone (I. F. Stone's namesake and spiritual heir) drew from the revisionist history of the Cold War. In *JFK* (1991) and *Nixon* (1995), the major events of the century are explained as the results of "black ops": covert operations by hidden conspirators so highly placed that they amount to a secret government that wielded the real power in the Republic, a secret government that Stone calls "the Beast."

JFK wove the Kennedy assassination into the venerable conspiracy theory of the Cold War as an American plot. Stone based his film on New Orleans district attorney Jim Garrison's *On the Trail of the Assassins,* in which Garrison raved: "What happened at Dealey Plaza in Dallas on November 22, 1963, was a coup d'état. I believe that it was instigated and planned long in advance by fanatical anti-Communists in the United States intelligence community . . . and that its purpose was to stop Kennedy from seeking détente with the Soviet Union and Cuba and ending the Cold War."[63] For Stone, the Kennedy assassination was part of a century-long plot to use the threat of Communism to protect the interests of America's ruling class. American anti-Communism was fascism, and it had been secretly running the country since World War II.

As the original political intent behind the search for government secrets slipped from memory, what survived of the politically rooted plot convention might be called postmodern secrecy mongering. Balzac said that the fundamental principle of popular writing is that behind every great fortune lies a great crime. Postmodern popular culture holds that behind every great political career lies a great scandal— a formula that provides the catharsis of discrediting the powerful, thereby vicariously empowering everyone else.

By way of example, there is television's wildly successful program *The X-Files*, which sends FBI special agents Fox Mulder (David Duchovny) and Dana Scully (Gillian Anderson) to hunt for government secrets about the extraterrestrial and the paranormal; their mottoes are "The truth is out there" and "Trust no one." The FBI in *The X-Files* is an organization suffused with paranoia and riven by plots and counterplots to frustrate Mulder and Scully from learning what is concealed in the bureau's X-Files, bureauspeak for cases too disturbing to be revealed to the public (unless they are concocted for the purpose of distracting the public from more important government conspiracies—sometimes the show's writers can't make up their minds).

The show's main plot device, a war between an FBI intent on concealing its guilty secrets and a citizenry determined to learn the truth, recalls the Church committee's portrayal of FBI director Hoover as the master blackmailer of American history who used secret files to promote his extremist political agenda. The series also draws on the faith of the era of the Pentagon Papers and the Nixon White House tapes: that the release of government secrets has the power to redeem American history and save the national soul.

The transformation of governmental secrecy and the historical theories based on it into popular entertainment formulas can also be seen in big-budget thrillers like *The Rock* (1996). Nicholas Cage plays an FBI agent–scientist at the bureau's laboratory in Washington; he is sent to San Francisco when terrorists take over the prison at Alcatraz and threaten to poison San Francisco Bay. But in postmodern FBI entertainment, it is no longer enough for the special agent–superhero to defend the nation against underworld conspiracies. *The Rock* also serves up a conspiracy *within* the bureau. Sean Connery plays a British operative held in a federal prison for stealing microfilms documenting the government's involvement in covering up UFO landings, planning the Kennedy assassination, and so on—all the standard fixtures of modern paranoia; the FBI's demented director plans to have Connery killed leading an assault on the island. But the characters played by Cage and Connery liberate the island, capture the terrorists, kill the director, and, as the picture ends, are about to release the microfilmed secrets that will save the world. Almost too much for one movie.

Postmodern secrecy mongering is part of what might be called postmodern paranoia, an aesthetic preference for "alternative" modes of thought that leads to a playful interest in conspiracy theories about government secrecy just for the hell of it. On the Internet, one site (www.conspire.com) is a spin-off from a book entitled *The Sixty Greatest Conspiracies of All Time*. Other, often ephemeral sites are named "Conspiracies, Cover-Ups, and Crimes"; "Secret No More," which posts FBI files obtained through the FOIA; and "Skeleton Closet," which tracks presidential hopefuls and reports "all the dirt on all the candidates—because character *does* matter." As I write this, the A&E Television Network is advertising a special program on conspiracies, a survey of the "hidden truths" of the great events of our time. As Art Linkletter liked to say, "People are funny." Maybe the culture of openness that Senator Moynihan proposes will finally let us laugh political paranoia out of American politics. It's a nice thought, but perhaps a trifle optimistic.

And as the original political motivation for the pursuit of government secrets devolves into the apolitical exploitation of scandal, earnest conspiracy theorists of the old school scold the popular culture for its obsession with the sex lives of the rich and powerful. When Anthony Summers described J. Edgar Hoover's supposed transvestism (in his biography *Official and Confidential*), some of Hoover's old enemies complained not just that the exposé was probably bogus, but that interest in the salacious side of the FBI would distract the public from the more serious political conspiracy theories about the bureau.[64] And while most historians noted that Seymour Hersh's revelations, in *The Dark Side of Camelot*, about JFK's sexual hijinks were unlikely to alter our evaluation of the Kennedy presidency, one reviewer, while contributing a few tidbits of his own, speculated darkly that the hubbub surrounding the book's publication amounted to an establishment plot to distract the public from the real Kennedy scandal: the media's complicity in the national security state's defeat of popular government.[65]

The history of secrecy has finally reached a point where people choose to believe in conspiracy theories—and even concoct their own—to satisfy aesthetic criteria, to purge themselves of personal demons, or just to have something to think and talk about. Some undertake their hunts for government secrets in order to resurrect lost causes, to vindicate positions taken during the Cold War, or to validate their status as certified victims of American fascism. Others simply cash in on secrecy because it once paid off and probably always will.

Sic transit gloria arcanorum.

The Irony of Secrecy

As political conspiracy theories about governmental secrecy devolved into the banality of commercial entertainment formulas, the accelerating declassification of Cold War secrets, often over the determined objection of the security agencies themselves, was taking an ironic—and, to some, an unwelcome—turn.

Over the years the Left had turned the Hiss and Rosenberg trials into case studies of its argument that the domestic Cold War had been a right-wing plot to repress radical reform and create an American empire. Central to this attack on Cold War orthodoxy was the claim that both Alger Hiss and the Rosenbergs had been put on trial, framed, and then unjustly punished to create hysterical public support for the Truman administration's containment strategy. These cases went to the heart of Washington's Cold War policies, both at home and around the world, because if the defendants were guilty as charged, it meant that the Soviet Union, far from being a friendly ally of the United States, had engaged in aggressive, hostile espionage against its American partner; that the American Communist Party was the willing and essential accomplice in Soviet espionage; that American Communism was not twentieth-century Americanism, as its 1930s slogan claimed, but a new form of treason. But if the charges were false, so were the government's justifications for the Cold War.

When historian Allen Weinstein began his study of the Hiss case in 1969, his position was that Hiss may have lied about not knowing Chambers but that Chambers "had falsely accused Hiss of Communist ties and espionage."[66] When Weinstein was denied the classified documents that he needed to test this hypothesis, he sued the FBI under the Freedom of Information Act. After three years of legal wrangling, he obtained more than thirty thousand pages of FBI files on Hiss and Chambers. Weinstein supplemented these with documents from archives in the United States and abroad, and he interviewed American and foreign members of Soviet espionage rings living in the Soviet bloc.

While Weinstein was pursuing this research, the Watergate crisis erupted. In an illogical but psychologically compelling association, some saw the Hiss case and Watergate as enmeshed: since Watergate refuted the patriotic belief that "the government would not lie, that law enforcement agencies would not fabricate evidence," the reasoning ran, "how much further would the Bureau have moved into illegality and fabrication when the spy mania was at its height and J. Edgar Hoover was in total control?" Since the point of raising the issue of secrecy was to prove a pattern of secret conspiracy, all government secrecy must be part of the pattern. Hiss's son recalled that there was "talk going around Washington . . . that all the recent political trials, beginning with the 'Hiss case,' were fixed."[67]

But at the end of his meticulously researched and argued study of the case, which finally appeared in 1978, Weinstein concluded that "the body of available evidence proves that [Hiss] did in fact perjure himself when describing his secret dealings with Chambers, so that the jurors in the second trial made no mistake in finding Alger Hiss guilty as charged."[68]

In some quarters this was the worst sort of bombshell, because it was friendly fire, and so the rage against Weinstein pulsed with a sense of betrayal. One historian wrote that Weinstein's sin was that he had demolished the fondest hopes of those who had used the Hiss case as their point of attack against the Cold War establishment: the belief among old and new leftists that establishing the innocence of Alger Hiss would redeem their history.[69]

In 1983, secret documents dealt an even more devastating blow to the revisionist position that government secrecy was evidence of anti-Communist plots. Like Weinstein, Ronald Radosh and Joyce Milton began their research for *The Rosenberg File* convinced that the government's secret documents must contain proof of the Rosenbergs' innocence. Radosh recalled that demonstrating against the Rosenbergs' executions was the beginning of his political education—it was "simply . . . an article of faith, an axiom, that Julius and Ethel Rosenberg were the victims of a government-sponsored conspiracy."[70]

But when Radosh gained access to the more than 200,000 pages of FBI, CIA, and navy documents released to the Rosenberg children in settlement of their FOIA lawsuit, he was amazed to find just the opposite. After dogged investigations and surprising discoveries that make their book the equal of the best true-crime reporting, Radosh and Milton concluded that the Rosenbergs, though unjustly executed, were guilty as charged: Julius had been a principal and Ethel his accomplice in one of the most important of Russia's espionage networks, and they had delivered valuable information about nuclear weapons to the Soviet Union.[71]

Radosh and Milton naively believed that their book would be salutary for the Left: "If the Rosenberg case has an ultimate moral, it is precisely to point up the dangers of adhering to an unexamined political myth." They did not expect bouquets, but they were unprepared for the rhetorical violence that greeted their book's publication. "To some veterans of the Old Left, merely to say in print that the Rosenbergs were involved in espionage," Radosh discovered, "was tantamount to calling for the resurrection of McCarthyism." During a public debate, their book was called the "fraud of the century," their scholarship "garbage in, garbage out."[72]

Since then, a wealth of evidence has accumulated to reinforce Radosh and Milton's conclusions, including documents from Soviet and American archives and information from new interviews with American spies who escaped prosecution by fleeing to the Soviet Union. Soviet case officer Aleksandr Feklisov of the KGB, for example, who formally signed up Rosenberg and directed him in his activities, has now confirmed Rosenberg's espionage activities. All this corroborates what Radosh and Milton wrote years ago, and in a new edition of their book they say: "If there is anything we have established, it is that the Rosenberg case resulted from a genuine effort to combat Soviet espionage; it was not a witch-hunt. It was not Julius Rosenberg's civil liberties that were being jeopardized but his espionage activities."[73]

It had been governmental secrecy that had allowed critics of the Rosenberg and Hiss cases to construct their elaborate theories about frame-ups and cover-ups. For years the Rosenbergs' defenders had demanded that the government reveal its secrets about the case, probably never dreaming that someday the files would land with a thump on their doorsteps. When the government gave in and released the documents, the secrets made the government's case even stronger. "Over the years," Radosh scoffs, "the Rosenbergs' defenders have loudly demanded the release of government documents on the case, only to deny the documents' significance once they are made public."[74] As the secret archives of the Cold War are released, the original case made against Soviet espionage in this country has received ever more conclusive corroboration. Secrecy raised doubts about the great internal-security cases of the Cold War; ending that secrecy has resolved them.

The release of secret Soviet documents after the collapse of the Soviet Union has also provided conclusive evidence of the American party's disloyalty, thus demolishing the theory that domestic anti-Communism was simply a conspiracy against the Left. In 1992 Harvey Klehr of Emory University traveled to Moscow to study the Russian archives on the Communist Party of the United States (CPUSA). On subsequent trips he was joined by John Earl Haynes of the Library of Congress. They collaborated with Fridrikh Igorevich Firsov of the Comintern archive at the Russian Center for the Preservation and Study of Documents of Recent History to produce *The Secret World of American Communism* (1995), part of Yale University Press's Annals of Communism series. Klehr, Haynes, and Firsov reprinted documents from the Russian archives that proved beyond doubt that the Soviet Union had heavily subsidized the CPUSA throughout its history, that prominent American radicals had laundered money for the Comintern, that the American party had maintained a secret espionage network in the United States with direct ties to Russian intelligence, that the testimony of former Communists like Whittaker Chambers and Elizabeth Bentley with regard to underground activity in the United States had been accurate in substance and in detail, that American Communists in government agencies had stolen secret documents and passed them to the American party, which forwarded them to the Soviet Union—and much more.

"It is no longer possible," Klehr, Haynes, and Firsov conclude, "to maintain that the Soviet Union did not fund the American party, that the CPUSA did not maintain a covert apparatus, and that key leaders and cadres were innocent of connection with Soviet espionage operations. Nowhere in the massive Comintern archives or in the American party's own records did the authors find documents indicating that Soviet or CPUSA officials objected to American Communists cooperating with Soviet intelligence or even having second thoughts about their relationship. Both the Soviet Union and the American Communist leadership regarded these activities as normal and proper. Their only concern was that they not become public."[75]

The most dramatic release of secret files from the Cold War, the publication of the Venona intercepts between July 1995 and August 1996, was another devastating blow to revisionist theories that minimized or dismissed the threat of Soviet espionage and the treasonous activities of American Communist spies. As noted earlier, "Venona" was the code name for one of the greatest cryptanalytical achievements in the history of espionage and counterespionage. Between 1940 and 1948, army code-breakers managed to decipher more than 2,900 messages between the Soviet Union and the United States, messages detailing the activities of the Soviet espionage networks in this country. A fantastic achievement, given the fiendishly difficult nature of the codes used.

As Moynihan notes, these intercepts provided a limited number of security professionals, including J. Edgar Hoover and his top associates, with fine-gauge descriptions of the activities of precisely the same Soviet spies who were named by defecting Soviet agents Alexander Orlov, Walter Krivitsky, Whittaker Chambers, and Elizabeth Bentley. In these coded messages the spies' identities were concealed beneath aliases, but by comparing the known movements of the agents with the corresponding activities described in the intercepts, the FBI and the code-breakers were able to match the aliases with the actual spies. Thus Julius and Ethel Rosenberg, Harry Dexter White, Klaus Fuchs, David Greenglass, and Theodore Alvin Hall were dragged, like moles from their tunnels, blinking in the bright light of history.

The prosecutors in the internal-security cases of the 1940s had not known, nor, until Venona, had we, that they had not been given all or even the best government evidence against the Rosenbergs et alia. The Venona materials would have been conclusive in establishing the cast of characters in the Soviet spy networks. But the documents were not handed over to the prosecutors to keep the Russians from learning that their codes had been broken. All in vain. As mentioned earlier, the Soviets had already found out, through the efforts of English spy Kim Philby. Thus information that could have corroborated the testimony of Whittaker Chambers and Elizabeth Bentley was denied not only to the government prosecutors and the American people but to the president himself. How, though not yet why, Harry S. Truman was denied this desperately needed information has been revealed for the first time in FBI documents obtained by Senator Moynihan in his research for this volume.

Not only have newly released secret documents undercut the charge that the government concocted the threat of Soviet espionage, but they have also discredited the claim that Washington deliberately (or unwittingly) misled the public about the Soviet threat to the United States, Europe, and Asia. John Lewis Gaddis, who is the Robert A. Lovett Professor of Military and Naval History at Yale University and is generally considered the most authoritative historian of the Cold War, has surveyed what can now be said about the history of this conflict. His book's title, *We Now Know*, refers to the fact that, whatever new information about the Cold War surfaces in the future, we now know *how* that war ended—the critical fact not known by writers of earlier Cold War histories.

It does Gaddis no favor to summarize his nuanced discussion in a few sentences, even if the sentences are his own. His main conclusion is that "the 'new' history [of the Cold War] is bringing us back to an old answer: that *as long as Stalin was running the Soviet Union a Cold War was inevitable*" (emphasis in original). Moreover, the conditions that made the Cold War inevitable did not end with Stalin's death, because Stalin "built a system sufficiently durable to survive not only his own demise but his successors' fitful and half-hearted efforts at 'de-Stalinization.'"[76]

"Who then was responsible [for the Cold War]?" Gaddis asks. "The answer, I think, is authoritarianism in general, and Stalin in particular." Gaddis drives home his point: "Did Stalin therefore seek a Cold War?" His answer: "Does a fish seek water?"[77]

Gaddis shows in case after case how the latest information from American and foreign archives tends to support the original explanations that Washington offered for its policies. Archival documents relating to "the hidden history of the Korean War," to use I. F. Stone's term, now show that the war was fully premeditated by North Korea and that the plans were approved by Stalin himself.[78] There is no documentary support for Stone's thesis that the Korean War was the result of a secret power struggle in Washington; instead, everything refutes it.

There is, moreover, no documentary evidence for the

most fundamental thesis of all Cold War revisionism—that the United States deliberately embarked on the conflict simply to increase its economic and political power. Not only do the recently released secret archives of the Cold War fail to support the revisionists, but the documentary evidence refutes them. Gaddis points to the crucial difference between what the revisionists call the American "empire" and Stalin's: Stalin forcibly constructed an empire with a brutality that ensured its instability, whereas the Europeans voluntarily sought refuge within an American empire. We now know that the savage behavior of the Red Army in Eastern Europe eliminated any possibility that the Russians could construct an empire by consent similar to that which evolved in the West. In the Soviet empire "there were few people left apart—from the party and official bureaucracies who ran it—who believed that they had anything to gain from living within a Soviet sphere of influence." In the American zone, "Europeans were meanwhile convincing themselves that they had little to lose from living within an American sphere of influence."[79]

The Soviet archives and the testimony of Soviet diplomats and agents also undercut the revisionists' fallback position: that even if Stalin and later Soviet leaders seemed to act aggressively, they were merely behaving in a manner customary to world powers, who all try to expand their influence and carve out spheres of influence. Far from relinquishing Lenin's goal of world revolution, Stalin's innovation was to view the Soviet Union as the center from which socialism would spread and eventually defeat capitalism: "The effect was to switch as the principal instrument for advancing revolution from Marx's idea of a historically determined class struggle to a process of territorial acquisition Stalin could control."[80] Soviet memoirs and archives furnish ample proof that what Gaddis calls Soviet leaders' "romantic" attachment to the world revolution continued to guide their actions. A paramount example of that continued attachment to revolutionary ideology was Khrushchev's dangerous and provocative support for Castro, which in turn led to the missile crisis.

In assigning responsibility for the Cold War to Stalin, Gaddis is careful not to say the United States and the West were blameless in their responses. "This argument by no means absolves the United States and its allies of a considerable responsibility for how the Cold War was fought," he writes. "Nor is it to deny the feckless stupidity with which the Americans fell into peripheral conflicts like Vietnam, or their exorbitant expenditures on unusable weaponry: these certainly caused the Cold War to cost much more in money and lives than it otherwise might have. Nor is it to claim moral superiority for western statesmen. None was as bad as Stalin—or Mao—but the Cold War left no leader uncorrupted: the wielding of great power, even in the best of times, rarely does."[81]

The irony of secrecy's impact on Cold War historiography is that, as documents from the Soviet archives and newly declassified materials from American agencies become available, there may be developing a historical consensus that will once again resemble the original justification for containment offered by Truman, Marshall, Kennan, Acheson, Nitze, and the other policy-makers. Once dubbed by revisionists the architects of illusion, these leaders are coming to be seen as having acted sensibly and responsibly in light of the knowledge available to them, and that knowledge now seems to have been accurate in view of what is now known about the intentions, character, and personality of Joseph Stalin and the system he created.

The End of Secrecy?

This seems to be the final irony of government secrecy in the Cold War: originally imposed largely as a ritual to delegitimize critics of Cold War policies, secrecy was transformed by revisionists into a counter-ritual to discredit America's role in the Cold War—only to end, when the secrets were finally revealed, as a vindication of the original architects of the war. The door swings both ways. It swings open. And it swings closed.

It would be too much to say that there the matter rests, because so much in Cold War history touches on basic human questions that will forever be disputed. But it would not be too rash to say that the inordinate role of secrecy in setting the terms of the historical debate is over. Throughout much of the Cold War, conjecture about secrets produced an adversarial alternative to the official explanation of American government policies. The end of secrecy has returned our view of Cold War history to facts instead of speculations about what is not known. The debate will go on, but it will be more honest.

Yet if the end of secrecy has confirmed that the substance of American Cold War policies was sound, it has confirmed just as strongly how wrong our leaders were to rely on secrecy in order to achieve their goals. The irony of secrecy is that it cut most deeply those who used it to stifle opposition to their policies. In the short term, secrecy may have made it easier for Washington to mobilize the country during the postwar crisis with Stalin. But the government's reliance on secrecy raised doubts about the wisdom and morality of policies that might well have been more solidly supported had the issues been fully aired in debate. What secrecy grants in the short run—public support for government policies—in the long run it takes away, as official secrecy gives rise to fantasies that corrode belief in the possibilities of democratic government. All because of secrets locked away foolishly and in the end, it would seem, needlessly. Secrecy is a losing proposition. It is, as Senator Moynihan has told us, for losers.

CHAPTER ONE

Secrecy as Regulation

Secrecy is a form of regulation. There are many such forms, but a general division can be made between those dealing with domestic affairs and those dealing with foreign affairs. In the first category, it is generally the case that government prescribes what the citizen may do. In the second category, it is generally the case that government prescribes what the citizen may know.

In the United States, secrecy is an institution of the administrative state that developed during the great conflicts of the twentieth century. It is distinctive primarily in that it is all but unexamined. There is a formidable literature on regulation of the public mode, virtually none on secrecy. Rather, there *is* a considerable literature, but it is mostly secret. Indeed, the modes of secrecy remain for the most part—well, secret. On inquiry there are regularities: patterns that fit well enough with what we have learned about other forms of regulation. But there has been so little inquiry that the actors involved seem hardly to know the set roles they play. Most important, they seem never to know the damage they can do. This is something more than inconveniencing to the citizen. At times, in the name of national security, secrecy has put that very security in harm's way.

How did secrecy and bureaucracy become so entwined—a vast secrecy system almost wholly hidden from view? What has it cost (no less than what it has achieved)? A clearer picture is emerging.

The Foreign Relations Authorization Act for Fiscal Years 1994 and 1995 created the Commission on Protecting and Reducing Government Secrecy to conduct "an investigation into all matters in any way related to any legislation, executive order, regulation, practice, or procedure relating to classified information or granting security clearances."[1] In truth, apart from atomic energy matters, there was only one such general statute—the Espionage Act of 1917 at the outset of World War I. As for inquiry, there had been but one other commission, the Commission on Government Security, created in 1955. This, of course, came in the aftermath of the Communists-in-government issue which convulsed American politics following World War II. The first commission, however, added nothing to our knowledge of that subject, and many of the issues were still out there. It seemed a good place for the new commission to begin.

It happened that the National Security Agency, our signals outfit—successor to the Army Signals Intelligence Service and the army security agency and under the leadership of its deputy director, William P. Crowell—was beginning to think it time to reveal some of the things that the army had learned about Soviet espionage in those years. After all, the Soviet Union had disappeared, and the code-breakers who had decrypted the secret messages were in their late years, still unacknowledged. And now there was this new commission. In short order it was determined to turn the Venona decryptions, as they were called, over to the commission. ("Venona" is a made-up word designating a Soviet code.)

In July 1995 the first set of documents was released at a

ceremony at the Central Intelligence Agency's headquarters in Langley, Virginia, and the story began to unfold. On February 1, 1943, the Signals Intelligence Service had begun transcribing Soviet cables (mostly KGB)* sent between Moscow and the United States (mainly to and from contacts in New York and Washington). The cables were both coded and enciphered, and it remains a marvel that any were ever broken. Not many were: only about 2,900 in all, a fraction of the many thousands intercepted. The arduous decoding work began in 1943 and was done at Arlington Hall, a former girls' school in Virginia; the setup resembled that of the Ultra project at Bletchley Park in wartime Britain, where German signals were intercepted and decoded.

But unlike the British team, which had a smuggled copy of the encoding machine used by the Germans, the American team had only the coded cables themselves. Led by Meredith Knox Gardner, the code-breakers put in much hard work during World War II, but they broke nothing. In the summer of 1946, however, Gardner managed to extract a phrase in a KGB message sent from New York to Moscow on August 10, 1944. Next was a report on the presidential election of 1944. Then, on December 20, 1946, a cable sent to Moscow two years earlier. It contained a list of the scientists working on the Manhattan Project, the secret U.S. government project that developed the first atomic bombs.

This decoded cable and the ones that followed were a revelation. As the monograph accompanying the 1995 release of the documents puts it, "The Venona decrypts were . . . to show the accuracy of Chambers' and Bentley's disclosures"—that is, the accuracy of the information about Soviet espionage that Whittaker Chambers (beginning in 1939) and Elizabeth Bentley (beginning in 1945) had provided to the American government. As more cables were decoded,

* For the sake of clarity, in this book the acronym KGB refers not only to the Komitet Gosudarstvennoi Bezopasnosti, or the Committee of State Security, which was established in the Soviet Union in 1954, but also to its predecessor organizations.

General Carter W. Clarke of army intelligence informed the FBI liaison officer that "the Army had begun to break into Soviet intelligence service traffic, and that traffic indicated a massive Soviet espionage effort in the U.S."[2]

"Massive" is a relative term. In all, the Venona decryptions came up with some two hundred names or code names of Americans who were passing secret information to Soviet agents. There were neighborhoods in New York City in which this number would have seemed surprisingly small, such were the politics of that time and place. (Possibly the most important of the atomic spies was a nineteen-year-old from the West Side of Manhattan, Theodore Alvin Hall, who betrayed his country's secrets quite on his own initiative. Indeed, he had to go looking for a Soviet agent to give the secrets to.) On the other hand, two hundred Communist spies might have seemed chilling to someone living in Kansas City, Missouri. Given that not a few Republicans were then attacking the New Deal as being soft on Communism, the charge could easily have been dismissed as domestic politics. Perhaps especially by the president of the United States, a Democrat from Missouri.

National politics and national security are always to some extent interrelated, but in the years of the Truman presidency the relationship became problematic. Trust leeched out of the political system, loyalties waned, betrayal became common. Communism—as an indigenous force, as yet another manifestation of diaspora politics, or as an instrument of Soviet policy—achieved astonishing influence not in its own right, much less on its own behalf, but as an agent for poisoning American politics. The effects were felt for a generation or more; the reverberations are felt even today, after the collapse of the Soviet Union. Government secrecy, as the commission was discovering, played a large role in all this.

Begin with the Federal Bureau of Investigation and its director, J. Edgar Hoover. At that time a prudent operative reported every hint of danger, and did so immediately. Consider Hoover's letter of May 29, 1946, sent to the director of what was then a powerful federal agency and meant to be shared with Truman; the commission retrieved the document, until now unpublished, from the Harry S. Truman Library.

Federal Bureau of Investigation
United States Department of Justice
Washington 25, D.C.
May 29, 1946

PERSONAL AND CONFIDENTIAL
BY SPECIAL MESSENGER

Honorable George E. Allen
Director
Reconstruction Finance Corporation
Washington, D.C.

Dear George:

I thought the President and you would be interested in the following information with respect to certain high Government officials operating an alleged espionage network in Washington, D.C., on behalf of the Soviet Government.

Information has been furnished to this Bureau through a source believed to be reliable that <u>there is an enormous Soviet espionage ring in Washington operating with the view of obtaining all information possible with reference to atomic energy, its specific use as an instrument of war,</u> and the commercial aspects of the energy in peacetime, and that a number of high Government officials whose identities will be set out hereinafter are involved. It has been alleged that the following departments and agencies of the United States Government handle the problem and current development of atomic energy and among these departments and agencies, the United States secret of atomic energy is held in trust. The names of the individuals in each department or agency who control such matters have been furnished as follows:

State Department—Under Secretary of State Dean Acheson
Assistant to the Under Secretary of State Herbert Marks
Former Assistant Secretary of War John J. McCloy

War Department—Assistant Secretary of War Howard C. Peterson

Commerce Department—Secretary of Commerce Henry A. Wallace

Bureau of the Budget—Paul H. Appleby
George Schwartzwalder

Bureau of Standards—Dr. Edward U. Condon

United Nations Organization—Alger Hiss
Abe Feller
Paul Appleby (who is being considered for transfer from the Bureau of the Budget to the United Nations Organization)

Office of War Mobilization and Reconversion—James R. Newman

Advisors to the Congressional Committee on Atomic Energy—James R. Newman
Dr. Edward U. Condon

The individual who furnished this information has reported that all of the above individuals mentioned are noted for their pro-Soviet leanings, mentioning specifically Alger Hiss of the United Nations Organization, Paul Appleby and George Schwartzwalder of the Bureau of the Budget, Dr. Condon of the Bureau of Standards, and John J. McCloy of the State Department.

The informant has stated that the McMahon Committee headed by Senator Brien McMahon of Connecticut is charged with formulating the policy concerning atomic energy[,] and serving as advisors to the Committee are <u>Dr. Condon of the Bureau of Standards, who, the informant states, is nothing more or less than an espionage agent in disguise, and James R. Newman, an employee of the Office of War Mobilization and Reconversion who is known to the informant to be a personal friend of Nathan Gregory Silvermaster,</u> who, you may recall, is one of the principal individuals known to have operated as an agent of the Soviet Government in U.S. Government offices for a considerable time until December, 1944. <u>It is known that Silvermaster obtained information through his associates in a Russian espionage network and such information was turned over to the Soviet Government.</u> The informant has indicated that Newman is also a friend of the news commentator <u>Raymond Gram Swing and columnist Marquis Childs. Newman is also reported to be the so-called ringleader of this particular Soviet espionage network</u> and through his employment with the Office of War Mobilization and Reconversion, he had access to material flowing from the <u>White House.</u> The informant stated that through Dr. Edward Condon at the Bureau of Standards, Newman has access to technical data concerning atomic energy. The informant further stated that Secretary of Commerce Henry A. Wallace knows of the background of Dr. Condon but condones his further employment in this highly strategic and important position.

<u>James Newman allegedly obtains from the War Department through the cooperation of Assistant Secretary of War Peterson highly technical information on the atomic bomb itself</u> and all matters relating generally to atomic energy. According to the informant, Newman has a direct line to Assistant Secretary Peterson's office.

With reference to the State Department, it was reported that Newman is in personal and daily contact with Dean Acheson, Herbert Marks, and on some occasions with John J. McCloy, and therefore, any knowledge of atomic energy and international relations with reference to it are immediately known to him. In so far as the international picture is concerned with respect to atomic energy, it was reported that Newman is in a position to obtain this information from Alger Hiss of the State Department who holds the position of advisor to Mr. Stettinius,* the American Representative to the United Nations Organization.

Concerning the Bureau of the Budget, the informant reported that Paul Appleby and sometimes George Schwartzwalder pass upon the recommendations of the Office of War Mobilization and Reconversion which are made to the President concerning the necessary appropriations to carry on experimental operations concerning atomic energy and particularly its relative position to that of a large Army and Navy. It was pointed out that in almost all cases the final decision at the Bureau of the Budget on such matters is passed upon by Paul Appleby.

The informant has drawn the conclusion that the entire setup of the McMahon Committee to investigate and recommend legislation on atomic energy and its use is a scheme to make available information concerning the atomic bomb and atomic energy, and that it all amounts to Soviet espionage in this country directed toward the obtaining for the Soviet Union the knowledge possessed by the United States concerning atomic energy and specifically the atomic bomb.

The informant stated that technical and exacting information which Newman desires to pass on to Russian principals is made available to Mr. Silvermaster, or, in those matters of a highly technical nature, Dr. Edward Condon of the Bureau of Standards contacts Silvermaster directly. The news commentator Raymond Gram Swing, according to the informant, is utilized for subtle propa-

* Edward R. Stettinius, Jr., served as U.S. secretary of state (1944–45) and as the first U.S. delegate to the United Nations (1945–46).

ganda with reference to agitation for release of atomic energy to the Allied Powers and that the same use is made of Marquis Childs, a feature Washington newspaper writer.

The informant is of the opinion that the entire setup has a use other than that of espionage for the Soviet Government, namely, the promotion of pro-Soviet propaganda, which, when reduced to its simplest form, advances the argument "why keep a large Army and Navy when the use of atomic energy eliminates the necessity for such a large force." In Government circles and among those handling the question of atomic energy, the unanimous argument of all and especially of those mentioned above is in agreement that a large Army and Navy are not necessary to the United States as the United States has exclusive knowledge and the "know how" of the atomic bomb.

It is known to this Bureau that Dr. Condon is a personal friend of Nathan Gregory Silvermaster, and although Silvermaster is presently under investigation by this Bureau, no information has been developed to substantiate the fact that Condon has turned over any information of a confidential nature to Silvermaster. It has also been made known to this Bureau through various sources in the past that the political views of Under Secretary of State Dean Acheson, Assistant Secretary of War Howard C. Peterson, and Secretary of Commerce Henry Wallace have been pro-Russian in nature, and therefore, it is not beyond the realm of conjecture that they would fit into a scheme as set out above. Alger Hiss of the United Nations Organization has been reported to this Bureau as a former member of the Communist underground organization operating within the Government in Washington, D.C.

Since James R. Newman has been described as the ringleader of this alleged espionage network and, further, since Herbert S. Marks is in close touch with information dealing with relations between the United States and Russia at the State Department in the office of Dean Acheson, investigations are being conducted by this Bureau concerning the activities of these two individuals. You may be assured that you will be kept advised of all developments in connection with the above allegations.

Sincerely yours,
Edgar[3]

This was baseless corridor talk. There were scraps of truth here, but in the main it was fantasy and dismissed as such. Both fantasies *and* truth.

We now know how it came about in those surreal times. John E. Haynes of the Library of Congress has unearthed the document that led to Hoover's bizarre compendium of May 29. The day before, the director had received a memorandum from D. Milton ("Mickey") Ladd, head of the FBI's security division. Ladd, the son of Senator Edwin Freemont Ladd of North Dakota, appears to have been an exemplary agent, later becoming assistant to the director. And he cleared his desk. The subject of Ladd's memorandum, which the director had requested, was Alger Hiss. Page after page laid out what was known about Hiss (including the fact that his wife, Priscilla, may have been a member of the League of Women Shoppers). Mostly atmospherics, but then, many a mafioso got in trouble for less. The serious charges were those leveled by Whittaker Chambers, who insisted that Alger Hiss was a member of "the underground organization of the Communist Party in Washington, D.C., as early as 1933." In New York no shortage of people knew what Chambers had been; now Washington was catching on. Ladd's memorandum was for the most part an admirable summation, but then it included this extraordinary claim:

> Mr. Joseph A. Panuch, Deputy to Assistant Secretary of State Russell, has reported to the Bureau that Alger Hiss together with Dean Acheson, Under Secretary of State; Herbert Marks, Assistant to the Under Secretary of State; John J. McCloy, former Assistant Secretary of War; Assistant Secretary of War Howard Peterson; Henry A. Wallace, Secretary of Commerce; Paul H. Appleby and George Schwartzwalder of the Budget Bureau; Dr. Edward U. Con-

don of the Bureau of Standards and the Senate Committee on Atomic Energy; James Newman of the Office of War Mobilization and Reconversion and also an advisor on the Committee on Atomic Energy and Abe Fuller of the Budget Bureau and UNO [United Nations Organization] are operating as an enormous espionage ring in Washington with the ultimate objective of obtaining all information concerning atomic energy, its specific use as an instrument of war and commercial aspects thereof in peacetime for the purpose of making such information available to the Soviet Union.[4]

Here Ladd grew a little careless. For starters, he didn't have the name of their source quite right. It was J. Anthony Panuch (pronounced "panic"), then deputy to the assistant secretary of state for administration, Donald S. Russell. Panuch was born in Prague, emigrated to the United States early, and graduated from Fordham University and Columbia University School of Law. Afterward he had a wide-ranging career, but he was evidently not welcomed at the higher reaches of the State Department. ("I knew him before he was nobody," recalls one contemporary.) His charges were loony, but the director of the FBI passed this lunacy on to the president of the United States the very next day.

Except there *was* the matter of Alger Hiss.

When the Commission on Protecting and Reducing Government Secrecy acquired the first Venona decryptions and a number of further releases now available in *Venona: Soviet Espionage and the American Response, 1939–1957,* the fine volume by Robert Louis Benson and Michael Warner, we were prompted to ask a simple, urgent, central question. As the Venona documents showed, by 1947 the United States was acquiring solid evidence of Communist espionage. The FBI knew all about this, for it fell to them, specifically to their brilliant agent, Robert Lamphere, to break the code names in the KGB cables. (Elizabeth Bentley, for instance, was "Good Girl.") Now then, did the director of the FBI, who had been quite prepared the year before to rush to the president a report of an all but fictional "enormous Soviet espionage ring in Washington," inform the president of the possibly less than enormous but *real* Communist spying when *real* evidence became available?

This seemed a simple matter to sort out. Surely the FBI's archives contained documents that would answer the question one way or another. The commission decided to ask the current director of the FBI, Louis J. Freeh, for help. This was done, and agents were immediately placed at the commission's disposal. Or rather, the agents came round one morning, professed not to know much about the matter, but promised to look into it. They were never heard from again.

Bureau "property," the commission members surmised. After the commission report was completed and published, I wrote, as chairman, to Director Freeh, recounting what had happened, or rather had not happened, expressing a measure of disappointment. Freeh was quietly indignant; a statutory commission had made a legitimate request for information and been stonewalled, as it were, by his own agents. He ordered his personal staff to sweep the basement. In short order they produced a loose-leaf binder of Top Secret files: some thirty-six documents, now at last available.

And we have our answer. President Truman was never told of the Venona decryptions.

It gives one pause to think now that all Truman ever "learned" about Communist espionage came from the hearings of the House Un-American Activities Committee, the speeches of Senator Joseph R. McCarthy, and the like. But, as the commission discovered, the decision not to tell the president was made not by J. Edgar Hoover, who hated Truman. It was made by Omar Nelson Bradley, chairman of the Joint Chiefs of Staff, who admired Truman in a most personal way and served him with the highest professional standards. The proof was in the binder. On October 18, 1949, an FBI agent, Howard B. Fletcher, sent to Ladd a memorandum describing a recent conference with General Carter W. Clarke, then chief of the army security agency, "regarding the dissemination of [Venona] material to the Central Intelligence Agency" (Figure 1).

General Clarke stated that when Admiral Stone* took over in charge of all cryptanalytical work he was very much disturbed to learn of the progress made by the Army Security Agency in reading [Venona] material. Admiral Stone took the attitude that the President and Admiral Hillenkoetter† should be advised as to the contents of all of these messages. General Clarke stated that he vehemently disagreed with Admiral Stone and advised the Admiral that he believed the only people entitled to know anything about this source were [deleted] and the FBI. He stated that the disagreement between Admiral Stone and himself culminated in a conference with General Bradley. General Bradley, according to General Clarke, agreed with the stand taken by General Clarke and stated that he would personally assume the responsibility of advising the President or anyone else in authority if the contents of any of this material so demanded. General Bradley adopted the attitude and agreed with General Clarke that all of the material should be made available to [deleted] and the FBI.

General Clarke stated the reason that he recently called upon you was for the purpose of informing you as to the difference of opinion between himself and Admiral Stone and to acquaint you with the opinion of General Bradley. He stated that he wanted to be certain that the Bureau was aware of this and to make sure that the Bureau docs not handle the material in such a way that Admiral Hillenkoetter or anyone else outside the Army Security Agency, [deleted,] and the Bureau are aware of the contents of these messages and the activity being conducted at Arlington Hall.[5]

Army "property." And so Truman was never told.

* Admiral Earl E. Stone was the head of the newly created Armed Forces Security Agency, which in 1952 became the National Security Agency.

† Admiral Roscoe H. Hillenkoetter was the first director of Central Intelligence (1947–50).

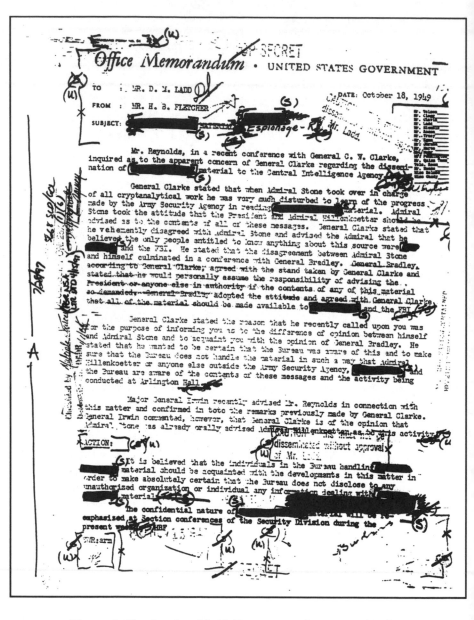

Figure 1. The October 18, 1949, memorandum reporting Omar Bradley's decision not to inform President Truman of the Venona decryptions. *Source:* Federal Bureau of Investigation, Washington, D.C.

Here we have government secrecy in its essence. Departments and agencies hoard information, and the government becomes a kind of market. Secrets become organizational assets, never to be shared save in exchange for another organization's assets. Sometimes the exchange is in kind: I exchange my secret for your secret. Sometimes the exchange resembles barter: I trade my willingness to share certain secrets for your help in accomplishing my purposes. But whatever the coinage, the system costs can be enormous. In the void created by absent or withheld information, decisions are either made poorly or not made at all. What decisions would Truman have made had the information in the Venona intercepts *not* been withheld from him?

The question tantalizes, for the president was hardly a passive figure. Claude D. Pepper would tell a story about Truman from the days when they were fellow senators; it now seems to suggest how different things might have been. One midday in the late 1980s, I was walking with the former senator from Florida back from the Senate to the House, he having returned to Congress as a member of the House of Representatives. We left the Senate chamber by the west entrance, turned left, and were soon passing S-224, one of those nameless rooms in the Capitol where members assemble for assorted activities (one of which, in an earlier time, was a morning tumbler of bourbon). "See that room?" Pepper remarked. "I was walking just where we are now one morning in 1940, when Harry Truman came out. 'Claude,' he said to me, 'don't you think we ought to get up a committee to look into the profits all these defense industries are making these days out of the Army and Navy? If we don't, the Republicans will!'"

By March 1, 1941, the year after this exchange, the Truman committee, formally known as the Committee to Investigate the National Defense Program, was created. It wasn't that many years later that Truman became president. It is surely logical to suppose that such a man would sense the political peril of a Communist espionage ring operating within his own government. If only he had known this—known for real, that is, from the likes of Bradley. If only political liberals had known. If only those in the universities had known. Seymour Martin Lipset has observed that at the height of the McCarthy era, an academic would be in worse trouble with his peers if he believed Chambers than if he believed Hiss. The Hiss perjury trial was a defining political event, as Richard Gid Powers observes in his Introduction. Allen Weinstein, in *Perjury: The Hiss-Chambers Case,* notes that even before Hiss went to prison, Hiss and Chambers and their "supporting casts" had achieved "the status of icons in the demonologies and hagiographies of the opposing camps." The result was a kind of unconscious obscurantism: "Contemporary arguments by politicians and intellectuals alike over the 'meaning' of the Hiss case, more than the evidence itself, set the direction and limits of subsequent historical investigation."[6] Affairs need not have been so misdirected. Secrecy ensured that they were.

And secrecy continues to flourish even now, with the Cold War ended and military outlays beginning, or in some instances continuing, to decline. Current projections for the year 2002 call for the number of military personnel to be reduced by one-third and military procurement, in constant dollars, to be reduced by one-half compared to 1985 levels.[7] Even today there are considerably fewer military officers and fewer "classification authorities" (or "original classifiers"), that is, individuals designated "in writing, either by the president or by selected agency heads, to classify information in the first instance." The 1996 report of the Information Security Oversight Office—part of the National Archives and Records Administration, which keeps track of classified information—summarized the year's trends as follows.

- The number of original classification authorities decreased by 959 to 4,420.
- Reported original classification decisions decreased by more than 62,000 to 105,163.

The numbers are declining, as one would expect in the post–Cold War era. But then the report summarizes the year's "derivative" (as opposed to original) classification decisions—documents classified because they incorporated, paraphrased, restated, or otherwise referred to classified information—and the year's total for all classifications, original and derivative. Here there is an increase.

- Reported derivative classification decisions increased by 2.2 million to 5,684,462.
- The total of all classification actions reported for fiscal year 1996 increased by 62 percent to 5,789,625.[8]

The CIA accounted for 52 percent of all classification decisions, the Department of Defense for 44 percent. It is hard to see how fewer military officers and fewer classification authorities could result in a stunning 62 percent *increase* in new secret documents—almost 6 million in all, and all of them deemed threats to national security if ever disclosed. Such is the grip of secrecy entwined with bureaucracy.[9]

Bureaucratic boundaries have also proliferated, although occasionally they have been surmounted by public servants of rare quality. In the case of the CIA and the FBI in the 1990s, John M. Deutch as director of the CIA, Jamie S. Gorelick as deputy attorney general, and Louis J. Freeh as director of the FBI have developed guidelines for sharing intelligence information and thereby have successfully reduced tensions between these two rivals. At the top, at all events. In the vaults and tunnels, however, the secret wars have gone on as before.

A notable example of this continuing conflict occurred in Berlin in the early 1990s, after the wall fell and East Germany reunited with West Germany. The CIA station in Berlin had begun obtaining files from the now defunct East German Stasi (domestic intelligence) and HVA* (foreign intelligence). The FBI, for its part, was just then beginning the mole

* The HVA, or Hauptverwaltung Augklärung (Main Department of Reconnaissance), was part of the Ministry of State Security.

hunt that would lead in 1994 to the arrest of Aldrich Ames (quite the most spectacular infiltrator in our nation's history and to all appearances completely apolitical; the traitors, at least, knew when the Cold War was over). But the CIA station chief in Berlin, dubbed by FBI agents "the Poison Dwarf," or so it was reported in the press, refused to provide access to the files.[10]

There was no misfeasance in this; the culture of the intelligence community was to develop sources and keep them in place, as was that of the law enforcement community. But this time the matter grew so contentious that the head of the Department of Justice's Office of Intelligence Policy and Review suggested that the FBI begin investigating whether the chief of the CIA Berlin station ought to be indicted by the U.S. government for obstruction of justice. In the end, the station chief retired and matters were resolved, but it seemed that some things had not changed since 1949.

Indeed, although the Central Intelligence Agency had been created only in 1947, in fairly short order it had acquired most of the institutional trappings of the military and diplomatic agencies it lived with. An "iron triangle" of sorts developed. In 1966, the Office of Legislative Counsel was established, with a staff of six for handling congressional relations. A decade later, after the House and Senate had established select committees on intelligence (one under Senator Frank Church, the other under Congressman Otis Pike), the staff was increased to thirty-two. Later renamed the Office of Congressional Affairs, it now has a staff of forty-five. The intelligence budget remained secret—Article 1, section 9, to the contrary—until 1997, when a gross number, $26.6 billion, was made known.[11]

But by that time, as Evan Thomas remarked on reading the Church committee reports, it seemed that the public knew more about the inner workings of the Central Intelligence Agency's Clandestine Service than it did about the Department of Health and Human Services.[12] Established in the mid-1970s, the CIA's Center for the Study of Intelligence had been at work. As described in its Web site (www.odci.gov/csi), the center conducts research on intelligence; publishes classified and unclassified editions of the journal *Studies in Intelligence*, as well as books, monographs, and a quarterly newsletter; hosts conferences and symposia on military, intelligence, and political history; manages the systematic declassification review of historically valuable CIA records; and coordinates a number of academic outreach programs.

Much of the vigor of this scholarly endeavor is the work and legacy of Sherman Kent, a Yale historian who joined the Office of Strategic Services during World War II and had moved on to the CIA. In 1955, in the first issue of *Studies in Intelligence*, Kent observed that "intelligence today is not merely a profession, but like most professions it has taken on the aspects of a discipline": a methodology, a vocabulary, a body of theory and doctrine, a set of refined techniques, a large professional following. But the intelligence community did not have its own literature. Kent set forth the ambitious but reasoned goal of establishing a literature on intelligence. "The most important service that such a literature performs is the permanent recording of our new ideas and experiences," he added. "When we record we not only make possible easier and wider communication of thought, we also take a rudimentary step towards making our findings cumulative."[13]

In 1992, the editors of *Studies in Intelligence* wrote that, in the nearly forty years since Kent had underscored the need for it, "a vast literature" on intelligence had been built up. They allowed that until just then much of the material had been unavailable to the public. Fair enough. Yet surely any attempt at a cumulative literature on intelligence must have circulated within the intelligence community itself. To little effect, it would seem. For all the daunting achievements of American statecraft during these years, the unstinting support of massive intelligence budgets, and the startling technological and scientific achievements, the overall quality of American intelligence may well have declined over time. Two statements, one anecdotal, the other analytic, argue the point.

First is Jeffrey Smith's account of the experience of General George Lee Butler, commander of U.S. Strategic Command (STRATCOM) from 1990 to 1994. As the one responsible for drafting the overall U.S. strategy for nuclear war, Butler had studied the Soviet Union with an intensity and a level of detail matched by few others in the West. He had studied the footage of the military parades and the Kremlin, had scrutinized the deployments of Soviet missiles and other armaments: "In all, he thought of the Soviet Union as a fearsome garrison state seeking global domination and preparing for certain conflict with the West. The only reasonable posture for the United States, he told colleagues, was to keep thousands of American nuclear weapons at the ready so that if war broke out, Washington could destroy as much of the Soviet nuclear arsenal as possible. It was the harrowing but hallowed logic of nuclear deterrence." But Butler began having doubts about this picture, upon which so much of U.S. foreign policy was based, by the time of his first visit to the Soviet Union, on December 4, 1988. When he landed at Sheremetyevo Airport, on the outskirts of Moscow, he thought at first that the uneven, pockmarked runway was an open field. The taxiways were still covered with snow from a storm two days earlier, and dozens of the runway lights were broken. Riding into downtown Moscow in an official motorcade, Butler noticed that the roads were ragged, the massive government buildings crumbling. He was astonished when the gearshift in his car snapped off in his driver's hand. After poring over thousands of satellite photos and thirty years' worth of classified reports, Butler had expected to find a modern, functional industrialized country; what he found instead was "severe economic deprivation." Even more telling was "the sense of defeat in the eyes of the people," Butler told Smith. "It all came crashing home to me that I really had been dealing with a caricature all those years."[14]

The second statement is by Admiral Stansfield Turner, director of the CIA from 1977 to 1981. In an article in *Foreign Affairs* in 1991, well after Butler's doubts had been confirmed by the collapse of the Soviet Union, Turner averred: "We should not gloss over the enormity of this failure to forecast the magnitude of the Soviet crisis. We know now that there were many Soviet academics, economists and political thinkers, other than those officially presented to us by the Soviet government, who understood long before 1980 that the Soviet economic system was broken and that it was only a matter of time before someone had to try to repair it, as had Khrushchev. Yet I never heard a suggestion from the CIA, or the intelligence arms of the departments of defense or state, that numerous Soviets recognized a growing, systemic economic problem." Turner acknowledged the "revisionist rumblings" claiming that the CIA had in fact seen the collapse coming, but he dismissed them: "If some individual CIA analysts were more prescient than the corporate view, their ideas were filtered out in the bureaucratic process; and it is the corporate view that counts because that is what reaches the president and his advisers. On this one, the corporate view missed by a mile. Why were so many of us insensitive to the inevitable?"[15]

The answer has to be, at least in part, that too much of the information was secret, not sufficiently open to critique by persons outside government. Within the confines of the intelligence community, too great attention was paid to hoarding information, defending boundaries, securing budgets, and other matters of corporate survival. Too little attention was paid to ethnic issues, both domestic and foreign. The Soviet Union, after all, broke up along ethnic lines. And *much* too little attention was paid to the decline of Marxist-Leninist belief, both here and abroad. The Red Scare was far less fearsome than many would have had us believe.

Government regulations dealing with domestic affairs derive from statute. Congress makes a law, entrusting its enforcement to a bureaucracy that issues rules and rulings to carry out the law. Since 1936 these regulations have been published in the *Federal Register,* there for all to see. But as for secrecy in foreign affairs, the statutory basis is slim—as noted, a handful of limited measures enacted in 1917 and 1947. Yet around these have developed an enormous intelligence bureaucracy, almost a secret government of its own, operating largely out of public view.

As new information about the Cold War emerges from the archives of the former Soviet Union and from American files, we can more easily trace the history of how secrecy and bureaucracy became enmeshed. We can see how, as the secrecy system took hold, it prevented American government from accurately assessing the enemy and then dealing rationally with them during this and other critical periods. Always excepting—the reader may take this as a personal bias—the scientists. They had little use for secrecy, but they put up with it. Among other things, in 1960 they put up the Corona reconnaissance satellite that enabled us, more or less literally, to keep track of every tank in the Soviet empire. If the Soviets had ever decided to launch an invasion through the celebrated Fulda Gap, we would have known about it weeks in advance, and it would not have succeeded. The first camera operated until 1972. Possibly, nay, probably, it was declassified and put on display as the commission proceeded with its work. That was a secret worth protecting—for a time—and that, too, is a theme of this study.

CHAPTER TWO

The Experience of
World War I

When Woodrow Wilson was inaugurated as president in 1913, he inherited a system of government that valued openness over secrecy. To be sure, the American Constitution—which had been drafted in closed, or, if you like, secret, sessions—presumes the need for secrecy in some matters. Article 1, section 5, provides that "each House shall keep a Journal of its Proceedings, . . . excepting in such Parts as may in their Judgment require Secrecy." (Not without a measure of prescience, Anti-Federalists argued that senators and representatives, who were given the power to fix their own salaries [Article 1, section 6], would do so in secret.)[1] The practice of closed deliberations was nothing unusual for the age, but it quickly lost its luster in the United States. Although Senate sessions were closed at first, in 1794 a resolution was adopted creating public galleries that were to remain open "so long as the Senate shall be engaged in their legislative capacity, unless in such cases as may, in the opinion of the Senate, require secrecy, after which the said galleries shall be closed."[2]

Openness in deliberation and not least in diplomacy came to be seen as something of a democratic virtue, even an aspect of national character. In 1860, one of Andrew Jackson's early biographers reported an anecdote that cast the general as the very embodiment of this virtue. When Jackson was told that one Augustus, a servant with the run of the White House, might be smuggling presidential papers to the general's opponents, Jackson responded: "They are welcome, sir, to anything they can get out of my papers. They will find there, among other things, false grammar and bad spelling; but they are welcome to it all, grammar and spelling included. Let them make the most of it. Our government, sir, is founded upon the intelligence of the people; it has no other basis; upon their capacity to arrive at right conclusions in regard to measures and in regard to men; and I am not afraid of their failing to do so from any use that can be made of any thing that can be got out of my papers."[3]

Apocryphal or not, the anecdote bespeaks what appears to have been a widely shared sentiment. Then with the onset of the Civil War we observe the surely unprecedented notion of openness as an instrument of foreign policy. On December 3, 1861, at the beginning of the second session of the Thirty-Seventh Congress, Abraham Lincoln accompanied his State of the Union message with 410 pages, all promptly printed, of dispatches to American ministers abroad. The dispatches dealt with the Confederate states' efforts to obtain recognition from foreign powers, notably Spain, France, and Great Britain. It was a fateful enterprise in which assertive openness was considered the most effective policy, and there is reason to judge that this proved to be the case. Openness communicated our threats as well as our entreaties, and it did so, in the case of Britain, not only to Whitehall but also to an increasingly literate and volatile public. The United States was dealing with insurrection at home; did Her Majesty's Government, did the British people, consider that this same misfortune might befall England? Or Ireland?*

This is not to say that American diplomacy of the Civil War was without its secret missions, messages, and the like. Even so, the American government began to espouse the concept of openness. One outcome of this policy was that the Department of State began publishing annual compilations of correspondence and similar material, in a series that became known as *Foreign Relations of the United States*. Something new under the sun. Hewing to a publishing schedule of one volume per year, the anonymous editors from the 1870s through the 1890s were surprisingly aboveboard when selecting and editing the documents at hand. The occasional coded communication was paraphrased. Portions of other communications were omitted in order to protect relations with a particular country or the sensitivity of ongoing matters, especially litigation. Otherwise, writes State Department historian William Z. Slany, "the immediateness of the publication confirmed the Department's lack of concern about issues of sensitivity or possible impact upon cur-

---

* Secretary of State William H. Seward could be subtle indeed in such matters. On June 19, 1861, he concluded a dispatch to Charles Francis Adams, the minister to Great Britain, with "a single remark" by way of persuading the British government to leave the United States to manage its "domestic controversy" on its own. "The fountains of discontent in any society are many, and some lie much deeper than others," Seward observed. "Thus far this unhappy controversy has disturbed only those which are nearest the surface. There are others which lie still deeper that may yet remain, as we hope, long undisturbed. If they should be reached, no one can tell how or when they could be closed. It was foreign intervention that opened and that alone could open similar fountains in the memorable French revolution" (*Executive Documents Submitted to the Senate*, 37th Cong., 2d sess. [Washington, D.C.: Government Printing Office, 1861–62], 1:109). The allusion to the fountains of discontent in Ireland was unspoken, but it was there. Seward, of Auburn, New York, was a vocal supporter of Irish freedom and would not have failed to note that the Fenian Brotherhood, an American support organization for revolutionary Irish nationalists, had been founded in his own state four years earlier. The brotherhood supported several attempts at insurrection in Ireland and several invasions of Upper Canada, the Niagara frontier well within Seward's regional sphere (for all that he would be remembered only for the purchase of Alaska).

rent negotiations. . . . The question of secrecy appears rarely to have arisen in the editing of published documents."[4]

Openness in foreign relations had clearly become an American theme. On January 8, 1918, in an address to Congress, Woodrow Wilson set forth the Fourteen Points to be used as a guide for a peace settlement. His first point stated the goal: "open covenants of peace, openly arrived at, after which there shall be no private international understandings of any kind but diplomacy shall proceed always frankly and in the public view."[5]

Wilson surely believed this, and he surely was believed. Yet as the twentieth century advanced, secrecy and conspiracy were to become primary instruments of statecraft even as states themselves attained unprecedented authority and presumption. Wilson's sixth point concerned Russia, which he assured "a sincere welcome into the society of free nations under institutions of her own choosing."[6] But Lenin had already seized power in what would become Leningrad. The United States was already at war, and it would continue to be at war in one form or another for most of the rest of the century. Amid the pressures of protecting national security, secrecy was to become pervasive within the American state.

Indeed, much of the structure of secrecy now in place in the U.S. government took shape in just under eleven weeks in the spring of 1917, while the Espionage Act was debated and signed into law. The Espionage Act had an antecedent in the Alien and Sedition Acts of 1798—three statutes dealing with aliens and one with sedition. These bills were passed by a Federalist Congress in order to silence opposition to war with France, which then seemed inevitable. (Neither country had declared war, but French and American ships had fought battles.) One measure required an alien to live in the United States for fourteen years before he could become a citizen; at the time, immigrants were mostly French and Irish natives who supported the Democratic-Republicans, who in turn tended to support France. Thomas Jefferson and James Madison both challenged the constitutionality of the acts, and the laws were a prominent issue in the 1800 election, which Jefferson ultimately won. Thereafter the acts expired, were repealed, or were amended out of existence.[7] It was the nation's first experience with how war or the threat of war changed the balance between private liberty versus public order, an instability that was eerily reenacted 119 years later.

It would be an exaggeration to state that from the outset of hostilities in 1914 the Democratic administration of Woodrow Wilson expected war with Germany. But its sympathies lay with Great Britain, as would those of the administration of Franklin D. Roosevelt, a spare two decades later. The plain fact is that the American governing classes have always—with the exception of an occasional Roosevelt, one Eisenhower, and one Kennedy—been ethnically English, Scottish, or Scotch-Irish. In 1861, when Secretary of State William H. Seward was doing his diplomatic best to ensure that Great Britain did not interfere with the civil crisis in the United States, he observed, "It would be a hazardous day for both the branches of the British race when they should determine to try how much harm each could do the other." This was a threat of war. But because the threat was between two "branches" of the same "race," war was surely unthinkable.[8]

Thus the pattern was established well before Wilson took office: the perception of civil order as subject to both external and internal threats, with the two connected primarily through ethnicity. At the outset of this century the United States had a considerable foreign-born population, concentrated mostly in a few urban centers; in 1910 about 40 percent of the populace of New York City were immigrants.[9] Many of these folks were caught up in diaspora politics, much of it difficult for natives to follow. (Fenians? Yes, that was a given. But Mensheviks?) Nor was this merely a first-generation preoccupation with the politics of the "old country." There came a figurative time, which W. S. Gilbert would have recognized, when "every boy and every gal" born in the Bronx was either a little Stalinist or else a little Trotskyite or Lovestonite or Shachtmanite.[10] Nathan Glazer has described his being *"socialist by descent"* (his emphasis) in the Bronx in the 1930s: "I was what would be called today a social democrat. Again, it was a matter of descent. My father . . . was strongly anticommunist. He was a member of the International Ladies Garment Workers Union and, after the fierce battle over control of the union in the 1920s, communists had as bad a reputation among ILGWU members as among middle Americans. Had he been a member of the Fur Workers Union, my politics by descent would very likely have been communist."[11] American socialism was by now respectable enough. For the rest, much of it was concealed, or partly concealed, behind language barriers and ghetto walls. And more.

One comment, however digressive, does seem in order here. Our conduct as a society has grown better, not worse, in a civil libertarian sense. The persecution of German Americans in World War I was atrocious and for the most part groundless. That of Japanese Americans, Italian Americans, and again German Americans in World War II was offensive but not uniformly hysterical. During and after World War II, a fair number of first- or second-generation Russian Jews were involved with Soviet espionage, but little was made of the ethnic (or, if you like, religious) dimension of this fact: Communism was the issue, and the ideological focus seemed all the clearer because there were, we may be thankful, a sufficient number of Protestant and even Catholic Marxists. More recently, Arab Americans have found themselves under suspicion as potential terrorists, but not by those whom we may call the authorities. There has been a learning process.*

* After Islamic terrorists bombed the World Trade Center in 1993, some in the American public and media lashed out at Arab Americans and Muslims. But on August 5, 1997, following the arrest of several Palestinians who allegedly planned to bomb crowded sites in New York City, Clyde Haberman of the *New York Times* recorded an atmosphere quite different from

In all this it helps to recall the tentativeness that attended much of American civic life during and after the Civil War. There was the war itself, of course—the fiercest in human history. When the war finally ended, the president was assassinated, his death part of a plot that extended to his secretary of state. (Seward, who was stabbed and pistol-whipped in his Washington home on the same evening that Lincoln was shot, was badly hurt but did survive.) Woodrow Wilson was born in Virginia in 1856, growing up amid secession and this aftermath. Another president was assassinated: William McKinley, slain in 1901 by a Polish anarchist, Leon F. Czolgosz, who thought all rulers deserving of death. Anarchism was a real enough threat, and its roots were foreign.

By contrast, the Industrial Workers of the World (IWW), the radical labor organization whose members were known as Wobblies, was very much an American movement, founded in Chicago in 1905. But industrial agitation inevitably involved foreign-born workers, and these were frequently in conflict with native workers. This was remarkably apparent at the strike in the silk mills of Paterson, New Jersey, in 1913, an event that aroused all manner of emotion across the nation. Even the famously radical Elizabeth Gurley Flynn, the "Rebel Girl," was struck by Paterson's "tenacious ethnic divisions," and John Reed, who was then a reporter covering the strike for the socialist newspaper *The Masses*, carried away from the city the same impressions. As historian Melvyn Dubofsky relates the encounter, Reed once asked a young Jew which nationalities were united in the

---

that following the 1993 attack. Haberman interviewed Hamed Nabawy, a Brooklyn grocer and a naturalized American from Egypt, who had endured "verbal violence" not only after the World Trade Center incident but also after others, like the Oklahoma City bombing, that had no known connection to the Middle East. But when the 1997 bomb plot was uncovered, Nabawy said, fewer people seemed ready to heap collective blame on Arab Americans: "Maybe we are a little less quick these days to point accusing fingers at an entire ethnic or religious group when something bad happens."

strike, and received the following reply: "'T'ree great nations stick togedder like dis.' He made a fist. 'T'ree great nations— Italians, Hebrews, and Germans.'" How about Americans? Reed inquired. But "the Jew shrugged his shoulders, grinned scornfully, and answered: 'English peoples not go on picket line. Mericans no lika fight!'" Reed concluded: "It is the English-speaking contingent that remains passive at Paterson, . . . while the 'wops,' the 'kikes,' the 'hunkies'—the 'degraded and ignorant races from Southern Europe'—go out and get clubbed on the picket-line and gaily take the medicine in Paterson jail."[12]

Compounding the ethnic divisions within the IWW was the IWW's division from the rest of the country. Of this period, Dubofsky writes: "From 1909 to 1919 a legend enveloped the IWW. Many Americans, especially during World War I and the postwar Red Scare, became convinced that the Wobblies were 'cut-throat, pro-German, or . . . bolshevik, desperadoes who burn harvest-fields, drive iron spikes into fine timber and ruin sawmills, devise bomb plots, who obstruct the war and sabotage the manufacture of munitions—veritable supermen, with a superhuman power for evil, omnipresent and almost omnipotent.' The hobo Wobbly had replaced the bearded, bomb-carrying anarchist as a bogeyman in the middle-class American's fevered imagination."[13]

Imperial Germany blundered here as elsewhere. In the face of proclaimed American neutrality, it set upon a campaign of espionage aimed at curtailing the American supply of armaments for the Allies, enlisting American ethnic elements for the purpose—typically Germans and Irish but also a new cadre, Indians from the subcontinent (mainly Punjabis) opposed to British rule in India. Thus it came about, on November 20, 1915, that Wilson's secretary of state, Robert Lansing, the most moderate of men (who before the outbreak of war had negotiated international arbitral tribunals that promised an era in which disputes between nations could be settled by law rather than by arms), urged the president to include in his forthcoming State of the Union address "some suggestion as to legislation covering foreign intrigues in our internal affairs such as conspiracies to blow up factories, to encourage strikes, to interfere with industrial operations, to gather information of this government's secrets, etc., etc."[14]

More than six months earlier, Wilson, the embodiment of the academic in politics (thoughtful, careful, devoted to reason), had told a Philadelphia audience, "There is such a thing as a man being too proud to fight."[15] Now, on December 7, 1915, in his State of the Union message to Congress, Wilson observed, speaking of the war in Europe, "We have stood apart, studiously neutral." But unprecedented events abroad called for unprecedented actions at home, and Wilson made a plea that astonishes still, as much for its passion as for what it proposes.

> There are citizens of the United States, I blush to admit, born under other flags but welcomed under our generous naturalization laws to the full freedom and opportunity of America, who have poured the poison of disloyalty into the very arteries of our national life; who have sought to bring the authority and good name of our Government into contempt, to destroy our industries wherever they thought it effective for their vindictive purposes to strike at them, and to debase our politics to the uses of foreign intrigue. . . . A little while ago such a thing would have seemed incredible. Because it was incredible we made no preparation for it. We would have been almost ashamed to prepare for it, as if we were suspicious of ourselves, our own comrades and neighbors! But the ugly and incredible thing has actually come about and we are without adequate federal laws to deal with it. I urge you to enact such laws at the earliest possible moment and feel that in doing so I am urging you to do nothing less than save the honor and self-respect of the nation. Such creatures of passion, disloyalty, and anarchy must be crushed out.[16]

No president had ever spoken like that before; none has since. Even during a half century of Cold War, when there were indeed persons of foreign birth living in the United States and actively involved in seditious activities on behalf of the Soviet Union, no president spoke like that. Others in public life did; many others in private life did, including not a few who knew what they were talking about. But the telling fact is that the intensity of fear and, yes, loathing of those years was never equaled later.

With war's arrival, securing loyalty and unearthing treason had never seemed more important. The first statute enacted by the First Congress had prescribed the oath of allegiance to be taken by officers of the American government. It was simply an oath to support the Constitution of the United States. In 1861, four months into the Civil War, it was amended: it was now an oath to "support, protect, and defend the Constitution and Government of the United States against all enemies, whether *domestic or foreign*" (emphasis added).[17] Note that the designation "domestic" comes first. The linkage never thereafter dissolved.

Assistant Attorney General Charles Warren was assigned the task of drafting the laws that Wilson had called for. And on June 3, 1916, seventeen separate bills were sent to Congress.[18] On February 3, 1917, Germany resumed unrestricted submarine warfare, and the United States broke diplomatic relations. On February 20, the Senate combined thirteen of the seventeen bills and passed that measure, but the House did not act. At a cabinet meeting on March 20, Attorney General Thomas W. Gregory asserted that "German intrigues" were afoot but complained of the "helplessness of his Department under existing laws."[19] In his address asking for a declaration of war, Wilson cited spying as an example of the hostile intent of the "Prussian autocracy": "From the very outset of the present war it has filled our unsuspecting communities and even our offices of government with spies and set criminal intrigues everywhere afoot against our national unity of counsel, our peace within and without, our industries and our commerce. Indeed it is now evident that its spies were here even before the war began."[20]

Following the procedure prescribed by the Constitution, President Wilson called a special session of the Sixty-Fifth Congress on April 2, 1917, asking a joint session for a declaration of war against Germany. On that same day, the chairman of the House Judiciary Committee, Edwin Y. Webb, Democrat of North Carolina, introduced H.R. 291, *A Bill to Punish Acts of Interference with the Foreign Relations, the Neutrality, and the Foreign Commerce of the United States, to Punish Espionage and Better to Enforce the Criminal Laws of the United States*. On April 3, Senator Charles A. Culberson, Democrat of Texas and chairman of the Committee on the Judiciary, introduced a similar bill in the Senate (S. 2). On April 4, the Senate adopted a Declaration of War. On April 5, the U.S. Civil Service Commission provided the president with a choice of executive orders for "excluding from the Government service any person of whose loyalty to the Government there is reasonable doubt."[21]

On April 6, the House declared war. On April 7, the president signed a confidential executive order concerning the loyalty of government employees. The debate on the Espionage Act continued through the spring. These bills were based on the legislation proposed by the attorney general the previous year. Both provided for press censorship. The Senate bill, chapter 2, section 2(c), read:

> Whoever, in time of war, in violation of regulations to be prescribed by the President, . . . shall collect, record, *publish*, or communicate . . . information relating to the public defense calculated to be, or which might be, useful to the enemy, shall be punished by a fine of not more than $10,000 or by imprisonment for not more than 10 years, or by both such fine and imprisonment: Provided, That nothing in this section shall be construed to limit or restrict, nor shall any regulation herein provided for limit or restrict, any discussion, comment, or criticism of the Government or its representatives, or the publication of the same: Pro-

vided, That no discussion, comment, or criticism shall convey information prohibited under the provisions of this section.[22] (Emphasis added.)

Section 4 of the House bill similarly provided that during wartime the president could, "by proclamation, prohibit the publishing or communicating of or the attempting to publish or communicate any information relating to the national defense which, in his judgment, is of such character that it is or might be useful to the enemy."[23]

To repeat, in the Sixty-Fourth Congress, the Senate had passed espionage legislation, including the press censorship provision, largely as proposed by the attorney general, but the House had not taken action when Congress adjourned on March 3. By April 2, then, the measure had been around for a few months, and now opposition appeared. In a definitive article for the *Columbia Law Review,* Harold Edgar and Benno C. Schmidt, Jr., sum up the objections to section 2(c): "First, opponents claimed that the provision would establish a system of prior restraint censoring newspaper publications of news about the war. Second, the provision was challenged as delegating unlimited power to the President to decide what information should be published. Third, objection was again made to the lack of a specific culpability standard."[24]

The Encyclopedia of the United States Congress records that the censorship portion of the Espionage Act "set off a storm of Congressional controversy," with House Speaker James Beauchamp (Champ) Clark declaring that censorship of the press was "in flat contradiction of the Constitution."[25] The issue was intermittently debated, and with some intensity, during a seven-week period in which much else was going on. The most important debate took place in the Senate, which had of course already passed the measure but now had the opportunity to reconsider.

A sample of the debate can be found in the *Congressional Record* of April 18, when Charles S. Thomas, Democrat of Colorado, spoke with some force against the measure: "Mr. President, that is not justice; that is not law; that is not liberty; that is the suppression of every field of legitimate inquiry in time of war. . . . Surely an expression of that kind should not go into a statute, and especially now, when we are acting upon a subject of far-reaching importance, without due deliberation." Thomas noted that although the law was one of the most important ever considered by the Senate, fewer than twenty or so senators were on hand to reconsider its consequences: "It strikes directly at the freedom of the press, at the constitutional exemption from unreasonable search and seizure, not to mention other provisions so sacred . . . that they should not be modified or imperiled, however great the exigency, except upon the most serious, far-reaching, and extended consideration. Yet we are going ahead with this as a war measure, although when enacted it will be permanent in its operation; and I very much fear that with the best of intention we may place upon the statute books something that will rise to plague us."[26]

Jacob Harold Gallinger of New Hampshire, chairman of the Republican caucus, interrupted to say he had been "somewhat disturbed in glancing over this bill" and was very interested in what the senator from Colorado had been saying. Gallinger then asked Thomas to yield so that he might ask for a quorum, as "more Senators ought to be here." Thomas replied that Gallinger knew as well as he did that when a quorum call is placed, "the Senators will simply come in and answer to their names and go out again." (At that time there was no watching of the debates on television.) Even so, it was agreed: a quorum was called, and the debate drifted on. Thomas offered an amendment to strike the provision; it failed.

On May 14, John Knight Shields, Democrat of Tennessee, offered a long legal brief on the First Amendment and the constitutionality of the administration proposal. Shields cited Henry Campbell Black's *Handbook on American Constitutional Law* (commonly known as *Black's Constitutional Law*) and Judge Joseph Story's great work upon the Constitution, where the nineteenth-century jurist declares that the language of the First Amendment "imports no more than every man shall have a right to speak, write, and print his opinions upon any subject whatsoever, *without any prior restraint*, so always that he does not injure any other person in his rights, person, property, or reputation, and so always that he does not thereby disturb the public peace or attempt to subvert the Government" (emphasis added). Shields also cited the Supreme Court of Ohio, which had defined the parallel between the private citizen and the press: "The liberty of the press, properly understood, is not inconsistent with the protection due to private character. It has been well defined as consisting in the right to publish with impunity the truth, with good motives and for justifiable ends, whether it respects government, magistracy, or individuals." Black writes, "It is now thoroughly understood that freedom of the press includes not only exemption from previous censorship but also immunity from punishment or sequestration after the publication, provided that the comments made keep within the limits of truth and decency and are not treasonable." Lest his point not seem forceful enough, he returns to the words of Judge Story: "In the United States no censorship of the press has ever been attempted or would for a moment be tolerated. It is clearly and indubitably prohibited by the constitutional provisions under consideration."[27]

William E. Borah, Republican of Idaho, was the stormiest in his opposition, and he had his history down. He began with the Sedition Act of 1798.

> Once before in the history of the Government we undertook to establish something in the nature of an abridgment of speech and of the press. It was a complete and ignominious failure. It did not serve the objects and purposes of those who fathered it. It accomplished nothing in the way of that which they desired to accomplish. That was in 1798. Then during the Civil War we undertook again, in an indirect way, to establish a censorship by suppressing cer-

tain publications and to prevent the distribution of certain printed material coming supposedly, and in fact at that time conceded to be, from those who were in sympathy with the southern side of the contention. That was an ignominious failure, conceded to be such. It served no purpose whatever and accomplished no good whatever. The historians writing upon the subject and some of the men who enforced it, even, before they died conceded and acknowledged that their attempt to suppress these publications served no benefit and in no way aided the Government in its work.[28]

Clearly the press had its defenders in this debate, but it also had its critics. The incorrigibility of journalists and publishers drew some attention. Senator Thomas James Walsh of Montana recalled that General Robert E. Lee was driven to distraction when his campaign plans were reported in the Richmond newspapers.[29]

On May 12, the Senate voted thirty-nine to thirty-eight in favor of a motion by Hiram W. Johnson, Republican of California, to strike the censorship provision.* A margin of one vote.

But opinion had shifted. A parliamentary move was made to salvage some part of the measure when Senator Lee Slater Overman, Democrat of North Carolina, introduced an amendment that had originally been submitted by opponents of the censorship provision in order to soften its effects but that had been defeated in a vote on April 20. Henry Cabot Lodge, Republican of Massachusetts, who two days before had opposed the Johnson amendment to strike the provision and who had earlier supported the language proposed by Senator Overman, reversed himself in a short statement on May 14: "I have come to the conclusion very distinctly that it would be far better not to have any legislation of this sort than to permit [the Bureau of Information] to exclude, as

---

* As for party affiliation, the vote was fifteen Democrats and twenty-four Republicans in favor, twenty-seven Democrats and eleven Republicans opposed. Not voting were twelve Democrats and seven Republicans.

they will have the power to exclude, practically anything from the newspapers of the country."[30]*

A complex conference with the House followed. President Wilson sent a letter to Edwin Yates Webb of North Carolina, the Democratic chairman of the House conferees, and reiterated the administration's position: "Authority to exercise censorship over the press to the extent that that censorship is embodied in the recent action of the House of Representatives is absolutely necessary to the public safety." Most newspapers would observe a "patriotic reticence" about publishing anything that could be injurious to national security, Wilson admitted, "but in every country there are some persons in a position to do mischief in this field who can not be relied upon, and whose interests or desires will lead to actions . . . highly dangerous to the Nation in the midst of a war." Wilson was adamant: "I want to say again that it seems to me imperative that powers of this sort should be granted."[31]

But despite Wilson's last-minute lobbying, the Espionage Act did not contain the censorship provision. The law was signed on June 15, 1917, and it remains the law. The two main provisions cover the unlawful obtaining of national defense information and the unlawful disclosure of such information to a foreign government or its agents. The criminal penalties are more severe for the second offense and

* Lodge's reference to a Bureau of Information, "if that is its name," as he put it in his May 14 statement, was surely to the Committee on Public Information, which Wilson had established by executive order a few weeks earlier. The committee had been proposed to Wilson on April 14 by Secretary of State Lansing, Secretary of War Newton Diehl Baker, and Secretary of the Navy Josephus Daniels, who had written of their concern about "premature or ill-advised announcements of policies" and the need to "safeguard all information of value to an enemy" (Lansing, Baker, and Daniels to Wilson, April 14, 1917, in *The Papers of Woodrow Wilson*, edited by Arthur S. Link [Princeton: Princeton University Press, 1984–92], 42:55). It would come to be known as the Creel committee for its chairman, George Creel, a newspaperman from the Midwest, and as an agency that promoted the administration's war aims, but it narrowly missed becoming the Bureau of Censorship. It was the age of burgeoning bureaus.

harsher in times of war than at other times. It did include a provision punishing certain "seditious or disloyal acts or words in time of war," but this did not satisfy the Wilson administration, or at all events Attorney General Gregory. The next year, accordingly, new provisions, known collectively as the Sedition Act of 1918, were added to the basic statute and signed into law by the president on May 16, 1918.

Whereas the 1917 act focused on different forms of conduct—obtaining, communicating, or publishing designated information, for example—the 1918 act focused on speech itself, making criminal an extensive variety of listed "utterances." It defined eight specific offenses punishable by up to twenty years' imprisonment and a ten-thousand-dollar fine, making it a crime to "utter, print, write, or publish any disloyal, profane, scurrilous, or abusive language about the form of government of the United States, or the Constitution of the United States." Another stricture, which prohibited those who would "urge, incite, or advocate any curtailment of production in this country of any thing . . . necessary or essential to the prosecution of the war," was aimed at left-wing labor unions. When Congress grew increasingly concerned that the 1918 amendment was too strenuous in its restrictions on speech, the Sedition Act was repealed in March 1921.[32]

The 1917 act was amended again in 1933 to prohibit government employees from publishing any foreign code or anything transmitted in such a code; this was a narrow provision that followed publication, by a former top signals intelligence official, of what became a popular book about the State Department's code-breaking activities against Japan. A 1938 amendment added two new sections to prohibit the taking and disseminating of photographs of military installations and equipment designated by the president.

In 1950 Congress added a new subsection to specifically cover the unauthorized possession of national defense information by persons *outside* the government. This amendment has proven confusing, primarily because it does not include any culpability requirement. The degree of "scienter," or guilty knowledge, required for behavior to be covered under the 1917 act had long been a source of controversy; now Congress appeared to be avoiding the issue entirely. Little wonder that Edgar and Schmidt judge the Senate report on the 1950 legislation "inexplicit" on this issue and the House report "inexplicable."[33] The statute has been amended several more times since 1950, but these instances have amounted to either technical updates of the list of protected information (such as adding spacecraft, satellite systems, and other advanced technologies) or modifications of penalties for those who violate the statute (such as adding a provision allowing forfeiture of their property).

In 1986 Samuel L. Morison, a civilian analyst with the Office of Naval Intelligence, was convicted of supplying photographs of a Soviet nuclear-powered aircraft carrier, then under construction, to *Jane's Defence Weekly* (July 1984). Morison was the first individual convicted under the 1917 Espionage Act for unauthorized disclosure of information to the press. No one has been convicted since.

The Atomic Energy Act of 1954 was a narrowly defined statute concerning nuclear data and its communication or disclosure "with intent to injure the United States" or "with reason to believe such data will be utilized to injure the United States or to secure an advantage to any foreign nation."[34] Penalties were prescribed for doing so. By contrast, the National Security Act of 1947, which created the Central Intelligence Agency, provided that the Director of Central Intelligence would be responsible for protecting intelligence sources and methods from unauthorized disclosure. But there are no penalties for not doing so. If there were, half of our national security advisors would have spent time in jail.

And so the modern age began. Three new institutions had entered American life: Conspiracy, Loyalty, Secrecy. Each had antecedents, but now there was a difference. Each had become institutional; bureaucracies were established to attend to each. In time there would be a Federal Bureau of Investigation to keep track of conspiracy at home, a Central Intelligence Agency to keep tabs abroad, an espionage statute and loyalty boards to root out disloyalty or subversion. And all of this would be maintained, and the national security would be secured, through elaborate regimes of secrecy. Eighty years later, at the close of the century, these institutions continue in place. To many they now seem permanent, perhaps even preordained; few consider that they were once new.

What is more, we began this age by trampling on liberty. And we did so at the behest of the most learned and liberal of presidents, who in short order was to become the world's standard-bearer for the right of all peoples to freedom under law. A president who envisioned a world league of nations governed by law. A president who could state with chilly precision what would be the alternative. Wilson sketched just such a scenario once, in 1919, when he was in St. Louis campaigning for the League of Nations and someone asked him what would happen if the treaty establishing the league were not ratified.

> Very well, then, if we must stand apart and be the hostile rivals of the rest of the world, then we must do something else. We must be physically ready for anything to come. We must have a great standing army. We must see to it that every man in America is trained to arms. We must see to it that there are munitions and guns enough for an army that means a mobilized nation; that they are not only laid up in store, but that they are kept up to date; that they are ready to use tomorrow; that we are a nation in arms; because you can't be unfriendly to everybody without being ready that everybody shall be unfriendly to you. . . .
>
> You have got to think of the President of the United States, not as the chief counselor of the Nation, elected for a little while, but as the man meant constantly and every

day to be commander in chief of the armies and navy of the United States, ready to order it to any part of the world where the threat of war is a menace to his own people. And you can't do that under free debate. You can't do that under public counsel. Plans must be kept secret. Knowledge must be accumulated by a system which we have condemned, because we have called it a spying system. The more polite call it a system of intelligence and you can't watch other nations with your unassisted eye. You have got to watch them by secret agencies planted everywhere. Let me testify to this, my fellow citizens. I not only did not know it until we got into this war, but I did not believe it when I was told that it was true, that Germany was not the only country that maintained a secret service. Every country in Europe maintained it, because they had to be ready for Germany's spring upon them, and the only difference between the German secret service and the other secret services was that the German secret service found out more than the others did. And therefore Germany sprang upon the other nations unawares, and they were not ready for it.

And you know what the effect of a military nation is upon social questions. You know how impossible it is to effect social reform if everybody must be under orders from the government. You know how impossible it is, in short, to have a free nation if it is a military nation and under military orders.[35]

As it turned out, it *was* possible. Not that the United States ever became a military nation, but for the longest while we have been a nation on constant military alert. Each of Wilson's successors has been followed everywhere by a man carrying "the football," that is, the black briefcase containing the nuclear missile launch codes. And as for spying and intelligence and secrets . . . well.

But the larger and more important development was of just the opposite character. Now a civil liberties movement that imposed a kind of prior restraint on government also entered American life. Gradually, over time, American government became careful about liberties. Due process appeared in our calculation of such matters as loyalty, and this in turn steadily eroded the base of radical rejection of American society. It was slow in coming, too slow. But it came, and in the process American democracy not only survived but prevailed. One could date this development from May 14, 1917, when Henry Cabot Lodge switched his vote on the issue of press censorship. In 1876 Lodge had been awarded the first Ph.D. in political science conferred by Harvard University; later he taught there. He was an authority on Alexander Hamilton and the age of American independence. And he likely would have known of Madison's letter to Jefferson of May 13, 1798: "Perhaps it is a universal truth that the loss of liberty at home is to be charged to provisions against danger, real or pretended, from abroad."[36]

In the meantime, though, there was a war to be won against Germany.

Then as now, the United States had a large population of Americans of German ancestry. German culture was widely admired, the German language was taught in public schools, and German political traditions were viewed as essentially democratic. Germany was arguably the most advanced culture in Europe. Early in the war, the Berlin government set out to use these attachments and attractions in order to strengthen opposition to entering the war. When war began in August 1914, the German ambassador arrived in the United States with $150 million in German treasury notes ($2.2 billion in current dollars) to pursue a propaganda campaign, purchase munitions for Germany, and conduct an espionage campaign aimed at denying war matériel to the Allies.[37] This last task was the province of the military attaché, Captain Franz von Papen.

In a fateful manner, while the British made friends, the Germans made enemies. Early on the morning of July 30, 1916, German agents, probably assisted by Irish nationalists, blew up a munitions dump at the Black Tom railroad

Figure 2. A bomb explodes at the National Storage Company's plant on Black Tom Island, Jersey City, July 30, 1916. The next day, the front page of the *New York Times* carried a photograph of the sabotage at New York Harbor. Reprinted courtesy of the *New York Times*.

yard and adjoining warehouses at New York Harbor (Figure 2). (The site is now Liberty State Park, the debarkation point for boats carrying tourists to the Statue of Liberty.) It was a stunning event in both magnitude and consequence. The first and most powerful blast, at 2:08 A.M., shook houses along the New Jersey shore, rocked skyscrapers in Manhattan, shattered windows from Brooklyn to Hoboken, and threw people from their beds miles away. The noise of the explosion was heard as far away as Maryland and Connecticut, and on both sides of the Hudson, people in their pajamas rushed to the streets to watch the sky glow red from the flames as more explosions thundered from the harbor.[38] Sabotage became a national issue.

Captain von Papen also provided support for the Ghadar movement (*ghadar* is Urdu for mutiny), which was composed mostly of Punjabi Indians seeking independence from British rule. It was based principally in California, to which Punjabi agricultural workers had migrated from Canada. Once the United States declared war on Germany, the government indicted 105 people of various nationalities for participating in the conspiracy. From the start, the "Hindoo conspiracy" was viewed as an "offshoot of the German neutrality plots": according to the *San Francisco Chronicle*, the complaint charged that those arrested had "conspired to 'Cripple, hinder and obstruct, the military operations of Great Britain' by sending Hindoos to India to stir up a revolt, and to help Germany by forcing Great Britain to withdraw troops from Europe for service in India to quell the revolt."[39] At the trial, the conspiracy was described as one that "permeated and encircled the whole globe."[40] Twenty-nine defendants were found guilty: fifteen Indians and fourteen German Americans or Germans, including Franz von Bopp, the German consul in San Francisco. The "Hindoo conspiracy" entered the national imagery.[41]

For all the energy and expenditure that these events represented, it is not clear what Berlin had to show for its elaborate and extensive espionage activity. At this time the United

States possessed only one genuine defense secret: that the American military was in no sense prepared for a major war with powerful adversaries. The U.S. Army was so under-equipped that when it arrived in France it had to borrow French artillery. But even this was an open secret, and in that regard the Espionage Act can be said to have accomplished little or nothing. German espionage (whether real or imagined) did, however, do great damage to German Americans and thereby to the American people at large.

As war approached, Wilson delivered a mordant fore-cast, one recorded by Frank Irving Cobb: "'Once lead this people into war,' he said, 'and they'll forget there ever was such a thing as tolerance. To fight you must be brutal and ruthless, and the spirit of ruthless brutality will enter into the very fibre of our national life, infecting Congress, the courts, the policeman on the beat, the man in the street.' Conformity would be the only virtue, said the President, and every man who refused to conform would have to pay the penalty."[42] Wilson seems not to have noticed his own excess, a failing not unknown in presidents. Remember, he had alerted Congress to the intrigues of the foreign-born pour-ing poison into "the very arteries of our national life." Whether he realized it or not, Wilson was forever showering civil liberties on Germans in Germany while taking them away from American citizens of German descent. In his mes-sage to Congress asking for a declaration of war, he was em-phatic: "We have no quarrel with the German people. We have no feeling towards them but one of sympathy and friendship."[43] Throughout the war, he pressed a policy of "war on the German government, peace with the German people."[44] Save, it appears, such Germans as might have mi-grated to Milwaukee.

Never before, never since, has the American govern-ment been so aroused by the fear of subversion, the com-promise of secrets, the danger within. In *The Growth of the American Republic*, Samuel Eliot Morison, Henry Steele Commager, and William E. Leuchtenburg write: "In

1917–19 the people of the United States abandoned themselves to a hysteria of fear of German conspiracies and of Communist subversion, and the government indulged in greater excesses than at any previous crisis of our history."[45] Again we see the linkage of ethnic identity and political radicalism, a connection that had been present in Wilson's 1915 message to Congress and his reference to "creatures of passion, disloyalty, and anarchy" who "must be crushed." Now it all broke out. As the historians note: "The war offered a great opportunity to bring patriotism to the aid of personal grudges and neighborhood feuds. The independent-minded sort of citizen who was known to his conforming neighbors as a 'Tory' in the Revolution, a 'Jacobin' in 1798, and a 'Copperhead' in the Civil War became a 'pro-German traitor' in 1917 and a 'Bolshevik' in 1918 and was lucky if he did not have garbled scraps of his conversation sent in to the Department of Justice or flashes from his shaving mirror reported as signals to German submarines." Even though no one had any reason to suspect the vast majority of German Americans, libraries withdrew German books from circulation, schools dropped German from their curricula, and some universities not only abolished their German departments but also revoked degrees conferred upon distinguished Germans. A number of German publications, feeling the pressure, went under cover. The governor of Iowa declared an English-only policy for conversations conducted in public places or even over the telephone, and the mayor of Jersey City refused to allow the Austrian-born violinist Fritz Kreisler to appear in concert.[46]

The last word, as it were, was left to former president Theodore Roosevelt in an address at Kansas City on October 1, 1917: "The men who oppose the war; who fail to support the government in every measure which really tends to the efficient prosecution of the war; and above all who in any shape or way champion the cause and the actions of Germany, show themselves to be the Huns within our own gates and the allies of the men whom our sons and brothers are crossing the ocean to fight."[47] It is well that Dwight D. Eisenhower graduated from West Point in 1915; had he been younger and had the war hysteria gone on much longer, an Eisenhower might not have been admitted to the U.S. Military Academy.

Back in Washington, Congress made some attempts to restrain the executive, although it might be more accurate to say that Congress simply lagged. Postmaster General Albert S. Burleson and Attorney General Gregory vied with each another in cracking down on those who were deemed to have made treasonable utterances, and soon the president proposed amendments to extend the Espionage Act to cover "profane, scurrilous, or abusive language about the form of government, . . . the Constitution, . . . or the flag of the United States, or the uniform of the Army and Navy." Thus it was that the Sedition Act became law on May 16, 1918. Although Congress allowed the law to expire in 1921, during the three years that the act was in force, pro-German newspapers, German speakers, and, more often, socialists and other antiwar radicals were suppressed or punished.[48]

Under the combined force of the Espionage Act and the Sedition Act, the government also instituted a widespread program of supervision and censorship of the press; prohibited two socialist newspapers from the mails; quashed the circulation of *The Public*, a tax journal that advocated using taxes to bear more of the costs of the war; and banned Thorstein Veblen's *Imperial Germany and the Industrial Revolution*. A film producer received a jail sentence of ten years for making *The Spirit of Seventy-Six*, a film whose subject, the American Revolution, was thought to inflame anti-British sentiments. A Vermont minister received a sentence of fifteen years for citing Jesus as an exemplar of pacifism.[49]

At this now considerable distance, it is difficult to appreciate the force of pacifism as a political movement of the late nineteenth and early twentieth centuries. It was international, based on creed, and given to association with socialism and other such commitments. There was nothing notably exotic in its doctrine, certainly not in the age of The Hague Peace Conferences—which were convened in Holland in 1899 and 1907 by the czar of Russia and which established the Permanent Court of Arbitration and fifteen other conventions on the customs and laws of war—and The Hague Peace Palace, the gift of Andrew Carnegie, built there between 1907 and 1913.

William Jennings Bryan, Wilson's first secretary of state, was a pacifist—in the words of his biographer, a "pacifist committed, with remarkably few reservations, to nonviolence in dealings between the nations." To this end, Bryan had set about negotiating some nineteen "cooling-off" treaties providing for international commissions to conciliate disputes when ordinary diplomatic methods failed.[50] (In the Hoover administration, Secretary of State Frank B. Kellogg would negotiate another nineteen such treaties.) Bryan resigned, gracefully, over the tone of Wilson's response after the Germans torpedoed the passenger ship SS *Lusitania* in 1915. Arthur Link observes that what Bryan could not accept was not so much what the president said as what he did not say about American neutrality: he did not say that the United States would do everything possible to avoid "even the possibility of war."[51] Josephus Daniels, Wilson's secretary of the navy, was a Bryan supporter and was certainly thought to be a pacifist; even his obituary noted as such.[52] When Wilson appointed Newton Diehl Baker as secretary of war, the *New York Times* ran an article with a rather pointed subtitle: "He Is Known as an Ardent Pacifist."[53]

Nonviolence had been advocated by Quakers in America since the seventeenth century. Of a sudden, such views became subversive and "foreign" and a penal offense. The United States grew reckless in its infringement of liberty. Consider the matter of Eugene V. Debs, who had run for president as the candidate of the Socialist Party of America in 1912. He had received 900,369 votes, 6 percent of all votes cast. (Wilson received only 41.9 percent.) On June 16, 1918, Debs delivered an antiwar speech in Canton, Ohio, expressing solidarity with three men—Wagenknecht, Baker, and Ruthenberg—who had been convicted of failing to register for the draft. He also condemned the conviction of Kate Richards O'Hare, who had been charged with obstructing the draft. Because such speech was now forbidden under the Espionage Act, Debs was tried, convicted, and sentenced to ten years' imprisonment on each of three counts, to be served concurrently.

The Supreme Court did not consider the constitutionality of the Espionage Act of 1917 and the Sedition Act of 1918 until after World War I. The enduring legal precedent established by the Court in its consideration of these acts comes from *Schenck v. United States*. In writing the opinion on behalf of the Court, Justice Oliver Wendell Holmes articulated the test of "clear and present danger." The ruling affirmed that Congress has a right to limit speech in an attempt to limit certain "evils." Holmes explained: "The most stringent protection of free speech would not protect a man in falsely shouting fire in a theatre and causing a panic. It does not even protect a man from an injunction against uttering words that may have all the effect of force . . . . The question in every case is whether the words used are used in such circumstances and are of such a nature as to create a clear and present danger that they will bring about the substantive evils that Congress has a right to prevent."[54] Subsequent to *Schenck*, Justice Holmes also wrote the opinion, for a unanimous court, upholding Debs's conviction on March 10, 1919.[55]

The American presidency, with the cooperation of Congress and the courts, was obstructing democracy to an unprecedented extent, and doing so in the name of defending it.

Democracy was not obstructed altogether, of course. In 1920, Debs was once again the presidential candidate of the Socialist Party of America, this time running from a penitentiary in Atlanta. He received more votes, 915,940, than in 1912, but a lower proportion of the electorate, 3.4 percent.

On Christmas Day 1921, President Warren G. Harding commuted Debs's sentence, and he was provided a railroad ticket from Atlanta to Washington. On December 26, Debs called first on Attorney General Harry M. Daugherty and then had a half-hour visit with President Harding at the White House. In the 1920 election, Harding had promised a return to normalcy, and he did his best. Just before Harding took office, on Wilson's last day as president, Congress had repealed the Sedition Act, the 1918 amendment to the Espionage Act. But nothing would be quite the same again.

CHAPTER THREE

The Encounter with Communism

Loyalty to country had appeared as a force in American affairs. The day after the declaration of war in 1917, Wilson had issued an executive order that in effect required government employees to support government policy, both in conduct and in sympathy. The order read: "The head of a department or independent office may forthwith remove any employee when he has ground for believing that the retention of such employee would be inimical to the public welfare by reason of his conduct, sympathies, or utterances, or because of other reasons growing out of the war. Such removal may be made without other formality than that the reasons shall be made a matter of confidential record, subject, however, to inspection by the Civil Service Commission." The order was intended to be in effect only temporarily—"this order is issued solely because of the present international situation, and will be withdrawn when the emergency is passed"—but in the manner of bureaucracies, the "emergency" lingered. The Civil Service Commission debarred persons from examinations for reasons relating to loyalty as late as 1921, years after the war had ended.[1]

Part of the reason for this lingering caution was that loyalty had become enmeshed with a kind of bureaucratic hoarding instinct. All bureaucrats have this instinct, and it intensifies during times of crisis. Moreover, as the concept of loyalty adopted in 1917 implied, the various federal departments and agencies did possess a great deal of information that could be used to injure the government or the national interest if revealed by disloyal persons with ties to hostile nations or to internal elements hostile to the American way of life.

Among these internal elements were impassioned anarchists, who believed that any form of regulation or government was immoral and who had formed an international movement in the nineteenth century.[2] In their terrorist mode, they had set about blowing up czars and such. After the assassination of President McKinley, the United States adopted a statute barring anarchists from entering the country. The arrest, imprisonment, and deportation to Russia of Russian-born American anarchist Emma Goldman was a celebrated case of the later Wilson years. Although no doubt idealists, the anarchists were also frequently violent and so threatened the necessary state monopoly on violence. Even so, there does not appear to have been any systematic search for anarchists at the federal level until passage of the Espionage Act of 1917. But shortly thereafter, bureaucracies were compiling dossiers and government officials were classifying information by various degrees of secrecy. It appears that the American military borrowed today's three-tier gradation in classifying documents—Confidential, Secret, and Top Secret (at that time, For Official Use Only, Confidential, and Secret)—from the system used by British forces in France.[3] Again, it all begins in 1917.

If 1917 was an eventful year in the United States, it was a momentous one in Russia. In a cabinet meeting on March 20, called after German submarines sank three American merchant vessels, President Wilson spoke of summoning Congress and, by implication, asking for a declaration of war. Secretary of State Lansing recorded that the president spoke of the situation in the belligerent countries, "particularly in Russia where the revolution against the autocracy had been successful."[4] Lansing took up the point to argue that "the revolution in Russia, which appeared to be successful, had removed the one objection to affirming that the European War was a war between Democracy and Absolutism"; further, American entry into the war "would have a great moral influence in Russia."[5] A moment all but erased from history by the events that followed.

That autumn, the Bolsheviks seized power and created the world's first totalitarian regime. On October 26 (in the Russian calendar), the day after the storming of the Winter Palace in St. Petersburg, Lenin pronounced in *Pravda* that the "dictatorship of the proletariat" had commenced. If hardly a democratic society, czarist Russia had been a reasonably open one (*Pravda* itself had been freely circulated since beginning publication on May 5, 1912). All this was now supplanted by terror, violence, and, above all, secrecy. If something like the Soviet regime had been envisioned, both by those who had great hopes for it and by those who instinctively feared it, no one seems to have anticipated that secrecy would be its most distinctive feature. Everything that went on in government was closed to public view. Civil society ceased to exist. Only the nameless masses and the reclusive leaders remained.

Soviet secrecy in domestic affairs carried over into foreign affairs. The new regime was both threatened and threatening. Early on, American, British, and French expeditionary forces were sent to overturn the new Bolshevik government and somehow keep Russia in the war. (It could be fairly remarked that the United States took this intervention rather too offhandedly. Nothing came of it, and we may be said to have assumed that it did not affect Soviet attitudes and conduct later on. As it was, the United States did not recognize the Soviet government and exchange ambassadors until 1933.)

Even while under attack, however, the Soviets began recruiting secret agents in foreign countries. They saw themselves as leaders of a worldwide movement—the red flag, symbol of universal brotherhood—and anticipated early success as other regimes began to collapse at the close of World War II. Some agents were under cover, some quite public, some both.

John Reed, a Harvard graduate of the class of 1910, was of the hybrid sort. In 1913, he joined the staff of *The Masses*, a socialist journal published in New York. (Its fame today is largely accounted for by its illustrations, created by John Sloan and other artists of the Ashcan school.) In August 1917, Reed published an antiwar article, "Knit a Strait-Jacket for Your Soldier Boy." This brought upon him prosecution for sedition under the Espionage Act and, with his acquittal, a measure of fame in his own circles.[6] But the great event was Reed's trip to Russia, where he witnessed the Bolshevik coup. His account of the revolution, *Ten Days That Shook the World,* appeared in 1919 (soon after his acquittal in *The Masses* trial) and proved a master work of what would come to be called agitprop. He also attended the All-Russian Soviet convention in January 1918. In the summer of 1919 he was expelled from the Socialist Party at its convention in Chicago and thereupon helped to found the Communist Labor Party. That same year, the Bolsheviks founded the Communist International, or Comintern, an association of national Communist parties that in theory were equals but in practice were always dominated by the Soviet party; Reed promptly returned to the Soviet Union to seek the Comintern's recognition of his new Communist Labor Party as *the* Communist party in the United States. He died of typhus in Moscow in October 1920 and was buried beside the Kremlin wall. Lenin, who had become Reed's close friend, wrote an introduction to one edition of Reed's book, although he did not live to see the movie (*Reds,* 1981).

Reed was a Soviet agent. On January 22, 1920, the Comintern gave him gold, jewels, and other valuables worth

1,008,000 rubles for party work in the United States.[7] The U.S. government did not know this, nor much else besides; it has only recently been discovered in the archives of the former Soviet Union. We now know that for the next seven decades the U.S. government would be the object of a sustained Soviet campaign of infiltration and subversion. In the United States the Soviets were to have a measure of success among elites, as they did in Great Britain (Kim Philby was, properly speaking, Harold Adrian Russell Philby), but in the pattern already seen, an ethnic factor—the workings of diaspora politics—was to be the most prominent.

In the beginning, most American Communists were Russians. The Communist Party of the United States of America (CPUSA) was organized at Moscow's behest in 1921, merging Reed's Communist Labor Party with the Communist Party of America, which had been organized by a former socialist, midwesterner Charles Emil Ruthenberg. The membership was not large and was overwhelmingly of foreign birth: Theodore Draper, in *The Roots of American Communism*, estimates that but 10 percent of the members spoke English.[8] Harvey Klehr, John Earl Haynes, and Fridrikh Igorevich Firsov, in *The Secret World of American Communism*, place that estimate at about 12 percent for the two parties that merged in 1921.[9] Draper comments that the American Communist movement began as a "predominantly Slavic movement," as immigrants brought their politics with them or responded sympathetically to political changes in their homelands.[10] This situation changed somewhat as "Americans" and "other nationalities" joined the movement.[11] But the ethnic dimension of American Communism never ceased, although at times it seems to have been overshadowed by the likes of Reed.

Perhaps a quarter of a million persons passed through the Communist Party between 1919 and 1960—with the emphasis on passing through.[12] Nathan Glazer estimates that at the peak of the movement's popularity there were "considerably fewer than 100,000 Communists."[13] Nor did the party, or parties in the first instance, have an auspicious beginning. Fear of radical revolutions got out of hand in 1919–20. There was a good deal of disorder and no small amount of criminal behavior. On May Day 1919, thirty-six bombs were mailed to prominent politicians, judges, and other "enemies of the Left." The *New York Times* wrote of a "nationwide bomb conspiracy." As noted, the Washington home of Attorney General A. Mitchell Palmer was damaged by a bomb that went off prematurely and blew up the bomber.[14]

All this would appear to have been a last surge of anarchism, but it was generally taken for Bolshevism. "Russian Reds Are Busy Here," ran a headline from the *Times*. Palmer, the "Fighting Quaker," responded with major cross-country raids—the Palmer Raids—on radical organizations, including the New York–based Union of Russian Workers, on November 7–8, 1919, the second anniversary of the Bolshevik Revolution. On January 2, 1920, federal agents in thirty-three cities arrested more than four thousand Communists as undesirable aliens deserving of deportation. The *Washington Post* warned, "There is not time to waste on hair-splitting over infringement of liberty." J. Edgar Hoover, then a twenty-five-year-old Justice Department official, located a U.S. Army transport, nicknamed the "Soviet Ark," and sent a shipload of radicals home, inviting members of Congress to see them off at Ellis Island. Hoover now emerged as a national figure, while his superior, the attorney general, began making plans to run for president and warning of likely strikes, bombings, and other terror on May Day.[15]

The unrest did not last. May Day 1920 passed without incident, damaging Palmer's credibility. His raids came to be seen as excessive, and his presidential aspirations faded. Most Americans had begun to agree with Warren G. Harding, who, while running for president against Democrat James Cox, had commented, "Too much has been said about

Bolshevism in America."[16] The Democratic administration, leaderless following Wilson's stroke on October 2, 1919, had become undisciplined and erratic.

Such intervals would recur, with both parties involved, but now a sense of civic order returned. Draper observes: "Ironically, the Palmer raids came as a blessing in disguise to the foreign-language federations. More than ever they were able to imagine themselves Russian Bolsheviks in America. Had not the Russian Revolution been forced to work illegally almost to the very eve of the seizure of power? Was there any fundamental difference between Palmer's prisons and the Czar's dungeons? . . . If the Russian road to the revolution was right, then the postwar repression in the United States merely offered additional proof that the American revolution was really approaching. The underground character of the movement became the supreme test of its revolutionary integrity."[17]

And now the new rulers of Russia turned their acolytes into agents. Klehr, Haynes, and Firsov write: "Soviet intelligence was able to make use of the Comintern and its operatives because, from its foundation, the Communist International had encouraged Communist parties to maintain both a legal political organization and an illegal or underground apparatus. Among the twenty-one conditions required for admission to its ranks, the Comintern in 1920 stipulated that all Communist parties create an illegal 'organizational apparatus which, at the decisive moment, can assist the Party to do its duty to the revolution.'"[18]

Intended both to protect the parties from police repression and to promote secret political subversion, these underground apparatuses conducted operations that were as inventive as they were extensive. Comintern representatives traveled with false passports, and they elaborated clandestine courier services, mail drops, and various codes and cryptographic systems for communicating with foreign Communist parties, which were urged to form secret units and to have safe houses and fake identification documents at the ready. And the Comintern representatives were prepared to assist these foreign Communist parties with cash and valuables. Before the United States officially recognized the USSR in 1933, Soviet money for American Communists was sent by way of secret couriers. The subsidy of valuables sent to Reed has already been mentioned; the document from the Soviet archives that mentions Reed's payment also details others sent to three other Communists in the United States in 1919–20, for a total subvention worth 2,728,000 rubles. As Klehr, Haynes, and Firsov comment, "This account reveals that in this period the Comintern supplied the tiny American Communist movement with the equivalent of several million dollars in valuables [that is, gold, silver, or jewels], an enormous sum in the 1920s."[19] In time the size of the subsidies fell off, but even so, they continued for decades afterward.[20]

American Communists were relatively isolated. Apart from circles in New York and a very few other metropolitan centers, and apart from elements in the American labor movement, Communists were almost unknown. Among intellectuals and especially within the labor movement, the encounter with Communism produced an often fierce anti-Communist response. (For the duration of the Cold War, the American Federation of Labor was unmatched in its understanding of Communism and its antagonism to it.) In time, an opposition appeared in the form of ex-Communists who had broken with the party. With a sure sense of things to come, Ignazio Silone predicted that "the final battle would be between Communists and ex-Communists," so great were the insight and loathing of the disillusioned.[21]

But because a measure of social distance separated most ex-Communists from the rest of the nation in these years, their tales, when told, often seemed too exotic to be true. They were easily dismissed as fantasists or worse. Such was the experience of Benjamin Gitlow, who had worked with Reed in founding the Communist Labor Party but who was expelled from the CPUSA in 1929, during one of the recurrent purges that followed Stalin's exile of Trotsky. In 1939 Gitlow testified before a congressional committee that the fledgling party in America had received Soviet subsidies, frequently in the form of diamonds and jewelry that it could convert to cash with the aid of sympathetic businessmen. But Gitlow, like other ex-Communists, was often seen as an unreliable witness. His testimony was discounted.[22]

Trotsky was an emblematic figure. He was living in Manhattan when the Bolsheviks came to power in St. Petersburg, whereupon he rushed home, became foreign minister, commanded armies, might have succeeded Lenin, was exiled by Stalin, and in time was assassinated in Mexico City. Sidney Hook, a professor at New York University and a one-time fellow traveler who, with many a New Yorker, followed Trotsky into opposition to Stalin, relates in his autobiography that it was one of his students, Sylvia Ageloff, who unwittingly communicated Trotsky's whereabouts to his assassin.[23] Ageloff's sister served for a time as Trotsky's secretary in Mexico City, and when Ageloff visited there, Trotsky and his wife grew fond of her. After Ageloff had returned to New York, she was "casually" offered a ticket to Paris by a female friend who said that she was not going to be able to use it. Ageloff readily accepted. In Paris she met a dashing young journalist who said he was from Belgium—her first love. He was in fact Ramón Mercader, whose mother, a leading member of the Spanish Communist Party, was then living in Moscow with a general in the Narodnyi Komissariat Vnutrennikh Del (People's Commissariat of Internal Affairs), a predecessor of the KGB. In 1940, with Ageloff's guileless help, Mercader traveled to Mexico City, insinuated himself into Trotsky's household, and, when the opportunity arose, murdered him.

Back in New York, there now commenced yet another raging battle between Stalinists and Trotskyites. Questions of who and whom devolved into an eternity of commissions and conventions and contentions. As ever, the party-line Communists lied about everything; we now know that

Ramón Mercader was indeed a KGB agent and that in 1943 the KGB even planned a commando raid to free him from the Mexican prison where he was being detained.[24] Life-and-death issues in New York City, they were little noticed in the rest of the nation.

In 1948, Whittaker Chambers, who had been a contributor to the Communist publications the *Daily Worker* and *The New Masses* in the early 1930s and was later an editor at *Time*, would startle most of the nation with what seemed an astonishing assertion: in the mid-1930s he had been an undercover agent of the Soviet Union and a member of a Washington "cell" that included, most prominently, Alger Hiss. A great controversy arose. Was Chambers telling the truth?

Sidney Hook recounts that "everyone" in New York in the 1930s knew about Chambers's past: "I assumed—and I am confident that I was not the only one—that Chambers was engaged in underground work after he left *The New Masses*."[25] Only after Chambers had broken with the party did he realize that the penalty for this divorce could be death. As Hook recalls: "Chambers was on the verge of hysteria, . . . convinced that, because he had become a faceless, nameless, unknown creature of the underground, his elimination either by murder or kidnapping would remain undetected. His goal was to become a *public* character again, to emerge under his own name and thus prevent his disappearance into the shadows."[26]

Hook devised a complicated "'life insurance' policy" whereby Chambers would "draw up a detailed list of all the Soviet operatives he knew, all the 'sleepers' in Washington and elsewhere who had given him information," and send this to Earl Browder, then head of the CPUSA, with the further message that, if Chambers were murdered, the list would be made public. Hook adds, "When Chambers first publicly identified his fellow-conspirators in 1948, the names were quite familiar to me." They were the same names that Chambers had given to a mutual friend, Herbert Solow, in 1938. They were the same names that he had given to Adolph Berle, then an assistant secretary of state, in 1939. Many years later, in 1953, when Hook asked Berle about the incident and its aftermath, Berle talked about how confusing life was in Washington when he met Chambers, at the beginning of World War II with the world "falling to pieces" all around. "Nonetheless," Hook notes, "despite his initial incredulity at the bizarre tale, Berle steadfastly insisted that he had sent word of Chambers' story to the White House. Berle himself ended up convinced that it was true. Fortunately Berle kept his notes of his meeting with Chambers, which listed the names Chambers had identified as his confederates."[27]

It is not difficult to imagine how a memo from Berle could have been ignored. The anti-Communist hysteria of 1919–20 was remembered, especially by those associated with the administration of Franklin D. Roosevelt, as something of an embarrassment. No one would have wanted to be accused of similar credulity. And so the interval of 1918–39 concluded, and the Great War resumed. During that time the Soviet Union had put in place a fairly elaborate espionage apparatus, more or less reflexively. From the Soviet perspective, the United States was a somewhat marginal power, but even so, spies here might prove useful in time— as indeed they would, however briefly. For its part, the U.S. government was not much interested in such matters.

Looking back on this period, David Riesman wrote in 1952: "Twenty and even ten years ago, it was an important intellectual task . . . to point out to Americans of good will that the Soviet and Nazi systems were not simply transitory stages, nor a kind of throwback to the South American way—that they were, in fact, new forms of social organization, more omnivorous than even the most brutal of earlier dictatorships. At that time, there were many influential people who were willing to see the Nazis as a menace but insisted that the Bolsheviks were a hope."[28] It is a matter of the first importance that the people whom Riesman refers to were concentrated in New York City.

Among them was Lionel Trilling, a native of the city,

who spent most of his life at Columbia University and was one of the nation's foremost literary critics. In 1947 he published his only novel, *The Middle of the Journey,* which turns on the relations between Gifford Maxim, a former spy seeking to establish a higher profile in order to avoid being liquidated (in the usage of that period), and an upper-class couple, Arthur and Nancy Croom, who, although fictional representatives of a certain time and place, bear a remarkable resemblance to Alger and Priscilla Hiss. It happens that Trilling knew Chambers. He later wrote that Chambers's political career, including its underground phase, was "the openest of secrets while it lasted." But Trilling had never met either Alger or Priscilla Hiss, nor did he know anyone who had. Yet in a sense they *all* had. A few months after the novel was published, the Hiss case broke, and the previously obscure Chambers became "a historical figure."[29]

The novel, as the author remarked with a measure of understatement in his introduction to the 1975 edition, "was not well received." In fact it was attacked as a faintly disguised and politically incorrect account of real-life events. Trilling was even asked by one of Hiss's lawyers to testify against Chambers in court. Trilling refused, saying, "Whittaker Chambers is a man of honour," an assertion that provoked the lawyer into an "outburst of contemptuous rage." But Trilling stood by his assessment: "Whittaker Chambers had been engaged in espionage against his own country; when a change of heart and principle led to his defecting from his apparatus, he had eventually not only confessed his own treason but named the comrades who shared it, including one whom for a time he had cherished as a friend. I hold that when this has been said of him, it is still possible to say that he was a man of honour."[30]

It was the times that were out of joint. Trilling acknowledged that, a mere three decades afterward, the mentality of the Communist-oriented intelligentsia of the 1930s and 1940s strained comprehension, even among those who had observed it firsthand:

That mentality was presided over by an impassioned longing to believe. . . . What the fellow-traveling intellectuals were impelled to give their credence to was the ready feasibility of contriving a society in which reason and virtue would prevail. A proximate object of the will to believe was less abstract—a large segment of the progressive intellectual class was determined to credit the idea that in one country, Soviet Russia, a decisive step had been taken toward the establishment of just such a society. Among those people of whom this resolute belief was characteristic, any predication about the state of affairs in Russia commanded assent so long as it was of a "positive" nature, so long, that is, as it countenanced the expectation that the Communist Party, having actually instituted the reign of reason and virtue in one nation, would go forward to do likewise throughout the world.[31]

Any characterization or evidence to the contrary was swiftly dismissed. Either the messengers were disparaged as being deficient in goodwill or the message itself was explained away. "Should it ever happen that reality did succeed in breaching the believer's defenses against it," Trilling wrote, "if ever it became unavoidable to acknowledge that the Communist Party, as it functioned in Russia, did things, or produced conditions, which by ordinary judgment were to be deplored, . . . then it was plain that ordinary human judgment was not adequate to the deplored situation, whose moral justification must be revealed by some other agency, commonly 'the dialectic.'"[32]

But in time even these seemingly unassailable defenses were forced to give way. Trilling recounted:

But there came a moment when reality did indeed breach the defenses that had been erected against it, and not even the dialectic itself could contain the terrible assault it made upon faith. In 1939 the Soviet Union made its pact with Nazi Germany. There had previously been circumstances—among them the Comintern's refusal to form a united front with the Social Democrats in Germany, thus allowing Hitler to come to power; the Moscow purge trials;

the mounting evidence that vast prison camps did exist in the Soviet Union—which had qualified the moral prestige of Stalinist Communism in one degree or another, yet never decisively. But now to that prestige a mortal blow seemed to have been given. After the Nazi-Soviet pact one might suppose that the Russia of Stalin could never again be the ground on which the hope of the future was based, that never again could it command the loyalty of men of good will.[33]

At the time of the Nazi-Soviet nonaggression pact, Richard Rovere, who later wrote the luminous "Letter from Washington" series in the *New Yorker,* was literary editor of *The New Masses* in New York. In his memoirs he recalls that, so great was his shock at the news, he cannot remember where he was during the next three or four days.[34] But as Trilling noted, even the Nazi-Soviet pact was not enough. War came; Hitler was the common enemy. The Soviets were allied with the West. And it was not until belief in the Soviet system had begun to fade in Moscow that something similar occurred in New York.

Now pay heed. New York City in the 1930s and early 1940s was the center of the country. It cast 7.3 percent of the votes in the 1944 presidential election. But it was not the capital. The capital was in Washington, D.C., a city that at this time was still provincial, with but little awareness of these matters. When the issue of Communists in government and Communists in general rose again, as it soon did, even Truman could easily dismiss it as reactionary hysteria. That he could do so was partly a consequence of the relative isolation of Communists in America.

There is another perspective, one perhaps best evoked by the anecdote told about Ernest Bevin, onetime head of the Transport and General Workers' Union in Britain and the British foreign secretary at the time of the Potsdam conference in 1945. When he returned from the conference, a fellow MP asked him what the Soviets were like. "Why," Bevin replied, "they're just like the bloody Communists!" By contrast, it is quite possible that Truman had never met a Communist until he sat down with Stalin at the same conference, and it is equally possible that Hoover had never knowingly met a Communist. This was a matter of regionalism in what was then a much more regionalist nation. The clandestine activities of the Communist Party of the United States of America were common knowledge within political and intellectual circles of Manhattan in the 1930s. They were a given. But they were almost completely unknown elsewhere, apart from a few midwestern industrial cities.

It may be wondered if Truman ever knew that he was chosen as the vice presidential candidate for FDR's 1944 reelection campaign by a cabal of Democrats whose leader was Edward J. Flynn of the Bronx. Flynn had encountered Communists at the polls in his borough. In 1944 the Liberal Party was founded to give antiorganization voters, Jewish for the most part, a "line" on which they could vote for Roosevelt. Previously the American Labor Party had served that purpose, but it was now under Communist control. These were serious matters to Democratic leaders. They judged that too many of these adversary organizations were too close to the incumbent vice president, Henry A. Wallace. Soon Wallace was out and Truman was in, thanks to Ed Flynn and his cohorts. These least sophisticated of politicians proved in some ways to be the most astute and prescient and, in the years ahead, crucial.

CHAPTER FOUR

The Experience of World War II

The Great War resumed in 1939. The combatants were much the same; war itself, however, was changing dramatically, perhaps most significantly with the advent of aerial bombardment. The very idea had once seemed repellent. The First Hague Conference of 1899 had banned bombing from balloons, but the Germans went ahead even so, using dirigibles to develop the first strategic aerial bombing force. Soon airplanes and actual bombers followed, for which the all-important appurtenance was the bombsight.

In the 1920s an American inventor, Carl L. Norden, had developed a sighting device that promised precise aiming for high-altitude bombs. The Norden bombsight became the army's most important secret in the original understanding of the Espionage Act of 1917, which was primarily directed to military equipment, deployment, and installations. By November 1937, German spies had stolen the plans. The theft was the work of a large espionage operation directed from Hamburg by Colonel Nikolaus Ritter—the Ritter Ring, it was called. The Norden operation was carried out by Hermann Lang, a thirty-six-year-old native of Germany who was by then a naturalized U.S. citizen living in a German-American neighborhood in Queens, New York. He worked as an assembly inspector at the Norden plant on Lafayette Street in downtown Manhattan. (An equivalent facility today would be located in New Mexico and surrounded by an electrified fence. But we were learning.) Lang evidently considered himself a German patriot, and he copied the bombsight plans as an act of German patriotism.[1]

Soon, however, the Federal Bureau of Investigation was onto the operation. Another participant in the ring was Fritz Duquesne, an Afrikaner of Huguenot descent who had been born in Cape Province and had witnessed the British quashing of Afrikaner republics in the Boer War. By the 1930s, he too was a naturalized U.S. citizen, but he was willing to spy against the United States if, in so doing, he would be working toward the downfall of his "hated enemy," England.[2] On June 29, 1941, the FBI arrested twenty-three members of the Ritter Ring—nineteen in New York and four in New Jersey. On Walter Winchell's weekly radio program, FBI director J. Edgar Hoover called it "the greatest spy roundup in U.S. history."[3]

Espionage was becoming the stuff of entertainment. *The House on Ninety-Second Street,* a film released in 1945, was loosely based on the activities of the Ritter Ring. The FBI had by now acquired a firm place in the national imagery as the bane of foreign subversives, with German and later Japanese spies assuming the roles that gangsters had played in the 1920s and early 1930s. This was due partly to the director's law-and-order persona but also to the public's innate fascination with espionage, the subject of a great many 1930s spy novels and moving pictures. Much of this was merely entertainment; some part of it reflected national anxieties. But it also reflected a fact of consequence: the U.S. government was acquiring, principally but not exclusively through the FBI, an organized capacity to defend against foreign attack and, most important, was beginning to learn the art of infiltration where there was a domestic component to the foreign attack.

Note the pattern set in 1917. First, twentieth-century war requires or is seen to require measures directed against enemies both "foreign *and* domestic." Such enemies, real or imagined, will be perceived in both ethnic and ideological terms. Second, government responds to domestic threats with regulations designed to ensure the loyalty of those within the government bureaucracy and the security of government secrets, with similar regulations designed to protect against disloyal conduct on the part of citizens and, of course, foreign agents.

We do well to be wary of rules concerning organizational behavior, and even more so for such rules in political affairs. But, then, should we not also be mindful of the view of the framers of the Constitution—that they had discovered, in Hamilton's phrase, a new "science of politics" for bringing stability to the government that they had contrived?[4]

The record of 1917 and the years immediately following is instructive. President Wilson looked up the rules—in this case, the law of the sea—and decided that Germany was in gross and criminal violation. Whereupon the U.S. government declared war. New laws and regulations were dutifully enacted to ensure proper behavior in wartime. Events got out of hand. As fears of Communist conspiracies and German subversion mounted, it was the U.S. government's conduct that approached the illegal. A reasonable explanation for this is that at the time the government had no organized means of assessing these dangers accurately and responding to them appropriately.

It is notable that, in great contrast to the experience of World War I, there was little anti-German hysteria (not too strong a word) during World War II. This may partly be accounted for by the fact that the German presence in American civil life had already been suppressed during the earlier period, which saw what the *Harvard Encyclopedia of Ameri-*

can Ethnic Groups calls "the rapid dismantling of the asso-
ciational structure of German America," from the drasti-
cally reduced readership of German-language publications
to the dissolving of the National German-American Alliance
in April 1918, under Senate investigation.[5]

Even so, German Nazis made a considerable effort to establish an American base. They had already begun recruiting by 1924, but the first large-scale American organization,
the Friends of the New Germany, was not founded until July
1933.[6] A new immigrant, Fritz J. Kuhn, promptly joined. By
1936, Kuhn had become leader of the German-American
Bund (Amerika-Deutscher Volksbund), which was formed
at Buffalo, New York, and was thenceforth a not insignifi-
cant and more or less national political presence. In 1939,
on George Washington's birthday, Kuhn and his allies organized a mass rally in Madison Square Garden in New York.
The newsreel coverage was stunning: a full-fledged Nazi
rally, complete with uniforms and salutes, all intended to
rouse the masses in the struggle against "Rosenfeld's [that
is, Roosevelt's] Jew Republic."

Robin Edwin Herzstein estimates that the Bund probably consisted of some 6,500 activists at this time, with a combined pool of 50,000 to 100,000 sympathizers, family, and
friends.[7] In other words, about the same number of people
as the early Communist Party. There were other parallels.
Herzstein describes a similar immigrant core with similar
apocalyptic fantasies:

> When the Depression struck, many of these newly arrived
> Germans found themselves in dire straits. Unemployed or
> engaged in menial tasks like dishwashing, these disap-
> pointed people found solace in the Bund. They could leave
> their cramped cold-water flats, head for a local *Stube*, and
> sit around drinking beer. The conversation often turned to
> the Jews and to the misery of living in Roosevelt's America.
> Tens of thousands of such people attended Bund meetings
> and rallies. Better-educated leaders, like Fritz Kuhn, found
> them easy to manipulate.

Kuhn and his associate Gerhard Wilhelm Kunze made themselves the spokesmen of these alienated recent immigrants. Like Hitler, they hoped that the United States would fragment into an ethnic free-for-all. As one of the Bundists put it: "This will happen here. It is inevitable. When that day comes, and it is probably not far-off, we must be prepared to fight for the right kind of government. We must win the masses to our side." When *der Tag* (the Day) arrived, the Bund had to be ready to grab its share of the loot.[8]

There was even a similar reaching out to other ethnic groups: White Russians, Italians, Irish. The differences, however, were decisive. At the end of 1939 Kuhn was jailed for embezzlement, by 1941 Nazi Germany had declared war on the United States, and by 1945 the Third Reich was crushed. There was not time to generate the kind of influence or recruit the range of receptive audiences that Soviet Communism had.

To say again, the onset of World War II found the United States significantly better *organized* to deal with subversion, real or imagined. After war broke out in Europe in 1939, the government posted FBI agents in embassies in Latin America to compile information on Axis nationals and sympathizers. A worldwide regulatory regime was put in place that thereafter continally expanded, albeit with different players.[9] The FBI was, of course, active at home as well as abroad. Within three days of the bombing of Pearl Harbor, 1,291 Japanese, 857 Germans, and 147 Italians had been taken into custody.[10]

It is fair to say that by this time the federal government had bureaucratized its mode of dealing with subversion. State and local governments had no such experience or organizational framework, so such matters as mass evacuation of foreign elements became the concern of the federal government. Politics, not routine, set the order of the day (to use that expression correctly for a change). This was nicely encapsulated in a memorandum Hoover sent to Attorney

General Francis Biddle on February 3, 1942. He observed that, in California, "the necessity for mass evacuation is based primarily upon public and political pressure rather than on factual data. Public hysteria and in some instances, the comments of the press and radio announcers, have resulted in a tremendous amount of pressure being brought to bear on Governor [Culbert L.] Olson and Earl Warren, Attorney General of the State, and on the military authorities. . . . Local officials, press and citizens have started a widespread movement demanding complete evacuation of Japanese, citizen and alien alike."[11] Which was indeed the case. Soon congressional representatives from western states were joining in. Ten days after Hoover's memo to Biddle, Congressman Clarence Lea of California, the senior West Coast representative, wrote to Franklin D. Roosevelt on behalf of all members of Congress from California, Oregon, and Washington, recommending "the immediate evacuation of all persons of Japanese lineage and all others, aliens and citizens alike, whose presence shall be deemed dangerous or inimical to the defense of the United States from all strategic areas." The congressmen also recommended that "strategic areas" be defined as the states of California, Oregon, and Washington and the territory of Alaska.[12] These views prevailed.

On February 19, 1942, the matter was dealt with according to the regulatory mode. Roosevelt issued Executive Order 9066, "Authorizing the Secretary of War to Prescribe Military Areas." The order gave the secretary of war the power to exclude persons from designated areas in order to provide "protection against espionage and against sabotage to national-defense material."[13]

The executive order did not single out any specific group, ethnic or otherwise, but the result was that Japanese aliens, American citizens of Japanese descent, and Alaskan Aleuts were prohibited from living, working, or traveling on the West Coast. Between May 8, 1942, and March 20, 1946, a total of 120,313 people of Japanese descent who had been living on the West Coast were interned in relocation camps established elsewhere in the West. At the behest of the United States, sixteen Latin American countries interned at least 8,500 Axis nationals. Where governments were reluctant, the United States did the job for them: Peru, for instance, deported about one thousand Japanese, three hundred Germans, and thirty Italians to the United States in 1942.[14] Although the last American relocation camp was closed by March 1946, some Japanese detainees were still in custody as late as 1949.

Some argued that Germans and Italians should be dealt with in much the same way. But the members of these groups were far more numerous, and their political influence was far more formidable. Interning them all seemed inadvisable if not impossible. On May 15, 1942, Secretary of War Henry L. Stimson recommended to the president at a cabinet meeting that particular individuals should be excluded from militarily sensitive areas, but not entire classes of Germans or Italians.[15] Five months later, on October 12, Columbus Day, Attorney General Biddle announced that unnaturalized Italian immigrants would no longer be classified as enemy aliens.[16] German subjects in the United States technically remained enemy aliens, although by January 1943 most of the restrictions on them had been removed. Granted, first Imperial Japan and then Nazi Germany and Fascist Italy had attacked or declared war on the United States, and fascism, broadly defined, did have adherents in this country. Even so, eventually the U.S. government would regret these responses to the crises.

At the time, though, there was little protest at the internment of Japanese and others during World War II.[17] The Roosevelt administration never experienced any loss of reputation; Earl Warren went on to become chief justice of the United States. Much later—more than four decades later—Congress sought to make amends by means of the Civil Liberties Act of 1988, which states that the Japanese internment was "carried out without adequate security reasons and without any acts of espionage or sabotage documented" and was "motivated largely by racial prejudice, wartime hysteria, and a failure of political leadership."[18] The act provided redress for about eighty thousand survivors of internment, each of whom was eligible to receive twenty thousand dollars. More important, they also received an apology from Congress on behalf of the American people.

Extend the term "racial prejudice" to include ethnic and religious prejudice, and we can see a pattern of response to crisis that seems to have become fixed by World War II. In 1943, Lieutenant General John L. DeWitt, western defense commander, issued a report on the 1942 Japanese evacuation in which he reaches a bizarre conclusion: "In the war in which we are now engaged racial affinities are not severed by migration. The Japanese race is an enemy race and while many second and third generation Japanese born on United States soil, possessed of United States citizenship, have become 'Americanized,' the racial strains are undiluted. . . . There are indications that [West Coast Japanese] are organized and ready for concerted action at a favorable opportunity. The very fact that no sabotage has taken place to date is a disturbing and confirming indication that such action will be taken."[19] The last statement verges on the clinically paranoid. Interpreting the absence of overt threat as a device for allaying suspicion can be the mark of a seriously troubled mind. *Vide* Erving Goffman.

There were many such statements during World War II, and how could there not be? The Japanese had attacked the United States without warning. The losses seemed severe (more severe than they actually were). Germany and Italy promptly joined in the war against us. Europe had been conquered; Britain seemed all but lost; only Canada remained. In point of fact we kept our heads pretty well. The supreme Allied commander in Europe was a German American, with no notice taken. And for all the Japanese internees, there were also Japanese Americans like Daniel K. Inouye and

Spark M. Matsunaga, who emerged from the U.S. Army as decorated officers and went on to become U.S. senators.

World War II did see a reprise of the issue of press censorship when the *Chicago Tribune* revealed Roosevelt's plans for fighting a world war even before the United States had become involved. "FDR's War Plans!" shrieked the headline on December 4, 1941: "Goal Is 10 Million Armed Men." Robert R. McCormick, the *Tribune*'s publisher, was an open foe of FDR's administration. Many thought that his paper's exposé was a demonstration of the press's impudence toward affairs of state. But in fact the incident may have been the first instance of the executive using the power of secrecy for his own purposes by "leaking" confidential information to the press.

In his biography of McCormick, Richard Norton Smith records the various sources that had provided the details about Roosevelt's "Victory Program," which the president had requested of the secretaries of war and navy five months earlier: "Citing 'a confidential report prepared by the joint Army and Navy high command by direction of President Roosevelt,' the *Tribune* revealed plans for total war on two oceans and three continents. An extensive air campaign against the German Reich, accompanied by offensive ground action in North Africa and the Near East, would theoretically culminate in a massive U.S.-led invasion of Fortress Europe no later than July 1, 1943." At a cabinet meeting two days after the story broke, Smith notes, Attorney General Biddle remarked that McCormick could perhaps be prosecuted under the Espionage Act of 1917. (He would not be the last attorney general to get this wrong.)[20]

The chief executive was surpassingly unperturbed. Smith speculates that Roosevelt might have seen McCormick's *Tribune* as having provided an opportunity. Michael Barone once suggested to the author that in this case Roosevelt's passivity, a matter that continues to perplex historians, was actually an example of government rationing secret information in order to affect third parties. By the 1960s, it would be routine for, say, the Johnson administration to give classified materials on the Vietnam War to friendly journalists and members of Congress, and almost certainly to friendly governments as well. But in this instance as in much else, it appears that FDR was the first to scout out the new territory. The essential "strategic" fact was that the secrets were created by executive regulation, and thereafter executives would feel free to use them as they might.

CHAPTER FIVE

The Bomb

W orld War II came to a close in August 1945, after the United States dropped two atomic bombs on Japan. The world now knew that the United States possessed the most fearsome secret in the history of warfare. In time, the United States would learn that the Soviet Union also possessed the secret, which had been spirited away by spies. The bomb changed international politics. It also changed the United States. Nothing has quite been the same since.

Prometheus-like, men had stolen fire from the gods. Maurice M. Shapiro, now chief scientist emeritus of the Laboratory for Cosmic Physics at the Naval Research Station in Washington, was one of the scientists who worked at the Atomic Research Laboratory at Los Alamos. He described the scene of the Trinity test, the first nuclear explosion, in the New Mexico desert on the morning of July 16, 1945: "At precisely 5:30 there was a blinding flash—brighter than many suns—and then a flaming fireball. Within seconds a churning multicolored column of gas and dust was rising. Then, within it, a narrower column of debris swirled upward, spreading out into an awesome mushroom-shaped apparition high in the atmosphere."[1]

But awe was almost immediately crowded out by "an oppressive sense of foreboding."[2] In his account of this moment, J. Robert Oppenheimer, then director of the Los Alamos laboratory, made an analogy often repeated since: "We waited until the blast had passed, walked out of the shelter and then it was extremely solemn. We knew the world would not be the same. A few people laughed, a few people cried. Most people were silent. I remembered the line from the Hindu scripture, the *Bhagavad-Gita:* Vishnu is trying to persuade the Prince that he should do his duty and to impress him he takes on his multi-armed form and says, 'Now I am become Death, the destroyer of worlds.' I suppose we all thought that, one way or another."[3]

The scientists at the site knew that if the test worked, not only would it end the war, as it did within the month, but it would forever change the nature of warfare. It was the culmination of four years of secret work, the fruit of the vast enterprise code-named the Manhattan Project. Before long we would learn that Communist sympathizers had stolen parts of the complex formula. *Our* punishment would now begin.

This was a complex fate. But then, so was that of Prometheus. For his audacity he was chained to a mountain where an eagle daily gnawed at his liver, which then healed itself every night. He was at length freed by Hercules. So, at length, would the United States be freed from the long torment of secrecy that followed, but only *after* a long ordeal and only to a degree.

The scientists present at the Trinity test had submitted to an unfamiliar and altogether uncongenial secrecy, for they knew what was at stake. (The physicists included some—Hans Bethe of Germany, Enrico Fermi of Italy, and James Chadwick of England, discoverer of the neutron and winner of the 1935 Nobel Prize for Physics—whose nationalities must have made them especially sensitive to what was in jeopardy.) Atomic fission itself was not a secret. German scientists knew of it; there are no secrets in science. Oppenheimer and his associates had "simply" figured out the techniques and found the resources to build the bomb before the Germans did. Later the Soviets did the same thing. But even in 1945, at that moment of profound concealment, scientific discourse was a remarkably open one, as Shapiro recorded: "While waiting for the rain to abate so that the test could begin, Dr. Bethe and I discussed his epochal discovery of the thermonuclear reactions that power the sun and stars. For me it was a memorable dialogue: we were about to witness the first massive fission explosion, yet we talked of controlled fusion—the steady burning of hydrogen in stars." Shapiro added, "We pointedly did not discuss the prospect of future H-bombs, also based on thermonuclear reactions."[4]

The H-bombs did come; it seemed that they had to come, once the A-bomb was no longer the American advantage. But even before then, in 1946, the United States did try to forestall a nuclear arms race. President Truman proposed to the United Nations a plan for international control of atomic energy. The Baruch Plan, as it came to be known (after Truman's representative Bernard M. Baruch), was blocked by the Soviet Union, whose leader Joseph Stalin was determined to have his own bomb.

And he soon had it. Thanks to successful espionage, the Russians tested their first atom bomb in August 1949, just four years after the first American test. Such alacrity on their part could mean only that they had somehow obtained at least part of our secret. And in fact the A-bomb that the Soviets detonated in August 1949 was a near-exact copy of "Fat Man," the American weapon that had destroyed Nagasaki in August 1945 (Figures 3 and 4).

Now the stakes were raised. When Truman and his advisors learned of the first Soviet test, they embarked on an intense, four-month, secret debate about whether to proceed with the hydrogen bomb project. A number of officials and atomic energy experts at the highest reaches of govern-

Figure 3. "Fat Man," the atomic bomb detonated over Nagasaki, Japan, on August 9, 1945. *Source:* National Archives and Records Administration, Washington, D.C.

Figure 4. Russian physicist Iulii Khariton with the first Soviet atomic bomb, detonated on August 29, 1949. Built according to designs stolen from the United States, the Soviet bomb was an almost exact copy of American weapon deployed four years earlier. Photograph by Victor Luk'yanov; printed courtesy of Dr. Alexey Semenov.

ment were quietly consulted, and then the president made his decision. In January 1950 Truman announced that the United States would continue researching and developing all forms of nuclear weapons, including H-bombs.

The arms race was on. Bethe described its first leg in a lecture, "My Road from Los Alamos," which he gave at the University of Maryland in December 1994. In the late 1940s, it was not clear whether a fusion weapon was technically possible. But in early 1951, a year after Truman's decision to accelerate the hydrogen bomb project, the mathematician Stanislaw Ulam and the physicist Edward Teller demonstrated that it was. Ulam and Teller's formulation was so "ingenious," so "convincing," Bethe recalled, "it was clear that not only the United States could make it but surely there were competent physicists in the Soviet Union who could do it as well": "And this being so, it was then clear that it had to be done, and in spite of my apprehension, I agreed to participate for a good half-year in developing the hydrogen bomb. We concluded it had to be done because the Soviets could, we believed, do it too." Then Bethe recounted, with the succinctness of the historical moment, what followed.

> First the U.S. tested a device which could not have been delivered in a war, which consisted of liquid deuterium. And it worked. It worked, in fact, impressively, giving a yield of some 10 megatons.
>
> This was followed in August 1953 by a Soviet test which [Andrei] Sakharov called the "layer cake," alternate layers of uranium and liquid deuterium to provide the nuclear fuel which is necessary for a fusion reaction. This would have been deliverable, its yield of energy of four-tenths of a megaton.
>
> In 1954 the United States made tests in the Pacific where they tested various variations, all with liquid deuterium, and developed some three or four different hydrogen bombs, each giving about 10 megatons.
>
> And finally in November 1955, there was an additional Soviet test. Sakharov had, in the meantime, hit upon the idea of Ulam and Teller, and produced a device just like

ours. They deliberately reduced the yield of it so they could deliver this bomb from a plane to the . . . test ground and the plane could get away. This could have been three megatons.

As Bethe's remarks make clear, the Soviet Union did not steal the Ulam-Teller method. Their own scientists discovered it, as scientists will do once certain principles are abroad. But the hydrogen bomb began, obviously, as a weapon, and because it was a weapon, details about it were kept, for the most obvious reasons, as secret as possible.

With, however, an all-important difference. There was no way to keep the whole world from knowing *about* the secret, for the simple reason that the bombs had to be tested. The weapons were new, there was much to be learned about them, and the only way to do so was to set them off. Thus began a series of tests by assorted nuclear powers that continues even to this day. But none has seized the world's imagination quite as much as did the underwater explosion in 1946 on Bikini, a small coral atoll in the Marshall Islands, an explosion designed to test the effect of the atom bomb on naval armament and equipment and on certain forms of animal life. The photographs were unforgettable. One caption read: "An awe-inspiring mushroom cloud rises above Bikini atoll in an underwater atomic bomb test. The mighty column of water dwarfs huge battleships." One ship captain, apprised of radioactive fallout, ordered the decks swabbed. Captain Cook might have done as much; no better remedy seemed at hand, such was the suddenness with which this new age had come upon us. The Bikini tests were followed in 1948 by tests of three weapons at Eniwetok atoll, two hundred miles west in what was termed the Pacific Proving Grounds.

The tension between great publicity and even greater secrecy finally led *Life* magazine to "tell all." In two lengthy articles, "The Atom" in May 1949 and "The Atomic Bomb" in February 1950, the fundamentals of the science and the particulars of the weapon were set forth in the language of laypeople. Americans were not yet used to all this secrecy—the kind of secrecy that we knew about, anyway. The editors of *Life* were clearly upset by the imbalance of what they called "necessary security and unnecessary secrecy." They were, even so, scrupulous. A headnote to the article "The Atomic Bomb" declares: "This article reveals no secrets. It is based on published, unclassified material that can be found by anyone, including the Russians, in public libraries." The article itself invokes a number of the nation's most respected journalists and commentators in support of the judgment that secrecy was getting out of hand.

> For the past five years the operations and results of the U.S. atomic weapons program have been almost completely unknown to the public. The critical facts about this greatest of all publicly owned enterprises have been withheld, partly because of essential security restriction. But a larger factor behind the present state of public ignorance is the extension of secrecy far beyond the limits of true security.
>
> This growing disparity between required security and officially imposed secrecy has recently come in for sharp criticism by many of the country's best-informed observers. Joseph and Stewart Alsop, writing about the world strategic situation and the H-bomb, say, "What the President has said [about the bomb] is not one third, or one tenth, of what it is his bounden duty to say." Hanson Baldwin, in the *New York Times*, writes, "Facts are the foundation of democracy—and facts we do not have."[5]

The Cold War had come. Americans were used to secrecy during wartime. The date of D day, for instance. But now a distinction was being made between a "hot war" like World War II and a "cold war" like the one then under way (the terms date from the 1940s), and secrecy was being presented as essential to both. This was wholly new. Profound aspects of the culture, even the nature of energy (the oldest of mysteries), were now to be known by a few but withheld from the rest. In a sense, it was the most primitive of arrangements in the most advanced of societies. The *Life* editors anguished: "So stifling are the effects of all-encompassing security that conscientious publications are unwilling to take the responsibility for presenting conclusions which they themselves could draw from the available, nonsecret literature. The government can and should take that responsibility—now, before it is too late."[6]

But it *was* too late—and for a complex of reasons, the most important being that the United States now had reason to fear for its security. Pearl Harbor had seemed devastating, but it represented an external threat, and that threat had passed. Now there appeared an *internal* threat in the form of American Communists serving as agents of the Soviet Union. What's more, the Soviet espionage attack, admittedly limited, had an unnerving capacity for penetrating key sites. Los Alamos, obviously. But also Arlington Hall, where Meredith Gardner and his fellow cryptographers (for the most part women, as it happens) were near to losing their minds decoding and deciphering the Venona cables, one arduous word at a time.

Looking over their shoulders was William W. Weisband, corporal, cipher clerk, spy. In 1945 he began work at Arlington Hall that made use of his fluency in Russian. Weisband was the first to tell the Soviet Union the critical information that its secret messages were being broken. In 1950 the U.S. Army discovered Weisband's treason, and, although he was suspended from his job, he was never prosecuted for espionage. Nothing was done, and no one outside the army and the FBI was informed. Bureaucracy has its uses.[7]

Here we come upon a large dilemma of our national life, one not readily if at all resolvable. We can but set forth the essentials and await some consensus—which may never come. The first essential concerns bureaucracy's tendency to amass official secrets, a tendency long ago noted by Max Weber. Although Weber's work was just being translated into English when the editors at *Life* produced their series on secrecy and the atom bomb, their critique could have been based on the Weberian model. *Wirtschaft and Gesellschaft*

(*Economy and Society*), published after Weber's death in 1920 but most likely written in part before World War I, includes a chapter entitled "Bureaucracy," where Weber delineates this tendency so clearly that the Commission on Protecting and Reducing Government Secrecy cited the following passage in its 1997 report.

> Every bureaucracy seeks to increase the superiority of the professionally informed by keeping their knowledge and intentions secret. Bureaucratic administration always tends to be an administration of "secret sessions": in so far as it can, it hides its knowledge and action from criticism. . . .
>
> The pure interest of the bureaucracy in power, however, is efficacious far beyond those areas where purely functional interests make for secrecy. The concept of the "official secret" is the specific invention of bureaucracy, and nothing is so fanatically defended by the bureaucracy as this attitude, which cannot be substantially justified beyond these specifically qualified areas. In facing a parliament, the bureaucracy, out of a sure power instinct, fights every attempt of the parliament to gain knowledge by means of its own experts or from interest groups. The so-called right of parliamentary investigation is one of the means by which parliament seeks such knowledge. Bureaucracy naturally welcomes a poorly informed and hence a powerless parliament—at least in so far as ignorance somehow agrees with the bureaucracy's interests.[8]

Clearly some aspect of this "sure power instinct" was behind the army's decision to keep Venona secret. It may be argued that the government ought to have been more open about these matters, ought to have made public what it knew about these spies: after all, we had rolled them up; their time was over. (As it was, the Soviet Union wasn't gaining much from its espionage efforts. In 1945 Bethe had estimated that the Soviets would be able to build their own bomb in five years; thanks to information provided by their agents, they did this in four. That was the edge that espionage gave them:

a year's worth, no more.) Yet who in the U.S. government could have made this information public? The president himself didn't know about it. And might not the public have panicked more than it did? Bethe, knowing that the Soviets would have the bomb in five years, began to believe that there would be atomic war in ten.[9] The ensuing arms race, along with war on the Korean peninsula, absorbed the energies of the executive. Too much was happening to expect something like a measured judgment. Instead, we began to accuse one another.

Trials arising from charges of espionage—perhaps most notably, the trials of Alger Hiss in 1949 and 1950—took place in quick succession. In Britain Klaus Fuchs confessed in January 1950 that he had been a Soviet agent at Los Alamos, setting in motion a chain of events that would expose the "Rosenberg ring." On February 9, 1950, in his infamous speech at Wheeling, West Virginia, Senator Joseph McCarthy announced that he was in possession of a list of 205 Communists serving in the Department of State. In time, he was to accuse even General George C. Marshall of treason.

Also in 1950, Harry Gold became a suspect after Fuchs described meeting with a courier in Santa Fe, New Mexico, five years earlier. On May 22, Gold confessed after FBI agents found a map of Santa Fe in his closet. Gold had indeed been Fuch's courier, but it turned out that once, when KGB compartmentalization had been breached, Gold had received information from a second Los Alamos agent whom he described as a young soldier. On June 15, Gold identified a picture of David Greenglass as being that of the soldier, thus uncovering the second Los Alamos agent, code-named Calibre, mentioned in the Venona decryptions. Greenglass confessed immediately and implicated his sister, Ethel, and her husband, Julius Rosenberg. The FBI quickly identified Julius Rosenberg as the agent code-named Antenna, later changed to Liberal, in the Venona cables.

Beginning March 6, 1951, in a trial that was followed

the world over, the Rosenbergs, Greenglass (who pleaded guilty and testified against them), and a codefendant, Morton Sobell, were charged under the Espionage Act of 1917. Federal judge Irving R. Kaufman sentenced both Rosenbergs to death under section 2 of the Espionage Act, 50 *U.S. Code* 32 (now 18 *U.S. Code* 794), which prohibits transmitting or attempting to transmit to a foreign government information "relating to the national defense." Sobell and Greenglass were given prison sentences. And thus the Rosenbergs became the first American civilians executed for wartime spying. A month later, in May, two British intelligence officials, Donald Maclean and Guy Burgess, defected to Moscow. Would treason never end?

But for every accusation there was a denial. And the American government and the American public were being confronted with possibilities and charges that were at once baffling and terrifying. For all who believed Whittaker Chambers when he said that Hiss was indeed a Communist spy, there appeared to be a corresponding number convinced of Hiss's innocence. The same was true regarding the Rosenbergs. And for all who agreed that there were Communists in government, there were as many who saw the government as contriving fantastic accusations against innocent people.

In the more balanced history of this period that is emerging, the first fact is that a significant Communist constituency *was* in place in Washington, New York, and Los Angeles, but in the main those involved systematically denied their involvement. This was the mode of Communist operations the world over. In his memoirs the diplomat and historian George F. Kennan is quite clear-sighted about this: "The penetration of the American governmental services by members or agents (conscious or otherwise) of the American Communist Party in the late 1930s was not a figment of the imagination. . . . It really existed; and it assumed proportions which, while never overwhelming, were also not trivial."[10] Kennan must be read closely: "conscious or otherwise," he says. American Communism could be no more than a mindset, but it mattered. Communist spies tracking the bomb were tiny in number; Communist sympathizers were many more. In between were a considerable number of real-enough agents with not enough to do. There were just not that many *political* secrets. Never are; can't be.

The second fact is that many of those who came to prominence by denouncing Communist conspiracy and by accusing suspected Communists and "Comsymps" clearly knew little or nothing of such matters—and often just as clearly couldn't care less. Hence the dubious character of the accusers ironically served to lend credibility to the accused.

Add to this the political subtext of much of the debate, which only muddled matters further. Often those who were telling the truth about Soviet espionage were discredited or discounted as readily as those who knew little but who would accuse others of anything. The consequent ridicule could be devastating, and there was plenty of it; as one popular ditty of the time mocked, "Who's going to investigate the man who investigates the man who investigates me?" A fault line appeared in American society that contributed to more than one political crisis in the years that followed. Belief in the guilt or innocence of Alger Hiss became a defining issue in American intellectual life. Parts of the American government had conclusive evidence of his guilt, but they never told. The "anti-anti-Communists," to use Richard Gid Powers's term, were left to rant on about "scoundrel time" and witch-hunts and blacklists.[11] In an odd way, government stayed out of the most heated political argument of the time.

With the publication of the Venona documents, the evidence of Hiss's guilt became public (Figure 5). Hiss was indeed a Soviet agent and appears to have been regarded by Moscow as its most important. A Soviet cable of March 30, 1945, identified an agent code-named Ales as having attended the Yalta Conference of February 1945. He had then journeyed to Moscow, where, according to the cable, he and "his whole group"—that is, his colleagues back home—were "awarded Soviet decorations." This man could have been only Alger Hiss, deputy director of the State Department's Office of Special Political Affairs; the other three State Department officials in the delegation from Yalta to Moscow are beyond suspicion.[12] The party was met by Andrei Vyshinsky, the prosecutor in the Moscow trials of 1936–38. By no later than June 1950, the U.S. Army was persuaded that Ales *was* Hiss. But, as they say in combat, it maintained strict radio silence.

With or without the army signals intelligence, the Hiss case has been argued for half a century. More instructive has been the complete silence, maintained for the same half century, concerning Theodore Alvin Hall, a nineteen-year-old Harvard undergraduate who was recruited to work at Los Alamos. He arrived there in January 1944 and was assigned to work with Bruno Rossi on nuclear implosion. Entirely on his own, Hall passed on to the Soviets crucial information about implosion. A walk-in, as the tradecraft has it.* In May 1950, D. M. Ladd of the Federal Bureau of Investigation received a memorandum summarizing important investigation developments in the espionage field. One section was devoted to Hall and his classmate Saville Sax.

THEODORE ALVIN HALL and SAVILLE SAX
    Recent information from [Venona] reflects that Theodore Hall, in November, 1944, was in New York City, where he was in contact with Saville Sax. Hall, at that time,

---

* John Lewis Gaddis observes that Klaus Fuchs was also a walk-in: "The Russians did not recruit Klaus Fuchs: he recruited them. The German émigré scientist, then in Britain, offered information about bomb development as early as the fall of 1941, and the Russians immediately accepted. This happened before anyone knew whether such a device could be made to work, and certainly prior to the 1944 Anglo-American agreement not to share atomic bomb information with 'third parties'; indeed there is reason to think that latter decision may have been influenced by preliminary indications that the Russians had already penetrated Manhattan Project security" (*The United States and the End of the Cold War: Implications, Reconsiderations, Provocations* [New York: Oxford University Press, 1992], p. 90).

MGB

From: WASHINGTON

To: MOSCOW

No: 1822

30 March 1945

Further to our telegram No. 283[a]. As a result of "[D% A.'s]"[i] chat with "ALES"[ii] the following has been ascertained:

1. ALES has been working with the NEIGHBORS[SOSEDI][iii] continuously since 1935.

2. For some years past he has been the leader of a small group of the NEIGHBORS' probationers[STAZhERY], for the most part consisting of his relations.

3. The group and ALES himself work on obtaining military information only. Materials on the "BANK"[iv] allegedly interest the NEIGHBORS very little and he does not produce them regularly.

4. All the last few years ALES has been working with "POL'"[v] who also meets other members of the group occasionally.

5. Recently ALES and his whole group were awarded Soviet decorations.

6. After the YaLTA Conference, when he had gone on to MOSCOW, a Soviet personage in a very responsible position (ALES gave to understand that it was Comrade VYShINSKIJ) allegedly got in touch with ALES and at the behest of the Military NEIGHBORS passed on to him their gratitude and so on.

No. 431   VADIM[vi]

Notes: [a] Not available.
Comments:
    [i] A.: "A." seems the most likely garble here although "A." has not been confirmed elsewhere in the WASHINGTON traffic.
    [ii] ALES: Probably Alger HISS.
    [iii] SOSEDI: Members of another Soviet Intelligence organization, here probably the GRU.
    [iv] BANK: The U.S. State Department.
    [v] POL': i.e. "PAUL," unidentified cover-name.
    [vi] VADIM: Anatolij Borisovich GROMOV, MGB resident in WASHINGTON.

Figure 5. Decrypted Soviet cable that identified the agent code-named Ales—"probably Alger Hiss"—as having attended the Yalta Conference of February 1945. *Source:* National Security Agency, Washington, D.C.

was employed by MED* at Los Alamos. At the recommendation of Sax, Hall agreed to supply to Soviet Intelligence information concerning work being done at Los Alamos. Hall delivered to Beck (unidentified) certain information, and Sax contacted an official at the Soviet Consulate and delivered to him certain information. Based on the foregoing, an intensive investigation has been instituted.

Theodore Alvin Hall, who is identical with the Hall mentioned in the [Venona] information, presently is employed at the University of Chicago at the Institute of Nuclear Physics.

Sax also is residing in Chicago, where he is operating a mimeographing business.

Further investigation is being conducted to determine the current activities of these individuals and to identify Beck.†

Hall and Sax were both sons of first-generation Russian immigrants who brought their politics with them, especially in Sax's case. His family, Russian Jews from Vinnitsa, Ukraine, had emigrated to America in 1914 after pogroms struck their village. Sax's father had previously gotten into trouble for publicly criticizing the czar, and the family always remained devoted to the cause of the Russian revolution. Like Hall's father, Sax's father became prosperous in America, but unlike the Halls, the Saxes did not assimilate into American society.[13] The Halls were Jewish also and had no fondness for the old regime in Russia, but they did seem concerned about fitting into American society. (Hall and his brother, apparently concerned about anti-Semitism, changed their surname, Holtzberg, early on.) At Harvard, Hall was a member of the John Reed Society, a convinced Marxist as well as a brilliant physicist. With the war over, he decided quite on his own that the United States must never

* The MED was the Manhattan Engineer District, one of the atomic research centers constructed by the U.S. Army Corps of Engineers. In June 1942, the MED was put in charge of building research laboratories and manufacturing facilities across the country. In time the entire project was code-named the Manhattan Project.

† "Beck" was later identified as Sergei N. Kournakoff.

have a nuclear monopoly, and he proceeded to help the Soviet Union to break it.[14] Not a word of this was known outside government until the Venona decryptions were made public beginning in July 1995 (Figure 6).

A handful of journalists studying the documents promptly made the connection between a single reference to Hall and later ones to an agent code-named Mlad (Russian for "young" or "youngster"). In September 1995 Joseph Albright and Marcia Kunstel of the Cox newspapers met with Hall in Cambridge, England, where he had been teaching since 1962, and he signed an agreement with them to do a series of embargoed interviews. Michael Dobbs of the *Washington Post*, working separately, also spotted the connection; he flew to England, made his way to Cambridge, knocked on Hall's door, and asked him if he was the agent Mlad. Hall did not deny it; he merely replied that all of that had been a long time ago.[15]

Hall was more forthcoming with Albright and Kunstel. Their book, *Bombshell: The Secret Story of Ted Hall and America's Unknown Atomic Spy Conspiracy*, contains his account of what motivated him in 1944. Hall insists that he acted entirely on his own, uninfluenced by any party, person, or hope for personal gain. His political views had been shaped during the economic depression of the 1930s, he said, and he had seen how prosperity was restored not by Roosevelt's New Deal but by World War II. "What would happen when the war was over?" he wondered: "At nineteen I shared a common belief that the horrors of war would bring our various leaders to their senses and usher in a period of peace and harmony. But I had been thinking and reading about politics since an early age, and had seen that in a capitalist society economic depression could lead to fascism, aggression and war—as actually happened in Italy and Germany. So as I worked at Los Alamos and understood the destructive power of the atomic bomb, I asked myself what *might* happen if World War II was followed by a depression in the United States while it had an atomic monopoly."[16] Appar-

USSR

RUDAI-2A

Ref No: S/NBF/T193

Issued: Z/C/21/5/1952

Copy No: 205

1. LIST OF SCIENTISTS ENGAGED ON THE PROBLEM OF ATOMIC ENERGY.

2. UNSUCCESSFUL EFFORTS OF AN UNIDENTIFIED PERSON (POSSIBLY "STAR") TO CONTACT NICHOLA NAPOLI AND "HELMSMAN".

From: NEW YORK

To: MOSCOW

No: 1699   2 Dec 1944

Conclusion of telegram No. 940 [sic][i].

Enumerates [the following][a] scientists who are working on the problem[ii] – Hans BETHE, Niels BOHR, Enrico FERMI, John NEWMAN, Bruno ROSSI, George KISTIAKOVSKI, Emilio SEGRÈ, G.I.TAYLOR, William PENNEY, Arthur COMPTON, Ernest LAWRENCE, Harold UREY, Hans STANARM, Edward TELLER, Percy BRIDGEMAN, Werner EISENBERG, STRASSENMAN
[7 groups unrecoverable]
our country addressed himself to NAPOLI[iii] and the latter, not wanting to listen to him, sent him to BECK [BEK][iv] as military commentator of the paper. On attempting to visit HELMSMAN [RULEVOJ][v] he was not admitted to him by the latter's secretary.

ANTON

Figure 6. The first Venona message indicating Soviet espionage, decrypted by Meredith Gardner. The message, which listed the scientists working at Los Alamos, was sent on December 2, 1944, and was decoded by Gardner on December 20, 1946. Eventually it was learned that the source for this information was Ted Hall, in his first act of espionage. *Source:* National Security Agency, Washington, D.C.

ently not liking the answers he was coming up with, Hall set about helping the Soviet Union break the monopoly. Afterward he was followed around a bit by the FBI before he finally decided to relocate to England. There he became a much-published physicist who traveled to and from the United States without concern.

It will require at least another generation to sort out the details of these incidents of subterfuge. But the facts now in hand surely attest that the U.S. government's pursuit of alleged sympathizers and spies in the post–World War II period did not amount to persecution, still less delusion. Not a few in fact were spies, and of these most were left untroubled. Never prosecuted, never named. Instead, the bureaucracies kept their secrets, especially the secrets that would not have held up in an American court.

Part of the reason for this reticence, as we have seen, was a reaction against the uproar over radical revolutionists in 1919–20, when there was a good deal of disorder and no small amount of government misconduct. Let us say now, in extenuation, that a world war, followed by what for a while seemed to be the onset of world revolution, required a fair amount of adjusting. A measure of balance did return, though, partly because of the isolationist bent that had appeared in national politics in reaction to Wilsonian activism but also because the legal profession had begun to brush up on the Bill of Rights.* Nothing like the Palmer Raids of

* On May 28, 1920, twelve of the nation's most respected lawyers and legal scholars (including Roscoe Pound, dean of Harvard Law School; Harvard law professors Felix Frankfurter and Zechariah Chafee, Jr.; and Francis Fisher Kane, former U.S. attorney for the Eastern District of Pennsylvania, who had resigned in protest over the Palmer Raids) issued a booklet entitled *Report upon the Illegal Practices of the United States Department of Justice*. The booklet, which has been called "the most authoritative denunciation of the anti-Red activities of the Justice Department yet made," documented that department's responsibility for a number of abuses of the Constitution—in particular, the Fourth, Fifth, and Eighth amendments (Robert K. Murray, *Red Scare: A Study in National Hysteria, 1919–1920* [Westport, Conn.: Greenwood Press, 1955], p. 25).

1919–20 would happen again in the United States; the trial of Sacco and Vanzetti, two anarchists, would take place in 1921, but it was a trial, not a raid. During the 1940s and 1950s, when the United States was going through much torment over Communism and Communist subversion, there were many displays of public alarm and political histrionics but few of the egregious excesses of the earlier period. No president since Wilson has sent a rival candidate to prison, whatever his party affiliation.

But another reason for the government's reticence was that secrecy had become the norm. As Weber had shown, a culture of bureaucracy will always tend to foster a culture of secrecy.

CHAPTER SIX

A Culture of Secrecy

The Cold War settled in, a winter of many discontents. American society in peacetime began to experience wartime regulation. The awful dilemma was that in order to preserve an open society, the U.S. government took measures that in significant ways closed it down. The culture of secrecy that evolved was intended as a defense against two antagonists, by now familiar ones: the enemy abroad and the enemy within. Fallout shelters were built not only on the South Lawn of the White House but also in urban and suburban neighborhoods across the country, preparing the population for a Soviet attack with weapons that had by then become obsolete in nuclear arsenals. Cabinet officers routinely went through evacuation exercises, rushing to shelters miles from Washington. Schoolchildren learned to duck under desks. As for the enemy within, by 1950 or thereabouts the Communist Party was essentially neutralized. It still existed in outward appearance, but sometimes seemed to linger merely as a device maintained by the U.S. government to trap the unwary.

In each of these cases, the government overresponded,

but in none can it be blamed harshly. The Soviet Union was by now developing a nuclear and missile capacity very much on its own, if one allows for the contributions made by expatriate German scientists (a resource that both sides shared). And the Soviets continued an espionage offensive, although after Los Alamos there were no major successes—a fairly steady yield of random information, but nothing of coherent consequence.

Indeed, the terms of trade, if that image may be used here, had quite reversed since the 1940s. It was the Soviets who were now forced to deal with an enemy within. Marxism was a belief system that could evoke intense attachment, but all of a sudden it failed. Judgments vary, but probably the last member of the Politburo to have studied Marx and Lenin and adhered to their worldview was Mikhail A. Suslov, who became a member in 1952 and served almost continuously for thirty years.[1] Now came bureaucracy, disillusion, dissent, defection. Among the most conspicuous instances of the last-mentioned came in 1967, when Joseph Stalin's daughter, Svetlana, defected to the United States.

Thus the U.S. government, which at an earlier moment and to an as yet unknown extent had indeed been infiltrated by persons with pro-Soviet leanings or even actively treasonable intent, now stood unassailable. Not so the Soviet government. Disillusion grew from within. The promise of Marxism-Leninism had not been kept; the contrast with the Western world, and especially the United States, grew ever more painful. There was a good bit of internal exile; as time went on, there was more and more open defection.

The West probably undervalued the advantage of this situation, having had so little experience with such regimes. In 1975, for example, Arkady M. Shevchenko, then undersecretary-general for political and security council affairs of the United Nations, defected to the United States. Shevchenko was the highest-ranking Soviet in the U.N. system. (By unspoken agreement, a Soviet held the position of undersecretary for security council affairs, while an American held that of the undersecretary for general assembly affairs. The postwar settlement, that is, embodied in bureaucratic rank.) Shevchenko was able and effective; some said that he was on the shortlist to succeed an aging Andrei A. Gromyko. Then one day, with no hint, no notice, Shevchenko whispered to an American working in the Secretariat that he would like to defect. This was arranged, but in the tradecraft of the time, nobody was to know. Shevchenko was "kept in place," but as a source for what? For the cables that he could read. In time, Moscow sensed that something was wrong, evidently narrowing the suspects to Shevchenko, Oleg Troyanovsky (now ambassador to the United Nations), or Anatoly Dobrynin (the Soviet ambassador in Washington). By now no one was beyond suspicion.[2]

But before all this, the United States had to live through the aftermath of Soviet espionage, which had crested at Los Alamos. Several laws were enacted. The most important was the Atomic Energy Act of 1946, which introduced the principle that certain information was "born classified," meaning that no assessment was needed in order for that information to be deemed secret. In August 1945, for example, the government had released a history of the Manhattan Project, *A General Account of the Development of Methods of Using Atomic Energy for Military Purposes Under the Auspices of the United States Government, 1940–1945*, commonly known as the Smyth report (General Leslie R. Groves, head of the Manhattan Project, had asked Henry DeWolf Smyth, a physics professor at Princeton University, to write the account).[3] The Smyth report noted that most of the information on the development of the atomic bomb could be obtained from unclassified sources. But in the context of the Atomic Energy Act, this hardly seemed to matter. Automatic classification was by now a pattern of governance, and indeed it remains such. During the 1940s and 1950s, government regulation expanded as greatly as it had during the New Deal.

But during the 1930s, both supporters and opponents of Roosevelt's New Deal programs had grown concerned about the scope of the executive branch's assertion and had passed laws to counter it. In 1938, Roscoe Pound, chairman of the American Bar Association's Special Committee on Administrative Law and former dean of Harvard Law School, had denounced the trend of turning "the administration of justice over to administrative absolutism, . . . a Marxian idea."[4] In 1939, in response to such criticisms as well as to calls for greater openness in government as a means for assuring fairness in proceedings,[5] President Roosevelt had asked Attorney General Homer Cummings to organize a committee to study existing administrative procedures and recommend reforms.

The attorney general's Committee on Administrative Procedure, chaired by Dean Acheson, submitted a final report in 1941. After the war, this committee's efforts and hearings in the Senate Judiciary Committee resulted in the Administrative Procedure Act (APA) of 1946. The APA rests on a constellation of ideas: government agencies should be required to keep the public informed of their organization, procedures, and rules; the public should be able to participate in the rule-making process; uniform standards should apply to all formal rule-making and adjudicatory proceedings; and judicial review should be available in certain circumstances. Taken together with the Freedom of Information Act, an amendment to the APA that was enacted in 1966 and added to in 1974, 1986, and 1996, the APA was intended to foster more open government through various procedural requirements and thus to promote greater accountability in decision making.

As enacted, the APA recognized few exceptions to the standard of crafting a more open government, but the important one was set out in section 3 of the 1946 statute, which addressed "any function of the United States requiring secrecy in the public interest." Government manuals began to distinguish between agencies' ordinary operations, about which the public had a right to know, and agencies' confidential operations.[6] By its own terms, the APA's procedural requirements for both rule making and adjudication do not apply "to the extent that there is involved a military or foreign affairs function of the United States."

This very broad walling off of military and foreign affairs was consistent with the Supreme Court's decision ten years earlier in *United States v. Curtiss-Wright Export Corporation*, where the Court supported a sweeping range of executive discretion in the conduct of foreign affairs: "In this vast external realm, with its important, complicated, delicate and manifold problems, the President alone has the power to speak or listen as the representative of the nation. . . . The nature of transactions with foreign nations, moreover, requires caution and unity of design, and their success frequently depends on secrecy and dispatch. . . . He has his agents in the form of diplomatic, consular and other officials. Secrecy in respect of information gathered by them may be highly necessary, and the premature disclosure of it productive of harmful results."[7] Richard Frank has commented that the dichotomy between domestic politics and foreign affairs could not have been clearer: "Even in 1936, during the only era in which delegation of authority in the domestic area was being found unconstitutional, the Court was prepared, in most generous terms, to grant the Executive great latitude in foreign affairs."[8] Now, however, the definition of foreign affairs was becoming so inclusive that the distinction between foreign and domestic was dissolving.

The encounter with espionage, some of it involving employees and even military personnel of the U.S. government, led inevitably to the issue of loyalty. Wilson's executive order of April 7, 1917, had introduced the concept of loyalty as a condition of government service. Years of civil service reform had been designed to remove "party affiliation," as the term was, from considerations of government employment. In 1939, however, an amended Hatch Act prohibited federal employees from "membership in any political party or organization which advocates the overthrow of our constitutional form of government in the United States."[9]

The Hatch Act in turn was implemented through Civil Service Commission regulations devised in 1940; they were modified in 1942 to include the question "Do you advocate or have you ever advocated, or are you now or have you ever been, a member of any organization that advocates the overthrow of the Government of the United States by force or violence?" In 1942, President Roosevelt had also issued War Service Regulation 2, which denied a civil service examination or appointment to anyone whose loyalty was in "reasonable doubt." This was used by the Civil Service Commission to deny federal employment to a wide variety of individuals, ranging from members of the Communist Party to those associated with the German Bund and other allegedly fascist causes. Other wartime regulations gave the secretaries of war and the navy the authority to summarily remove employees considered risks to national security; after the war, this authority was extended to the Department of State and other departments. In 1944, the Civil Service Commission established a loyalty rating board to handle cases, referred by regional commission offices, involving "derogatory information" with regard to loyalty.[10]

Even so, during World War II the standards and procedures for conducting a loyalty program were not uniform; the development of such a program was left until after the war.[11] In March 1947 President Truman issued Executive Order 9835, establishing the Federal Employee Loyalty Program. The program set up uniform investigation procedures, authorized loyalty review boards across the government, and directed that federal employment be denied where "there is a reasonable doubt as to the loyalty of the person involved." Despite the wartime regulations, "personnel security" was still largely a new discipline. The Atomic Energy Act of 1946 had mandated a security program for its newly established Atomic Energy Commission and had directed the FBI to investigate employees' "character, associations, and loyalty," and in 1950 Congress had empowered certain agency heads to summarily suspend those deemed security risks. Nevertheless, most federal agencies still did not subject their employees to any formal security screening. Lieutenant General Leslie R. Groves, who had served in the army for thirty-two years and directed the Los Alamos project, put it succinctly when he testified in 1954 before the AEC board reviewing the suspension of J. Robert Oppenheimer's security clearance: "The Army as a whole didn't deal with matters of security until after the atomic bomb burst on the world because it was the first time that the Army really knew there was such a thing [as security]." A combination of the bomb's consequences and the growing fears about Communist and related threats to internal security led to a new "demi-jurisprudence" of security clearance procedures.[12]

The Truman order made loyalty a concern across the federal government. The approach generally proved popular, although a cross-section of legal scholars, including Zechariah Chafee, Jr., and Erwin Griswold, did criticize the lack of procedural safeguards and clear standards for assessing prospective and current government employees.[13]

In March 1948, the celebrated "Attorney General's List" was first promulgated. Seventy-one organizations and eleven schools viewed as "adjuncts of the Communist Party" were identified as "subversive," although in no case was the subversion defined. The list, published in the *Federal Register,* stated that "it is entirely possible that many persons belonging to such organizations may be loyal to the United States." But a striking aspect of the listing is the prominence of Japanese and German organizations, years after World War II. Similar diaspora groups—the American-Polish Labor Council, the Hungarian-American Council for Democracy, the Macedonian-American People's League—also appear. Some listings seem unlikely: Sakura Kai (the Patriotic Society, or the Cherry Association, for veterans of the Russo-Japanese War), the Dante Alighieri Society, even the Ku Klux Klan. But the list also included well-established Communist-front organizations (Figure 7).

It was a short step from proscribing organizations deemed subversive to querying government employees about their membership. The political pressure to establish a broader, more comprehensive security program—subsuming loyalty as one key criterion—had increased in 1950 with the passage of legislation "to protect the national security of the United States by permitting the summary suspension of employment of civilian officers and employees of various departments and agencies."[14] Moreover, during the 1952 presidential campaign, Eisenhower vowed to root out Communists and other security risks from the government and the defense industry, suggesting that their presence had been tolerated too easily by the Truman administration. In his first State of the Union address, Eisenhower promised a new system "for keeping out the disloyal and the dangerous." Executive Order 10450 followed within three months. It provided that the appointment of each federal employee would be subject to an investigation and that each agency head would be responsible for ensuring that the employment of each subordinate was "clearly consistent with the interests of the national security."[15] While abolishing the loyalty program of the Truman order, which had been criticized as both ineffective and inefficient,[16] the new order also made it clear that "the interests of the national security require that all persons privileged to be employed in the departments and agencies of the Government, shall be reliable, trustworthy, of good conduct and character, and of complete and unswerving loyalty to the United States."[17] Senator Joseph McCarthy praised the new order: "Altogether it represents a pretty darn good program. I like it."[18] The *New York Times* observed that the new program meant "a new investigation of many thousands of employees previously investi-

FEDERAL REGISTER

VOLUME 13   1934   NUMBER 56

Washington, Saturday, March 20, 1948

American League Against War and Fascism.
American Patriots, Inc.
American Peace Mobilization.
American Youth Congress.
Association of German Nationals (Reichsdeutsche Vereinigung).
Black Dragon Society.
Central Japanese Association (Beikoku Chuo Nipponjin Kai).
Central Japanese Association of Southern California.
The Central Organization of the German-American National Alliance (Deutsche-Amerikanische Einheitsfront).
Communist Party of U. S. A.
Congress of American Revolutionary Writers.
Dai Nippon Butoku Kai (Military Virtue Society of Japan or Military Art Society of Japan).
Dante Alighieri Society.
Federation of Italian War Veterans in the U. S. A., Inc. (Associazione Nazionale Combattenti Italiani, Federazione degli Stati Uniti d' America).
Friends of the New Germany (Freunde des Neuen Deutschlands).
German-American Bund (Amerikadeutscher Volksbund).
German-American Vocational League (Deutsche - Amerikanische Berufsgemeinschaft).
Heimusha Kai, also known as Nokubei Heiaki Gimusha Kai, Zaibei Nihonjin, Heiyaku Gimusha Kai, and Zaibei Heimusha Kai (Japanese Residing in America Military Conscripts Association).
Hinode Kai (Imperial Japanese Reservists).
Hinomaru Kai (Rising Sun Flag Society—a group of Japanese War Veterans).
Hokubei Zaigo Shoke Dan (North American Reserve Officers Association).
Japanese Association of America.
Japanese Overseas Central Society (Kaigai Dobo Chuo Kai).
Japanese Overseas Convention, Tokyo, Japan, 1940.
Japanese Protective Association (Recruiting Organization).
Jikyoku lin Kai (Current Affairs Association).

Kibei Seinen Kai (Association of U. S. Citizens of Japanese Ancestry who have returned to America after studying in Japan).
Kyffhaeuser, also known as Kyffhaeuser League (Kyffhaeuser Bund), Kyffhaeuser Fellowship (Kyffhaeuser Kameradschaft).
Kyffhaeuser War Relief (Kyffhaeuser Kriegshilfswerk).
Lictor Society (Italian Black Shirts).
Mario Morgantini Circle.
Michigan Federation for Constitutional Liberties.
Nanka Teikoku Gunyudan (Imperial Military Friends Group or Southern California War Veterans).
National Committee for the Defense of Political Prisoners.
National Federation for Constitutional Liberties.
National Negro Congress.
Northwest Japanese Association.
Nichibei Kogyo Kaisha (The Great Fuji Theatre).
Protestant War Veterans of the U. S., Inc.
Sakura Kai (Patriotic Society, or Cherry Association—composed of veterans of Russo-Japanese War).
Shinto Temples.
Silver Shirt Legion of America.
Sokoku Kai (Fatherland Society).
Suiko Sha (Reserve Officers Association, Los Angeles).
Washington Book Shop Association.
Washington Committee for Democratic Action.
Workers Alliance.
Under Part III, section 3, of Executive Order No. 9835, the following additional organizations are designated.
American Polish Labor Council.
American Youth for Democracy.
Armenian Progressive League of America.
Civil Rights Congress and its affiliated organizations, including: Civil Rights Congress for Texas. Veterans Against Discrimination of Civil Rights Congress of New York.
Tom Paine School of Social Science, Philadelphia, Pa.
Tom Paine School of Westchester, New York.
Walt Whitman School of Social Science, Newark, N. J.

The Columbians.
Communist Party, U. S. A., formerly Communist Political Association, and its affiliates and committees, including: Citizens Committee of the Upper West Side (New York City). Committee to Aid the Fighting South. Dennis Defense Committee. Labor Research Association, Inc. Southern Negro Youth Congress. United May Day Committee. United Negro and Allied Veterans of America. Connecticut State Youth Conference. Council on African Affairs.
Hollywood Writers Mobilization for Defense.
Hungarian-American Council for Democracy.
International Workers Order, including People's Radio Foundation, Inc.
Joint Anti-Fascist Refugee Committee.
Ku Klux Klan.
Macedonian-American People's League.
National Committee to Win the Peace.
National Council of American-Soviet Friendship.
Nature Friends of America (since 1935).
New Committee for Publications.
Photo League (New York City).
Proletarian Party of America.
Revolutionary Workers League.
Socialist Workers Party, including American Committee for European Workers' Relief.
Veterans of the Abraham Lincoln Brigade.
Workers Party, including socialist Youth League.
Attention is also directed to certain organizations which are operated as schools. While the Attorney General is not of the view that any institution of learning, devoted to the advancement of knowledge, is subversive, it appears that these organizations are adjuncts of the Communist Party. They are as follows:
Abraham Lincoln School, Chicago, Ill.
George Washington Carver School, New York City.
Jefferson School of Social Science, New York City.
Ohio School of Social Sciences.
Philadelphia School of Social Science and Art.
Samuel Adams School, Boston, Mass.
School of Jewish Studies, New York City.
Seattle Labor School, Seattle, Wash.

Figure 7. A portion of the "Attorney General's List," a compilation of organizations and schools seen as "adjuncts of the Communist Party," published in the *Federal Register* 13 (March 20, 1948).

gated, as well as many more thousands who have had no security check."[19]

In the months to follow, concerns about personnel security heightened. In early November 1953, Attorney General Herbert Brownell alleged that President Truman had nominated a Soviet agent, Harry Dexter White, to serve as the executive director of the International Monetary Fund, despite knowing of White's involvement in Soviet espionage.* On December 3, President Eisenhower directed that a "blank wall be placed between Dr. [J. Robert] Oppenheimer and secret data," marking the beginning of the process that led to the AEC's suspension of Oppenheimer's security clearance later in December and its four-to-one decision on June 28, 1954, against restoring the clearance.

Thus the personnel security system that remains in place today, notwithstanding a fair amount of tinkering to ensure greater due-process protections, developed against the background of these deep concerns about loyalty and ideological associations. Edward Shils, writing in 1956, captured the moment: "The present system is centered around the assumption that spies are recruited from among those who feel an ideological kinship with the Soviet Union and from those who can be blackmailed or personally influenced or who by loose and careless talk disclose the secrets which have been entrusted to them."[20]

The concept of loyalty necessarily involved the notion of secrecy. Disloyal employees would reveal secrets; loyal employees would not. In such a setting apprehension rose,

---

* This squalid episode—White was five years' dead, and Brownell was thinking Republican politics—is described in Richard Gid Powers's *Secrecy and Power: The Life of J. Edgar Hoover.* Former president Truman remarked, in an undated note written on stationery from the Waldorf-Astoria Hotel, where he stayed November 8–12, 1953, that his information on White had consisted of a report based on "statements made to the FBI by a crook and a louse, Mrs. Bentley and Whittaker Chambers" ("Post-Presidential File," box 619, Harry S. Truman Papers, Truman Library, Independence, Mo.).

as did the dimension of secrecy. More and more matters became classified. At about the same time that some were becoming concerned about public regulations involving mostly domestic activities, others were becoming worried about this newest form of regulation—classified secrets pertaining to foreign affairs.

This anxiety resulted in the first congressional inquiry. On January 18, 1955, Senators John C. Stennis and Hubert H. Humphrey introduced Senate Joint Resolution 21, an act to establish the Commission on Government Security.[21] In a floor statement, Humphrey put it bluntly: "Our present total Government mechanism for assuring security does not inspire confidence." He stated the reason for the proposed measure: "Not since 1917, when the Espionage Act was under consideration by the Congress, has there been full-dress consideration by the Congress of the problems of protecting national secrets, and national defense generally, against subversive penetration." After discussing particular problems in the administration of the personnel security system, Humphrey observed: "As a practical matter, our present security system is a phenomenon of only the past decade. We have enacted espionage laws and tightened existing laws; we have required investigation and clearance of millions of our citizens; we have classified information and locked it in safes behind locked doors, in locked and guarded buildings, within fenced and heavily guarded reservations. But each of these actions has been taken sporadically and independently and not as part of a rational overall master plan for security." Humphrey posed these questions: "What are we trying to protect, and against what? What can we effectively protect? What specific measures will give us the degree of protection we want or need? What price are we willing to pay for security?"[22]

Having cited the duplication and contradiction among the "complex of Government security statutes, regulations, and procedures," Humphrey then noted how limited congressional involvement had been.

To the extent Congress has legislated at all in this area, it has been primarily concerned with the problems of espionage and unauthorized disclosure of national defense secrets. The basic statute is the Espionage Act of 1917. We have amended this statute a number of times to tighten it in the light of current needs, but we have never really studied it to make sure that a statute written in 1917 to reflect the political, military, and technological problems of that era is adequate in the era of hydrogen bombs, radar, and guided missiles, and the world's most infamous conspiracy, the international Communist conspiracy, which surely is not comparable in its ramifications, its subtleties, and its treachery, to some of the old tyrannies of years gone by.[23]

We encounter here (yes, even in the Congress) the bureaucratic desire for uniformity and predictability—"each of these actions has been taken sporadically and independently and not as part of a rational overall master plan"— but also and equally a concern for civil liberties, a fear of too much government with too few restraints. Loyd Wright, former president of the American Bar Association, was named chairman of the commission, with Senator Stennis as vice chairman. The spirit of the enterprise may be seen from President Eisenhower's appointments, which included the likes of Franklin D. Murphy, then chancellor of the University of Kansas, and James P. McGranery, who had served as attorney general under President Truman.

The commission set about reviewing and studying all phases of the government's security and loyalty programs, which it called a "vast, intricate, confusing and costly complex of temporary, inadequate, uncoordinated programs and measures designed to protect secrets and installations vital to the defense of the Nation against agents of Soviet imperialism." There had been a reason for the welter of programs that had sprung up between 1947 and 1955: "the ceaseless campaign of the Soviet Union and international communism to infiltrate our Government, industry, and other vital areas and to subvert our citizenry for purposes of espionage and sabotage." But now a stricter, more orderly approach was called for. The *Report of the Commission on Government Security,* published in June 1957, called for a "sound Government program" to establish the following: "procedures for security investigation, evaluation, and, where necessary, adjudication of Government employees, and also appropriate security requirements, with respect to persons privately employed or occupied on work requiring access to national defense secrets or work affording significant opportunity for injury to national security"; "vigorous enforcement of effective and realistic security laws and regulations"; and "careful, consistent, and efficient administration of this policy in a manner which will protect the national security and preserve basic American rights."[24]

The commission report—all 807 pages of it—was encyclopedic and fair-minded. It revealed a clear concern that the idea of loyalty not mutate into a caste system dividing the born-again from the untouchable. The commission distinguished between "the loyalty problem" and the problem of suitability and security, recognizing that "all loyalty cases are security cases, but the converse is not true." Someone who talks too freely when in his cups or someone whose personal life makes them vulnerable to blackmail may be a security risk but may also be a loyal American. The commission recommended that "as far as possible such cases be considered on a basis of suitability to safeguard the individual from an unjust stigma of disloyalty."[25]

In the end, however, the commission had only two legislative proposals: first, to penalize unlawful disclosures of classified information by persons outside as well as within the government (in the past, only disclosures by government employees had been punishable); second, to make admissible in court evidence of subversion that federal agencies had obtained by wiretapping.[26]

Little came of the commission's work. The proposal to outlaw disclosures of classified information by anyone, federal employee or no, was quickly perceived as prior restraint on the press: censorship. Responses from journalists and editorial boards were at once swift and predictable. Four days after the commission had issued its report, James Reston wrote an article for the *New York Times*, "Security Versus Freedom: An Analysis of the Controversy Stirred by Recommendation to Curb Information." Reston's article is notable for its specificity.

> The history of recent years is full of illustrations of the dangers of such broad legislative proposals.
>
> Franklin D. Roosevelt's deal with Joseph Stalin at Yalta to bring the Ukraine and Bylo-Russia into the United Nations was classified "top secret." Elaborate efforts were made to conceal the arrangement. The late Bert Andrews, Washington correspondent of the *New York Herald-Tribune*, found out about it.
>
> He "willfully," even gleefully, reported it, knowing full well that it was classified "top secret." Under the proposals of the Commission on Government Security, if law at the time, he would have been subject to a fine of $10,000 and five years in jail. . . .
>
> This newspaper also published the original plans of the United States, Britain, France and the Soviet Union on the formation of the United Nations. Again, they were marked "top secret" and the Federal Bureau of Investigation was called in to make an official investigation of disclosure.
>
> In this case, though the Government maintained that publication would block formation of the United Nations, the main result was a long debate on the Big Five veto power and the assumption that the five major powers could agree on a post-war settlement. This, in turn, helped clarify the issue and contributed to some modifications of the Charter, but under the legislation now proposed by the Commission on Government Security, it would have been a clear case for criminal action.[27]

(In this last-mentioned case, we would note that the potential felon would have been Reston himself, who had a friend in the Chinese delegation.)

Reston's assumption that journalists would act responsibly in such matters had a certain innocence. So did Wright's opposing assumption that, by making secret information public, the instigator was in effect a traitor: "The purveyor of information vital to national security, purloined by devious means, gives aid to our enemies as effectively as the foreign agent."[28]

Now then. Even at that time, the most frequent purveyors of "information vital to national security" obtained it, not by "devious means," but through routine channels. Officials often provided classified information to journalists, sometimes to enhance their own prestige, sometimes to gain advantage in an internal dispute, sometimes to let the public know something that the purveyor thought the public had a right to know. The matter has never been quantified, but it is reasonable to think that most "leaking" was coming from the higher reaches of the system. (We have Kennedy's testament that the Ship of State is the only ship that leaks from the top.) As Max Frankel of the *New York Times* has observed, presidents soon came to realize that "even harmless secrets were coins of power to be hoarded."[29]

It was beyond the range of a commission report to speculate on the allure of secrecy, but this must never be discounted. The official with a secret *feels* powerful. And is. In 1960, three years after the *Report of the Commission on Government Security* was published, the Committee on Government Operations of the House of Representatives declared: "Secrecy—the first refuge of incompetents—must be at a bare minimum in a democratic society, for a fully informed public is the basis of self-government. Those elected or appointed to positions of executive authority must recognize that government, in a democracy, cannot be wiser than the people."[30] Which is very likely true, but not of necessity widely believed by those in authority, howsoever brief.

The Commission on Government Security was not as bold or explicit in stating the problem, but it did attempt, in its most instructive proposal, to provide a solution. As a remedy for "one of the principal deficiencies of past loyalty and security programs"—the "shortage of trained, qualified personnel to administer them"—the commission recommended an independent central security office in the executive branch. The first duty of its director would be "to select eminently qualified personnel, including hearing examiners to conduct loyalty hearings under the Federal civilian employee program and security hearings under the industrial, atomic energy, port and civil air transport programs."[31] This strategy fit well with public administration doctrine of this time. It could well have been proposed by one of the several Hoover commissions of the postwar period. Like the Civil Service Commission, the new federal agency would operate according to uniform rules administered by trained, qualified, well-managed personnel.

But this, too, ran athwart the changed political culture of Washington. It was turning out that secrets were an asset not to be centralized and shared.

Organizations with the morale, incentives, and structure enabling them to hold information closely were increasingly disinclined to cooperate with organizations that were not. This is perhaps too generous. A less charitable view is that secrets had become assets; organizations hoarded them, revealing them sparingly and only in return for some consideration. Such as these wanted no part of some central security office busying itself with their internal affairs. This, of course, is conjecture, but it is certainly true that no central security office emerged.[32]

Instead, the dispersal of secrecy centers within the government continued. The Federal Bureau of Investigation began operations, as against investigations, overseas. This was a logical extension of its internal task of keeping abreast of domestic espionage and, from an organizational perspective, provided an opportunity of considerable import.

A dramatic instance of this extension can be seen in the interesting relationship that the FBI developed with a naturalized American named Morris Childs, born Moishe

Chilovsky in the Ukraine in 1902 of Jewish parents. His father, who had been engaged in anticzarist activities and had been exiled to Siberia, fled to the United States in 1910, and his family came the following year. Morris Childs later became a charter member of the Communist Party of the United States of America. Following the expulsion of Jay Lovestone (born Jacob Liebstein in 1898 in Lithuania), Childs became a party official under Browder; in 1929 he was sent to Moscow for further training. In 1934, he became a member of the American Central Committee, and in 1945 he succeeded Budenz as managing editor of the *Daily Worker*. In 1947, Childs returned to Moscow, where he learned of the repression there and specifically of Stalin's persecution of Jews. Thoroughly disillusioned, he was "turned" by the FBI in the early 1950s. In 1957, Childs became deputy head of the CPUSA and the primary contact with Soviet, Chinese, and other parties abroad, traveling regularly to Moscow and Peking. He led the U.S. delegation to the Twenty-First Party Congress in Moscow in 1959. Reportedly a source of considerable information about Kremlin politics and especially of Sino-Soviet tensions, Childs's role as an American agent was kept entirely within the FBI until President Gerald R. Ford was informed in 1974. In 1987, he was awarded the National Security Medal in a ceremony held *in camera* at FBI headquarters.

Meanwhile, the Eisenhower administration began an inquiry of its own. In August 1956 Secretary of Defense Charles E. Wilson established the five-member Committee on Classified Information, chaired by Charles A. Coolidge, a former assistant secretary of defense. (The other four members were retired high-ranking military officers.) In his letter establishing the committee, Secretary Wilson stated that he was "seriously concerned over the unauthorized disclosure of classified military information"; he called on the committee to examine the adequacy of all laws and regulations on classification and the safeguarding of classified information, as well as the procedures utilized at the Defense Department in this area and the department's ability to "fix responsibility" for unauthorized disclosure of classified information.

Three months after it was set up, on November 8, 1956, the Coolidge committee issued a report containing twenty-eight recommendations—ten covering overclassification, eleven relating to unauthorized disclosures of information, and the remaining seven relating to department policies vis-à-vis Congress, industry, and the press. The first recommendation—based on a finding that Defense Department officials had a tendency to "play it safe" and classify too much—called for "a determined attack" on overclassification, "spearheaded by the responsible heads within the Department of Defense, from the Secretary of Defense down." Another called on senior officials to "throw back over-classified matter received from subordinates." The committee also urged the department to make clear that the classification system "is not to be used to protect information not affecting the national security, and specifically prohibits its use for administrative matters." What the committee did not propose was any disciplinary action when classification procedures were abused. And in July 1957, when Secretary Wilson issued a new directive consolidating the department's rules for classification, it did not impose any procedures to address the matters that he had caused to be so strikingly set forth.

In addition to the several commissions organized to examine the security classification system, in 1955 the House of Representatives created the Special Government Information Subcommittee of the Government Operations Committee. The subcommittee was created because some representatives were concerned about the growth of postwar secrecy, especially the Eisenhower administration's establishment in November 1954 of the Office of Strategic Information, in the Commerce Department. The new agency was responsible for formulating policies about production and distribution of "unclassified scientific, technical, industrial, and economic information, the indiscriminate release of which may be inimical to the defense interests of the United States."[33]

In 1953, Representative John Moss, a freshman Democrat on the House Post Office and Civil Service Committee, had raised the issue of public access to government information. He had sought information from the Eisenhower administration's Civil Service Commission to verify its claim that 2,800 federal employees had been fired for "security reasons"; he wanted to know whether these reasons were based on allegations of disloyalty or espionage or on other matters that could also be grounds for discharge—like a misstatement on a job application. The commission refused to release the information, and Moss found that he had no means to compel its release. Two years later, he urged the creation—and subsequently was made chairman—of the Special Government Information Subcommittee, tasked with monitoring executive secrecy.

The Moss subcommittee undertook a lengthy inquiry (spanning the duration of both the Coolidge committee and the Wright commission) of the classification system's administration and operation and, more generally, the availability of information from agencies and departments. Among its chief concerns was the lack of any action against overclassification of information: "In a conflict between the right to know and the need to protect true military secrets from a potential enemy, there can be no valid argument against secrecy. The right to know has suffered, however, in the confusion over the demarcation between secrecy for true security reasons and secrecy for 'policy' reasons. The proper imposition of secrecy in some situations is a matter of judgment. Although an official faces disciplinary action for the failure to classify information which should be secret, no instance has been found of an official being disciplined for classifying material which should have been made public. The tendency to 'play it safe' and use the secrecy stamp has, therefore, been virtually inevitable."[34] But aside from effecting some attention to declassification of historical documents, the subcommittee's recommendations—including those intended to provide disincentives for overclassification and to establish a security classification system based in statute—were "largely ignored" by the executive branch.[35]

The Moss subcommittee did, however, remain at the forefront of legislative efforts to enhance public access to government information. Beginning in the mid-1950s, it focused more attention on how the security classification system related to the rights of both Congress and the public to obtain information from the executive branch. This would lead in 1966, after eleven long years, to enactment of the Freedom of Information Act (FOIA), which established any person's statutory right of access to all federal records except those falling into one of nine listed categories.

In 1958, Moss succeeded in narrowing the use of the 1789 "housekeeping" statute, an oft-litigated provision that had allowed government agencies to withhold information. In 1962, he helped persuade President Kennedy to narrow the use of "executive privilege" in denying the release of records. And in 1965 Moss, with Representative Donald Rumsfeld, introduced legislation to establish a presumption that, with only narrow exceptions, executive-branch documents should be available to the public and that judicial review should be available as a check on agency decisions to withhold information. By 1966, bipartisan support for the effort had grown, and it appeared that the issue of public access to information might even come up in the fall congressional elections. The legislation passed the Senate first, then the House. On July 4, 1966, President Johnson signed the FOIA into law. It went into effect exactly one year later, in order to give the executive branch time to prepare for its implementation.

Notable as that achievement was and remains, it did not much change the practices of the bureaucracy. In 1972, the

House Foreign Operations and Government Information Subcommittee, now chaired by Representative William Moorhead of Pennsylvania, concluded that "the efficient operation of the Freedom of Information Act has been hindered by five years of foot dragging by the Federal bureaucracy." Agency procedures were deficient and employees untrained, large fees were charged in order to deter requests, responses were long in coming, and the exemption categories were being applied too broadly. Again Congress responded. With Moorhead's leadership, the FOIA was amended substantially in 1974 (the amendment became law after Congress voted overwhelmingly to override a presidential veto) to close some of the loopholes and strengthen several provisions.

Notwithstanding the accomplishments of Representatives Moss and Moorhead and their colleagues, an inevitable conflict remains between the right of access prescribed in the FOIA and the authority of the executive branch to preserve certain secrets. The very first exception to the general FOIA principle of public access applies to matters that are "specifically authorized under criteria established by an Executive order to be kept secret in the interest of national defense or foreign policy" or to matters that are "in fact properly classified pursuant to such Executive order."[36] This exception is not surprising; as noted, such matters had been treated differently in the original Administrative Procedure Act. The difference now is the availability of procedures, including use of the courts, to review bureaucrats' decisions to deny the release of information requested under the FOIA.[37]

From the onset of the atomic age there had been a tension between the defense establishment (generally defined) and the scientific community over the nature of secrecy in science. From the time of the Smyth report and the arguments of Bethe and others as to the inevitability of a Soviet H-bomb, the level of irritation between the two camps was not inconsiderable. The scientists had said that the United

States could not hide nature from Russians. Now an argument arose about the disutility of trying to hide nature from Americans. As noted earlier, the Wright commission was on to this, stressing "the dangers to national security that arise out of overclassification of information which retards scientific and technological progress, and thus tends to deprive the country of the lead time that results from the free exchange of ideas and information."[38]

This aspect of the Wright commission's report was echoed in resounding fashion thirteen years later. In July 1970, a special task force on secrecy, convened by the Defense Science Board and led by Frederick Seitz of Rockefeller University, issued its final report on how to address problems with the system for classifying scientific and technical information.[39] The task force, whose members included Edward Teller and Jack P. Ruina of the Massachusetts Institute of Technology, deemed it unlikely that any classified scientific and technical information would remain secure for as long as five years; more likely, the information would become known to others in as little as one year by means of "independent discovery" or clandestine disclosure.[40] The report also cited the costs of classification, urging that its effect in inhibiting the flow of information should be considered, and balanced against the benefits, when classification decisions were made. If greater care was taken to classify fewer documents and for shorter periods, the task force concluded, the amount of scientific and technical information that was classified could be reduced by as much as 90 percent.

In its most telling passage, the Seitz task force wrote that "more might be gained than lost" if the United States were to adopt "unilaterally, if necessary—a policy of complete openness in all areas of information." Recognizing, however, that this proposal was not practical in light of prevailing views on classification, it recommended instead a "rigid schedule" for automatic declassification, with a general period of one to five years, subject to exemptions for specified categories.[41] That nothing came of this recommendation speaks to the culture of secrecy that was settling on Washington. This task force was not a band of outsiders; its members included Teller and Ruina, men who had designed and built the weapons under scrutiny. In matters of constructing weaponry their judgment was unquestioned, but by some bizarre dissociation, their judgment could not be trusted where secrecy was concerned.

Nor did time mellow these attitudes. To the contrary: "The security classification of information became in the 1980s an arbitrary, capricious, and frivolous process, almost devoid of objective criteria." Thus was the conclusion of Glenn T. Seaborg, co-discoverer of plutonium and chairman of the Atomic Energy Commission from 1961 to 1971. During this time he kept a journal, much of it consisting of a diary written at home each evening, the rest containing correspondence, announcements, minutes, and the like. Seaborg was careful about classified matters; nothing was included that could not be made public. While he was at the AEC, the portions of his journal relating to the Kennedy and Johnson administrations were microfilmed and placed in the appropriate presidential libraries. Before he left the AEC, Seaborg had the entire journal cleared virtually without deletion.

Then lunacy descended. Or, rather, the Atomic Energy Commission became the Department of Energy and bureaucracy got going. Seaborg writes of all this in an article, "Secrecy Runs Amok," published in *Science* in 1994. It seems that in 1983 the chief historian of the department asked to borrow one of two sets of the journal, some twenty-six volumes in all, for work on a history of the commission. By the time Seaborg got his journal back, passage after passage had been redacted, much of it explicitly public information (like the published code names of nuclear weapons tests), some of it purely personal (like his account of going trick-or-treating with his children on Halloween).[42]

The twenty-six volumes of the journal, "in expurgated form," as Seaborg puts it, are now available in manuscript archives of the Library of Congress. But where does one go for sanity? Seaborg notes that, "with the beginning of the Reagan administration, the government had begun to take a new, much more severe and rigid position with regard to secrecy."[43] The balance between the right of the public to know and the right of the nation to protect itself was simply lost as (often apologetic) investigators pored over the papers of one of the great Americans of our time.

Again to the theme that organizations in conflict—make that "competition"—become like one another. By the 1990s the Central Intelligence Agency had created a history staff at the Center for the Study of Intelligence. (History staffs were by then standard appurtenances of Washington agencies.) The center engaged a young scholar, Nick Cullather, to write a history of the agency's early involvement in Guatemala. In 1994, the CIA published a redacted version of Cullather's *Operation PBSUCCESS: The United States and Guatemala, 1952–1954*. One of the redacted portions: a passage quoted from President Eisenhower's memoirs.[44]

CHAPTER SEVEN

The Routinization of Secrecy

$\mathbb{A}$s the Cold War gathered, the United States, in no wise the aggressor, had to organize itself to deal with aggression from a different kind of adversary. The Soviet Union's very name reflected the new phenomenon: a federation of soviets, towns or village councils made up of workers and peasants. The hamlet as nation-state as international movement. The red flag knew no boundaries: it represented mankind, and the Supreme Soviet in Moscow spoke for mankind. This was not German or Japanese nationalism. It was something wholly new, and now the United States organized itself in a wholly new fashion.

The Cold War is probably best understood as the third in a succession of civil wars in Western civilization. The first began in 1914, the second in 1939. The third began in Central Europe, as had the two earlier conflicts, with the Soviets pressing to expand their dominion in the wreckage of previous regimes. In 1949 Communists triumphed in a civil war in China; suddenly, the conflict became global.

In all this the United States, as the preeminent world

power, began to recognize that it would be managing disputes, and very likely engaged in warfare, around the world and indefinitely. As a consequence, a large peacetime military establishment began to take shape. Foreign policy began to anticipate, rather than merely react to, conflicts. Seeing that the United States would inevitably be drawn in if the Soviets were to invade West Germany, we chose to become engaged in advance, helping to formulate the North Atlantic Treaty in 1949; for the first time in our history, we entered a peacetime alliance committing us to war if others were attacked. In 1955 the Soviets organized the Warsaw Pact, and the symmetry was complete. Central Powers versus Allied Powers, Axis Powers versus Allied Powers, Warsaw Pact versus North Atlantic Treaty Organization.

The extraordinary fact of the final stage of this hundred years' war is that warfare never broke out between the major contesting powers. Proxy conflicts of all sorts did occur. U.S. forces did see action. Still, this time, global confrontation did not result in global war. The reason, of course, was the atomic bomb and the strategic thinking that began with the onset of the atomic age. American strategic doctrine, with its emphasis on "second-strike" capability—on developing a nuclear-weapons force able to withstand nuclear attack and deliver a retaliatory attack—was surely key in ultimately achieving nuclear stability. But during the Cold War this outcome was by no means clear. As ideological conflict between the two powers raged, so did efforts to gain tactical advantage through espionage or subversion. Both parties organized alliances, built conventional forces and strategic forces, cultivated dissent among adversaries, hoarded information, and built up intelligence forces of unprecedented size and global reach.

As we have seen, part of the U.S. response to what seemed a new world order was to rationalize, modernize, and routinize its intelligence operations. The National Security Act of 1947 created the National Security Council to advise the president about all domestic, foreign, and military policies relating to national security and the Department of Defense, bringing American armed forces under unified command. It also created the Central Intelligence Agency to provide "national intelligence"—"timely, objective, independent of political considerations, and based upon all sources available to the intelligence community"—to the president and agency heads.[1] Thus the CIA essentially began its life as a committee. It was to make sense of the cable traffic, publish the *National Intelligence Daily* for the president and a few others, keep an eye out for the unexpected. Truman had originally understood that the agency would work "for the benefit and convenience of the President of the United States . . . [so that] instead of the President having to look through a bunch of papers two feet high, the information was coordinated so that the President could arrive at the facts."[2]

In short order, however, the CIA became a worldwide organization involved with espionage, insurgency, and counterinsurgency—operations of every sort. By the late 1950s, it had grown to about the size of the State Department, with some twenty thousand employees. After setting up in temporary buildings on Navy Hill, across the road from the State Department, it acquired its magnificent headquarters on the banks of the Potomac, at Langley, Virginia. (Senate lore has it that Senator Richard B. Russell of Georgia slipped the building into a defense appropriations bill in the guise of an aircraft carrier.) And with the vast expansion in bureaucratization came a remarkable routinization of secrecy. Until 1997, the intelligence budget was secret; even now that the total budget is public information, its details remain classified. Covert operations, often paramilitary, became a signature activity. A half century after the CIA was founded, a newly confirmed director told the press, and, by indirection, agency employees, that the mission of the CIA was "to pursue the hardest targets that threaten American interests around the world": "At the end of the day, this is an espionage organization. . . . Otherwise I don't know why we are here."[3]

As we shall see, there were several reasons for the CIA's having embraced concealment as a modus vivendi. But the routinization of secrecy worked against the very purpose it was designed to serve: to see clearly the nature of the Soviet threat, and to respond accordingly.

In his magisterial summa *Bureaucracy: What Government Agencies Do and Why They Do It*, James Q. Wilson states: "An organization is like a fish in a coral reef. To survive, it needs to find a supportive ecological niche." If an organization's niche is not specified by law, as it was with the Social Security Administration or the Internal Revenue Service, its founding executives can sometimes achieve that autonomy by other means. Wilson uses the CIA as the prime example of how this transformation can be brought about: "First, [the founding executives must] seek out tasks that are not being performed by others. . . . The first directors of the Central Intelligence Agency faced plenty of rivals—the military services as well as the State Department had active intelligence services. This fact . . . led it to define a new role for itself in the area of covert operations."[4]

The agency lost little time in defining this role. Its reach, it determined at the outset, would be global. In *Operation PBSUCCESS*, Nicholas Cullather records that CIA agents arrived in Guatemala in March 1947, just months after the agency was created; they were to keep an eye on Peronists and Communists and, in time, start a civil war.[5] This operation became the model for the Cuban operation that culminated in the Bay of Pigs. In the meantime, the Eisenhower administration used covert actions to build a government in South Vietnam and support a separatist movement in Sumatra.[6] The activities in Iran are now well known (though the full story will never be known, as the agency destroyed the files in 1960s). There were others, less dramatic but no less adventurous.

But of course the CIA was chiefly concerned with carving out its sphere of influence with regard to the Soviet

Union. And in the drive to pursue an active agenda, it often disregarded voices that seemed to argue for a quieter approach. In July 1947, three months after CIA agents had arrived in Guatemala, the magazine *Foreign Affairs* published "The Sources of Soviet Conduct," by a writer identified only as "X." Although the piece was attacked and even grossly misread by those with interventionist leanings, it was surely the most prescient position paper in the history of modern American diplomacy. Its author, George F. Kennan, who at that time was head of the State Department's policy planning staff, argued the case for containment as a largely passive policy. There was no urgency, he asserted, for the simple reason that Soviet doctrine itself decreed there was none. Marxism-Leninism had famously declared that capitalism contains the seeds of its own destruction, that its inescapable result was a revolutionary transfer of power to the working class. A final phase would lead to war and revolution, but all in good time. In tracing intentions from ideology, Kennan perceived that the Soviet leadership may have been less aggressively expansionist than many assumed: "We have seen that the Kremlin is under no ideological compulsion to accomplish its purposes in a hurry. Like the Church, it is dealing in ideological concepts which are of long-term validity, and it can afford to be patient. . . . The very teachings of Lenin himself require great caution and flexibility in the pursuit of Communist purposes."[7]

Moreover, the faith was dying at home. Kennan saw that Soviet Communism contained its own seeds of destruction: the hardships of Soviet rule, especially with regard to human freedoms, and the hardships of the troubled Soviet economy. The Russian people, he observed, "are disillusioned, skeptical and no longer as accessible as they once were to the magical attraction which Soviet power still radiates to its followers abroad. The avidity with which people seized upon the slight respite accorded to the Church for tactical reasons during the war was eloquent testimony to the fact that their capacity for faith and devotion found little expression in the purposes of the régime."[8]

As for the Russian economy, some parts of it had developed—notably, the metallurgical and machine industries (which would be crucial in producing nuclear weapons). But for the rest, it was a backward economy devastated by war and hobbled by an increasingly outdated infrastructure (a primitive railroad system, an inadequate highway network, a rudimentary air transport industry). Kennan clearly foresaw the consequences: "The future of Soviet power may not be by any means as secure as Russian capacity for self-delusion would make it appear to the men in the Kremlin." He recalled Thomas Mann's analogy in the great novel *Buddenbrooks:* human institutions, like stars, often appear to shine most brilliantly when their inner decay is in reality farthest advanced. "And who can say with assurance that the strong light still cast by the Kremlin on the dissatisfied peoples of the western world is not the powerful afterglow of a constellation which is in actuality on the wane? This cannot be proved. And it cannot be disproved. But the possibility remains (and in the opinion of this writer it is a strong one) that Soviet power, like the capitalist world of its conception, bears within it the seeds of its own decay, and that the sprouting of these seeds is well advanced."[9]

Kennan, of course, wrote at a time when the United States was pursuing a postwar policy of accommodation with the Soviet Union.[10] But he was warning of obstacles ahead. We were in for a time of trouble, but we needed to keep it in perspective; it was trouble that we could handle.

All this seemed to change in August 1949, with the intelligence reports that the Soviet Union had "probably" achieved a successful nuclear explosion.[11] Truman directed the State Department and Defense Department to conduct a joint study of nuclear weapons policy, including the advisability of proceeding with not just developing but stockpiling nuclear weapons. The resulting text, called NSC-68, was principally associated with Paul H. Nitze, who replaced Kennan as head of the State Department's policy planning staff. It proposed that the nation move to the more aggressive footing that we now associate with the Cold War: the Soviets were to be rolled back, not merely contained.

In his biography of Allen Dulles, Eisenhower's first director of Central Intelligence, Peter Grose suggests that the assessment in NSC-68 was all but unbalanced: "Democrats and Republicans both believed that the Free World confronted a global adversary that would yield to nothing less than an overwhelming counterforce. This conviction had been enshrined in NSC-68, . . . which perceived the world through a Manichaean prism."[12] Looking back in 1997, Nitze recalled that the drafters of NSC-68 relied on threat assessments from the intelligence community, and that parts of the assessments turned out to be "significantly inflated." He gave the example of a CIA report that put the number of combat-capable Soviet divisions at 175, when in fact only a third of these divisions were at full strength, another third were at half strength, and the rest were only skeletal.[13]

This misinformation regarding Soviet military strength also colored the debate about Soviet intentions. Among those involved with NSC-68, neither Kennan nor Charles E. "Chip" Bohlen were swayed.* They argued that the leaders of the Soviet Union were first of all concerned with maintaining their own power, then with keeping control of Soviet satellites; global expansion of socialism came last. They raised their objections, and Nitze explains that NSC-68 was modified to some extent, though never to Kennan and Bohlen's satisfaction.[14]

Withal, NSC-68 echoed Kennan's basic assessment: "The greatest vulnerability of the Kremlin lies in the basic nature of its relations with the Soviet people. That relationship is characterized by universal suspicion, fear and denuncia-

* At the time, Bohlen was a specialist in Russian affairs, while Kennan was a special assistant to the secretary of state. Both would go on to become ambassador to Russia: Kennan in 1952, Bohlen from 1953 to 1957.

tion. It is a relationship in which the Kremlin relies, not only for its power but its very survival, on intricately devised mechanisms of coercion. The Soviet monolith is held together by the iron curtain around it and the iron bars within it, not by any force of natural cohesion."[15]

The policy of containment that NSC-68 described was one of seeking, "by all means short of war," to block further expansion of Soviet power, expose Soviet pretensions, induce retractions of the Kremlin's control and influence, and "so foster the seeds of destruction within the Soviet system that the Kremlin is brought at least to the point of modifying its behavior to conform to generally accepted international standards."[16]

The history of American foreign policy in the second half of the twentieth century could be written in terms of how this message was lost.[17] One component, surely, is that during this time so much became secret. Kennan's views were published in *Foreign Affairs*. But in the years that followed, typically as one administration succeeded another, most documents, studies, and other informed assessments were classified. NSC-68 itself was classified until 1975. Policy planners moved about in a fog of secrecy so thick that they did not entirely recognize when they had changed directions. Thus, by the time of the Nixon administration, the movement from containment to détente was based on an assumption of the Soviet regime's permanence and power. American government had lost touch with the concept that the Soviet Union was bound to self-destruct in time.* (As Nixon himself commented in his book *The Real War* (1980), "During all of my presidency we were engaged in a 'war' with the Soviet Union," predicting that the struggle with the Soviets "will continue to dominate world events for the rest of this century.")[18]

A few did recognize that the haze of secrecy was growing denser, especially at the CIA, and they warned of its dan-

* The author so attests. In 1976, he was fired from Ford's cabinet for thinking otherwise.

gers. One such moment came during the McCarthy period, after the senator's committee had begun targeting the agency. On July 9, 1953, McCarthy's staff summoned William P. Bundy, a CIA employee and son-in-law of Dean Acheson, to testify that very morning about his four-hundred-dollar contribution to Alger Hiss's legal defense fund. (Before joining the agency, Bundy had informed his new superiors of his contribution; Hoover had come upon the information and almost certainly passed it on to McCarthy.) On the spot, Director Dulles decided that his officers were not to testify before Congress. Irate, McCarthy took to the Senate floor. But the next day, Dulles made his way to Capitol Hill. Remaining pleasant but firm, he asked Vice President Nixon to call McCarthy off, which Nixon did, at a small dinner gathering with committee members.[19]

The fallout for the CIA was a good bit of public criticism. Walter Lippmann wrote, speaking of Dulles's stand, "Secrecy is not a criterion for immunity." The agency had to submit to congressional accountability just like every other executive agency: "The argument that the CIA is something apart, that it is so secret that it differs in kind from the State Department or, for that matter, . . . the Department of Agriculture, is untenable." Hanson W. Baldwin of the *New York Times* went further, warning of "a philosophy of secrecy and power, of the ends justifying the means, of disagreeable methods for agreeable ends."[20] These critics were not outsiders, radicals denouncing the government in New York's Union Square or in Chicago's Haymarket Square. They were personal friends, Dulles and Lippmann having been at the Paris Peace Conference together in 1919. They were journalists of reputation and experience, setting high standards for public affairs. Secrecy seemed out of place to them. *Fin de ligne*.

But even had the government been inclined to heed warnings like these, the routinization of concealment would have prevented assessments from receiving a fair hearing. Not long after the Bundy episode, former president Herbert

Hoover announced that, as part of the work of the Second Commission on Organization of the Executive Branch of the Government, he had named General Mark W. Clark to a task force to look into the "restructure and administration" of the CIA.[21] President Eisenhower evidently became concerned that Clark's inquiry might get too close to sensitive matters, so he asked Lieutenant General James H. Doolittle, who had led the bombing raid on Tokyo in April 1942, to head a panel of consultants to review the agency's covert activities. In a letter of July 26, 1954, Eisenhower told Doolittle that the Clark task force, in keeping with the Hoover commission's mandate, was to concern itself with means "to accomplish the policy of Congress to promote economy, efficiency, and improved services." Because that work was to get under way shortly, the president suggested that the two generals confer in order to avoid "unnecessary duplication." Then Eisenhower gave explicit instructions. "The distinction between the work of your Study Group and of the Hoover Task Force is this: 'You will deal with the covert activities of the CIA, . . . and your report will be submitted to me.' . . . . Reports of the Hoover Commission are made to the Congress."[22] Doolittle's report was to be secret.

The sixty-page report, marked Top Secret, was delivered to the president on September 30, 1954—two months' work, but a great divide. Doolittle was confident about his assessment of CIA tactics. "Infiltration by human agents" wasn't working: "The information we have obtained by this method of acquisition has been negligible and the cost in effort, dollars and human lives prohibitive." It was time to explore "every possible scientific and technical avenue of approach to this scientific problem."* There was a tendency at CIA "to

---

* The first U-2 test flight took place one year later, on August 1, 1955. The first operational flight, targeting Moscow and Leningrad, took place in early July 1956. Francis Gary Powers's U-2 was shot down on May 1, 1960. This would seem an average life for a technical secret. Satellites came next, whereupon both sides knew that both sides knew what was going on in the Fulda Gap, or wherever. This was the great intelligence feat that brought stability to the Cold War.

over-classify documentary data originating in the Agency, a condition which operates in derogation of the security classification system as a whole." Translation: secrets are hoarded. "The Armed Services should be allowed to engage in espionage and counterespionage operations." Translation: the military was still here; there must not be a civilian monopoly on intelligence. Doolittle's most significant recommendation, however, is found in the first few pages of his report: containment would not do; the United States was at war. "We must develop effective espionage and counterespionage services and must learn to subvert, sabotage and destroy our enemies by more clever, more sophisticated and more effective methods than those used against us," he urged. "It may become necessary that the American people be made acquainted with, understand and support this fundamentally repugnant philosophy."[23]

The American people would not be "made acquainted" with this outlook. Only the president and a few others read the report. Nothing of substance was leaked. On October 14, 1954, Baldwin did file a long story in the *New York Times*, "Doolittle Heads Inquiry into CIA," noting that General Clark was also leading a similar inquiry. But not much of substance was reported—certainly not a profound shift away from containment as national policy.

The Clark report—actually two reports, one public, one classified—was finished the following May 1955 and transmitted to Congress in June by the Hoover commission. It was a credible exercise in the never-ending quest for efficiency in American government. Although it found Director Dulles in possession of many admirable qualities, the report concluded that he had taken on too many duties and responsibilities. The CIA as a whole was spread too thin. The task force recommended that the agency focus on collecting intelligence on Communist China and Russia and her satellites, not allowing itself to get distracted by operations elsewhere around the globe. "The task force is deeply concerned over the lack of adequate Intelligence data from behind the

Iron Curtain. . . . The glamor and excitement of some angles of our Intelligence effort must not be permitted to overshadow other vital phases of the work or to cause neglect of primary functions."[24] Thus the judgment of the Clark report was in line with that of the Doolittle report: covert action was getting in the way of intelligence.

The Clark report seems not to have been well received at the agency. In a memorandum of July 19, Frank O. Wisner, then the cia's deputy director of plans—which is to say, covert action—took a more than defensive tone. The "Clark Committee," he charged, had "solicited advice from Senator McCarthy, and the more or less public solicitation of any and all adverse information concerning cia and its personnel." Wisner wasn't in the mood for this, and he responded much as J. Edgar Hoover would have done. He concluded his three-page Secret memorandum by lumping the investigations of General Clark together with those of Senator McCarthy and portraying the cia as an embattled organization: "The personnel of this Agency are entitled to feel very reassured and, in fact, proud to belong to an organization which has so successfully withstood the acid test of these *unprecedented* investigations. I consider that we are entitled to hold our heads high and to indulge ourselves in a modest amount of self-congratulation. Certainly there is no longer any reason for the personnel of this Agency to feel that the Agency is under the gun or required to offer apologies. . . . I believe that we should let it be understood that the 'open season' on cia is closed and that it is no longer a fashionable or profitable pursuit to sling mud at our people."[25]

Wisner and his colleagues did have some reason to be indignant. Here they were, devoting their careers to the struggle against Communism, routinely risking their lives in the endeavor (some, like William Buckley in Beirut years later, were tortured to death), while the likes of Senator McCarthy had the audacity to question their loyalty. But this surely was not General Clark's purpose, and his task force was onto something. Secrecy was beginning to cause problems. The agency was seen to be deceptive. In early 1967 it was revealed that the agency had secretly funded the Congress for Cultural Freedom, whose journal, *Encounter*, was first edited in London by Irving Kristol and Stephen Spender. The journal was assertively anti-Communist, but more liberal than conservative. Kristol was wholly unapologetic. Correct opinion in New York was not reassured. The CIA? Indeed, the U.S. government? By far the most important of the task force's critiques concerned "the quality and quantity of the Agency's intelligence on the Soviet Union." Was there insufficient room in the CIA's ecological niche, as Wilson calls it, for *intelligence?* In two years' time, the U.S. government was to adopt the view of Soviet capabilities and prospects that argued the task force's case in stunning terms.

For all the distraction of covert action and military engagement on the periphery of Eurasia and in parts of what was coming to be known as the Third World, the central, all-consuming task of statecraft during the Cold War was to establish an effective system of deterrence by which the Soviet Union would be dissuaded from nuclear war. The big "secret" of the American government during the early and middle years of the Cold War was that Soviet economic and military power was advancing at a rate that made deterrence problematic at best. In 1957, a Top Secret report, "Deterrence and Survival in the Nuclear Age," warned of the Soviets' "spectacular progress" in achieving substantial parity in the essentials of military strength, forecasting a crossover, as the term was: a time when the USSR would achieve military superiority over the United States. Soviet growth was so phenomenal that a crossover could also be anticipated for Soviet economic superiority.

The document, known as the Gaither report, for H. Rowen Gaither, Jr., then head of the Ford Foundation, was a product of the Security Resources Panel of the president's Science Advisory Committee. (PSAC as it would be known, had been created by President Eisenhower to provide science advice independent of Pentagon counsels.)* The National Security Council had requested the report, and the job was done in six months. It was forwarded to the president just weeks after the October 4, 1957, launching of Sputnik. The conclusions were stark to the point of startling:

> The Gross National Product (GNP) of the USSR is now more than one-third that of the United States and is increasing half again as fast. Even if the Russian rate of growth should decline, because of increasing difficulties in management and shortage of raw materials, and should drop by 1980 to half its present rate, its GNP would be more than half of ours as of that date. This growing Russian economic strength is concentrated on the armed forces and on investment in heavy industry, which this year account for the equivalent of roughly $40 billion and $17 billion, respectively, in 1955 dollars. Adding these two figures, we get an allocation of $57 billion per annum, which is roughly equal to the combined figure for these two items in our country's current effort. If the USSR continues to expand its military expenditures throughout the next decade, as it has during the 1950s, and ours remains constant, its annual military expenditures may be double ours. . . .
>
> This extraordinary concentration of the Soviet economy on military power and heavy industry, which is permitted, or perhaps forced, by their peculiar political structure, makes available economic resources sufficient to finance both the rapid expansion of their impressive military capability and their politico-economic offensive by which, through diplomacy, propaganda and subversion, they seek to extend the Soviet orbit.

The charts that followed were uncompromising. The first showed the Soviets reaching toward U.S. production levels in coal and steel and already producing twice the number of machine tools. This while the United States frittered away resources on consumer goods like automobiles, wash-

* This, at all events, was the understanding of committee members in later years. The author was a member from 1971 to 1973.

ing machines, and refrigerators. The second showed that the military effort of the USSR was about to surpass that of the United States.

The assertion that the Soviet GNP was growing "half again as fast" as that of the United States was traumatic. In 1956, nominal growth in the United States was 5.5 percent, which would give the Soviets a nominal rate of 8.25 percent. The former rate was in line with the forecasts prepared by the Council of Economic Advisers, which had been estimating long-run real growth of 3.5 percent, with inflation at about 2 percent. And so the "crossover" date would be 1998. By the end of the century, the Soviet Union would have a larger economy than the United States would and presumably vastly greater military strength as well.[26]

The intelligence community accepted and "improved" the assessment of the Gaither commission. In May 1958, Director Dulles spoke to the annual meeting of the Chamber of Commerce of the United States. His talk was entitled "Dimensions of the International Peril Facing Us," and he described these as formidable: "Whereas Soviet gross national product was about 33 percent that of the U.S. in 1950, by 1956 it had increased to about 40 percent, and by 1962 it may be about 50 percent of our own. This means that the Soviet economy has been growing, and is expected to continue to grow through 1962, at a rate roughly twice that of the economy of the United States. Annual growth overall has been running between 6 and 7 percent, annual growth of industry between 10 and 12 percent." Dulles then provided more statistics showing that Soviet consumption as a proportion of GNP was significantly lower than U.S. consumption, whereas Soviet investment was significantly higher. Furthermore, investment funds in the USSR were plowed back into expansion of electric power, the metallurgical base, and producer goods. Defense expenditures, as a proportion of GNP in the USSR, were significantly higher than in the United States, "in fact about double." Soviet industrial production was rapidly expanding, increasing 11 percent in 1957–58; in comparison, industrial production had declined 11 percent in the United States. The output of coal in the Soviet Union was about 70 percent of that in the United States. In steel production, reported Dulles, "In the first quarter of 1958, the Sino-Soviet Bloc has for the first time surpassed the United States. . . .The three months figures show that the USSR alone turned out over 75 percent of the steel tonnage of the U.S."[27]

At a 6 percent growth rate for the USSR, the crossover date would be 1992. At 7 percent, 1983. As best this now receding history can be reconstructed, the Department of State was almost alone in questioning such fantasy. In 1962, Walt Rostow, then head of the policy planning staff, privately demurred that he was not one of those "6 percent forever" people.[28]*

The Gaither report remained Top Secret until 1973. But, of course, it had leaked well before then. On November 5, 1957, two days before it was forwarded to the president, the *New York Times* reported that a secret study of the entire scope of national defense was about to be sent to the NSC;

---

* Also in 1962, G. Warren Nutter, an economist of the Chicago school, published *The Growth of Industrial Production in the Soviet Union* (Princeton: Princeton University Press, National Bureau of Economic Research, 1962). As was often the case with those of the Chicago school at this time, Nutter was wholly at odds with the general disposition of the academic profession. He judged that Soviet growth rates did not equal those of the czarist period, preceding the 1917 revolution, and did not at all match growth rates in contemporary West Germany and Japan. He dismissed Soviet statistics as propaganda. Withal, he was no less alarmed by the state of affairs. As Paul Craig Roberts would later write: "Nutter's studies of the Soviet system also foretold that serious economic problems would not constrain the Communist leadership from building a military machine that was openly aggressive and a formidable threat to the rest of the world" ("Warren Nutter: An Economist for All Times," in *Ideas, Their Origins, and Their Consequences: Lectures to Commemorate the Life and Work of G. Warren Nutter* [Washington, D.C.: American Enterprise Institute for Public Policy Research, 1988], p. 159). From 1969 to 1973 Nutter served as assistant secretary of defense in the Nixon administration but felt not the least sympathy for the administration's détente approach to the Soviet Union. It would, he felt, only embolden the Soviet military.

then, on December 23, the *Washington Post* published a detailed article.[29] The term "missile gap" now appeared. The report had been explicit in this matter: "By 1959, the USSR may be able to launch an attack with ICBMs carrying megaton warheads, against which SAC [Strategic Air Command] will be almost completely vulnerable under present programs. By 1961–1962, at our present pace, or considerably earlier if we accelerate, the United States could have a reliable early-warning capability against a missile attack, and SAC forces should be on a 7- to 22-minute operational 'alert.' The next two years seem to us critical. If we fail to act at once, the risk, in our opinion, will be unacceptable."[30]

It is not clear whether the Gaither panel had access to the U-2 photographs then available, which evidently showed no sign of a massive ICBM buildup. In any event, President Eisenhower did know about the photographs and was disinclined to see a crisis. Probably Senator John F. Kennedy did not know about them, and so the "missile gap" entered the rhetoric of the 1960 presidential election. Journalist Joseph Alsop knew all manner of leading figures within the intelligence community. In August 1958 he had written: "At the Pentagon they shudder when they speak of the 'gap,' which means the years 1960, 1961, 1962, and 1963. They shudder because in these years, the American government will flaccidly permit the Kremlin to gain an almost unchallenged superiority in the nuclear striking power that was once our specialty."[31]

In 1976, the Congressional Joint Committee on Defense Production published the Gaither report. In an introduction to the volume, Senator William Proxmire wrote, "Few documents have had as great an influence on American strategic thinking in the modern era."[32] The missile gap turned out not to exist, but nearly four decades later the United States is still contemplating modes of missile defense.[33] *Civil* defense has pretty much disappeared from policy debates, but in weapons negotiations and appropriations, the aftermath of the scare echoes on.

The question must be asked: what was gained by secrecy? What would have been lost had the report been made public, as Senator Lyndon B. Johnson requested at the time? For fifty years, as Bryan Hehir has observed, the United States confronted a direct, unambiguous issue: "how to deter a conscious, rational choice to use nuclear weapons against American territory."[34] Given the nature of the issue—a rational choice—a case surely can be made that our deliberations ought to have been more public. Save for the Smyth report of 1946, this case was never made. The bomb created a mystique of secrecy that resisted a disposition to openness.

To be sure, vigorous public debate about nuclear strategy did occur, principally at universities and various think tanks. But within government, decision making proceeded on the basis of tightly held (unless deliberately leaked) classified information and analysis. Of the roughly one hundred people associated with the Gaither report, few were economists. None of the principals had any specialized knowledge about the Soviet system, certainly not enough to add "investment in heavy industry" to outlays on the armed forces to produce an index of Soviet geopolitical strength defined as nuclear strike power. These passages from the report now seem absurd. What seems merely painful is the image of physicists measuring the overall strength of an economy in terms of coal and steel production, thirteen years after one of the first computers began operating at Harvard University.

Now, it would be an exaggeration to say that government secrecy alone caused this muddled state of affairs. The disposition put in place in the Eisenhower years—to see the Soviets as a modern industrial economy growing ever stronger—resulted partly from accepting Soviet data at face value. In July 1990, one year before the collapse of the Soviet regime, Nicholas Eberstadt of the American Enterprise Institute testified before the Senate Committee on Foreign Relations, and he was careful to acknowledge that, for estimates on Soviet economic output, the "most comprehensive and authoritative" were those produced by the U.S. government, principally under the auspices of the Central Intelligence Agency. "In fact," he added, "I believe it may be safe to say that the U.S. Government's effort to describe the Soviet economy may be the largest single project in the social science research ever undertaken." But the project had shortcomings, contradictions that were evident "even in a fairly cursory assessment of the published research." Eberstadt pointed first to the problems attendant upon using the notoriously inflated statistics provided by the Soviet Union. "The limitations of these official statistics are well known," he said. But "very often the U.S. analysis took these figures at face value, with only minor adjustments." The consequences of such credulousness were seen in the latest CIA *Handbook of Economic Statistics*, which suggested that the per-capita output of milk was higher in the USSR than in the United States, "making the Soviet Union not only a nuclear power, but a dairy superpower." What's more, "these estimates suggest Soviet meat output in the late 1980s to be about the same as in the United States in 1960, during the Eisenhower years." Such estimates, of course, were totally out of step with impressions of Western tourists and Soviet citizens alike. "Now, it is widely believed that the Soviet Government routinely hides many of its efforts from outside view," Eberstadt granted. "But where, one wonders, are the hidden stockpiles and reserves of Soviet meat?"[35]*

Using Soviet data was one problem; another was that the tendency to overestimate Soviet strength was pandemic. At the same hearing of the Senate Committee on Foreign Re-

* Poorly stocked grocery stores and the long queues outside them were just part of the story. By the 1960s, it was commonplace for journalists and other visitors to return from Moscow with tales about Soviet hotels, particularly the Stalinist behemoth known as the Ukraine. *Always* get a room on a lower floor, the advice was, as the elevators *never* worked. A former defense official in the Kennedy administration proposed the ironic theory that such scenes were part of a demonic device by which Soviet officials concealed the vibrant, progressive society in which everyday Russians actually lived.

lations that Eberstadt spoke at, Michael J. Boskin, then chairman of the Council of Economic Advisers, estimated that the economy of the Soviet Union was "about one-third" that of the United States.[36] At this time, the official *Handbook of Economic Statistics* put the ratio at 52 percent.[37] The disposition to overstate, which had begun with the Gaither-era projections, was still much in evidence. The U.S. GDP for 1990 was $4.8 trillion. The intelligence community put Soviet GDP at $2.5 trillion. The president's chief economist made it more like $1.6 trillion. The difference, $900 billion, would buy a lot of missiles.

But the CIA, which had made its estimates of Soviet GDP public as early as 1959, did have company. Many economists failed to grasp the stagnation that had settled on the Soviet economy after a brief post–World War II spurt in industries beloved of Heroes of Soviet Labor. Dale W. Jorgenson writes that "this has to be one of the great failures of economics—right up there with the inability of economists (along with everyone else) to find a remedy for the Great Depression of the 1930s."[38] Henry S. Rowen of Stanford University, whose distinguished government service included his chairmanship of the National Intelligence Council (1981–83), has echoed this sentiment; Sovietologists both within the intelligence community and in academia, trained to rely on the same general assumptions and data, had engaged in a form of "group think" that resulted in a monumental failure of analysis. In 1985, Rowen circulated a paper to senior officials in the Reagan administration, outlining his conclusion that actual Soviet economic growth was close to zero; in 1986, he expressed his views directly to the president and vice president.[39] Even so, the analytic system failed, and the United States paid a price.

Moreover, the system had failed from the beginning. In 1997, the CIA's Center for the Study of Intelligence convened a conference to coincide with the release of intelligence estimates prepared between 1946 and 1950. In addressing the conference, Kennan noted that intelligence assessments of

Soviet military intentions began suffering from "a certain deterioration" beginning in late 1948: "There were evidences of the assumptions, and the tendency to overrate allegedly blindly aggressive military commitments on the Soviet side, commitments quite divorced from the political restraints and awareness of the basic weaknesses in the civilian and economic backgrounds that inevitably modified Soviet diplomacy."[40] To repeat Stansfield Turner's query of 1991, "Why were so many of us so insensitive to the inevitable?"[41]

The answer has to be, at least in part, that too much of the information was secret. The intelligence community's valuations were not sufficiently open to the critique of the likes of Eberstadt or the Swedish economist Anders Åslund, who for a long time described the Soviet Union as "a reasonably well developed Third World country, calling to mind Argentina, Mexico, or Portugal."[42] In 1997, the European Comparison Project, looking at Soviet per capita GDP for 1990, estimated it to be only 32 percent of U.S. per capita GDP. Åslund calculates this at 30 percent lower than the U.S. intelligence estimate. And thus the crossover somehow never came about. This, of course, is just what Kennan had been saying, but that message had been lost.

There was an element of organizational aggrandizement in all this routinization of secrecy. By the 1990s, the budget of the intelligence community was five times that of the State Department. By the late 1990s, the military budget of the United States would about equal those of Russia, China, Japan, France, Germany, and the United Kingdom combined (the countries with the six next largest defense budgets).[43] In an address to the National Press Club in 1997, President Gerald R. Ford looked back on his early days in the House of Representatives, where for twelve years he was a member of the Defense Appropriations Committee. Every year, before the committee began hearings in preparation for putting together a defense bill, the members were briefed by the CIA. The director and his analysts "were very prestigious, they were acknowledged to be the wisest, brightest people we had in the government," Ford recalled. "They had charts on the wall, they had figures. And their conclusion was that in ten years, the United States would be behind the Soviet Union in military capability, in economic growth, in the strength of our economy. It was a scary presentation." But as it turned out, they were wrong by 180 degrees. "These were the best people we had, the CIA so-called experts," Ford mused. "How they could be so in error, I don't understand, but they were. Thank goodness they were wrong."[44]

Better to have overspent than otherwise, one might argue. But what was the good of getting the Soviet trajectory so very wrong? A good deal was put at risk in all this, and we ought to learn something from it.

Risks still persist, among them the relations between Russia and the former members of the Soviet Union as well as among nationality groups within Russia. But recent history suggests that lessons still need to be learned. The differences among these groups of the former Soviet Union are so profound that the Strategic Arms Reduction Treaty (START), the most important weapons-reduction agreement of the nuclear age, might not have gone forward at all. Yet START was negotiated without the least awareness that the Soviet Union might break up by the time the negotiations were completed.

NSC-68 had alerted us to the fact that "the Soviet system might prove to be fatally weak": "the well-known ills of colonialism" were compounded by the Kremlin's demands that its satellites not only accept its authority but believe in and proclaim its ideological primacy and infallibility. "These excessive requirements can be made good only through extreme coercion," the authors observed. "The result is that if a satellite feels able to effect its independence of the Kremlin, as Tito was able to do, it is likely to break away."[45]

But such sagacity got lost. In the 1980s, George P. Shultz, a masterful secretary of state, began to sense that the new Soviet leader, Mikhail Gorbachev, was interested in great reductions in nuclear weapons. (We would at least get START I.) The cultural exchanges seemed to be getting off the ground. The word from Moscow was positive. Not so from Langley. As Schultz later recounted, "In Washington, and especially from the CIA and its lead Soviet expert, Bob Gates, I heard that the Soviets wouldn't change and couldn't change, that Gorbachev was simply putting a new face on the same old Soviet approach to the world and to their own people. 'The Soviet Union is a despotism that works,' Gates said."[46] Soviet despotism would stop working in about four years; by then, Gates would be director of the CIA. Somehow it came to be that that is how a career officer rose to the top.

When the START treaty—with four different countries—came to the Senate Committee on Foreign Relations, the negotiators conceded that the thought of a Soviet break had never occurred to them. At a committee hearing on the treaty in 1992, I asked one of the negotiators, Ambassador Ronald F. Lehman, then director of the U.S. Arms Control and Disarmament Agency: "When did you, as negotiators, first contemplate the possibility that you would be signing a treaty with four countries and not one?"

Lehman replied, "Well, if you mean informal speculation, it probably began about two years ago [June 1990]. In terms of would this actually have come to pass, I think at the time of the Moscow coup [August 1991] people began to realize that some of the themes we were hearing around the Soviet Union might begin moving very quickly."

"Two years ago you began to think it might be possible; one year ago it became very real?" I asked.

"I think it became quite obvious that we had to step up to the issue with the dissolution of the Soviet Union in December of last year," said Lehman.

In other words, the negotiators had to begin dealing with the proposition of the dissolution of the Soviet Union in December of 1991, when the Soviet Union was already dissolving. I then asked Ambassador Linton F. Brooks whether anyone had suggested that by 1992 they would be negotiating with four governments, not one. He replied, "Senator, I certainly do not remember that . . . . I think very few of us on our end of the street predicted the collapse."[47]

Now, it was not the negotiators' job to follow the internal dynamics of the Soviet regime. Their concern was with throw weights. But they were entitled to intelligence, some whiff of caution, and they got none.[48] An age that began with state papers of unequaled clarity and prescience ended in a bureaucratic mode that never devised an effective mode of self-correction.

CHAPTER EIGHT

A Culture of Openness

T‌he Cold War ended; secrecy as a mode of governance continued as if nothing had changed. On the premise that data is the plural of anecdote, a small incident: early in 1993, the Senate Committee on Foreign Relations asked to be briefed on the conflict that had broken out in Bosnia and adjacent countries. A sizable contingent of generals arrived, accompanied by civilians. In the manner of President Ford's briefings decades earlier, the man from the agency began. But first the question: is everybody here cleared? One asked oneself: cleared for what? Premature Chetnik sympathies? Latent Titoist tendencies? We *had* no secrets about the Balkans. But this was now government routine.

The routine is best represented by the annual report of the Information Security Oversight Office (ISOO) of the National Archives and Records Administration. Every year since 1979, ISOO has counted the number of secrets created by various agencies of government. The report for 1996, a model of clarity and concision, provides a two-page listing of agency acronyms and abbreviations. Seventy-six in all, including exotica like MCC, for the Marine Mammal Commission. But in 1996, after years of expanding secrecy, there now appeared some evidence of shrinkage. As noted, the number of government officials who could classify a document had indeed been reduced; presumably this would have reduced the number of classifications, but the number of classifications *increased* by nearly two-thirds (see Chapter 1). The report was the first under the regime of Executive Order 12958, "Classified National Security Information," which was signed by President Clinton April 17, 1995, and which was, as the report states, "a radical departure from the secrecy policies of the past."[1] Original classifications were to be cut back, documents were to be released. But on the first count, results were surely mixed.

Credit to Clinton and his aides, notably John D. Podesta, sometime professor at the Georgetown University Law Center. They had acted on the slowly cumulating perception in Washington that secrecy could be the ruin of presidents and could put at risk the constitutional order itself. This was clear enough in the Iran-Contra affair but most dramatic, if not always perceived as such, in the resignation of Richard M. Nixon, which began with an effort to protect inane government secrecy.

In a well-worn story, Robert S. McNamara, toward the end of his tenure as secretary of defense, ordered a study of American intervention in Vietnam. In 1971, the documents known as the Pentagon Papers made their way to the *New York Times* and the *Washington Post,* both of which decided to publish. Nixon, grievously ill advised, decided to go to court to prevent publication. On the anniversary of the event in 1996, Max Frankel of the *Times* wrote: "Twenty-five years ago today, reporters, editors and owners of *The Times* stood accused in Federal court of treasonous defiance of the United States. We had begun to publish a 10-part series about the Pentagon Papers, a 7,000-page study of how four Administrations became entrapped in Vietnam—progressively more committed and more frustrated than they dared at every stage to admit to the public. Although the documents were historical and lacking any operational value, they were stamped 'Top Secret' and therefore withheld, like trillions of other Government papers, from public, press, Congress and even Executive officials not duly 'cleared' into the priesthood of 'national security.'"[2] The problem, as the writings of Henry Cabot Lodge, Sr., could have told Nixon, is that no law prohibited publishing documents like these. Such a law had been proposed by a previous president—Wilson—but Congress, having considered it, had decided against it. By roll call vote. Somehow this memory, if it had ever taken hold (recall Biddle and the *Chicago Tribune*), had evanesced.

Harold Edgar and Benno C. Schmidt, Jr., have exhausted the subject in their analysis of the earlier espionage laws, published in 1973 against the backdrop of the Pentagon Papers litigation. The courts found that there was literally "no law" to prevent publication. The problem could be traced to the time of creation, 1917, when Wilson failed in his efforts to achieve a sweeping ban on publication of defense information. The U.S. espionage laws, as Edgar and Schmidt had showed, are "in many respects incomprehensible," with the result being that "we have lived since World War I in a state of benign indeterminacy about the rules of law governing defense secrets."[3]

Most of the executive orders on national security information issued in succession since 1951 do not even refer to espionage law. And, as in the case of the Commission on Government Security's proposal in 1957, Congress has not been willing to make unauthorized disclosure of classified information an action subject to criminal sanctions without consideration of the *intent* of the communicator. This being so difficult to prove, such cases have been all but impossible to prosecute. As a former assistant general counsel of the CIA concluded (in an unpublished paper cited by Edgar and

Schmidt): "An individual who simply reveals to the public at large classified data is for all practical purposes immune from prosecution since his defense, of course, would be that he thought the American public had a right to know and the Government would not be able to prove intent to aid a foreign government or to harm the United States. The fact that any reasonable man would know that revelation to the general public ipso facto reveals to foreign governments is immaterial. Even if the one making the exposure is a government employee well versed in the rules governing classified information, there can be no presumption of intent which would bring him within the terms of present espionage laws."[4]

President Nixon's attempt to suppress the Pentagon Papers was doomed from the start. And indeed what followed was all so hapless. It was no secret that the United States was involved in a war in Vietnam. If we could publish our correspondence with Britain in 1861, we were surely in a position to reveal much less consequential matters with assorted lesser powers in 1971. And just as surely was Justice Hugo L. Black correct when he wrote, in the Pentagon Papers case, "The guarding of military and diplomatic secrets at the expense of informed representative government provides no real security for our Republic."[5]

How sensitive was the material in the Pentagon Papers? Erwin N. Griswold, who had been President Nixon's solicitor general at the time of the crisis and accordingly had argued the government's case before the Supreme Court, summed it up well nearly two decades later: "I have never seen any trace of a threat to the national security from the publication. Indeed, I have never seen it even suggested that there was such an actual threat. . . . I doubt if there is more than a handful of persons who have ever undertaken to examine the Pentagon Papers in any detail—either with respect to national security or with respect to the policies of the country relating to Vietnam." Like vast numbers of other classified materials, the Pentagon Papers were kept secret not so much to prevent harm to national security but to prevent "governmental embarrassment of one sort or another." Griswold concluded: "There may be some basis for short-term classification while plans are being made, or negotiations are going on, but apart from details of weapons systems, there is very rarely any real risk to current national security from the publication of facts relating to transactions in the past, even the fairly recent past. This is the lesson of the Pentagon Papers experience."[6]

This is an apt critique of the culture of secrecy. It is a belief system, a way of life. It can be, as it was during the Cold War, all consuming. Judgment blurs. And so, three days after the *New York Times* began printing the Pentagon Papers on June 13, 1971, the Nixon administration obtained a temporary restraining order against further publication; a mere fifteen days later, the Supreme Court rejected the president's attempt at prior restraint, and the newspaper resumed its publication of the Papers. One month later, Nixon created "the Plumbers," a White House unit with a mission to prevent leaks of classified material.

Leonard Garment writes that Nixon's political demise began with Daniel Ellsberg's massive dump of the Pentagon Papers: "Nixon let his anger undermine his political judgment."[7] William Safire concurs: "The Pentagon Papers case led [Nixon] into an overreaction that led to his most fundamental mistakes." The breach of *secrecy*, however inconsequential, caused him "to lose all sense of balance, to defend his privacy at the expense of everyone else's right to privacy, and to create the climate that led to Watergate."[8] The Plumbers commenced domestic covert operations, which continued into the 1972 presidential campaign. In 1974, Nixon would become the first president in American history to resign.

What would become known as the Iran-Contra affair began as a matter of agency routine. But one determining difference separated this from earlier covert operations abroad: the House of Representatives and the Senate had each now established a select committee on intelligence. These had come about in the aftermath of the Church and Pike committees, which, in studying the intelligence community, had found that agencies too often abused the civil rights of American citizens and pursued activities in violation of law. In May 1976, one month after the Church committee issued its report, the Senate created the Select Committee on Intelligence, the measure passing by a vote of seventy-two to twenty-two. The following year, the House established a comparable committee. The resolution creating the Senate committee (S. Res. 400, Ninety-Fourth Congress) stated that the heads of intelligence agencies should keep the committee "fully and currently informed" of their agencies' operations, including "any significant anticipated activities."*

Three years later in Nicaragua, in July 1979, the regime of Anastasio Somoza fell to a general uprising, after which the Marxist-led Sandinista National Liberation Front took power. The following November in Iran, the U.S. embassy in Tehran was seized by Islamic extremists, and fifty-two Americans were taken hostage. The events marked the onset of a new era, the fading of another. Islamic hostility to the West, part of what Samuel P. Huntington would describe as the "clash of civilizations," was emerging. Marxism as a political force was waning. Nicaragua would appear to have been the site of the last classically Marxist revolutionary regime to seize power anywhere. When an idea dies in Madrid, it can take two generations for word to reach Managua. (Word never did reach Langley. A reasonable American response to the new Communist government in Managua would have been a statement of condolence. We

* The author was a member from February 1977 to January 1985, the last four years as vice chairman, with Senator Barry Goldwater of Arizona as chairman.

regretted the misfortune that had visited the people of Nicaragua: in the event of earthquakes, they could be assured of American aid; when the first crop failure came, however, they would need to look to Havana. In the meantime, no, repeat no, Soviet aircraft or missiles.)

A visit to Nicaragua in December 1983 induced this thought. Managua had been leveled by an earthquake. The cathedral was a ruin. The one new building, nine or ten stories high in the best international style, was the Ministry of the Interior. One fine morning, I set out to pay a visit to Commandant Tomas Borge, who was at work in his suite on the top floor. On the sidewalk outside, television cameras greeted the arriving guest. But before the elevators had been reached, the power had gone off, and there followed something of a climb. In the commandant's suite an hour of dialectic ensued, after which lunch was suggested. The commandant turned to theretofore silent aides; in unison, they proposed that the barrio Sandino, a farmers' market with a restaurant, would be just the place. A bus happened to be waiting. At the restaurant, a table happened to be set. The visitor declined the tureen of goulash that was promptly served, along with the obligatory Pepsi Cola (soft drink of the people), asking instead for rice and beans. While waiting for the requested dish, the guests were treated to a quarter hour of street theater, in which a succession of workers and peasants came to express assorted disaffections in the best polemic mode. The week previous, the new orthopedic hospital, or whatever, had been opened in barrio Guavera, and the commandant had not shown the elementary courtesy of being on hand for the ceremony. Another delegation reported that the new irrigation system in Las Palmas, or wherever, was not yet working at full capacity. Still another group complained that the new highway to León was at least five weeks behind schedule. The commandant assertively acknowledged his failings but firmly resolved to change his ways and those of the regime. The people were correct: mistakes had been made; there would be no more of this. He asked forgiveness. That concluded, a somewhat hesitant aide came up to report that no beans were to be had.

This and other reports ought to have been enough to indicate to the American government the likely longevity of this regime, if left on its own. But counterrevolution was now agency routine, and the new Reagan administration was all for it. (The Carter administration had at first rather welcomed the revolution and sent food aid, much as Wilson had done with Russia in 1917.) And so to the jungles again, this time with neighboring Honduras providing a cooperative military regime. The idea was addled. The new Sandinista regime was already beginning to show its colors, but the United States seemed to be recruiting opposition from supporters of a previous, no less vile regime. The airport apron at Tegucigalpa, capital of Honduras, was littered with abandoned Nicaraguan air force transport planes in which assorted Somozan officials had fled, now presumably to organize a counterrevolution.

For the moment the United States needed a rationale for intervention. On March 3, 1986, President Reagan would allow that we might have to make our final stand at Harlingen, Texas. A prospect of some portent—the missing evidence for which was soon enough produced. The Sandinistas were providing arms to a Marxist guerrilla faction in El Salvador. The long march north had commenced.

In the end, nothing of the kind was ever proved. Heroic surveillance measures were put in place; outside the occasional pickup truck or small boat, nothing showed up. While in the capital, San Salvador, in 1983, I asked to see the rector and vice rector of the Central American University (both were Basque Jesuits subsequently murdered by the regime). I put the question to them directly: "Were the Sandinistas shipping arms to the Salvadoran insurgents?" "No," replied the rector. "But they had been?" "True." "Then why no longer?" "Because you are doing it now."* And, indeed, American equipment costing millions of dollars was being flown down, along with American military advisors. We had even built a small gem of a central intelligence agency, complete with fountains in the lobby. In the way of that world, the arms were being shared.

President Reagan saw a global issue at stake. In January 1984, he approved a CIA plan to mine harbors on the west coast of Nicaragua. That the mines were thereafter laid was no secret, but it was assumed the Contras had done it. On April 6, however, David Rogers of the *Wall Street Journal* reported that, in a covert operation, the CIA had mined the harbors. A constitutional crisis now commenced.

As noted, the statute creating the Senate Select Committee on Intelligence stated that the committee would be informed of any "significant anticipated events," meaning covert actions. The committee had not been informed. On April 9, Chairman Goldwater sent a furious letter to Director of Central Intelligence William J. Casey: "[How can I] most easily tell you my feelings about the discovery of the President having approved mining some of the harbors of Central America[?] . . . I am pissed off!" The letter, which went on at some length, contained two sentences contributed by the vice chairman: "This is an act violating international law. It is an act of war."[9]

The letter made it to the *Washington Post*, and tumult followed. The administration lied. First it lied about Goldwater: getting on, don't you know—memory problems. Then Robert C. McFarlane, national security advisor, lied to cadets at the U. S. Naval Academy—something never to be done. On April 15, the author resigned from the committee. Two weeks later, in an honorable act, Casey apologized to the

---

* Six years later, in November 1989, not only the rector, Ignacio Ellacuria, and the vice rector, Ignacio Martin-Baro, but also four other Jesuits, their cook, and her fifteen-year-old daughter were shot and brutally dismembered by government agents.

vice chairman and to the committee. It seemed a crisis had been avoided.

A legitimate question arose. In the statute providing that the committees were to be told in advance of "significant anticipated activities," what was meant by "significant?" We suggested that the term be defined as anything personally approved by the president. This understanding was dutifully drawn up and signed by all parties, the president included.

In the meantime, Congress, at the behest of Edward P. Boland, chairman of the House Select Committee on Intelligence and close associate of House Speaker Thomas P. "Tip" O'Neill, Jr., imposed a ban on further aid to the Contras. The administration set about secretly raising funds abroad; in the end they would sell arms to the ostensibly untouchable Iranians. The Casey Accord, as our agreement had come to be known, was ignored; the committees, again, were told nothing. Instead, it happened that the nation found out about the arms deals from a magazine published in Beirut.

There was a chilling, systemic quality to the event. Despite the statute, despite the accord, the executive kept quiet about its activities, which were certainly "significant." Nor should the executive have been concerned that the committees were politically unfriendly, for there were no politics, at least not on the Senate side. Goldwater was a Reagan loyalist, thought of the president as a protégé. His letter to Casey asked how was he going to defend the president's foreign policy if he wasn't told what it was. Goldwater and I had worked together to get the intelligence community pretty much whatever it felt it had to have, especially by way of satellites.

We escaped, you could say. The administration did not. Secrecy almost ruined yet another presidency. Off it went to buy arms abroad, with the National Security Council now opting for covert action of its own, all hidden by secrecy.

Whatever the intelligence community might have done, it was done by professionals. And the president was kept out of it. Now lieutenant colonels and the like were putting the presidency of the United States at risk. It was only luck that when it all finally came out, as it did in the subsequent joint congressional investigation, there seemed no point in destroying a popular president in his final years in office. No one wanted to replay the denouement of an all-too-recent Watergate. And yet, secrecy had got us into difficulties unlike any we had ever known.

Had it not been possible for those involved with Iran-Contra to act under a vast umbrella of secrets, they would have been told to stop. Recall that most of what they were doing was kept from the rest of the government. (It is still not clear what the CIA knew, outside the director himself.) During the congressional investigation Senator Paul S. Sarbanes of Maryland used the term "junta," something never known to American government. Hardly hyperbole. The behavior of the CIA and especially its director in the Nicaraguan mining episode was nothing less than the outset of a challenge to American constitutional government, the "first acts of deception that gradually mutated into a policy of deceit," as I told Theodore Draper for his history of the event, *A Very Thin Line;* the Iran-Contra affair two years later was the culmination of this insidious policy. I also told Draper that I didn't believe the American republic had ever seen so massive a hemorrhaging of trust and integrity. The very processes of government were put in harm's way by a conspiracy of faithless or witless men—sometimes both.[10]

In an earlier essay on the tormented congressional hearings, Draper began: "If ever the constitutional democracy of the United States is overthrown, we now have a better idea of how this is likely to be done. That may be the most important contribution of the recent Iran-Contra congressional hearings."[11] In his book *Firewall: The Iran-Contra Conspiracy and Cover-Up*, Lawrence E. Walsh, the independent counsel in the Iran-Contra investigation, concluded:

"What set Iran-Contra apart from previous political scandals was the fact that a cover-up engineered in the White House of one president and completed by his successor prevented the rule of law from being applied to the perpetrators of criminal activity of constitutional dimension."[12] Walsh uses the term "national security crime."[13]

In all this we need to be clear that those involved never set out to be criminals; they were trapped in a system. In his study, *The National Security Constitution: Sharing Power After the Iran-Contra Affair,* Harold Hongju Koh agrees that we saw "a nearly successful assault upon the constitutional structures and norms that underlie our postwar national security system." But it was not a case "of bad people violating good laws . . . or of good people violating bad laws . . . but of seriously misguided people violating seriously ineffective national security laws."[14] In Koh's judgment, the American government has not found a stable mode of national security decision making, and the likes of the Iran-Contra crisis—the parallel, in his view, being not Watergate but Vietnam—"waits to afflict us anew."[15] Surely this is true, and just as surely is it an element in this ongoing crisis, for only secrecy enables a constitutionally weak executive to bypass the legislature in making decisions that the legislature will not support when things go wrong.

A more serious development was that operations displaced intelligence and in fact became, in James Q. Wilson's phrase, "the culture-defining task of the CIA."[16] Many operations endeavors were more trouble than they were worth. Trouble not least at home, for Americans were never able to resign themselves to such CIA projects as how-to manuals on political assassinations. Nor were the national nerves appreciably improved by "The Routinization of Crisis Government," as Donald L. Robinson described it in 1974,[17] which had taken its toll in Vietnam. The intelligence community— the whole of it, not merely the CIA surely failed to impress on the White House (Congress, again, was left out) that the Red Chinese and the Soviet Union were not engaged in a great sweep down the perimeter of Asia and up the Bay of Bengal to Calcutta, through which, as Trotsky had decreed, the road to Paris ran. While we were in the jungles hoping to stop this, the Soviets and the Chinese were all but going to war with one another. In 1978 Robert Novak had a long interview with Deng Xiaoping in which the Chinese leader declared his desire "to join the Americans in confronting the Soviet Union." Taiwan could rest easy; he "had no objection to U.S. troops in South Korea."[18] And later, not four years after the fall of South Vietnam to what had been represented as an international Communist alliance, the People's Republic of China invaded the North. It is not clear that U.S. foreign policy agencies quite follow this even now.

The Cold War has bequeathed to us a vast secrecy system that shows no sign of receding. It has become our characteristic mode of governance in the executive branch. Intelligence agencies have proliferated and budgets grown even as the military has subsided. As old missions fade, the various agencies seek new ones. In 1967, Anthony Downs described this process whereby a government bureau, as it ages, becomes willing to modify its original formal goals in order to survive: a bureau's more senior officials "would rather alter the bureau's formal goals than admit that their jobs should be abolished because the original goals have been attained or are no longer important."[19] Exactly thirty years later, in September 1997, some wondered whether a similar process was taking place at the Central Intelligence Agency. The occasion was the fiftieth anniversary of the agency's founding, and the event was celebrated at Langley with a ceremony, complete with a display of "lipstick pistols" and other devices of spycraft. The *Washington Post* reported, matter-of-factly: "These artifacts were standard fare during the Cold War, an era from which critics say the CIA has yet to fully emerge. CIA analysts failed to forecast the Soviet Union's collapse, and some on Capitol Hill have questioned whether the agency, which has an estimated 16,000 employees, has adequately redefined its mission for a new era."[20]

President Clinton spoke on the occasion, setting forth the agency's future mission as outlined in an earlier directive. He repeated his top priorities for focusing intelligence resources "in the areas most critical to our national security": "First, supporting our troops and operations, whether turning back aggression, helping secure peace or providing humanitarian assistance. Second, providing political, economic, and military intelligence on countries hostile to the United States so we can help to stop crises and conflicts before they start. And, third, protecting American citizens from new trans-national threats such as drug traffickers, terrorists, organized criminals, and weapons of mass destruction."[21] The first task is ambiguous at best. The military supports the military and uses military intelligence. The second task is quite in order. That is the mission the agency acquired during the Cold War. The third task, as regards "trans-national threats" like drug traffickers and weapons dealers, is an invitation to marginalization or worse. There are already several dozen federal agencies engaged with drugs and crime (none of them with notable success). To nudge its way in, the CIA would have to begin competing with the Bureau of Alcohol, Tobacco and Firearms. As Downs had forecast.

At the time Clinton spoke, the CIA had had five chiefs in ten years, not to mention several aborted nominations. By contrast, the Federal Bureau of Investigation had had one director for its first forty-eight years: J. Edgar Hoover, who died in office. In an organizational mode not perhaps sufficiently appreciated, he had spent much of that time trying to keep his agency away from tasks that it couldn't perform. Tasks at which no organization could expect much success. Hoover "was strong enough to resist for many years FBI involvement in organized crime and civil rights cases,"* as

---

* As an aide to Governor Averell Harriman of New York in the 1950s, I became interested in the subject of organized crime after it was discovered that an extraordinary assembly of mob leaders from around the country

James Q. Wilson notes, "but when the time came, in his eyes, to change, he was also strong enough to make the organization change with him."[22]

It may be too much to suppose that other organizations will learn on their own. There was only one Hoover. Now is the time for law. Eighty years from the onset of secrecy as an instrument of national policy, now is the time for a measure

---

had convened in the hamlet of Apalachin in southern New York State. I also worked peripherally with Robert F. Kennedy, who was pursuing the subject as a Senate staffer. In July 1961, I published an article, "The Private Government of Crime," in *Reporter* magazine, arguing that what could reasonably be termed "organized crime" had its roots in Prohibition, that it was serious, and that no government bureau had found a way of dealing with it because doing so would have offered insufficient organizational rewards. Almost in passing, I noted that the FBI, which had "not hesitated to take on the toughest problems of national security," had "successfully stayed away from organized crime." It would have given Hoover nothing but institutional trouble.

By now I had joined the Kennedy administration as an aide to Arthur J. Goldberg, then secretary of labor. In a matter of weeks after the article appeared, the Department of Labor building was literally raided by G-men. In unison they hit our floor, went door to door, told everyone save the hapless author but including the secretary himself that a dangerous person had infiltrated their ranks, clearly implying that the secretary should go. I can't demonstrate this but offer the judgment that at any other department at this time in Washington, the person in question would have gone. Hoover had files on everyone, or so it was said.

The Department of Labor was different only insofar as Arthur J. Goldberg was different. On August 2, just after my article appeared, C. D. "Deke" DeLoach of the FBI had informed the secretary that "it would appear to be impossible to deal with Moynihan on a liaison basis in view of his obvious biased opinion regarding the FBI." The secretary called me in, told me that I had a problem, and sent me to explain my point of view to the director. The next day, DeLoach agreed to see me but made plain he could barely stand the sight. In my FBI file is a three-page, single-spaced memorandum of the meeting, sent to the director through John Mohr. It concludes: "Moynihan is an egghead that talks in circles and constantly contradicts himself. He shifts about constantly in his chair and will not look you in the eye. He would be the first so-called 'liberal' that would scream if the FBI overstepped its jurisdiction. He is obviously a phony intellectual that one minute will back down and the next minute strike while our back is turned. I think we made numerous points in our interview with him, however, this man is so much up on 'cloud nine' it is doubtful that his ego will allow logical interpretation of remarks made by other people." The director appended a handwritten notation, "I am not going to see this skunk." I was put on the "Not to Contact" list.

of definition and restraint. In 1997, the Commission on Protecting and Reducing Government Secrecy proposed a statute for achieving just these ends, noting the wisdom of John F. Kennedy's remark, "The time to repair the roof is when the sun is shining."

The Secrecy Commission noted that after the U.S. Army had adopted the three-level classification model used by the British—For Official Use Only, Confidential, and Secret (later Confidential, Secret, and Top Secret)—just what any of the various terms meant was never defined. With the beginning of the Cold War, presidents took to issuing executive orders about classification: Eisenhower, E.O. 10501; Kennedy, E.O. 10964; Nixon, E.O. 11652; Carter, E.O. 12065; Reagan, E.O. 12356; and Clinton, E.O. 12958. The one criterion conspicuously missing from all but President Carter's was a balancing test of the public's right to know and the government's need to protect national security. The Secrecy Commission proposed a simple enough framework for a statute that would do just that. First, information shall be classified only if its protection is demonstrably in the interests of national security, with the goal of keeping classification to an absolute minimum. Standards shall be established to determine whether information should be or remain classified, and these standards shall weigh the benefit from public disclosure against the need for its initial or continued protection; where doubt exists, information shall not be classified. Next, as a parallel program to the classification system, a declassification system shall be established. Information shall remain classified for no longer than ten years, unless it is specifically reclassified because of current risks; all information shall be declassified after thirty years, unless it is shown that doing so will harm an individual or ongoing government activities. Finally, a National Declassification Center shall be established to coordinate, implement, and oversee these declassification policies and practices. The commission report was unanimously endorsed by its members; the congressional members, one each of both parties from both bodies, have introduced legislation to establish this new framework.

The proposed National Declassification Center may seem a matter of concern mainly to scholars, but it is more of a national interest even than that. Secrecy has come at a price. As we have seen, the nation paid heavily in the McCarthy moment, when, as Shils wrote, "the phantasies of apocalyptic visionaries attained the level of a reasonable interpretation of events." Not for another forty years would government tell what it actually knew about the Communist conspiracy: there had indeed been one, but it had never been massive; it had first been contained, then suppressed. A democracy does not leave its citizens uninformed in these matters. As Paul McMasters comments, "The Government's obsession with secrecy creates a citizen's obsession with conspiracy."[23]

By coincidence, in 1997, forty-seven years after Senator Joseph McCarthy's famous speech in Wheeling, West Virginia, a new conspiracy was uncovered in the same city. James Rogers, a member of a right-wing extremist group, the Mountaineer Militia, was convicted of trying to help terrorists blow up an FBI fingerprint-records complex in nearby Clarksburg. Rogers had photographed blueprints that detailed the FBI complex and given the photographs to Floyd Looker, founder of the Mountaineer Militia. Looker then sold the pictures to an FBI agent posing as an explosives expert who worked for Middle East terrorists. Looker is reported to have told the agent, "That installation is a threat to national security. I don't care who knocks it out."[24]

Rogers was convicted under the Antiterrorism and Effective Death Penalty Act of 1996. The law is not a pretty thing. Among its provisions is one mandating that prisoners sentenced to death have but six months to file habeas corpus petitions after all state appeals are exhausted and, with few exceptions, allowing for consideration of only one habeas corpus petition. It also requires federal judges to defer to the findings of state courts unless their rulings are "unreasonable." In sum, it holds that in these cases constitutional protections do not exist unless they have been unreasonably violated—an idea that would have confounded the framers. No such law, nothing approaching such a law, was ever enacted during the Cold War. We are reminded of Richard Gid Powers's observation that the McCarthy experience had persuaded some people that the general public was too unsophisticated, too easily inflamed, to be informed of the real underlying issues of the Cold War; in similar fashion, the American government, almost as a matter of policy, left its citizens to think what they chose about international threats for fear that they might find out the truth or react unpredictably. Now, with the Cold War behind us, Congress got serious. There was to be no bombing of FBI records plants. Measures of a severity hardly contemplated and certainly never enacted during earlier crises now became statute with a minimum of objection. The Antiterrorism and Effective Death Penalty Act of 1996 passed the U.S. Senate by a vote of ninety-one to eight.

As Richard Hofstadter and others have recorded, conspiracy theories have been part of the American experience for two centuries, but they appear to have grown in dimension and public acceptance in recent decades. The most notorious conspiracy theories, of course, play upon the unwillingness of the vast majority of the American public to accept that President Kennedy was assassinated in 1963 by Lee Harvey Oswald. In 1964 the United States President's Commission on the Assassination of President John F. Kennedy, commonly called the Warren commission, released its report concluding that Oswald had acted alone. In 1964, a poll found that 36 percent of respondents accepted this finding, whereas 50 percent believed others had been involved in a conspiracy to kill the president. In 1978 only 18 percent responded that they believed the assassination had been the act of one man; fully 75 percent believed there had been a broader plot. The numbers have remained relatively steady since; a 1993 poll also found that three quarters of those surveyed believed (consistent with the film *JFK*, released that year) that there had been a conspiracy: the CIA had murdered the president in order to prolong the war in Vietnam.[25]

More painful yet was the 1997 request by the family of Martin Luther King, Jr., that the federal government establish a commission to offer amnesty to anyone with new information on the assassination of Dr. King. His son Dexter has alleged that Dr. King was killed "by Army intelligence, the Federal Bureau of Investigation and the Central Intelligence Agency, with the probable knowledge of President Lyndon Johnson."[26] This view is evidently shared by Dr. King's widow.

To go from assassination conspiracies to coverups of unidentified flying objects and extraterrestrial life is to trivialize the matter, but apparently the leap doesn't seem that great to the 80 percent of Americans who, according to a CNN-*Time* poll of June 15, 1997, believe that their government is hiding knowledge of the existence of extraterrestrial life forms.

Lest these be thought merely cases of mass dementia or the personal torment of survivors, keep in mind that for some decades into the Cold War (and since?), many of the men and women who ran the American government had a lively conviction that the government was spying on *them*.*

---

* In 1977, having been elected to the U.S. Senate, I took the precaution of asking for my own FBI file. In short order I had a three-inch stack of folders, 561 pages in all, including a Confidential report of an investigation conducted by the air force in 1952. Part of the report contained enclosures indicating "possible communist tendencies on the part of PATRICK J. MOINYHAN, DAY Civilian." The setting is London, where I had arrived as a Fulbright scholar in 1951. Wanting to stay a bit longer in Europe, and half expecting to be called back into the navy, I had taken a job at an air force installation on the outskirts of London. All of which, and more, are duly noted: "MOINYHAN, an American citizen, was employed in Air Installations sometime in the fall of 1951. His employment was due to the efforts of DANA M. HICKS, Major, A0912552, former Air Installations Officer. . . . Prior to his present employment MOINYHAN was doing research and study in the UK under a Fulbright scholarship. 'His thesis was something to do with labor.' HICKS had alleged that during his research, MOINYHAN had access to US Em-

Evan Thomas, writing of the early years of the CIA, speculates that such a conviction may have been behind Kennedy's swift reappointment of Allen Dulles as director of the CIA and J. Edgar Hoover as director of the FBI. Both men were "legends," explained the newly elected president; they were better left undisturbed. "His deference may have been encouraged by the knowledge that the CIA and FBI had thick files on the president-elect's past, including his brief affair with a German spy during World War II," observes Thomas. "The family patriarch, Joseph Kennedy, had urged his son to play it safe by reappointing Hoover and Dulles."[27]

We are not going to put an end to secrecy, nor should we. It is at times legitimate and necessary. But a culture of secrecy, a culture of the sort that we associate with Dulles and Hoover, need not remain the norm in American government as regards national security. It is possible to conceive that a competing culture of openness might develop, and that it could assert and demonstrate greater efficiency. The central fact is that we live today in an Information Age. Open sources give us the vast majority of what we need to know in order to make intelligent decisions. Decisions made by people at ease with disagreement and ambiguity and tenta-

---

bassy records. Some time after his employment at Air Installations, MOINYHAN was observed by informant to be reading the 'Daily Worker.' Informant reported that fact to HICKS who stated 'It's been looked into and it's all right.' HICKS also stated that MOINYHAN was permitted to 'go to the Unity Theatre.' U-OI-1 informed the writer that the Unity Theatre was run by communists and presented anti-American and Anti-Conservative (British Political Party) reviews. HICKS did not qualify any of his statements concerning SUBJECT. ROSENFELD [a colleague] remarked that all Communists should be lined up and shot. MOINYHAN quickly defended communism and told ROSENFELD that he was as bad as the communists to advocate such treatment. The discussion became heated. . . . MOINYHAN maintained his defense of communism . . . [and seemed] sincere in his defense of communism and they gained the impression that MOINYHAN was either a communist or a communist sympathizer."

In retrospect I suppose I ought not to have brought a copy of the *Daily Worker* to work, but I was young. On the other hand, the Unity Theater *was* good vaudeville, albeit of a pinkish cast.

tiveness. Decisions made by those who understand how to exploit the wealth and diversity of publicly available information, who no longer simply assume that clandestine collection—that is, "stealing secrets"—equals greater intelligence. *Analysis,* far more than secrecy, is the key to security.

There is no way to make certain that this new model of decision making will happen, yet the competitive spirit *can* be put to work here. In seeking victories where others had failed, policy-makers may begin to see that their devotion to secrecy has not served them well. An example, on a subject that still troubles U.S. foreign relations, is the Bay of Pigs invasion of Cuba in April 1961. Planned and carried out in secret, the object was to arouse a popular revolt against the regime of Fidel Castro, which had become unmistakably Communist in its orientation. No such uprising occurred, and the events set in motion arguably led to the Cuban missile crisis of 1962, the closest the United States and the Soviet Union came to a nuclear exchange during the Cold War.

It need never have happened. The Bay of Pigs debacle could have been avoided if foreign policy experts in the United States had but paid attention to published research already available to them. In the spring of 1960, Lloyd A. Free of the Institute for International Social Research at Princeton had carried out an extensive public opinion survey in Cuba. The polling techniques now common to American politics were then being developed by scholars such as Free and his associate Hadley Cantril. Free had asked one thousand Cubans to rank their well-being at that moment in time, five years previously, and five years hence. The Cubans reported that they were hugely optimistic about the future; many dreaded the return of Castro's predecessor, the dictator Fulgencio Batista. Free's report ended on an unambiguous note: Cubans "are unlikely to shift their present overwhelming allegiance to Fidel Castro."[28] His colleague Cantril later recalled: "This study on Cuba showed unequivocally not only that the great majority of Cubans supported Castro, but that any hope of stimulating action against him or exploiting a powerful opposition in connection with the United States invasion of 1961 was completely chimerical, no matter what Cuban exiles said or felt about the situation, and that the fiasco and its aftermath, in which the United States became involved, was predictable."[29] Free's report, published July 18, 1960, was readily available in Washington. (Indeed, the Cuban embassy sent for ten copies.) It is difficult not to think that the information in the public opinion survey might have had more influence had it been secret. In a culture of secrecy, that which is not secret is easily disregarded or dismissed.*

Now open sources compete with covert ones. The Cuban missile crisis provides the example of the shift in intelligence sources. As is well known, a key event of the crisis turned on the photographs taken by American U-2 planes, which showed unequivocally that the Soviets had landed and were beginning to assemble missiles in Cuba. These overflights were an important American secret for many years. After the spy planes came the spy satellites and the National Reconnaissance Organization, whose very name was a secret until 1992. But in the late 1990s, governments' monopoly on spying from space came to an end. An American firm, EarthWatch, in partnership with a Japanese firm, Hitachi, and others, built the spacecraft *Earlybird 1*, which was launched from Svobodny Cosmodrome, a military base in eastern Russia. The Russian booster was formerly a military missile known as *Start 1*, for the control talks that restricted

---

* In October 1961, six months after the Bay of Pigs, Lyman B. Kirkpatrick, inspector general of the CIA, prepared a detailed "Survey of the Cuban Operation," twenty copies in all. It was as blunt as such documents ever get: the Bay of Pigs was as painful a failure as the United States had yet experienced in the Cold War (and would lead step by step to the Cuban missile crisis). The survey, made public in 1997, stated that the CIA "failed to collect adequate information on the strengths of the Castro regime and the extent of the opposition to it; and it failed to evaluate the available information correctly." However, there is no mention of Free's survey, which was known to the agency and might have spared the United States, Cuba, the world, the trauma of the moment and the ultimate peril that followed. Open sources simply had no standing.

them. Fifteen minutes after launch, a ground station in Norway reported that the satellite was doing a fine job of taking pictures of the earth, distinguishing features as small as cars and trucks. EarthWatch sells these digital images over the Internet (www.digitalglobe.com), and at quite reasonable prices—$300 to $725 an image. Other such satellites will follow, and other pictures of high-definition, golf-ball-on-the-green precision cannot be long in coming to a Web site near you. Surely times have changed.

They have assuredly changed in Moscow. On December 26, 1997, the Moscow *Rossijskaya Gazeta*, an official journal of the Council of Ministers, published a 14,500-word "Russian Federation National Security Blueprint," with the subtitle "Russia Within the World Community." It is a singular document. It can be described as liberal in the traditional understanding of the term. As translated by the Foreign Broadcast Information Service and broadcast on the Internet, the "National Security Blueprint" acknowledges, for example, that the Russian Orthodox church and the churches of other confessions play "a most important role in the preservation of traditional spiritual values." In a section entitled "Russia's National Interest," the document declares: "The system of Russia's national interests is determined by the aggregate of the basic interests of the individual, society, and the state." (The basic interests of the individual consist in "the real safeguarding of constitutional rights and freedoms and personal security, in improved quality of life and living standards, and in physical, spiritual, and intellectual development." The interests of society include "the consolidation of democracy, the attainment and maintenance of social accord, the enhancement of the population's creative activeness, and the spiritual renaissance of Russia." The interests of the state lie in "the protection of the constitutional system, the sovereignty and territorial integrity of Russia, the establishment of political, economic, and social stability, . . . and the development of international cooperation on the basis of partnership.")[30] The document is open about ethnicity and the "centrifugal tendencies of Russian Federal components" to an extent few regimes would contemplate. Or risk: "The ethnic egotism, ethnocentrism, and chauvinism that are displayed in the activities of a number of ethnic social formations help to increase national separatism and create favorable conditions for the emergence of conflicts."[31] And the document is all but brutally candid about the deterioration of Russian conventional forces, "manifested in the extremely acute nature of social problems in the Russian Federation Armed Forces and other troops and military formations and organs, the critically low level of operational and combat training, . . . the intolerable decline in the level of . . . weapons and military equipment, and in general the reduction of the state's potential for safeguarding the Russian Federation's security."[32]

And so to the only remaining source of Russian power—nuclear weapons. Here the policy paper is not alarmist: "The threat of large-scale aggression against Russia is virtually absent in the foreseeable future." The blueprint refers repeatedly to international law. But, then, NATO is expanding. Wars along the federation's borders keep breaking out. So "until the nonuse of force becomes the norm in international relations, the Russian Federation's national interests require the existence of a military might sufficient for its defense." But the blueprint's description of how this will be achieved by the hollow Russian military is sobering: "The most important task for the Russian Federation Armed Forces is to ensure nuclear deterrence in the interests of preventing both nuclear and conventional large-scale or regional wars. . . . In order to perform this task the Russian Federation must have nuclear forces with the potential to guarantee the infliction of the required damage on any aggressor state or coalition of states."[33]

Thus, for a moment in the 1980s, it appeared that the nuclear era might slowly recede, that a weaponless world was at least conceivable. No longer, or at least not soon. President Boris Yeltsin of the Russian Federation had issued the "National Security Blueprint" less than two weeks after the Duma had declined to take up the START II treaty, the embodiment of a "building down" strategy. The treaty (which may yet be ratified by Moscow) had come about after long decades in which NATO developed a military doctrine of graduated, or flexible, response to a Soviet threat: weapons systems would escalate, but a full-scale nuclear exchange was to be the very last resort. The Soviet planners had begun to think in much the same terms (yet again to the theme of organizations in conflict). Then came the 1980s, when both the Soviet Union and the United States could contemplate serious cutbacks in strategic nuclear weapons. Then came the collapse of the Soviet system. Now the Russian core has reverted to a doctrine of inflexible response. One false step and it's nuclear war.

The "what-ifs" are intriguing. What if the United States had recognized Soviet weakness earlier on and accordingly kept its own budget in order, so that upon the breakup of the Soviet Union a momentous economic aid program could have been commenced?

What if we had better calculated the forces of ethnicity so that we could have avoided going directly from the "end" of the Cold War to a new Balkan War, leaving little attention and far fewer resources for the shattered Soviet empire?

There it rests, with the one remaining large and positive possibility. Openness. East and West paid hideous costs for keeping matters of state closed to the people whom the states embodied. The Russian policy paper, it should be noted, calls for "an appropriate statutory legal base" for dealing with "security tasks." Whether that should ever happen in the Russian federation is for others to say. It *can* happen here. In order for a culture of openness to develop within government, the present culture of secrecy must be restrained by statute. Let law determine behavior, as it did in the case of the Administrative Procedure Act. A statute defining and limiting secrecy will not put an end to overclassification and needless classification, but it will help.

After all, a huge proportion of the government's effort at

classifying is futile anyway. Let Kennan have the last word. In a letter of March 1997 he writes: "It is my conviction, based on some 70 years of experience, first as a government official and then in the past 45 years as an historian, that the need by our government for *secret* intelligence about affairs elsewhere in the world has been vastly over-rated. I would say that something upwards of 95% of what we need to know about foreign countries could be very well obtained by the careful and competent study of perfectly legitimate sources of information open and available to us in the rich library and archival holdings of this country." As for the remaining 5 percent, we could easily, and nonsecretively, find most of that in similar sources abroad. Kennan concludes: "There may still be areas, very small areas really, in which there is a real need to penetrate someone else's curtain of secrecy. All right. But then please, without the erection of false pretenses and elaborate efforts to deceive—and without, to the extent possible—the attempt to maintain 'spies' on the adversary's territory. We easily become ourselves, the sufferers from these methods of deception. For they inculcate in their authors, as well as their intended victims, unlimited cynicism, causing them to lose all realistic understanding of the interrelationship, in what they are doing, of ends and means."[34]

A case can be made, not different from that of Seitz and his fellow scientists a generation ago, that secrecy is for losers. For people who don't know how important information really is. The Soviet Union realized this too late. Openness is now a singular, and singularly American, advantage. We put it in peril by poking along in the mode of an age now past. It is time to dismantle government secrecy, this most pervasive of Cold War–era regulations. It is time to begin building the supports for the era of openness that is already upon us.

Notes

Introduction

1. Theodore Draper, "Getting Irangate Straight," *New York Review of Books*, October 8, 1987, p. 47; see also Draper, *A Very Thin Line* (New York: Touchstone, 1991).

2. Daniel Patrick Moynihan, letter to Richard Gid Powers, July 22, 1997.

3. Daniel Patrick Moynihan, "The United States in Opposition," *Commentary*, March 1975, p. 42.

4. DPM to RGP, July 22, 1997.

5. Daniel Patrick Moynihan, "Letter from Peking," January 26, 1975, intended for publication in the *New Yorker* but not printed due to Moynihan's appointment to the United Nations.

6. Daniel Patrick Moynihan, "Will Russia Blow Up?" *Newsweek*, November 19, 1979, p. 144.

7. Ibid.

8. Ibid.

9. Daniel Patrick Moynihan, commencement address at New York University, May 24, 1984.

10. DPM to RGP, July 22, 1997.

11. Ibid.

12. Max M. Kampelman, letter to DPM, December 3, 1991.

13. Conference on the future of intelligence, Washington, D.C., sponsored by the Richard M. Nixon Library, Yorba Linda, Calif., March 12, 1992.

14. Henry A. Kissinger, letter to DPM, April 2, 1992.

15. Daniel Patrick Moynihan, "Secrecy as Government Regulation," the Marver H. Bernstein Lecture, Georgetown University, Washington, D.C., March 3, 1997, p. 11.

16. Daniel Patrick Moynihan, "How America Blew It," *Newsweek*, December 10, 1990, p. 14.

17. Ibid.

18. Ibid.

19. The other commissioners were John M. Deutch, the former director of Central Intelligence; Martin C. Faga, the former director of the National Reconnaissance Office and assistant secretary of the Air Force for Space; Alison B. Fortier, former staff director of the National Security Council; Richard K. Fox, Jr., former ambassador and career foreign service officer; Representative Lee H. Hamilton of Indiana; Senator Jesse Helms of North Carolina; journalist Ellen Hume; Samuel P. Huntington, professor at Harvard University and former coordinator of security planning for the National Security Council; John D. Podesta, White House deputy chief of staff for the Clinton administration; and Maurice Sonnenberg, of Clinton's Foreign Intelligence Advisory Board. Eric R. Biel of the Senate Finance Committee staff served as director of the commission's staff of sixteen, which had several members on loan from the Departments of State and Defense, the Central Intelligence Agency, and the National Security Agency.

20. Commission on Protecting and Reducing Government Secrecy, *Secrecy: Report of the Commission on Protecting and Reducing Government Secrecy* (Washington, D.C.: Government Printing Office, 1997), p. xxi.

21. Ibid., p. xiii.

22. Edward A. Shils, *The Torment of Secrecy: The Background and Consequences of American Security Policies* (1956; reprint, Chicago: Ivan R. Dee, 1996).

23. Herbert J. Gans, "Best-Sellers by Sociologists: An Exploratory Study," *Contemporary Sociology* 26, no. 2 (March 1997): 134.

24. Daniel Patrick Moynihan, introduction to Shils, *Torment of Secrecy*, pp. x–xi.

25. Commission on Protecting and Reducing Government Secrecy, *Secrecy*, p. xxi.

26. Moynihan, introduction to Shils, *Torment of Secrecy*, p. xxi. The economist was Anders Åslund.

27. Commission on Protecting and Reducing Government Secrecy, *Secrecy*, p. xxi.

28. For a detailed discussion of the Venona project, see Robert Louis Benson and Michael Warner, *Venona: Soviet Espionage and the American Response* (Washington, D.C.: National Security Agency, Central Intelligence Agency, 1996).

29. Moynihan, introduction to Shils, *Torment of Secrecy*, p. xvi.

30. See, for example, Richard Hofstadter, *The Paranoid Style in American Politics and Other Essays* (1964; reprint, Chicago: University of Chicago Press, 1979); David Brion Davis, *The Fear of Conspiracy: Images of Un-American Subversion from the Revolution to the Present* (Ithaca: Cornell University Press, 1971).

31. For an overview of the events of these years and J. Edgar Hoover's activities, see Richard Gid Powers, *Not Without Honor: The History of American Anticommunism* (New York: Free Press, 1995), chap. 2, and *Secrecy and Power: The Life of J. Edgar Hoover* (New York: Free Press, 1987), chaps. 3–4.

32. For classic examples of early Red Web conspiracy theories, see Blair Coan, *The Red Web, 1921–1924* (1925; reprint, Boston: Western Islands, 1969); Richard Whitney, *Reds in America* (1924; reprint, Belmont, Mass.: Western Islands, 1970).

33. R. G. Brown et al., *Report upon the Illegal Practices of the United States Department of Justice* (1920; reprint, New York: Arno, 1969), generally referred to as the "Lawyers' Report."

34. The definitive account of the Brown Scare of the late 1930s and early 1940s is Leo P. Ribuffo, *The Old Christian Right: The Protestant Far Right from the Great Depression to the Cold War* (Philadelphia: Temple University Press, 1983).

35. Elizabeth Dilling, *The Red Network* (Kenilworth, Ill.: published by author, 1934), and *The Roosevelt Red Record and Its Background* (Chicago: published by author, 1936); J. B. Matthews, *Odyssey of a Fellow Traveler* (New York: Mt. Vernon, 1938); Eugene Lyons, *The Red Decade: The Stalinist Penetration of America* (Indianapolis: Bobbs-Merrill, 1941); Daniel Aaron, *Writers on the Left* (New York: Avon, 1961); William L. O'Neill, *A Better World: The Great Schism, Stalinism, and the American Intellectuals* (New York: Simon and Schuster, 1982).

36. John Roy Carlson [Avedis Derounian], *Undercover: My Four Years in the Nazi Underground in America* (New York: Dutton, 1943).

37. For a survey and refutation of Pearl Harbor conspiracy theories, see Gordon Prange, *Pearl Harbor: The Verdict of History* (New York: McGraw-Hill, 1986). For the 1944 sedition trial, see Ribuffo, *Old Christian Right;* Lawrence Dennis and Maximilian St. George, *A Trial on Trial: The Great Sedition Trial of 1944* (New York: National Civil Rights Committee, 1945).

38. The standard account of McCarthy and his career is David M. Oshinsky, *A Conspiracy So Immense: The World of Joe McCarthy* (New

York: Free Press, 1983). McCarthy published his notorious speech on Marshall in *America's Retreat from Victory: The Story of George Catlett Marshall* (1951; reprint, New York: Devin-Adair, 1962).

39. For an account of this episode, see Powers, *Not Without Honor,* chap. 10. For the notorious biography of Eisenhower, see Robert Welch, *The Politician* (1963; reprint, Belmont, Mass.: Western Islands, 1964).

40. Stanley Mosk and Howard H. Jewel, "The Birch Phenomenon Analyzed," *New York Times Magazine,* August 20, 1961, p. 12.

41. See Powers, *Not Without Honor,* chap. 10.

42. For Goldwater's own bitter account of these episodes, see Barry M. Goldwater with Jack Casserly, *Goldwater* (New York: Doubleday, 1988), pp. 143–44, 171, 176, 205.

43. See Powers, *Not Without Honor,* pp. 333–39; Peter Schrag, *Test of Loyalty: Daniel Ellsberg and the Rituals of Secret Government* (New York: Touchstone, 1964); Sanford J. Ungar, *The Papers and the Papers: An Account of the Legal and Political Battle over the Pentagon Papers* (1972; reprint, New York: Columbia University Press, 1989).

44. Neil Sheehan, introduction to Sheehan et al., eds., *The Pentagon Papers* (New York: Bantam, 1971), p. xii.

45. Ibid., pp. xiii, xv.

46. Gravel is quoted in Ungar, *The Papers and the Papers,* p. 37.

47. Mark Felt, *The FBI Pyramid: From the Inside* (New York: Putnam's, 1979), pp. 88, 93, 98. For an account of the raid at Media, Pennsylvania, see Powers, *Secrecy and Power,* pp. 464–66. See also Cathy Perkus, ed., *COINTELPRO: The FBI's Secret War on Political Freedom* (New York: Monad, 1975).

48. For detailed accounts of the Senate and House investigations of the intelligence agencies, see Loch K. Johnson, *A Season of Inquiry: The Senate Intelligence Investigation* (Lexington: University Press of Kentucky, 1985); Kathryn S. Olmsted, *Challenging the Secret Government* (Chapel Hill: University of North Carolina Press, 1996); Senate Select Committee to Study Governmental Operations with Respect to Intelligence Activities, *Final Report,* 64th Cong., 2d sess., H. Rept. 94–755.

49. Senate Select Committee to Study Governmental Operations, *Final Report,* book 3, p. 376.

50. Ibid., book 3, p. 3.

51. House Select Committee on Intelligence, testimony of retired special agent Arthur Murtagh, *Hearings Before the Committee on Intelligence,* 94th Cong., 1st sess., November 18, 1975, part 3, p. 1048.

52. Olmsted, *Challenging the Secret Government.*

53. Quoted in ibid., pp. 66, 79.

54. William Appleman Williams, *Tragedy of American Diplomacy* (Cleveland: World, 1959); Denna Fleming, *The Cold War and Its Origins* (New York: Doubleday, 1961); Gabriel Kolko, *Politics of War: The World and United States Foreign Policy, 1943–1945* (New York: Random House, 1968); Lloyd C. Gardner, *Architects of Illusion: Men and Ideas in American Foreign Policy, 1941–1949* (Chicago: Quadrangle, 1970); Gar Alperovitz, *Atomic Diplomacy: Hiroshima and Potsdam, the Use of the Atomic Bomb, and the American Confrontation with Soviet Power* (New York: Simon and Schuster, 1965). The quotation is from Gardner, *Architects of Illusion*, p. 317.

55. David Horowitz, *Free World Colossus: A Critique of American Foreign Policy in the Cold War*, rev. ed. (New York: Hill and Wang, 1971), pp. 4–6.

56. Robert James Maddox, *The New Left and the Origins of the Cold War* (Princeton: Princeton University Press, 1973), p. 19.

57. Gerald Posner, *Case Closed: Lee Harvey Oswald and the Assassination of JFK* (New York: Random House, 1993), p. 241.

58. Natalie Robins, *Alien Ink: The FBI's War on Freedom of Expression* (New York: William Morrow, 1992); Buckley's comment appears as a blurb on the back of the jacket.

59. Herbert Mitgang, *Dangerous Dossiers: Exposing the Secret War Against America's Greatest Authors* (New York: Donald I. Fine, 1988), p. 314.

60. Bud Schultz and Ruth Schultz, *It Did Happen Here: Recollections of Political Repression in America* (Berkeley: University of California Press, 1989), p. 413; Griffin Fariello, *Red Scare: Memories of the American Inquisition* (New York: Norton, 1995); Athan G. Theoharis and John Stuart Cox, *The Boss: J. Edgar Hoover and the Great American Inquisition* (Philadelphia: Temple University Press, 1988); and Ellen Schrecker, *The Age of McCarthyism* (New York: Bedford, 1984).

61. Edward Pessen, *Losing Our Souls: The American Experience in the Cold War* (Chicago: Ivan R. Dee, 1993), p. 11.

62. Bruce Cummings, foreword to I. F. Stone, *The Hidden History of the Korean War, 1950–1951* (1952; reprint, Boston: Little, Brown, 1988), pp. xi–xii.

63. Jim Garrison, *On the Trail of the Assassins* (New York: Warner, 1988), p. 324.

64. Anthony Summers, *Official and Confidential: The Secret Life of J. Edgar Hoover* (New York: Putnam's, 1993); Athan Theoharis, *J. Edgar Hoover, Sex, and Crime* (Chicago: Ivan R. Dee, 1995).

65. Seymour Hersh, *The Dark Side of Camelot* (Boston: Little, Brown, 1997); Gore Vidal, "Coached by Camelot," *New Yorker*, December 1, 1997, pp. 85–92.

66. Allen Weinstein, *Perjury: The Hiss-Chambers Case* (New York: Knopf, 1968), p. xvii.

67. Ibid., pp. 548–49.

68. Ibid., p. 565.

69. O'Neill, *A Better World*, p. 367.

70. Ronald Radosh and Joyce Milton, *The Rosenberg File*, 2d ed. (New Haven: Yale University Press, 1997), pp. 471–72.

71. Ibid., pp. 450–51.

72. Ibid., pp. 453, ix.

73. Ibid., pp. xxv, xxix–xxx.

74. Ibid., p. xxi.

75. Harvey Klehr, John Earl Haynes, and Fridrikh Igorevich Firsov, *The Secret World of American Communism* (New Haven: Yale University Press, 1995), pp. 18–19.

76. John Lewis Gaddis, *We Now Know* (New York: Oxford University Press, 1997), pp. 292–93.

77. Ibid., pp. 294, 25.

78. Ibid., pp. 74–75.

79. Ibid., p. 49.

80. Ibid., p. 14.

81. Ibid., pp. 293–94.

Chapter 1: Secrecy as Regulation

1. Foreign Relations Authorization Act for Fiscal Years 1994 and 1995, 50 *U.S. Code* 401.

2. Robert Lewis Benson, *Introductory History of Venona and Guide to the Translations* (Fort George G. Meade, Md.: Center for Cryptologic History, National Security Agency, 1995), pp. 3, 6.

3. J. Edgar Hoover, letter to George E. Allen, May 29, 1946, file "FBI–Atomic Bomb," in subject file "President's Secretary's File," Harry S. Truman Papers, Truman Library, Independence, Mo.

4. D. M. Ladd, memorandum to J. Edgar Hoover, May 28, 1946, Library of Congress.

5. H. B. Fletcher, memorandum to D. M. Ladd, October 18, 1949, archives of the Federal Bureau of Investigation.

6. Allen Weinstein, *Perjury: The Hiss-Chambers Case* (New York: Random House, 1978; reprint, New York: Random House, 1997).

7. Office of Management and Budget, *Historical Tables: Budget of the United States Government, Fiscal Year 1998* (February 1997); calculations are based on constant 1998 dollars.

8. Information Security Oversight Office, *1996 Report to the President* (Washington, D.C.: Information Security Oversight Office, 1996), p. ii.

9. Ibid.

10. James Risen and Ronald J. Ostrow, "East Germany's Spy Files at Center of FBI-CIA Clash," *Los Angeles Times*, October 25, 1995.

11. Tim Weiner, "For First Time, U.S. Discloses Spying Budget," *New York Times*, October 16, 1997.

12. Evan Thomas, "A Singular Opportunity: Gaining Access to CIA's Records," *Studies in Intelligence* 39 (1996): 19.

13. Sherman Kent, "Studies in Intelligence," September 1955, in *Studies in Intelligence, Index 1955–1992*.

14. R. Jeffrey Smith, "The Dissenter," *Washington Post Magazine*, December 7, 1997, pp. 18–20.

15. Stansfield Turner, "Intelligence for a New World Order," *Foreign Affairs* 70 (Fall 1991): 162.

Chapter 2: The Experience of World War I

1. John A. Rohr, *To Run a Constitution: The Legitimacy of the Administrative State* (Lawrence: University Press of Kansas, 1986), p. 156.

2. Floyd M. Riddick and Alan S. Frumin, *Riddick's Senate Procedure: Precedents and Practices*, 101st Cong., 2d sess., 1992, S. Doc. 101–28, p. 275.

3. James Parton, *Life of Andrew Jackson* (New York: Mason Brothers, 1860), 3:607.

4. William Z. Slany, "Draft History of the Foreign Relations Series," p. 4.

5. Wilson, "An Address to a Joint Session of Congress," January 8, 1918, in *The Papers of Woodrow Wilson*, edited by Arthur S. Link (Princeton: Princeton University Press, 1984–92), 45:536.

6. Ibid., p. 537.

7. *World Book Encyclopedia*, 1994 ed., s.v. "Alien and Sedition Acts," by Jerald A. Combs.

8. William H. Seward, letter to Charles Francis Adams, 1861, in *Annual Message of the President*, 37th Cong., 2d sess., S. Doc. 21, serial 1117, 1:108.

9. David M. Halbfinger, "Political Role of Immigrants Is Still Lagging," *New York Times*, December 1, 1997.

10. Sir William Schwenck Gilbert, *Iolanthe*, libretto by W. S. Gilbert, edited by William-Alan Landes (Studio City, Calif.: Players Press, 1997).

11. Nathan Glazer, "From Socialism to Sociology," in *Authors of Their Own Lives: Intellectual Autobiographies*, edited by Bennett M. Berger (Berkeley: University of California Press, 1990), p. 191.

12. Melvyn Dubofsky, *We Shall Be All: A History of the Industrial Workers of the World* (Chicago: Quadrangle Books, 1969), p. 271.

13. Ibid., p. 146, quoting Lewis S. Gannet.

14. Robert Lansing to Wilson, November 20, 1915, *Papers of Woodrow Wilson* 35:230.

15. Wilson, "An Address in Philadelphia to Newly Naturalized Citizens," May 10, 1915, *Papers of Woodrow Wilson* 33:147–50.

16. Wilson, "Annual Message on the State of the Union," December 7, 1915, *Papers of Woodrow Wilson* 35:306–7.

17. *An Act Requiring an Oath of Allegiance and to Support the Constitution of the United States, to Be Administered to Certain Persons in the Civil Service of the United States*, 12 Stat. 326 (August 6, 1861).

18. U.S. Department of Justice, *Annual Report of the Attorney General, 1916* (Washington, D.C.: Government Printing Office, 1916), pp. 12–20.

19. Robert Lansing, memorandum, March 20, 1917, *Papers of Woodrow Wilson* 41:442.

20. Wilson, "Address to a Joint Session of Congress," April 2, 1917, in *Papers of Woodrow Wilson* 41:524.

21. McIlhenny and others to Woodrow Wilson, April 5, 1917, in *Papers of Woodrow Wilson* 41:546.

22. S. 2, chap. 2, sec. 2(c).

23. H.R. 291, sec. 4.

24. Harold Edgar and Benno C. Schmidt, Jr., "The Espionage Statutes and Publication of Defense Information," *Columbia Law Review* 73, no. 5 (May 1973): 950–51.

25. *The Encyclopedia of the United States Congress* (New York: Simon and Schuster, 1995), 2:774.

26. *Congressional Record* 55, pt. 1:789 (April 18, 1917).

27. Ibid., pt. 2:2263 (May 14, 1917).

28. Ibid., pt. 2:2119 (May 11, 1917).

29. Ibid., pt. 1:787–88 (April 18, 1917).

30. Ibid., pt. 3:2262 (May 14, 1917).

31. Ibid., pt. 3:3144 (May 31, 1917).

32. Sedition Act of 1918, 40 Stat. 553.

33. Edgar and Schmidt, "Espionage Statutes," p. 1023.

34. 42 U.S. Code 2274.

35. Wilson, speech of September 5, 1919, *Papers of Woodrow Wilson* 63:46–47.

36. Madison to Jefferson, May 13, 1798, *The Republic of Letters: The Correspondence Between Thomas Jefferson and James Madison, 1776–1826*, edited by James Morton Smith (New York: W. W. Norton, 1995), 2:1048.

37. Jules Witcover, *Sabotage at Black Tom: Imperial Germany's Secret War in America, 1914–1917* (Chapel Hill, N.C.: Algonquin, 1989), p. 42; Captain Henry Landau, *The Enemy Within: The Inside Story of German Sabotage in America* (New York: G. P. Putnam's Sons, 1937), pp. 7–8.

38. Marc Mappen, "Jerseyana," *New York Times*, July 14, 1991.

39. "Ram Chandra in Toils with Four Hindoo Plotters," *San Francisco Chronicle*, April 8, 1917.

40. Joan M. Jensen, "The 'Hindu Conspiracy': A Reassessment," *Pacific Historical Review* 48 (February 1979): 65.

41. Ibid.

42. John L. Heaton, *Cobb of "The World"* (New York: Dutton, 1924), p. 270.

43. Wilson, "Address to a Joint Session of Congress," April 2, 1917, in *Papers of Woodrow Wilson* 41:523.

44. Samuel Eliot Morison, Henry Steele Commager, and William E. Leuchtenburg, *The Growth of the American Republic*, 6th ed. (New York: Oxford University Press, 1969), 2:383.

45. Ibid.

46. Ibid., 2:386.

47. *Theodore Roosevelt Cyclopedia*, edited by Albert Bushnell Hart and Herbert Ronald Ferleger (New York: Roosevelt Memorial Association, 1941).

48. *Encyclopedia of the United States Congress* 2:774.

49. Morison, Commager, and Leuchtenburg, *American Republic* 2:384.

50. Louis W. Koenig, *Bryan: A Political Biography of William Jennings Bryan* (New York: G. P. Putnam's Sons, 1971), pp. 502–3.

51. Arthur S. Link, *Wilson: The Struggle for Neutrality, 1914–1915* (Princeton: Princeton University Press, 1960), p. 420.

52. "Josephus Daniels Dies at Age of Eighty-Five," *New York Times*, January 16, 1948.

53. "Baker to Be New Secretary of War," *New York Times*, March 7, 1916.

54. *Schenck v. United States*, 249 U.S. 47 (1919).

55. *Debs v. United States*, 249 U.S. 211 (1919).

Chapter 3: The Encounter with Communism

1. Wilson's executive order of April 7, 1917, is quoted in Paul P. Van Riper, *History of the United States Civil Service* (Evanston, Ill.: Row, Peterson, 1958), p. 266; for the actions of the Civil Service Commission after the war, see pp. 265–67.

2. *World Book Encyclopedia*, 1994 ed., s.v. "Anarchism," by James D. Forman.

3. "General Orders No. 64, General Headquarters, American Expeditionary Force," November 22, 1917, in Harold C. Relyea, *The Evolution of Government Information Security Classification Policy: A Brief Overview (1775–1973)*, Congressional Research Service, September 11, 1973, p. 22.

4. Robert Lansing, memorandum, March 20, 1917, *The Papers of Woodrow Wilson*, edited by Arthur S. Link (Princeton: Princeton University Press, 1984–92), 41:438.

5. Ibid., p. 440.

6. Robert A. Rosenstone, *Romantic Revolutionary: A Biography of John Reed* (Cambridge: Harvard University Press, 1990), p. 330.

7. Harvey Klehr, John Earl Haynes, and Fridrikh Igorevich Firsov, *The Secret World of American Communism* (New Haven: Yale University Press, 1995), p. 22.

8. Theodore Draper, *The Roots of American Communism* (Chicago: Ivan R. Dee, 1957), p. 189. Draper also reproduces a breakdown of the total membership of the CPUSA, estimated at 26,680 members: English, 1,900 (including 800 from the Michigan organization, which soon dropped out); Estonian, 280; German, 850; Hungarian, 1,000; Jewish, 1,000; Lettish, or Latvian, 1,200; Lithuanian, 4,400; Polish, 1,750; Russian, 7,000; South Slavic, 2,200; Ukrainian, 4,000; and members from nonfederation countries, 1,100 (ibid.).

9. Klehr, Haynes, and Firsov estimate that fewer than 4,000 members of both the Communist Party of America (about 24,000 members) and the Communist Labor Party (about 10,000 members) spoke English (*Secret World*, p. 5).

10. Draper, *Roots of American Communism*, p. 191.

11. Ibid.

12. Ibid., p. 323.

13. Nathan Glazer, *The Social Basis of American Communism* (New York: Harcourt, Brace, and World, 1961), p. 3. Maurice Isserman estimates that in the years before World War II, there were 50,000 to 75,000 CPUSA members in the United States (Isserman, *Which Side Were You On? The American Communist Party During the Second World War* [Middletown, Conn.: Wesleyan University Press, 1982], p. 18).

14. Stanley Coben, *A. Mitchell Palmer: Politician* (New York: Da Capo Press, 1972), pp. 203-7.

15. "Russian Reds Are Busy Here," *New York Times*, June 8, 1919; Robert K. Murray, *Red Scare: A Study in National Hysteria, 1919–1920* (Minneapolis: University of Minnesota Press, 1955), p. 213; "The Red Assassins," *Washington Post*, January 4, 1920.

16. Roberta Strauss Feuerlicht, *America's Reign of Terror: World War I, the Red Scare, and the Palmer Raids* (New York: Random House, 1971), p. 108.

17. Theodore Draper, *The Roots of American Communism* (Chicago: Ivan R. Dee, 1957), p. 207.

18. Klehr, Haynes, and Firsov, *Secret World*, p. 21.

19. Ibid., p. 24.

20. In fact, the Soviet subsidies to American Communists continued into the 1980s, by which time the CPUSA scarcely existed. Moscow evidently did not realize this, perhaps assuming that most of the party members had gone underground—and inadvertently illustrating the truism that, in clandestine operations, it is ever difficult to check one's facts.

21. Ignazio Silone, *The God That Failed: Six Studies in Communism*, edited by Richard Crossman (London: Hamish Hamilton, 1950), p. 16.

22. Klehr, Haynes, and Firsov, *Secret World*, pp. 5, 7, 24–25. Robert A. Katzmann, who read a draft of the manuscript of this book, notes: "Gitlow was also a central figure in *Gitlow v. New York* (1925), in which Justice Edward T. Sanford, speaking for the Court, held that because 'a single revolutionary spark may kindle a fire that, smoldering for a time, may burst into a sweeping and destructive conflagration, [the state] may, in the exercise of its judgment, suppress the threatened danger in its incipiency' (268 U.S. at 669)."

23. Sidney Hook, *Out of Step: An Unquiet Life in the Twentieth Century* (New York: Harper and Row, 1987), p. 241.

24. National Security Agency, fourth Venona release, July 17, 1996, vol. 3, nos. 174–76 (December 29, 1943).

25. Hook, *Out of Step*, p. 281.

26. Ibid.

27. Ibid., p. 285.

28. David Riesman, *Abundance for What?* (Garden City, N.Y.: Doubleday, 1964; reprint, New Brunswick, N.J.: Transaction, 1993), p. 80.

29. Lionel Trilling, *The Middle of the Journey* (London: Secker and Warburg, 1975), p. viii.

30. Ibid., pp. x–xi. See also Daniel Patrick Moynihan, "Address to

the Entering Class at Harvard College, 1972," in *Coping: Essays on the Practice of Government* (New York: Random House, 1973), p. 405.

31. Trilling, *Middle of the Journey*, pp. xviii–xix.

32. Ibid., p. xix.

33. Ibid.

34. Daniel Patrick Moynihan, review of *Final Reports*, by Richard Rovere, *New Yorker*, September 17, 1984, pp. 134–40.

Chapter 4: The Experience of World War II

1. Art Ronnie, *Counterfeit Hero: Fritz Duquesne, Adventurer and Spy* (Annapolis, Md.: Naval Institute Press, 1995), pp. 208–9.

2. Ibid., p. 214.

3. Quoted in ibid., p. 2.

4. Publius [Alexander Hamilton], Federalist No. 9, in *The Federalist Papers*, edited by Clinton Rossiter (New York: New American Library, 1961), p. 72.

5. *The Harvard Encyclopedia of American Ethnic Groups*, s.v. "Germans," by Kathleen Neils Conzen.

6. Ibid.

7. Robert Edwin Herzstein, *Roosevelt and Hitler: Prelude to War* (New York: Paragon House, 1989), p. 189.

8. Ibid., p. 190.

9. Don Whitehead, *The FBI Story* (New York: Random House, 1956), p. 212.

10. By February 16, 1942, these numbers had expanded to a total of 2,192 Japanese, 1,393 Germans, and 264 Italians (Commission on Wartime Relocation and Internment of Civilians, *Personal Justice Denied* [Washington, D.C.: Government Printing Office, 1992], p. 55).

11. Ibid., p. 73.

12. Ibid., p. 81.

13. Franklin D. Roosevelt, "Authorizing the Secretary of War to Prescribe Military Areas," Executive Order 9066, *Federal Register* 7 (February 19, 1942): 38.

14. Commission on Wartime Relocation, *Personal Justice Denied*, p. 308.

15. Ibid., p. 287.

16. Stephen Fox, *The Unknown Internment: An Oral History of the Relocation of Italian Americans During World War II* (Boston: Twayne, 1990), p. 136.

17. Charles A. Horsky, having served as assistant prosecutor at the

Nuremberg war crimes trials, argued a case before the Supreme Court that challenged the wartime internment of Americans of Japanese ancestry. "I was trying to persuade the Court that there was no legitimate basis for the Army to arrest citizens," said Horsky in a 1989 interview with the *Washington Post*. "I couldn't get enough information to make it stick" (quoted in Irvin Molotsky, obituary of Charles A. Horsky, *New York Times*, August 24, 1997).

18. Civil Liberties Act of 1988, 102 Stat. 94. U.S. citizens of Aleutian descent were also relocated; of them the act said, "The United States failed to provide reasonable care for the Aleuts, and this resulted in widespread illness, disease, and death among the residents of the camps."

19. Quoted in Commission on Wartime Relocation, *Personal Justice Denied*, p. 82.

20. Richard Norton Smith, *The Colonel: The Life and Legend of Robert R. McCormick, 1880–1955* (Boston: Houghton Mifflin, 1997), p. 417.

Chapter 5: The Bomb

1. Maurice M. Shapiro, "Echoes of the Big Bang," *New York Times*, July 15, 1995.

2. Ibid.

3. J. Robert Oppenheimer's account is quoted in Richard Rhodes, *The Making of the Atomic Bomb* (New York: Simon and Schuster, 1986), p. 676.

4. Shapiro, "Echoes of the Big Bang."

5. "The Atomic Bomb," *Life*, February 27, 1950, p. 91.

6. Ibid., p. 100.

7. Weisband was convicted of contempt of court for failing to attend a grand jury hearing on Communist Party activity; in November 1950 he was sentenced to one year in prison (Robert Louis Benson and Michael Warner, eds., *Venona: Soviet Espionage and the American Response, 1939–1957* [Washington, D.C.: National Security Agency, Central Intelligence Agency, 1996], p. xxviii).

8. Max Weber, "Bureaucracy," in *Essays in Sociology*, translated and edited by H. H. Gerth and C. Wright Mills (New York: Oxford University Press, 1946), pp. 233–34.

9. Senate Committee on Foreign Relations, *The START Treaty: Hearings Before the Committee on Foreign Relations*, 102d Cong., 2d sess., S. Hrg. 102–607, pt. 1, p. 96.

10. George F. Kennan, *Memoirs: 1950–1963*, vol. 2 (Boston: Little, Brown, 1972), p. 191.

11. See, for example, Lillian Hellman, *Scoundrel Time*, with an introduction by Garry Wills (Boston: Little, Brown, 1976).

12. The three others were Edward R. Stettinius, Jr., secretary of state; H. Freeman Matthews, director of the Office of European Affairs; and Wilder Foote, assistant to the secretary of state (Edward R. Stettinius, Jr., *Roosevelt and the Russians: The Yalta Conference* [Garden City, N.Y.: Doubleday, 1949], p. 30).

13. Joseph Albright and Marcia Kunstel, *Bombshell: The Secret Story of Ted Hall and America's Unknown Atomic Spy Conspiracy* (New York: Times Books, 1997), p. 58.

14. Ibid., pp. 89–90.

15. Michael Dobbs, "Code Name 'Mlad,' Atomic Bomb Spy," *Washington Post*, February 25, 1996. See also Dobbs, "New Documents Name American as Soviet Spy," *Washington Post*, March 6, 1996.

16. Albright and Kunstel, *Bombshell*, p. 90.

Chapter 6: A Culture of Secrecy

1. Suslov joined the Politburo (then called the Presidium) in October 1952 but left in 1953 after Stalin's death. He rejoined in 1955 and remained a member until his death on January 25, 1982.

2. Daniel Patrick Moynihan, *A Dangerous Place* (Boston: Little, Brown, 1978), pp. ix–x.

3. Henry DeWolf Smyth, *A General Account of the Development of Methods of Using Atomic Energy for Military Purposes Under the Auspices of the United States Government, 1940–1945* (Washington: Government Printing Office, 1945). That same year Smyth published *Atomic Energy for Military Purposes: The Official Report on the Development of the Atomic Bomb Under the Auspices of the United States Government, 1940-1945* (Princeton: Princeton University Press, 1945); new editions of this work have been brought out by other publishers in 1976, 1978, and 1989.

4. Roscoe Pound, quoted in *Annual Report of the American Bar Association* 63 (1938): 340.

5. Erwin Griswold, "Government in Ignorance of the Law: A Plea for Better Publication of Executive Legislation," *Harvard Law Review* 48 (1934): 198. Griswold argued that, because administrative regulations "equivalent to law" had become so important in the ordering of everyday life, executive legislation should be published and thus made available to the public. A year after Griswold's essay appeared, Congress enacted the Federal Register Act of 1935, 49 Stat. 500.

6. Attorney General Tom Clark interpreted this exception to the APA's public-information provision in his 1947 *Manual on the Administrative Procedure Act:* "This would include the confidential operations

of any agency, such as the confidential operations of the Federal Bureau of Investigation and the Secret Service and, in general, those aspects of any agency's law enforcement procedures the disclosure of which would reduce the utility of such procedures. . . . It should be noted that the exception is made only to the extent that the function requires secrecy in the public interest. Such a determination must be made by the agency concerned. To the extent that the function does not require such secrecy, the publication requirements apply. Thus, the War Department obviously is not required to publish confidential matters of military organization and operation, but it would be required to publish the organization and procedure applicable to the ordinary civil functions of the Corps of Engineers."

7. *United States v. Curtiss-Wright Export Corporation,* 299 U.S. 304, 319 (1936).

8. Richard Frank, "Enforcing the Public's Right to Openness in the Foreign Affairs Decision-Making Process," in *Secrecy and Foreign Policy,* edited by Thomas Franck and Edward Weisband (New York: Oxford University Press, 1974), pp. 272–73.

9. Hatch Act, 53 Stat. 1148 (1953). Previously, under the Pendleton Act of 1883 and the Lloyd-LaFollette Act of 1912, civil service investigations of government employees had focused on issues of general character and ability. The 1912 act provided that employees could be removed only when doing so would promote the efficiency of the civil service. It also established specific procedures for notifying employees of any charges against them and allowing them to respond to such charges. The federal government's employment policies centered on the need to maintain a trustworthy and efficient civil service, one based on the core principle of "suitability" for federal employment, defined in the 1883 statute as "a requirement or requirements for government employment having reference to a person's character, reputation, trustworthiness, and fitness as related to the efficiency of the service" (22 Stat. 403 [1883]). Today, all government employees must still meet a standard of suitability that tracks the original 1883 definition; those requiring access to national security information must also be found "security-eligible" as defined in the Eisenhower Executive Order 10450.

10. Commission on Government Security, *Report of the Commission on Government Security* (Washington, D.C.: Government Printing Office, 1957), pp. 3–6; Eleanor Bontecou, *The Federal Loyalty-Security Program* (Westport, Conn.: Greenwood Press, 1953), p. 14.

11. Commission on Government Security, *Report,* p. 6.

12. Harold Green, "The Oppenheimer Case: A Study in the Abuse of Law," *Bulletin of Atomic Scientists* 33 (September 1977): 12, 61.

13. Among the critics were several Harvard law professors, including Zechariah Chafee, Jr., who had spoken out against Attorney General Palmer nearly three decades before, and Erwin Griswold, in

"The Loyalty Order: Procedure Termed Inadequate and Defects Pointed Out," *New York Times*, April 13, 1947. See also Bontecou, *Federal Loyalty-Security Program*, pp. 30–31.

14. Public Law 81–733, 64 Stat. 476 (1950).

15. Dwight D. Eisenhower, "Security Requirements for Government Employees," Executive Order 10450, *Federal Register* 18 (April 29, 1953): 2489.

16. Attempting to respond to the criticism, President Truman had amended his executive order in July 1951, lowering the standard of proof for disloyalty: "The standard for the refusal of employment or the removal from employment in an Executive department or agency on grounds relating to loyalty shall be that on all the evidence, *there is reasonable doubt* as to the loyalty of the person involved" (emphasis added; Harry S. Truman, Executive Order 10241, *Federal Register* 16 [April 28, 1951]: 3690). Then in 1952, the president convened a committee charged with merging "the loyalty, security, and suitability programs, thus eliminating the overlapping, duplication, and confusion which apparently now exist" (Truman, letter to the chairman of the Civil Service Commission, August 8, 1952, *Public Papers of the Presidents of the United States: Harry S. Truman* [Washington, D.C.: Government Printing Office, 1966], p. 513). But the often partisan attacks on his loyalty program persisted, and a single, unified program for reviewing applicants for government positions and existing employees was never established—even after the Wright Commission in 1957 criticized the Eisenhower structure as an "unnatural blend" and a "hybrid product, . . . neither fish nor fowl, resulting in inconclusive adjudications, bewildered security personnel, employee fear and unrest, and general public criticism" (Commission on Government Security, *Report*, p. 44).

17. Under Executive Order 10450, the *scope* of an investigation could vary, depending on an individual's position and how sensitive it was to national security.

18. Anthony Leviero, "New Security Plan Issued: Thousands Face Re-Inquiry," *New York Times*, April 28, 1953.

19. Ibid.

20. Edward A. Shils, *The Torment of Secrecy*, with an introduction by Daniel P. Moynihan (Glencoe, Ill.: Free Press, 1956; reprint, Chicago: Ivan R. Dee, 1996), pp. 213–14. Shils goes on to offer a strong critique of the system: "This seems a narrow and doctrinaire conception of the motives of treasonable conduct. It is this narrow doctrinairism which makes the present system so inefficient, even though it may well be fairly effective. Although it might catch a few potential spies, it hurts many innocent persons. The resources marshalled against the potential spy are usually almost equally dangerous to the innocent."

21. Public Law 304, 84th Congress.

22. *Congressional Record*, January 18, 1955, pp. 463–64.

23. Ibid.

24. Commission on Government Security, *Report*, pp. xiii–xiv.

25. Ibid., p. xvii.

26. Ibid., p. xxiii.

27. James Reston, "Security Versus Freedom: An Analysis of the Controversy Stirred by Recommendation to Curb Information," *New York Times*, June 25, 1957.

28. Commission on Government Security, *Report*, p. 688.

29. Max Frankel, "Top Secret," *New York Times Magazine*, June 16, 1996.

30. House Committee on Government Operations, *Availability of Information from Federal Departments and Agencies*, 86th Cong., 2d sess. (July 2, 1960), H. Rept. 86–2084, p. 36.

31. Commission on Government Security, *Report*, p. xvii.

32. In an even-tempered, respectful dissent to the proposal for establishing a central security office, former attorney general McGranery wrote of "the inherent evil of the pyramiding of administrative devices, the superimposing of agency upon agency and the empire-building proclivities which frequently go hand in hand with the creation of overseers," noting that "no problem is solved by shifting primary executive responsibility from agencies and officials having that primary responsibility to superimposed administrative creations," even those described as advisory (and for whom "the power to suggest too easily becomes the power to demand"). After all, there was no guarantee that a new agency would work any better than the old ones had. What was needed instead, McGranery continued, was a correction of existing procedures that failed to achieve national security "with minimum delay and maximum protection of the civil rights of the loyal employee," a desire to make the corrected procedures work, and a willingness to fix responsibility for mistakes of judgment and to seek to avoid their recurrence. "This can best be done," he added, "by holding accountable those officials and agencies having the primary responsibility" (ibid.).

33. Harold C. Relyea, *The Evolution of Government Information Security Classification Policy: A Brief Overview (1775–1973)*, Congressional Research Service, September 11, 1973, p. 50; Robert O. Blanchard, "Present at the Creation: The Media and the Moss Committee," *Journalism Quarterly* 49 (Summer 1972): 272.

34. House Special Government Information Subcommittee, H. Rept. 85–1884 (1958), p. 152.

35. House Committee on Government Operations, *Executive Classification of Information: Security Classification Problems Involving Exemption (b)(1) of the Freedom of Information Act* (1973), H. Rept. 93–221, p. 21.

36. 5 *U.S. Code* 552 (1966).

37. Even so, significant concerns remain about both the effectiveness and the efficiency of the procedures used under the FOIA. For example, at a roundtable program on May 16, 1996, the Commission on Protecting and Reducing Government Secrecy heard testimony from journalist Terry Anderson concerning his efforts to use the FOIA to reconstruct the history of his seven years' captivity in Lebanon. What he encountered from his own government—outright denials of requested information and expressions of regret for the long delays, documents that had been completely blacked out, and piles of foreign newspaper clippings on Middle Eastern terrorism that had somehow come to be classified once they entered agency files—led him to tell the commission, "It's not the law that has to be changed but the culture of non-cooperation among the bureaucrats."

38. Commission on Government Security, *Report*, p. xx.

39. Defense Science Board, *Final Report of the Defense Science Board Task Force on Secrecy* (July 1, 1970). Ironically, given its tone and recommendations, the task force report was marked "For Official Use Only," apparently in an effort to control its distribution.

40. The task force noted that "never in the past has it been possible to keep secret the truly important discoveries, such as the discovery that an atomic bomb can be made to work" (ibid., pp. 3–4).

41. Ibid.

42. Glenn T. Seaborg, "Secrecy Runs Amok," *Science*, June 3, 1994, p. 1410.

43. Ibid.

44. Nick Cullather, letter to author, July 2, 1997.

Chapter 7: The Routinization of Secrecy

1. National Security Act of 1947, 61 Stat. 495.

2. Merle Miller, *Plain Speaking: An Oral Biography of Harry S. Truman* (New York: Berkeley, 1973), p. 392n.

3. Walter Pincus, "CIA Veteran Tapped to Run Operations," *Washington Post*, July 22, 1997.

4. James Q. Wilson, *Bureaucracy: What Government Agencies Do and Why They Do It* (New York: Basic Books, 1989), pp. 188–89.

5. Nicholas Cullather, *Operation PBSUCCESS: The United States and Guatemala, 1952–1954* (Washington, D.C.: Central Intelligence Agency, Center for the Study of Intelligence, 1994), p. 7.

6. Ibid., p. 84.

7. X [George F. Kennan], "The Sources of Soviet Conduct," *For-*

eign Affairs, July 1947, reprinted in Hamilton Fish Armstrong, ed., *Fifty Years of Foreign Affairs* (New York: Praeger, 1972), p. 197.

8. Ibid., p. 200.

9. Ibid., p. 203.

10. Robert M. Laskey, editor's introduction to NSC-68, *Naval War College Review* 27 (May–June 1975): 52.

11. Ibid., p. 51.

12. Peter Grose, *Gentleman Spy: The Life of Allen Dulles* (Boston: Houghton Mifflin, 1994), p. 347.

13. Paul H. Nitze, "Reflections on the Origins of NSC-68" (remarks delivered at a seminar, "Assessing the Soviet Threat: The Early Cold War Years," sponsored by the Central Intelligence Agency, Washington, D.C., October 24, 1997).

14. Ibid.

15. Laskey, "NSC-68," p. 62.

16. Ibid., p. 68.

17. In *Strategies of Containment* (New York: Oxford University Press, 1982), John Lewis Gaddis distinguishes among five "distinct geopolitical codes" between 1947 and 1980: Kennan's original containment strategy (1947–49); NSC-68 and the Korean War (1950–53); the Eisenhower-Dulles "New Look" (1953–61); the Kennedy-Johnson "flexible response" strategy (1961–69); and détente (1969–79). In describing the first of these, Gaddis notes Kennan's belief that "the breakup of international communism was an irreversible trend" because it "was subject to many of the same self-destructive tendencies of classic imperialism" (p. 47). Kennan's containment strategy was designed to exploit these weaknesses and hasten the decline of Soviet influence beyond its borders by applying U.S. economic and technological advantages in key areas of the world. NSC-68 represented the second distinct phase of containment strategy, one that emphasized much more strongly than Kennan had the buildup of U.S. military strength to counter that of the Soviet Union. Moreover, although the drafters of NSC-68 still recognized important Soviet weaknesses (including vulnerability to nationalism within its own borders and in "satellite" states), Nitze and his colleagues were more pessimistic about Soviet capabilities and what it would take to counter these. In addition, NSC-68 raised concerns about future trends in relative military strength, though it also emphasized the extent of U.S. economic superiority. Eisenhower's New Look strategy was premised on asymmetrical response—on reacting to an adversary's challenges in ways calculated to apply one's strengths against the other side's weaknesses, even if this meant shifting the nature and location of the confrontation. Kennedy's "flexible response" shifted back to a symmetrical response—to deter-

ring all wars, be they general or limited, nuclear or conventional, large or small. This philosophy also stressed a decreasing reliance on nuclear weapons in favor of conventional military deterrence and covert action. Gaddis describes the fifth stage of containment, détente, as seeking "to change the Soviet Union's concept of international relations, to integrate it as a stable element into the existing world order," by applying a combination of pressure and inducements that would, if successful, persuade the Russians that stability was in their interests (p. 289).

18. Richard M. Nixon, *The Real War* (New York: Warner Books, 1980), p. 2.

19. Roy Cohn, *McCarthy* (New York: New American Library, 1968), p. 64.

20. Quoted in Grose, *Gentleman Spy*, p. 346.

21. The members of the Task Force on Intelligence Activities were General Mark W. Clark, chairman; Richard L. Conolly; Henry Kearns; Edward V. Rickenbacker; Donald S. Russell; and Ernest F. Hollings, then lieutenant governor of and later a senator from South Carolina.

22. James H. Doolittle, "Report on the Covert Activities of the Central Intelligence Agency, September 30, 1954," located at the National Archives and Records Administration, College Park, Maryland.

23. Ibid., p. 7.

24. Task Force on Intelligence Activities, "A Report to the Congress by the Commission on Organization of the Executive Branch of the Government," June 1955, p. 14.

25. Frank O. Wisner to Colonel Matthew Baird, CIA director of training, memorandum, July 19, 1955, p. 3.

26. If real, as against nominal, growth rates are used, the "crossover" does not occur until 2021, but the Soviets would have, by any such calculation, long since established a potential military superiority.

27. Allen W. Dulles, "Dimensions of the International Peril Facing Us," address to the U.S. Chamber of Commerce, Washington, D.C., April 28, 1958, published in *Vital Speeches of the Day* 24, no. 15 (May 15, 1958): 454.

28. Walter W. Rostow, conversation with author, 1962.

29. John Prados, *The Soviet Estimate: U.S. Intelligence Analysis and Soviet Strategic Forces* (Princeton: Princeton University Press, 1982), p. 74.

30. The Gaither Report of 1957, formally known as U.S. Congress, Joint Committee on Defense Production, *Deterrence and Survival in the Nuclear Age*, 94th Cong., 2d sess., 1976, Committee Print, p. 25.

31. Prados, *The Soviet Estimate*, p. 80; Joseph Alsop, "Our Government's Untruths," *New York Herald-Tribune*, August 1, 1958.

32. Gaither Report, p. iii.

33. In 1997, for example, the Clinton administration began developing an $11 billion fleet of Boeing 747s equipped with lasers that could destroy enemy missiles from a few hundred miles away. Because this laser anti-missile technology is unsuitable for long-range attacks, it does not violate the Anti-Ballistic Missile Treaty, and so it has enjoyed some bipartisan support. But the laser fleet has been attacked by congressional investigators as being so flawed that it might not work in wartime. See William J. Broad, "Plan for Airborne Laser Weapon Is Attacked," *New York Times*, September 30, 1997.

34. Bryan Hehir, *The Uses of Force in the Post–Cold War World* (Washington, D.C.: Woodrow Wilson Center for Scholars, 1996), p. 3.

35. Senate Committee on Foreign Relations, *Estimating the Size and Growth of the Soviet Economy: Hearing Before the Committee on Foreign Relations*, 101st Cong., 2d sess., July 16, 1990, p. 49.

36. Ibid., p. 33.

37. Central Intelligence Agency, National Foreign Assessment Center, *Handbook of Economic Statistics, 1990* (Washington, D.C.: Central Intelligence Agency, 1990), p. 38.

38. Dale W. Jorgenson, letter to author, March 18, 1991.

39. While concluding that this failure of analysis was not unique to the intelligence community, Rowen has also noted at least four major aspects of the Soviet economy in which the CIA's assessments "differed markedly from those of observers outside the community": the Soviet economy's overall size, its performance, its military burden (as a proportion of the Soviet GDP), and what he calls the "costs of empire." See, for example, Henry S. Rowen and Charles Wolf, Jr., letter to the editor, "The CIA's Credibility," *National Interest* 42 (Winter 1995–96): 111–12, which was written in response to an article defending the CIA's analysis.

40. George Kennan, "Assessing the Soviet Threat: The Early Cold War Years," Center for the Study of Intelligence, Washington, D.C., October 24, 1997.

41. Stansfield Turner, "Intelligence for a New World Order," *Foreign Affairs*, Fall 1991, p. 162.

42. Anders Åslund, "The CIA Versus Soviet Reality," *Washington Post*, May 19, 1988.

43. *The Military Balance, 1996–1997* (London: Oxford University Press, 1996), pp. 306–11.

44. Former president Gerald R. Ford, address to the National Press Club at a luncheon for the Ford Foundation Journalism Awards for Presidential and National Defense Reporting, June 2, 1997.

45. Laskey, "NSC-68," p. 63.

46. George P. Shultz, *Turmoil and Triumph: My Years as Secretary of State* (New York: Charles Scribner's Sons, 1993), p. 703.

47. Senate Committee on Foreign Relations, *The START Treaty: Hearings Before the Committee on Foreign Relations*, 102d Cong., 2d sess., 1992, pp. 67–68. The questions were posed by the author.

48. See Daniel Patrick Moynihan, *Pandaemonium* (Oxford: Oxford University Press, 1994), p. 51.

Chapter 8: A Culture of Openness

1. Information Security Oversight Office, *1996 Report to the President* (Washington, D.C.: Information Security Oversight Office, 1996), p. ii.

2. Max Frankel, "Top Secret," *New York Times Magazine*, June 16, 1996.

3. Harold Edgar and Benno C. Schmidt, Jr., "The Espionage Statutes and Publication of Defense Information," *Columbia Law Review* 73, no. 5 (May 1973): 934, 936. See also Chapter 2.

4. John D. Morrison, "The Protection of Intelligence Data," as quoted in ibid., p. 1055 n. 346. The uncertainties surrounding the legislative intent of the 1917 act (as well as of its most significant amendment, in 1950) were to have significant consequences more than half a century later. Edgar and Schmidt note that "no prosecution premised on publication has ever been brought under the espionage laws" and that the abandoned prosecution of Daniel Ellsberg and his colleague Anthony Russo for unlawful retention of the Pentagon Papers "was the first effort to apply the espionage statutes to conduct preparatory to publication." In October 1984, Samuel Loring Morison, a civilian analyst with the Office of Naval Intelligence, was arrested for supplying a classified photograph—a picture of a Soviet nuclear-powered carrier under construction—to *Jane's Defence Weekly*, which subsequently published it. In October 1985, Morison became the first person convicted under the 1917 Espionage Act for an unauthorized disclosure of classified defense information to the press. His conviction was upheld in 1988, and the Supreme Court declined to hear the case.

The Morison prosecution remains unique; no other individual has been prosecuted on such grounds since. While the core provisions of the espionage laws have been used with some frequency to prosecute government and defense-contractor employees for actual or attempted communication of national defense information to a foreign agent as well as conspiracies toward that end (thus reaching the conduct of now-notorious spies like Aldrich Ames), according to data gathered by the Department of Justice, there were sixty-seven indictments under the espionage laws between 1975 and August 1996. Figures compiled by the Department of Defense Security Institute show eighty-six new espionage cases *reported* between 1975 and 1995. Ames was indicted under 18 *U.S. Code* 794(c) of the Espionage Act for conspiracy "to directly or indirectly communicate, deliver or transmit . . . documents and information related to the national defense . . . to a foreign government or a representative or officer thereof . . . with the intent or reason to believe such information could be used to the injury of the United States or to the advantage of a foreign government." His wife, Rosario Ames, was also indicted for conspiracy under a separate provision of the act, 18 *U.S. Code* 793(g): for "a willful combination or agreement" with her husband "to communicate, deliver or transmit . . . documents relating to the national defense . . . to persons not authorized to receive them." Both were also indicted for tax fraud. Both subsequently pled guilty. Aldrich Ames was sentenced to life imprisonment without parole; Rosario Ames, to a five-year term.

5. *New York Times Company v. United States,* June 30, 1971, in vol. 403 of *United States Reports,* compiled by Henry Putzel, Jr. (Washington, D.C.: Government Printing Office, 1972), p. 719.

6. Erwin N. Griswold, "Secrets Not Worth Keeping," *Washington Post,* February 15, 1989.

7. Leonard Garment, *Crazy Rhythm: My Journey from Brooklyn, Jazz, and Wall Street to Nixon's White House, Watergate, and Beyond* (New York: Times Books, 1997), pp. 296–97.

8. William Safire, *Before the Fall: An Inside View of the Pre-Watergate White House* (Garden City, N.Y.: Doubleday, 1975), pp. 358, 552.

9. Barry M. Goldwater, letter to William J. Casey, April 8, 1984, quoted in Daniel Patrick Moynihan, *Came the Revolution: Argument in the Reagan Era* (San Diego: Harcourt Brace Jovanovich, 1988), pp. 178–79.

10. Theodore Draper, *A Very Thin Line: The Iran-Contra Affairs* (New York: Hill and Wang, 1991), p. 22.

11. Theodore Draper, "Getting Irangate Straight," *New York Review of Books,* October 8, 1987, p. 47.

12. Lawrence E. Walsh, *Firewall: The Iran-Contra Conspiracy and Cover-Up* (New York: W. W. Norton, 1997), p. 531.

13. Ibid., p. 518.

14. Harold Hongju Koh, *The National Security Constitution: Sharing Power After the Iran-Contra Affair* (New Haven: Yale University Press, 1990), pp. 2–3.

15. Ibid., p. 2.

16. James Q. Wilson, *Bureaucracy: What Government Agencies Do and Why They Do It* (New York: Basic Books, 1989), p. 189.

17. Donald L. Robinson, "The Routinization of Crisis Government," *Yale Review* 63 (Winter 1974): 161.

18. Robert D. Novak, "China's Savior," *Washington Post*, February 24, 1997.

19. Anthony Downs, *Inside Bureaucracy* (Boston: Little, Brown, 1967), p. 19.

20. John F. Harris, "On CIA's 50th, Clinton Praises 'Quiet Patriotism,'" *Washington Post*, September 17, 1997.

21. Office of the Press Secretary, White House press release, "Remarks by the President at the Fiftieth Anniversary of the Central Intelligence Agency," September 16, 1997, www.whitehouse.gov.

22. James Q. Wilson, *The Investigators: Managing FBI and Narcotics Agents* (New York: Basic Books, 1978), p. 202.

23. Paul McMasters, quoted in Eleanor Randolph, "Is U.S. Keeping Too Many Secrets?" *Los Angeles Times*, May 17, 1997.

24. Dennis Cauchon, "Militiaman Convicted Under Anti-Terrorism Law," *USA Today*, August 26, 1997.

25. National polling data (from Gallup Organization; Louis Harris and Associates, ABC News/*Washington Post*; Time/CNN/Yankelovich; CBS News/*New York Times*; and Gallup/CNN/*USA Today* surveys) provided by the Assassination Records Review Board and on file with the commission. Congress in 1992 established the Assassination Records Review Board to review all records related to the Kennedy assassination and make them available to the public (subject to narrow exemptions) as soon as possible. It is likely that the efforts of the board will greatly clarify the historical record concerning the assassination and the activities of Oswald and others; it is far less likely, however, that they will have much impact on opinion.

26. Editorial, "The Amnesty Option," *New York Times*, July 6, 1997.

27. Evan Thomas, *The Very Best Men, Four Who Dared: The Early Years of the CIA* (New York: Simon and Schuster, 1995), p. 239, citing Thomas C. Reeves, *A Question of Character: A Life of John F. Kennedy* (New York: Free Press, 1991), pp. 217–18. See also Michael Beschloss, *The Crisis Years: Kennedy and Khrushchev, 1960–1963* (New York: HarperCollins, 1991), p. 103.

28. Lloyd A. Free, "Attitudes of the Cuban People Toward the Castro Regime," Institute for International Social Research, Princeton University, 1960, p. 26.

29. Hadley Cantril, *The Human Dimension: Experiences in Policy Research* (New Brunswick, N.J.: Rutgers University Press, 1967), p. 5.

30. "Russian Federation National Security Blueprint," December 17, 1997, printed in Moscow *Rossijskaya Gazeta*, December 26, 1997, translated by Foreign Broadcast Information Service, pp. 3–4.

31. Ibid., p. 8. The "National Security Blueprint" continues: "The factors intensifying the threat of the growth of nationalism and na-

tional and regional separatism include mass migration and the uncontrolled reproduction of human resources in a number of regions of the country. The main reasons for this are the consequences of the USSR's breakup into national-territorial formations, the failures of nationalities policy and economic policy, . . . and the spread and escalation of conflict situations based on national and ethnic grounds. Other factors are the deliberate and purposeful interference by foreign states and international organizations in the internal life of Russia's peoples, and the weakening of the role of Russian as the state language of the Russian Federation. The adoption by Russian Federation components of normative legal acts and decisions that are at variance with the Russian Federation Constitution and federal legislation is becoming an increasingly dangerous factor eroding the single legal area of the country. The continuing violation of Russia's single spiritual area, economic disintegration, and social differentiation provoke the escalation of tension in relations between the regions and the center, thereby constituting a patent threat to the federal structure of the Russian Federation."

32. Ibid., p. 10.

33. Ibid., p. 18. Russia rejected the "no-first-use" nuclear doctrine on November 2, 1993, when the "Basic Provisions of the Military Doctrine of the Russian Federation" was approved by President Yeltsin.

34. George F. Kennan, letter to author, March 25, 1997. The spell of secrecy is hard to break. Open sources are often discounted still. In May 1998, India detonated a number of nuclear devices, including a hydrogen bomb. The newly formed Hindu nationalist government had all but announced that it would do this. The Bharatiya Janata Party (BJP) 1998 Election Manifesto read, "The BJP rejects the notion of nuclear apartheid and will actively oppose attempts to impose a hegemonistic nuclear regime. We will not be dictated to by anybody in matters of security and in the exercise of nuclear option." When the option *was* exercised, the Department of State asked why the Central Intelligence Agency hadn't told them in advance. *Newsweek* reported, "The intelligence failure 'ranks right up there with missing the collapse of the Soviet Union,' says a senior State Department official" (Evan Thomas, John Barry, and Melinda Liu, "Ground Zero," *Newsweek*, May 25, 1998, p. 29).

Index

Acheson, Dean, 57, 64, 68, 157, 186
Administrative Procedure Act (APA), 157–58, 174, 226
Albright, Joseph, 150
"Ales," 146–48. *See also* Hiss, Alger; Venona
Alien and Sedition Acts of *1798*, 94–96
Allen, George E., 63
Alsop, Joseph, 141, 194
Alsop, Stewart, 141
American Bar Association, 165
American Civil Liberties Union (ACLU), 24
American Communist Party, 15, 49, 145
American Federation of Labor, 117
American Historical Association, 10
Ames, Aldrich, 76
"Antenna," 144. *See also* Rosenberg, Julius and Ethel; Venona
Anti-Communism, 4, 6, 15, 36, 52
Appleby, Paul H., 63–68 *passim*
Arlington Hall, 15–16, 61, 71, 142. *See also* National Security Agency; Venona
Arms Control and Disarmament Agency, 200
Army Signals Intelligence Service, 60

Army Signals Security Agency, 15, 71. *See also* National Security Agency; Venona
Åslund, Anders, 198
Atomic bomb. *See* Nuclear weapons
Atomic Energy Act of *1946*, 156, 160
Atomic Energy Act of *1954*, 98, 156
Atomic Energy Commission, 160, 176
"Attorney General's List," 160, 162

Baker, Newton Diehl, 107
Baldwin, Hanson W., 186, 188
Barone, Michael, 134
Baruch Plan, 137
Bay of Pigs, 181, 222–23
Benson, Robert Louis, 69
Bentley, Elizabeth, 53, 54, 61, 69
Berle, Adolph, 119, 120
Bethe, Hans, 136–44, 174
Bevin, Ernest, 123
Biddle, Francis, 129, 131, 133, 204
Black, Hugo L., 205
Black Tom, explosion at, 101
Bohlen, Charles E. "Chip," 184
Boland, Edward P., 211
Bolshevism, 113–16 *passim*, 118, 120
Borah, William E., 94

Boskin, Michael J., 197
Bradley, Omar Nelson, 70, 71
Brooks, Linton F., 200
Buckley, William F., Jr., 43
Bundy, William P., 186
Bureaucracy, 155, 181, 201; in fed-
eral government, 129, 165; and
the Freedom of Information Act,
173; and intelligence, 80; Max
Weber on, 142–43, 153; and se-
crecy, 60, 80, 152, 180
Burgess, Guy, 145
Burleson, Albert S., 106
Butler, George Lee, 78, 79

Cantril, Hadley, 222, 223
Carter, Jimmy, 8, 209
Casey, William J., 3, 210
Castro, Fidel, 57
Center for the Study of Intelligence,
76, 177
Central Intelligence Agency (CIA), 7,
9, 37–38, 43, 51, 76, 180, 187–90,
214; creation of, 76, 98, 180; and
estimates of Soviet economy, 7,
13–14, 196–98; and Iran-Contra
affair, 3, 210–12; and Kennedy
assassination, 220–21; and NSC-
68, 184; operations of, 213; and
secrecy, 181, 185–86; and
Venona, 15, 61. See also Center
for the Study of Intelligence
Chadwick, James, 136
Chambers, Whittaker, 49, 53–54,
61, 68, 119, 121, 145
Chicago Tribune, 133–34, 204
Childs, Morris, 169–70
China, 188, 198
Church committee, 36–37, 46, 76,
207
Church, Frank, 36, 76
Civil Liberties Act of 1988, 131
Civil Service Commission, 91, 110,
159, 161, 169, 172
Civil War (U.S.), 22, 82, 83
Clark, James Beauchamp (Champ),
92
Clark, Mark W., 187–89
Clarke, Carter W., 62, 70

classification procedures, 171–73.
See also declassification procedures
Clinton, William Jefferson, 203, 215
COINTELPROS, 35, 37
Cold War, 9, 17, 90, 141, 178–79,
184, 190, 219–20, 226; and
atomic bomb, 179; beginning of,
39–40, 141, 154; and Church
committee, 36–37; and conspiracy theories, 21, 33, 36; Edward
Shils on, 12–13, 15; and fascism,
44–45; in findings of Commission on Protecting and Reducing
Government Secrecy, 16–17; history of, 16–20, 31, 55–58 passim;
and Pentagon Papers, 31–34; and
secrecy, 1–2, 34, 214, 217, 227;
and Soviet military outlays, 74;
and Joseph Stalin, 57, 58
Commager, Henry Steele, 104
Commission on Government Security (Wright commission), 60,
164, 167–68, 172, 175, 204; report of, 166
Commission on Protecting and Reducing Government Secrecy,
9–11, 16, 62–63, 143; on loyalty
programs, 165–66, 168; conclusions and recommendations of,
14, 217–18
Committee on Administrative Procedure, 157
Committee on Classified Information (Coolidge committee), 170
Committee to Investigate the National Defense Program (Truman
committee), 73, 95
Communism, 40, 86; domestic
communism, 15–17 passim, 24,
62, 146. See also Communist
Party of the United States
Communist International (Comintern), 23, 52–53, 113, 116–17,
122
Communist Labor Party, 113, 128
Communist Party of the United
States (CPUSA), 25, 35, 52–53,
114, 117, 119, 124, 128, 154, 159,

160, 170; and Soviet Communist party, 122
Condon, Dr. Edward U., 63–68 *passim*
Congress, U.S., 31, 35–36, 98, 106, 109, 171, 174, 194. *See also* House of Representatives; Senate
Congress for Cultural Freedom, 190
Conspiracy, 18, 23, 47, 50, 84, 98, 103; Communist, 28, 165; theories of, 22–27 *passim*, 29, 34–49
Constitution, U.S., 34, 81, 92, 127
containment doctrine, 6, 33, 49, 57, 182–85, 188
Contras. *See* Iran-Contra affair
Coolidge, Calvin: administration of, 171–72
Council of Economic Advisors, 192, 197
Cromwell, William P., 60
Cuba, 46, 222–23
Culbertson, Charles A., 91
Cullather, Nicholas, 177, 181
Cummings, Homer, 157
Czolgosz, Leon F., 87

Daily Worker, The, 119, 170
Daugherty, Harry M., 109
declassification procedures, 11, 80, 173
Debs, Eugene V., 107–9
Defense Science Board, 175
Department of Defense, 75, 171, 180, 183; Security Institute, 10
Department of Energy, 176
Department of Justice, 23, 24
Department of State, 10, 83, 97, 181, 183–84, 186, 193, 198
Deutch, John M., 75
DeWitt, John L., 132
diaspora politics, 62, 85
Dies, Martin, Jr., 25
Dobbs, Michael, 150
Doolittle, James H., 187–89
Draper, Theodore, 3, 114, 116, 212
Dubofsky, Melvyn, 87–88
Dulles, Allen, 38, 184, 186, 188, 192–93, 221

Duquesne, Fritz, 126
Durkheim, Emile, 12

Eberstadt, Nicholas, 195–98
Edgar, Harold, 92, 204
Eisenhower, Dwight D., 8–9, 28, 85, 161, 163, 165, 170, 177, 181, 187, 191, 194; administration of, 15, 181
Ellsberg, Daniel, 29–30, 32
El Salvador, 209–10
England, 82, 85, 103, 114, 126, 132, 144, 150, 152, 144
espionage, 80, 126, 100, 180; domestic, 16, 188; German, 103; protection against, 130; Soviet, 15–17, 49, 51, 53, 54, 60–62, 70, 86, 137, 143, 144, 155–56, 166
Espionage Act of *1917,* 60, 84, 91–92, 96, 104, 106–9 *passim,* 111, 125, 133, 145–46, 164–65
ethnicity: in the Soviet Union, 4–5, 79, 224, 226; in the United States, 12, 18, 85–90, 105, 114, 127–28, 130, 132
Executive Order 9066 (Roosevelt), 130
Executive Order 9835 (Truman), 159
Executive Order 10450 (Eisenhower), 161
Executive Order 10501 (Eisenhower), 217
Executive Order 10964 (Kennedy), 217
Executive Order 11652 (Nixon), 217
Executive Order 12065 (Carter), 217
Executive Order 12356 (Reagan), 217
Executive Order 12958 (Clinton), 203, 217

Federal Register, 80, 160–61
Federal Bureau of Investigation (FBI), 99, 152, 160, 169–70; and assassination of Martin L. King, Jr., 220; as competitor of CIA, 75–76; in conspiracy theories,

Federal Bureau of Investigation
(FBI) (continued)
48–49; criticisms of, 34–37,
46–47; files of, 2, 19, 41–45, 51;
in findings of Commission on
Protecting and Reducing Govern-
ment Secrecy, 9–10; and J. Edgar
Hoover, 24, 48, 62, 215–16, 221;
and Venona, 16–17, 54, 142
Fermi, Enrico, 136
First Amendment, 93–94
Fletcher, Howard B., 70
Flynn, Edward J., 124
Flynn, Elizabeth Gurley, 87
Ford, Gerald R., 170, 198, 202
Foreign Relations Authorization
Act for Fiscal Years 1994 and
1995, 60. See also Committee on
Protecting and Reducing Govern-
ment Secrecy
France, 82, 84, 104, 198
Frankel, Max, 168, 203
Free, Lloyd A., 222
Freedom of Information Act (FOIA):
and Administrative Procedure
Act, 157; and FBI, 35, 41–42, 44,
47, 49; and federal bureaucracy,
174; and Moss subcommittee,
172–73
Freeh, Louis J., 70, 75
Fuchs, Klaus, 54, 144
Fulbright, J. William, 28

Gaddis, John Lewis, 55–57
Gaither, H. Rowen, Jr., 8, 190
Gaither report, 190–98
Gallinger, Jacob Harold, 93
Gardner, Meredith Knox, 61, 142,
151
Garment, Leonard, 206
German Communist Party, 25
German Americans, 18, 86, 104–6,
131
German-American Bund, 128, 159
Germany, 29; in conspiracy theo-
ries, 23, 25; during World War I,
85, 88, 90–91, 101–104; during
World War II, 132–33, 150
Gilbert, W. S., 85

Gitlow, Benjamin, 117
Glazer, Nathan, 12, 86, 114
Gold, Harry, 144
Goldman, Emma, 111
Goldwater, Barry, 3, 28–29, 207,
210, 211
"Good Girl," 69. See also Bentley,
Elizabeth
Gorbachev, Mikhail, 200
Gorelick, Jamie S., 75
Greenglass, David, 54, 144–45
Gregory, Thomas W., 90, 97, 106
Griswald, Edwin N., 205
Groves, Leslie R., 160
Guatemala, 181–82

Hague peace conferences, 125–26
Hall, Theodore Alvin, 54, 62, 147,
149, 151–52
Hamilton, Alexander, 101
Harding, Warren G., 109, 115
Hatch Act, 159
Haynes, John E., 68
H-bomb. See Nuclear weapons
Hehir, Bryan, 195
Hillenkoetter, Roscoe H., 71
Hiss, Alger, 64, 68–69, 74, 119, 121,
144, 146–47, 186; case against,
50, 52; trial of, 49
Hiss, Priscilla, 68, 121
Hitler, Adolf, 25, 123, 129, 134
Holmes, Oliver Wendell, 108
Hook, Sidney, 118–20
Hoover, Herbert, 187
Hoover, J. Edgar, 34, 43, 50, 54, 115,
126, 189; and Church committee,
46, 47; and FBI, 215–16, 221; and
Francis Biddle, 129–30; and
George E. Allen, 62–68; and se-
crecy, 22–24, 37, 40; and Truman,
70
Housekeeping Statute of 1789, 173
House of Representatives, U.S., 9,
90–92, 207; and Defense Appropriations Committee, 198–99;
and Foreign Operations and Government Information Subcommittee, 174; and House Un-American Activities Committee, 25, 70;

and Select Committee on Assassinations, 40; and Select Committee on Intelligence, 41, 211; and Special Government Information Subcommitee of Government Operations (Moss subcommittee), 171–72
Humphrey, Hubert H., 164

India, 3, 88, 103
Industrial Workers of the World (IWW), 87–88
Information Security Oversight Office (ISOO), 74, 202
Inouye, Daniel K., 132
Inter-Continental Ballistic Missile (ICBM), 194
Iran-Contra affair, 3, 206–13

Jackson, Andrew, 82
Japan, 97, 198
Japanese Americans, internment of, 131–33
Jefferson, Thomas, 84–85
John Birch Society, 28, 29
Johnson, Hiram W., 95
Johnson, Lyndon B., 173, 195, 220; administration of, 28–29, 33, 134, 176
Jorgenson, Dale W., 197

Kampelman, Max, 6
Kaufman, Irving R., 145
Kennan, George F., 57, 145, 182–84, 197, 198, 227. See also containment doctrine
Kennedy, John F., 46, 48, 85, 168, 194; administration of, 28, 33, 176; assassination of, 40, 41, 45, 219
KGB, 51, 61, 118
Khrushchev, Nikita, 79
King, Martin Luther, Jr., 220
Kissinger, Henry, 6, 32
Kristol, Irving, 190
Kuhn, Fritz J., 128, 129
Kunstel, Marcia, 150

Ladd, D. Milton "Mickey," 147
Lang, Hermann, 125–26

Lansing, Robert, 88, 112
Lea, Clarence, 130
League of Nations, 99
Lee, Robert E., 95
Lehman, Ronald F., 200
Lenin, 23, 56, 84, 112, 118, 155, 182
Leuchtenburg, William E., 104
"Liberal," 144. See also Rosenberg, Julius and Ethel; Venona
Liberal Party, 124
Life magazine, 140–42
Lincoln, Abraham, 82
Link, Arthur, 107
Lippman, Walter, 186
Lipset, Seymour Martin, 74
Lodge, Henry Cabot, 95, 101, 204
Los Alamos, Atomic Research Laboratory, 142, 147, 151, 155, 156, 160
Loyalty, 18, 111; and disloyalty, 18, 52, 105, 172; ensuring, 127; as grounds for dismissal, 91; oath of, 90; programs for, 15, 159, 161, 163, 165, 169; in report of Commission on Government Security (Wright commission), 166; and secrecy, 98, 163

Maclean, Donald, 145
Madison, James, 84
Manhattan Project, 61, 136, 156
Marks, Herbert, 64, 68
Marshall, George C., 27, 57
Masses, The, 87, 113. See also New Masses, The
Matsunaga, Spark M., 133
McCarthy, Joseph R., 16–17, 19, 27, 51, 70, 144, 163, 186, 189, 219
McCloy, John J., 64, 68
McFarlane, Robert C., 210
McKinley, William, 87
McNamara, Robert, 7, 28–29, 203
"Mlad," 150. See also Hall, Theodore Alvin; Venona
Moorhead, William, 174. See also Freedom of Information Act
Morison, Samuel L., 98
Moss, John, 172–74
Moss subcommittee, 172–74

National Archives and Records Administration, 10, 74, 202
National Declassification Center, 217–18
National Intelligence Council, 197
National Intelligence Daily, 180
National Reconnaissance Organization, 223
National Security Act of *1947*, 98, 179
National Security Agency (NSA), 7, 9, 60. *See also* Arlington Hall; Venona
National Security Council, 3, 179, 191, 193, 211
Naval Research Station, 135
Nazi-Soviet nonaggression pact, 123
Nazis, 120, 128
New Masses, The, 119
Nicaragua, 208–12
Nitze, Paul H., 57, 184
Nixon, Richard M., 35, 185–86, 203; administration of, 185–86, 203, 204; and Pentagon Papers, 32–33, 204–5; and Watergate, 33, 206
Norden, Carl L., 125–26
North Atlantic Treaty, 179
North Korea, 55
NSC-68, 183–85, 199
Nuclear weapons, 28, 42, 51, 183–84, 195, 225–26; and the atom bomb, 135–42, 150, 179, 195; and the H-bomb, 137–40, 174; Soviet espionage in, 143–44; in wartime, 78, 144, 190
Nutter, G. Warren, 193

Office of Naval Intelligence, 98
Office of Strategic Information, 171
Office of Strategic Services, 77
Operation PBSUCCESS (Cullather), 177, 181
Oppenheimer, J. Robert, 136, 160, 163
Overman, Lee Slater, 89, 95

Palmer, A. Mitchell, 23, 115
Palmer Raids, 115–16, 152

Panuch, J. Anthony, 68, 69
Papen, Franz von, 101–2
Pearl Harbor, 142
Pentagon Papers, 29, 31–33, 40, 47, 203–6
Pepper, Claude D., 73
Philby, Kim, 16, 54, 114
Pike, Otis, 36
Pike committee, 36, 37, 207
Podesta, John D., 203
Pound, Roscoe, 157
Powers, Richard Gid, 74, 146, 219
President's Science Advisory Committee, 190, 192
Press: censorship of, 91, 96, 106, 133, 167; freedom of, 37, 93–94
Proxmire, William, 194

Reagan, Ronald, 210; administration of, 8, 209
Reed, John, 87–88, 113–14; and Communist Labor Party, 114; and John Reed Society, 149
Regulation: secrecy as, 13, 59, 79, 164; in wartime, 154
Reston, James, 167–68
Ritter Ring, 125–26
Roosevelt, Franklin D., 25, 38, 167; administration of, 85, 120, 130, 150, 157; war plans of, 133
Roosevelt, Theodore, 105
Rosenberg, Julius and Ethel, 49, 51, 54, 144–45
Rossi, Bruno, 147
Rostow, Walt, 193
Rowen, Henry S., 197
Rovere, Richard, 123
Ruina, Jack P., 175
Rumsfeld, Donald, 173
Russell, Richard B., 180
Russia, 22–23, 84, 107, 111–13 *passim*, 188, 198–99, 224–26. *See also* Soviet Union
Ruthenberg, Charles Emil, 114

Sakharov, Andrei, 138
Sarbanes, Paul S., 212
Sax, Saville, 147, 149
Schmidt, Benno C., 92, 204

Seaborg, Glenn T., 176–77
Secrecy, 1, 12, 27, 41, 45–47, 185, 203, 212, 222, 227; and Administrative Procedure Act, 158; and bureaucracy, 111, 153; and CIA, 186; and classification decisions, 11, 74–75, 172; after Cold War, 80, 202; during Cold War, 15–20, 58, 74, 154, 214; and conspiracy, 50, 98; cost of, 218; culture of, 154, 206, 221, 223, 226; and declassification decisions, 170–77, 217–18; and findings of Commission on Protecting and Reducing Government Secrecy, 10, 14; and Freedom of Information Act, 42; in government, 11, 47, 49, 73, 168, 202; as government regulation, 13, 59, 79, 164; and the legislature, 213, 216; and national security, 3, 8; and nuclear weapons, 136, 141, 195; power of, 21–22; and the presidency, 133, 211; as ritual, 29, 43; routinization of, 180, 198; and science, 174–75; in Soviet Union, 112; during Watergate era, 29–33, 35
Security Resources Panel, 190
Sedition Act of *1918*, 97. *See also* Alien and Sedition Acts of 1798
Seitz, Frederick, 106–9, 175, 227
Senate, U.S., 9, 81, 90–95; Judiciary Committee, 157; Committee on Foreign Relations, 195–97, 200, 202; Select Committee on Intelligence, 3, 210; Joint Resolution *21*, 164
Seward, William H., 85, 87
Shapiro, Maurice M., 135
Sheehan, Neil, 29–32
Shevchenko, Arkady M., 155–56
Shields, John Knight, 93–94
Shils, Edward, 12–15, 18, 21, 163, 218
Shultz, George P., 199–200
Silone, Ignazio, 117
Slany, William Z., 83
Smith, Jeffrey, 78
Smyth, Henry DeWolf, 156

Smyth report, 156, 174
Social Security Administration, 181
Solzhenitsyn, Alexander, 5–6
Soviet Union, 117, 155, 178, 181–82, 213, 226–27; archives of, 52–53, 80; and CIA, 181–82, 190; and Cold War, 44, 46, 49, 78, 183–85; and Comintern, 113–14; economy of, 4–8, 13–14, 79, 190–93, 195–201; and espionage, 51–56, 90, 119–20, 140, 143, 163, 165; U.S. relations with, 39, 43; and Venona, 60, 150–52
Spender, Stephen, 190
Sputnik, 9
Stalin, Joseph, 25, 39, 55–58, 137, 167
Stennis, John C., 164–65
Stimson, Henry L., 131
Stone, Earl E., 71
Stone, Harlan, 24
Story, Joseph, 93–94
Strategic Air Command, 194
Strategic Arms Reduction Treaty I (START I), 6, 199–200
Strategic Arms Reduction Treaty II (START II), 226
Strategic Command, U.S., 78
Studies in Intelligence, 77
Supreme Court, U.S., 158, 206

Teller, Edward, 139
Thomas, Charles S., 92–93
Thomas, Evan, 221
Torment of Secrecy, The (Shils), 12
Trilling, Lionel, 120–23
Trotsky, Leon, 118, 214
Truman, Harry S., 17, 45, 54, 57, 62–63, 70–71, 73, 137, 159, 161, 180; administration of, 15, 38, 49, 160, 162; Executive orders of, 159–61
Turner, Stansfield, 79

Ulam, Stanislaw, 139
United States v. Curtiss-Wright Export Corporation, 158
United Nations, 4, 137, 155, 167

Venona, 15–17, 53–54, 60–62, 69–71, 143–46, 150–51. *See also* Arlington Hall; National Security Agency
Vietnam War, 19–20, 28–34, 39, 57

Wallace, Henry A., 64, 124
Walsh, Thomas J., 95
Warner, Michael, 69
Warren, Charles, 90
Warren commission, 40, 219
Warsaw Pact, 179
Watergate, 20, 32–35, 50, 212, 213
Webb, Edwin Y., 91, 96
Weber, Max, 12, 142–43, 153
Weinstein, Allen, 49–50, 74
Weisband, William W., 142
White, Harry Dexter, 54, 163
Wilson, Charles E., 170

Wilson, James Q., 181, 213, 216
Wilson, Woodrow, 87, 110, 190, 204, 209; and Espionage Act, 89–90, 96–97; Executive order of, 158–59; and openness in foreign relations, 81, 84; and war with Germany, 85, 91
Wisner, Frank O., 189
World War I, 16, 88, 125, 127, 204
World War II, 77, 86, 113, 120, 127, 141, 150, 152, 161; end of, 135; and loyalty programs, 159; and Japanese internment, 130–32; and press censorship, 133; and Russia, 39
Wright, Loyd, 165
Wright commission. *See* Commission on Government Security

Young, Milton, 27